Biography Today

Profiles of People of Interest to Young Readers

1996
Annual
Cumulation

Laurie Lanzen Harris
Executive Editor

Cherie D. Abbey
Associate Editor

Omnigraphics, Inc.

Penobscot Building
Detroit, Michigan 48226

Laurie Lanzen Harris, *Executive Editor*
Cherie D. Abbey, *Associate Editor*
Helene Henderson, Kevin Hillstrom, Laurie Hillstrom,
Sue Ellen Thompson, *Sketch Writers*
Barry Puckett, *Research Associate*

Omnigraphics, Inc.

* * *

Matt Barbour, *Production Manager*
Laurie Lanzen Harris, *Vice President & Editorial Director*
Peter E. Ruffner, *Vice President, Administration*
James A. Sellgren, *Vice President, Operations and Finance*
Jane Steele, *Marketing Consultant*

* * *

Frederick G. Ruffner, Jr., *Publisher*

Copyright © 1997 Omnigraphics, Inc.

ISBN 0-7808-0070-2

Printed in the United States

Contents

5

Preface

Biography Today is a publication designed and written for the young reader—aged 9 and above—and covers individuals that librarians and teachers tell us that young people want to know about most: entertainers, athletes, writers, illustrators, cartoonists, and political leaders.

Biography Today is available as a magazine and as a hardbound annual. In its first year (Volume 1, 1992) *Biography Today* was published four times. Beginning with Volume 2, 1993, *Biography Today* will be published three times a year, in January, April, and September. We have made this change to adapt our publishing schedule more closely to the school year. Despite this change in frequency, the total number of pages will not change. We had initially planned to produce four issues of approximately 100 pages each; now we plan three issues of approximately 150 pages each, with a hardbound cumulation of approximately 400 pages.

The Plan of the Work

The publication was especially created to appeal to young readers in a format they can enjoy reading and readily understand. Each issue contains approximately 15 sketches arranged alphabetically; this annual cumulation contains entries on 39 individuals. Each entry provides at least one picture of the individual profiled, and bold-faced rubrics lead the reader to information on birth, youth, early memories, education, first jobs, marriage and family, career highlights, memorable experiences, hobbies, and honors and awards. Each of the entries ends with a list of easily accessible sources designed to lead the student to further reading on the individual and a current address. Obituary entries are also included, written to provide a perspective on the individual's entire career. Obituaries are clearly marked in both the table of contents and at the beginning of the entry.

New Feature—Brief Entries

Beginning with Volume 3, *Biography Today* will include Brief Entries of approximately two pages each. These entries cover people who may not have had as much extensive media coverage as the subjects of our other profiles. Examples of people profiled in Brief Entries in Volume 4 include Vicki Van Meter, who became the youngest person to pilot a plane across the U.S. and to Europe. All brief entries are clearly marked in the table of contents and at the beginning of the entry.

Biographies are prepared by Omni editors after extensive research, utilizing the most current materials available. Those sources that are generally available to students appear in the list of further reading at the end of the sketch.

Indexes

To provide easy access to entries, each issue of *Biography Today* contains a Name Index, a General Index covering occupations, organizations, and ethnic and minority origins, a Places of Birth Index, and a Birthday Index. These indexes cumulate with each succeeding issue. The three yearly issues are cumulated annually in the hardbound volume, with cumulative indexes.

Our Advisors

Biography Today is reviewed regularly by an Advisory Board comprised of librarians, children's literature specialists, and reading instructors so that we can make sure that the concept of this publication—to provide a readable and accessible biographical magazine for young readers—stays on target. They have evaluated the title as it developed, and their suggestions have proved invaluable. Any errors, however, are ours alone. We'd like to list the Advisory Board members, and to thank them for their efforts.

Sandra Arden	Assistant Director, Retired Troy Public Library Troy, MI
Gail Beaver	Ann Arbor Huron High School Library and the University of Michigan School of Information and Library Studies Ann Arbor, MI
Marilyn Bethel	Pompano Beach Branch Library Pompano Beach, FL
Eileen Butterfield	Waterford Public Library Waterford, CT
Linda Carpino	Detroit Public Library Detroit, MI
Helen Gregory	Grosse Pointe Public Library Grosse Pointe, MI
Jane Klasing	School Board of Broward County, Retired Fort Lauderdale, FL
Marlene Lee	Broward County Public Library System Fort Lauderdale, FL
Judy Liskov	Waterford Public Library Waterford, CT
Sylvia Mavrogenes	Miami-Dade Public Library System Miami, FL
Carole J. McCollough	Wayne State University School of Library Science Detroit, MI

| Deborah Rutter | Russell Library
Middletown, CT |
| Barbara Sawyer | Groton Public Library and Information Center
Groton, CT |
| Renee Schwartz | School Board of Broward County
Fort Lauderdale, FL |
| Lee Sprince | Broward West Regional Library
Fort Lauderdale, FL |
| Susan Stewart | Birney Middle School Reading Laboratory
Southfield, MI |
| Ethel Stoloff | Birney Middle School, Librarian, Retired
Southfield, MI |

Our Advisory Board stressed to us that we should not shy away from controversial or unconventional people in our profiles, and we have tried to follow their advice. The Advisory Board also mentioned that the sketches might be useful in reluctant reader and adult literacy programs, and we would value any comments librarians and teachers might have about the suitability of our magazine for those purposes.

New Series

In response to the growing number of suggestions from our readers, we have decided to expand the *Biography Today* family of publications. Five new series—*Biography Today Author Series, Scientists and Inventors Series, Artists Series, Sports Series,* and *Leaders of the World Series*—will be published in 1996. Each of the special subject volumes will be 200-pages and will cover approximatley 15 individuals of interest to the reader aged 9 and above. The length and format of the entries will be like those found in the regular issues of *Biography Today,* but there will be *no* duplication among the series.

Your Comments Are Welcome

Our goal is to be accurate and up-to-date, to give young readers information they can learn from and enjoy. Now we want to know what you think. Take a look at this issue of *Biography Today,* on approval. Write or call me with your comments. We want to provide an excellent source of biographical information for young people. Let us know how you think we're doing.

And here's a special incentive: review our list of people to appear in upcoming issues. Use the bind-in card to list other people you want to see

9

in *Biography Today*. If we include someone you suggest, your library wins a free issue, with our thanks. Please see the bind-in card for details.

And take a look at the next page, where we've listed those libraries and individuals that received a free issue of *Biography Today* in 1996 for their suggestions.

Laurie Harris
Executive Editor, *Biography Today*

CONGRATULATIONS!

Congratulations to the following individuals and libraries, who received a free issue of *Biography Today*, in 1996 for suggesting people who appear in Volume 5:

Alberta Smith Elementary School Library
Midlothian, VA
Nancy Stough

Bastrop High School Library
Bastrop, LA
W. Davenport

Tiffany-Jenelle Bates
Machesney Park, IL

Bloomfield High School
Media Center, Bloomfield, CT
Lisa Pitek

Colleen Branigan
Munnsville, NY

Anya Brown
Aliquippa, PA

Brownsburg Public Library
Brownsburg, IN

Lauren Caggiano
Ft. Wayne, IN

Camden Fairview Middle School Library
Camden, AR
Marva M. Marks

Brian Carlos
East Providence, RI

Central Middle School Library
Dover, DE

Charlene Chan
Scarsdale, NY

Wendy Chen
Garden Grove, CA

Thomas Chue
Glendale, CA

City of Inglewood Public Library
Ingelwood, CA
Hazel Ridgeway and Kay Ikuta

Joey Clark
Battle Creek, MI

Cohannet School
Taunton, MA
Ian Lewis

Pam Cordell
Chambersburg, PA

Kayla Courneya
Bay City, MI

Alicia Croson
Warrenton, VA

Mary D'agostino
East Syracuse, NY

Danville Public Library
Danville, IN
Cynthia S. Rutledge

Stephanie Davis
Toledo, OH

Alina Degtyar
Kew Gardens, NY

DuBois Area Senior High School
DuBois, PA

Dunkell Middle School Library
Farmington Hills, MI
Lindsey Drasin

East Detroit High School Library
Eastpointe, MI
Susan Kott

Eastover Elementary School Library
Charlotte, NC

Eastway Junior High School Library
Charlotte, NC
Linda Johnson

Linda Eveleth
Valencia, CA

Exposition Park-Bethune Regional Library
Los Angeles, CA
Jerry Stevens

Nicole Ferrara
Camillus, NY

Adam Finkel
Bloomfield Hills, MI

Franklin County Library
Rocky Mount, VA
Shirley A. Reynolds

Caitlin Frates
Los Altos, CA

Daisy and Nancy Gonzalez
Newark, CA

Jessica Gottschalk
Imlay City, MI

Joseph Hankins
Jacksonville, FL

Hillcrest Elementary
Holland, PA
Dara Levin and Terri Napierkowski

Frank Juarez
Santa monica, CA

Melissa Kramer
Bellmore, NY

Lake Dolloff Elementary
Auburn, WA
Melissa Zastrow

David and Tracy Liao
San Francisco, CA

Serena Liu
Rego Park, NY

Haydee Llanos
Brooklyn, NY

Novella S. Lopes
Miami FL

Velia Marsh
Phoenix, AZ

McCune Attendance Center
McCune, KS
Martha Tilton

Qiana McKay
Opa-Locka, FL

Helen Mengstu
Florissant, MO

Middletown Public Library
Middletown, IN
Patricia Jessup

Mark Murray
Arnold, MD

Nord Junior High
Amherst, OH
Matt Stipe

Chad Passage
Adams Center, NY

Pattengill Middle School
Lansing, MI
J.M. Force

Jessica Pollnow
Manchester, CT

Pat Popolizio
Niskayuna, NY

Pulaski County Public Library
Somerset, NY
Louann Hardy

Queens Borough Public Library
Youth Services
Jamaica, NY

Seth Rall, Stoughton, WI

Amanda M. Rezente, Cameron Park, CA

Ridgeview School
Olathe, KS

Riverhead High School Library
Riverhead, NY
Keylonda Miller

Kathleen Ruggiero, Middle Village, NY

Saratoga Public Library
Saratoga Springs, NY
Children's Room
Rebecca O'Dunne

Jake Scheiterlein, Clinton Township, MI

Adam B. Shahon, Parsippany, NY

Shaw High School
Cleveland OH
Jacqueline R. Avery

Frances and Jo-Lin Shih
Woodhaven, NY

Rose Sibble, Ames IA

Patricia Singh, Queens, NY

Pooja Sinha, Upper Brookville, NY

Abby Sprague, Columbus, IN

Spring-Ford Middle School
Royersford, PA
Jeanne M. Havarilla

Austin Stanley, Independence, MO

Joanne Stewart
Saratoga Springs, NY

Sturgis Public Library
Sturgis, MI

Rose Talbert, Laytonville, CA

Thomas Taque, Charlotte, NC

Sacheen A. Torres, Pico Rivera, CA

Hue Tran, Garden Grove, CA

Jacinda Treadway, San Jose, CA

S. Walker, Charlotte, NC

Washington Elementary School
Caldwell, ID

Watertown Public Library
Watertown, WI
Kelly Raatz

West Linn Public Library
West Linn, OR

David Xiao, New York, NY

Aung San Suu Kyi 1945-
Burmese Political Leader and Human
Rights Activist
Winner of the 1991 Nobel Peace Prize

BIRTH

Aung San Suu Kyi (AWNG SAHN SOO CHEE) was born June
19, 1945, in Rangoon, Burma. Her father was Burmese independence leader Aung San, who was assassinated when Suu Kyi was
two years old, and her mother was Khin Kyi, a former Burmese
ambassador to India. Suu Kyi was the youngest of three children.
Of her two brothers, the elder brother currently resides in the
United States; the younger one is deceased. In Burma, there is
no family-naming system. Parents give each child his or her own
personal name. Burmese names are alphabetized by the first letter

in the first word of the name because no part of the name is considered a last name. Also, Burmese women do not change their names when they marry, which is why Suu Kyi's parents do not have the same last name. Suu Kyi added her father's name to her own as a matter of choice.

HISTORY OF BURMA

Suu Kyi's experiences growing up are intimately tied to the history of the Burmese nation. Burma is about the size of Texas and borders Thailand, China, Tibet, and India. The Burmese people are made up of several ethnic groups speaking more than a hundred different languages. The Burmans are the largest ethnic group, residing mainly in the central region of the country, while the other groups tend to live around its mountains and coasts. The mostly Buddhist country was governed by monarchies for centuries, though it has always had a strong egalitarian tradition where people valued equal opportunities for education and spiritual growth for all.

During the 17th century, European invaders began encroaching on various places in the world, including Burma, and violently disrupting peoples' ways of life. By 1886, after three major armed resistance struggles, Burma had become a British colony. During the early decades of the 20th century, the movement for independence from Britain grew among Buddhist monks and university students at Rangoon, the capital city. By the 1930s one among the latter group emerged as the leader of the independence movement—Aung San, Suu Kyi's father, who was a law student at the time. When World War II broke out, Aung San and his close associates embarked on a mission some would regard in later years as highly controversial, but which others would consider more a desperate action on behalf of a free Burma. They left Burma to fight on the side of Japan to oust the British. When they realized that Japan would not then readily negotiate for Burma's freedom, they went to the other side and fought with the British to defeat the Japanese.

After the war, Aung San and his fighters obtained Britain's agreement that Burma could become a free nation. A democratic election was held in January 1947, and Aung San's party won an overwhelming majority. But its leader did not live to see the moment he struggled for; he and his new cabinet members were killed by a political assassin in July 1947 as they met to draft a constitution. A new government was elected to replace them, and the new Constitution making Burma an independent republic took effect. Burma became officially independent on January 4, 1948.

Over the years the military that Aung San founded grew stronger and many politicians served in its offices. In 1962 a military coup overthrew the elected government, and General Ne Win took control of the country. He ruled for almost 30 years in a military-led dictatorship. This period was characterized by political uprisings and economic instability. During this time, Burma went from being one of the most prosperous Asian nations to one of the poorest. By 1987, the United Nations officially considered Burma to be on a par with Ethiopia and Bangladesh. In addition to being governed by a repressive, abusive dictatorship, the country suffers from economic devastation, the fourth highest infant mortality rate in the area, and an absence of active universities (the military closed them down in 1988 when students began leading public demonstrations against its rule). In 1989 the military government changed the name of the country to "Myanmar" and the city of Rangoon became officially known as "Yangon."

YOUTH

This was the political environment in which Suu Kyi grew up. After her father was killed, the Burmese government arranged for a home for his widow and children on the banks on Inya Lake, an area of Rangoon in which many prominent political and military people live. The household was frequently visited by soldiers, former comrades of Aung San. Suu Kyi's mother went to work as the government's Director of Social Welfare.

EDUCATION

Suu Kyi's mother's family was composed of both Christians and Buddhists, so she was exposed to both traditions while growing up. She was sent to convent schools, and also took horseback riding, sewing, cooking, piano, and Japanese flower-arranging lessons.

When her mother was appointed Burmese ambassador to India in 1960, the family moved to New Delhi, where Suu Kyi attended high school. Her new Indian friends included Rajiv and Sanjay Gandhi, the sons of India's former prime minister Indira Gandhi. Family friends have described the teenaged Suu Kyi as very serious, correct, and interested in politics.

After finishing high school, Suu Kyi attended St. Hugh's College, part of Oxford University, in England. She majored in philosophy, politics, and economics (often known as PPP). Years later she commented that "I would much prefer to have read English, Japanese or forestry, but I [studied PPP] because economics seemed to be of most use for a developing country. . . . I would much prefer to be a writer. But once I had committed myself then I had to accept that I would end up in a political party. It is not what I wanted at all, but there cannot be any half measures."

At college, Suu Kyi lived in a dorm, but she often visited Paul and Patricia Gore-Booth while at Oxford. Sir Paul Gore-Booth was the British High Commissioner in New Delhi. The family had become acquainted with Suu Kyi's family during Paul Gore-Booth's previous appointment as British ambassador to Burma. When it was decided where Suu Kyi would go to college, the Gore-Booths offered to be her "family away from home." During one of those visits she first met her future husband, Michael Aris, a family friend of the Gore-Booths, though it was years after that meeting before they married.

Serving others has been a strong and valued tradition in Suu Kyi's family, and at different times in her life she kept that tradition alive. During one summer vacation, she went to visit a family friend in the newly independent nation of Algeria. While there, she devoted part of her vacation to participating in a project to build houses for families who had lost their husbands and fathers in Algeria's long struggle for independence from France.

At college, Suu Kyi lived by a strict personal moral code that included no drinking, no smoking, and no sex before marriage. It stood in stark contrast to the climate around her during the late 1960s, when freer attitudes about sex and drugs were the norm. Suu Kyi graduated from Oxford in 1967 with a B. A. in political science, philosophy, and economics.

EARLY LIFE: MARRIAGE AND CAREER

After finishing college, Suu Kyi went to New York. Though her original plan was to do postgraduate work at New York University, she instead interviewed for and obtained a job in 1969 at the United Nations as Assistant Secretary on the Advisory Committee on Administrative and Budgetary Questions.

She and Michael Aris kept in touch with many letters while she was working at the U.N. in New York and he was working as a tutor for the royal family in Bhutan. In 1972 they married and moved to Bhutan, where Suu Kyi got a job for the Ministry of Foreign Affairs in Bhutan. For the next decade or so Suu Kyi was both a scholar and a housewife, raising their two sons, Alexander and Kim. In 1975, the family returned to England, and she began work as the cataloguer of Burmese books and manuscripts at the Bodleian Library at Oxford. Over the years she authored some scholarly works on Burmese culture and history and continued her studies at various educational institutions.

Living at Oxford she was regarded as something of an eccentric, according to British newspaper reports, noted for riding her bike around the neighborhood accompanied by her dog who rode in a bicycle basket. She had failed the driving test, so in order to take her sons to school or run other errands, she would either have to bike or walk.

Friends from that time differ on whether she had political ambitions back then. One said he "didn't get the sense that here was someone plotting . . . to get back to Burma in a great political role." Another noted, however, that as her children got older, she was getting restless about what she was doing with her life.

CAREER HIGHLIGHTS

DEMOCRACY MOVEMENT IN BURMA

In April 1988, Suu Kyi was doing postgraduate work at the School of African and Oriental Studies in London when her mother had a stroke. She immediately returned home to take care of her. Suu Kyi came home to a country in turmoil. Since March thousands of Burmese people—led by university students and Buddhist monks, as during the independence movement against the British—had been mobilizing demonstrations against General Ne Win's oppressive dictatorship.

As Aung San's daughter, Suu Kyi was soon besieged by people asking for her support in the struggle. She remembers: "I obviously had to think about it. But my instinct was, 'This is not a time when anyone who cares can stay out.' As my father's daughter, I felt I had a duty to get involved."

The Burmese people heard Suu Kyi's basic political philosophy and vision when she gave her first public speech on August 26, 1988. Addressing an enormous crowd gathered in Rangoon, she called for a multiparty democracy, unity, basic human rights, and above all non-violence, following in the tradition of non-violent civil disobedience practiced by Mohandas Gandhi and Martin Luther King, Jr. Of that occasion, she told a reporter, "I'm not a public speaker, but I was not really nervous. I just did not have time to be. I was far more worried about actually getting there. . . . Just to arrive on the platform was the most tremendous relief. But I can't say I would describe it as an enjoyable experience."

During the summer of 1988 numerous mass protests took place, and the army killed thousands of protesters during those demonstrations. Observers estimate that from three to five thousand protesters were killed. On September 18 the military government imposed martial law under a specially assembled council called the State Law and Order Restoration Council (SLORC). The SLORC quickly became known for massive arrests, tortures, executions, enforcing slave labor, and forcing entire areas of people to destroy their homes and move. Signs were erected everywhere with such messages as "Crush Every Disruptive Element." One was posted outside Suu Kyi's home.

On September 24, 1988, in response to the formation of SLORC, the National League for Democracy (NLD) was formed by Suu Kyi and two former army officers who opposed Ne Win's rule. It is the largest political party in Burma that is recognized by the military regime. Suu Kyi then spent the next several months traveling around Burma and campaigning for the party.

Suu Kyi's mother died in January 1989. After her mother's death, Suu Kyi became even more active in the struggle for democracy. She publicly denounced Ne Win and led numerous demonstrations, even though public assemblies of more than five people were outlawed by the military. During the campaign, she had a harrowing experience when, as she and a group of supporters walked along a road, they were stopped by a group of soldiers. She walked on ahead alone, and the soldiers were ordered to shoot. Before they could, however, a higher ranking officer canceled the order. She later said, "It seemed so much simpler to provide them with a single target than to bring everyone else in." (A film entitled *Beyond Rangoon*, released in the U.S. in 1995, depicts this incident.)

UNDER HOUSE ARREST

On July 20, 1989, Lieut. Gen. Khin Nyunt, head of military intelligence for the regime in power, came to her house to put her under house arrest. The official charges were inciting civil unrest and breaking security laws. Tanks surrounded the grounds of her house, barbed wire was placed around the boundary, and bayonet-armed soldiers were posted outside.

At this point, her husband and sons were still in England, where they remained for their own safety. The military government revoked her sons passports in September 1989 and allowed no phone calls or visits with anyone including her husband and children. The SLORC told her she could be released if she agreed to leave the country. She informed the SLORC that she would leave if the military transferred its power to the democratically elected civilian party, all political prisoners were released, she were allowed 50 minutes of air time on TV and radio, and she were permitted to walk to the airport. The SLORC refused.

Though she was detained in her own home, life was not very easy. When she heard that others who had been arrested were being tortured she went on a hunger strike, demanding the end to torture. The military gave in after two weeks.

Suu Kyi gradually was forced to sell most of her possessions in order to buy food. She would not take money from her British husband, because Burmese politicians can be disqualified for accepting money from foreigners. When asked how she endured house arrest and separation from her family, she would explain that her suffering was not much compared to her countrymen, who were imprisoned under much harsher conditions. During her detention, she says, "my biggest concern was what is happening to my sons, how are they coping? I was hoping they wouldn't need me." But she adds that at least she knew her family was safe in England; many others who were imprisoned had no such assurance.

Suu Kyi also gathered strength from a regular daily schedule of meditation, listening to the radio, reading, and exercise. She asserts that, the whole time, "I never felt I was in prison. I felt I was very free. I felt as long as my mind was free they couldn't do anything to me." She adds, "I didn't feel lonely. Sometimes I did feel depressed. But as time went on, even the depression went away. I got used to it."

During Suu Kyi's detention, a national election was held, as promised in 1989 by the SLORC. On May 27, 1990, the NLD won, taking 81 percent of the vote. More than 72 percent of voters turned out to cast ballots. Still their leader remained under house arrest.

Suu Kyi was awarded the Nobel Peace Prize in 1991 for her nonviolent efforts to bring democracy to Burma. The Nobel Committee statement read: "Suu Kyi's struggle is one of the most extraordinary examples of civil courage in Asia in recent decades. She has become an important symbol in the struggle against oppression." At the December 10 award ceremony, Suu Kyi's oldest son, Alexander, accepted the prize for her. She learned of her honor on the radio. The $1 million prize money is being kept, Suu Kyi says, for the people of Burma.

In 1992, her husband was allowed to visit her for the first time in three years. After his first visit, he reported that she'd lost weight because she had little to eat. Suu Kyi later said of this time that sometimes she was

so malnourished and weak her hair fell out and she couldn't leave her bed: "Every time I moved, my heart went *thump-thump-thump,* and it was hard to breathe. . . . I thought to myself that I'd die of heart failure, not starvation at all."

Former Nobel Peace Prize winners, including Bishop Desmond Tutu and the Dalai Lama, attempted to travel to Burma in February 1993 in an effort to win her freedom. They were refused visas to enter the country, so they went to neighboring Thailand and interviewed Burmese refugees.

Suu Kyi's first visitor besides her family and captors was U.S. Representative Bill Richardson of New Mexico, who was permitted to meet with her in February 1994. He urged that she and Lieutenant General Khin Nyunt sit down and talk. She agreed to talks; Khin Nyunt did not respond right away. After nearly five years of forced solitude, she said of the regime's leaders, "I don't care if they deprive me of all of my privileges. They should not think that by making my personal conditions easier for me that this would in any way induce me to give up my convictions." Finally, though, such a meeting did take place, on September 20, 1994.

RELEASE FROM HOUSE ARREST

Suu Kyi was released on July 9, 1995, after six years of house arrest. Her husband and one son were allowed to visit in August 1995. It is not exactly clear why the SLORC allowed Suu Kyi to go free, but experts on Burma consider it doubtful that international pressure had much to do with it; the military government historically has been extremely isolationist and suspicious of foreigners. Suu Kyi's freedom is still conditional. Her family has remained in England, and she fears that if she leaves the country to visit them, she will not be allowed to return. Her phone is tapped and her activities are monitored by the military government. In addition, her lines of communication with the outside world are tenuous; a BBC radio interview she gave in August was jammed.

Burma, now officially called Myanmar, is still ruled by the military, which has been publicizing a convention it is sponsoring in order to write a constitution. One new law included is that anyone married to a foreigner is not eligible to hold office, a provision designed to exclude Suu Kyi from legitimate political life. Meanwhile, it is estimated that hundreds of supporters of democracy remain imprisoned.

In October 1995 her party, the NLD, officially proclaimed Suu Kyi its leader, but the military government ruled that to be an illegal action, citing a law that prevents political parties from changing leadership without its permission. In November the NLD announced it would boycott the military's constitution-writing convention. Recently, as the party has been gathering power, the military government has been again arresting NLD members.

Since her release, Suu Kyi's home has been the regular site of large groups of people—reporters, tourists, supporters, and food vendors. She addresses a huge crowd every weekend. One of the first speeches she gave upon release was videotaped and sent to the Nongovernmental Organizations Forum on Women that was held in China in August 1995. It served as the keynote address for the conference.

An associate of Suu Kyi has remarked on the change in her after six years of house arrest: "Her sense of mission grew when they placed her under house arrest, and it came to her even more strongly when she won the Nobel Peace Prize. . . . [Before her arrest] she looked like a schoolgirl. Today she looks like a much older woman than she is."

At this time, the future of Suu Kyi and of her country remains uncertain. What is clear, though, is her remarkable courage and commitment to the struggle for human rights in the face of political oppression. One of Suu Kyi's notable contributions to the study and practice of non-violent dissent is her description of the relationship between fear and corrupt power in society. She lists the fears that hold people back from fighting for human rights: "fear of imprisonment, fear of torture, fear of death, fear of losing friends, family, property or means of livelihood, fear of poverty, fear of isolation, fear of failure. A most insidious form of fear is that which masquerades as common sense or even wisdom, condemning as foolish, reckless, insignificant or futile the small, daily acts of courage which help to preserve man's self-respect and inherent human dignity."

Suu Kyi has been an inspiration to many people around the world, but most importantly to those in Burma. A statement she made in a 1989 interview helps to illustrate her personal appeal: "I try to put heart into the people because a lot of them are frightened that if they do anything, they ll be imprisoned or harassed. I tell people, 'If you give in to intimidation, you ll go on being intimidated.'" As for her own personal safety, she says that "is not a question that interests me very much."

MARRIAGE AND FAMILY

Suu Kyi and Michael Aris were married in 1972 in a Buddhist ceremony at the Gore-Booth home in London. Aris is a Research Fellow in Tibetan Studies at Oxford's St. Anthony's College; he has also spent time as a visiting professor at Harvard University. Their two sons, Alexander and Kim, were born in 1973 and 1977. Since her release from house arrest, Suu Kyi has said, "I hope to be with my family as much as possible, but I think I will not be able to have a normal family life for a very long time."

WRITINGS

Aung San, 1984
Aung San of Burma, 1991

Freedom from Fear and Other Writings, 1991 (edited by Michael Aris)
Let's Visit Burma, 1985 (juvenile)
Let's Visit Nepal, 1985 (juvenile)

HONORS AND AWARDS

Sakharov Prize for Freedom of Thought (European Parliament): 1990
Thorolf Rafto Prize for Human Rights (Norway): 1990
Nobel Peace Prize: 1991
Jawaharlal Nehru Award (Indian Council on Cultural Relations, India): 1995

FURTHER READING

BOOKS

Clements, Alan, and Leslie Kean. *Burma's Revolution of the Spirit: The Struggle for Democratic Freedom and Dignity*, 1994
Columbia Encyclopedia, 1993

PERIODICALS

Chicago Tribune, Oct. 15, 1991, p.10; July 10, 1995, p.2; Aug. 31, 1995, p.2
Christian Science Monitor, Sep. 5, 1995, p.1
Financial Times (London), Oct. 24, 1988, p.50; Aug. 22, 1995, p.5
Gazette (Montreal), Oct. 27, 1991, p.B5; July 15, 1995, p.H6
Independent (London), Dec. 6, 1992, p.15; Aug. 21, 1995, p.9
Los Angeles Times, July 10, 1990, p.H2
New York Times, Feb. 20, 1994, p.E4; Sep. 21, 1994, p.A3
New York Times Biographical Service, Oct. 1991, p.1092
New York Times Magazine, Jan. 7, 1996, p.32
Philadelphia Inquirer, May 9, 1989, p.A3; Aug. 16, 1992, p.B8
Time, July 24, 1995, p.48
Times of London, July 9, 1995, Overseas news section; July 16, 1995, Overseas news section; Mar. 2, 1996, Features section
Vanity Fair, Oct. 1995, p.120
Vogue, Oct. 1995, p.318
Washington Post, Sep. 1, 1995, p.A25

OTHER

"Weekend Edition," Transcript from *National Public Radio*, Sep. 2, 1995

ADDRESS

Aung San Suu Kyi
c/o British Embassy
Yangon, Myanmar

BOYZ II MEN

Michael McCary   1971-
Nathan Morris   1971-
Wanya Morris   1973-
Shawn Stockman   1972-
American Singers

EARLY YEARS

The popular singing group Boyz II Men includes four members: Michael "Bass" McCary, born on December 16, 1971; Nathan "Alex Vanderpool" Morris, born on June 18, 1971; Wanya (pronounced wan-yea) "Squirt" Morris (no relation to Nathan), born on July 29, 1973; and Shawn "Slim" Stockman, born on September 26, 1972.

Not a lot is known about the early years of the members of Boyz II Men; many details of their family histories are not available. Some reviewers have conjectured that they guard their privacy in order to maintain a certain public image. According to one report, their families have been instructed not to speak with the media. Whatever the reason, the flow of information to the public has been very tightly controlled.

It is known, though, that all four were born in Philadelphia, Pennsylvania, and grew up in urban neighborhoods in and around that city: Michael is from Logan, Nathan is from South Philadelphia, Wanya is from North Philadelphia, and Shawn is from Southwest Philly. Each of the four spent much of their childhood in single-parent households run by their mothers. None of their families had very much money. Despite the difficulties their families faced, the members of Boyz II Men all talk about the strong values they learned in their homes and the important role that religion played in their lives. Here, each of the four Boyz talks about some of their experiences growing up.

Wanya: "We are all from urban neighborhoods in Philly. These were loving communities that turned a corner during our lifetimes. As we grew up, the neighborhoods got worse. Bad things were all around us. Gangs and drugs were on the rise. Drugs were as available as a pack of cigarettes. I sat there and watched a lot of things happening. I saw my boys die. A lot of them. . . . Drugs got the best of my mother, just like my boys who I was hanging around with. It got the best of them. . . . You can't help a person doing drugs. It made our life hard, very hard. . . . I wasn't scared because everybody knew me, and I never did anything bad to anybody, but I was growing up fast because there was nobody else to raise us. I was still young, didn't know what was going on, but you do what you have to do. A lot of things happened during the years my mom was on drugs and was trying to get off. For a time, we were on welfare. Welfare was cool. I was still Wanya. I learned to look at everything carefully, to analyze everything. I was raised by everybody living in the projects. That's what grew me up. Growing up in the projects made me grow older more quickly than anybody."

Michael: "My mom always worked, but in between jobs, she made sure we were taken care of. Even though we didn't have much, we were always all right. There was food, a roof over our heads, and lots of love. There were drugs and violence outside—people on the corner selling drugs. People slinging dice. But that didn't mean you had to get involved. The difference was our upbringing. The need for attention is what makes people do bad things. They want quick money, flash. While they were out there doing that, we were studying our books. Mom taught us that the way to get all the things that you want in life is through books, not slinging any dice."

Nathan: "I'm from a family of two sisters and one brother. I was the youngest. When I was about nine or ten, my mom and dad were going through a divorce. Things weren't all that great. We didn't have everything we wanted to have. There were times when there was no electricity and no gas or water. But my mom tried to make the situation better. We moved in with my grandmother for a while until my mom found something better. After that we moved to South Philly. Now that we have a better life—an easier life—I remember all we went through. It was tough on both of my parents, and they never gave up trying, trying to take care of their family. It makes me remember what it is I'm here to do. Things may be easier now, but the values don't change. I always remember where I'm from. We all do. There is no pretending to be something special, something high and mighty, when you know your roots."

Shawn: "I'm from a typical black neighborhood that you'll find in southwest Philly. I lived with my mother and three brothers and sister. Everybody knew each other. Everybody looked out for each other. Yes, there were things out there to trip you up. But you didn't have to do those things. My mother taught me to read and write and to read the Bible. She instilled in me the sense of what is right and what is wrong. It lasted in me enough so that I was able to avoid trouble. If I didn't feel comfortable doing something, if it didn't feel right next to what my mother taught me, I wouldn't do it."

EDUCATION

The four members of Boyz II Men didn't know each other when they were very young, and yet there was one striking similarity to all their childhoods: all loved music from an early age. They all reminisce about the music they listened to as children. Their families played music all the time, and they listened to gospel, soul, rhythm and blues, and the Motown sound. They all started singing along at an early age, too.

That passion for music soon led each of them to audition for, and to win acceptance to, the High School for Creative and Performing Arts in Philadelphia, a magnet school for talented young students. It was a revelation, they've said, to find themselves in a school filled with students equally passionate about music. It was also a revelation to learn that the school's demanding curriculum featured classical music, jazz, and music composition and theory. "Coming from the neighborhoods we came from," Nathan recalls, "we weren't used to hearing a lot of classical music and jazz and opera. We saw the school as being like the TV show 'Fame,' but when we got there and heard people singing classical music, it was 'This ain't what I saw.' But when you get into it, you realize there are similarities between everything. Knowing all that just makes you a well-rounded musician." Shawn agrees, saying, "It opened our minds and our ears to different things, helped us write our music in different ways." As Wanya adds, "With classical as your roots, and experience behind you, then you can sing anything. We took that training and put it into what we do, and that's what gives us our uniqueness."

FORMING THE GROUP

It was while in high school that the group got together. But they weren't friends at first. They first met because they were singing in the choir at school. Shawn was a nerd, he says, always reading comic books and listening to metal music. Nathan was the cool one, hanging around with all the popular kids and the good singers.

Nathan was trying to get a group together, as he explains here. "We were sort of organizing a singing group, using different members of the choir. Finally we had Shawn, Wanya, a friend named Marc Nelson, and myself together, singing as a group. We hadn't met Michael yet. One day, the four of us were singing in the bathroom, practicing in there. The song was 'Can You Stand the Rain?' by New Edition. Michael happened to come in and, without anyone saying a word, he started singing, adding the bass note. It was what we needed, tied the whole thing together."

The acoustics in the bathrooms were so good, in fact, that that's where they could often be found practicing, as recounted here by Ellen Savitz, their former vice principal. "They are four of the nicest young men. A lot of the time, they'd be in the bathrooms harmonizing instead of going to class, because sometimes they thought they wouldn't need math or physics because they were going to make it big in music. But even when I made them go back to class, they were always polite and cooperative." Savitz also remembers "riding them to death because they'd be three minutes late for a class because of harmonizing—or flirting—but there was never an attitude from any of them. I used to have to kick them out of the auditorium in the late afternoon because they'd always be rehearsing. And you just knew they were going to make it—they had all of the confidence that was needed."

After several months of practice, they gave their first performance at a school talent show in 1989. It confirmed all their hopes about the future. As Wanya tells it, "The curtains opened, and we sang, and there was a bunch of people we'd known for the longest time, screaming like they'd never seen us before. Suddenly, we thought, 'This could be a career.'" Michael confirms it. "We didn't expect to get that kind of response. [The other students] had heard us numerous times—in the bathroom, in the lunchroom, on the roof, the hallways—but they said it was like a whole different group up there—a lot of the girls we dealt with said they were melting, falling out of their seats as if it was an actual concert."

GETTING DISCOVERED

They were still in school, singing in the bathrooms, in subway stations, and on street corners, when they got their big break. They sang all about it on their first hit, "Motownphilly." The Boyz attended a concert in Philadelphia and snuck backstage just as Michael Bivens walked through. Bivens, formerly with New Edition and at that time with Bell Biv DeVoe, had recently been offered a deal to develop new talent. When the Boyz saw Bivens, they knew it was their big chance. They asked if they could sing for him, and without waiting for a reply, launched into the New Edition hit, "Can You Stand the Rain." A crowd gathered around as they sang a cappella, or without instrumental accompaniment. When they finished, they expected to get the brush-off. Instead, Bivens gave his phone number to Nathan. "I was curious where they stood as far as stage presence," Bivens later recalled. "I wasn't seeing the complete package. But I could see that they had the most important piece, which a lot of groups were missing at the time—the vocals."

As it turned out, Will Smith, the rapper Fresh Prince, was one of those listening that night. He invited the group to come back to his house to sing at a party. "Everybody just kept requesting songs, and we just kept on singing," Shawn recalls. "That was a very magical night."

Nathan started calling Bivens every day until he finally agreed to represent them. He got them a deal with Motown Records, and they started out by singing background vocals. Bivens also helped them develop the collegiate boy-next-door image for which they are known today. He based it on a preppie character named Alex Vanderpool from his favorite soap opera, "All My Children." They started dressing in matching preppie outfits, wearing conservative things like cardigan sweaters, button-down shirts, ties, Bermuda shorts, khaki pants, and leather loafers. The look was designed to separate them from the hard-core "gangsta" rappers, to help them broaden their appeal to a large group of fans, and to make them look clean-cut, charming, polite, wholesome, humble, and friendly. It worked.

CAREER HIGHLIGHTS

The music of Boyz II Men is based, first and foremost, on their beautiful singing voices and their gorgeous, lush harmonies. Soul, rhythm & blues, funk, and hip hop all find their way into the music—in fact, their music has been called "hip-hop meets doo-wop." They write the lyrics and arrange the harmonies for most of the songs they record themselves. Despite the influences of modern music, electronic synthesizers and dubbing and mixing never steal the focus from their clear vocals.

No single lead singer predominates in Boyz II Men. Instead, Shawn, Nathan, and Wanya alternate singing lead, with Mike providing the bass.

Here, Wanya describes their individual sounds: "Shawn has a soft, sultry type of voice, and brings out the sound of a classically trained singer. Nathan's voice has the R & B bottom and a pop-soul feel. I bring a stronger gospel flavor to my voice and ad libs. And Mike is the (true) bottom, the bass, the thing that links us. So together we contain elements that can appeal to any kind of ear." Indeed, the music brings together fans of different ages, races, and backgrounds.

Their debut album, *Cooleyhighharmony,* came out in 1991. It quickly won them a bevy of new fans and a host of awards, including three Grammy Awards, two NAACP Image Awards, five Soul Train Awards, and three American Music Awards. Their first single "Motownphilly," which told the story of the group's history and described their musical style, placed in the Top 5 on the Singles charts. That was followed by "It's So Hard to Say Goodbye to Yesterday," a haunting, lyrical, and nostalgic a cappella ballad from the early 1970s film *Cooley High.* Then "End of the Road" came out, a single from the soundtrack to the Eddie Murphy film *Boomerang.* It set a record by holding the No. 1 spot on the Top Singles chart for 13 straight weeks, breaking the previous 12-week record set by Elvis Presley's 1956 hit, "Don't Be Cruel." (Boyz II Men's record was later broken by Whitney Houston's "I Will Always Love You.")

After several years of touring and an album of holiday songs, *Christmas Interpretations*, Boyz II Men went back to the studio in 1994 and recorded

a new album, *II*. The album features soulful vocals, lush, four-part harmonies, funky R & B beats, and the help of some of the top music producers, including Babyface, Dallas Austin, Jimmy Jam, and Terry Lewis. The album speaks about love in all its forms, on such hits as "I'll Make Love II You," "Water Runs Dry," "On Bended Knee," and their soulful remake of the Beatles song "Yesterday." Again, the album was a huge hit. "I'll Make Love II You" spent 14 weeks at the No. 1 spot on the charts, tying the record set by Whitney Houston. Ironically, "I'll Make Love II You" was bumped from the No. 1 spot by another Boys II Men tune, "On Bended Knee."

The combined sales of their recordings, to date, total more than 17 million. The success of this group, in such a short time, has been phenomenal. Boyz II Men currently has plans to continue touring through the end of 1995. What could be next for this popular group? The members of Boyz II Men are all still young—in their early 20s—and their fans certainly hope that they will continue to record and tour for many years to come. When asked which direction they will head after this, Shawn says that they may diversify: "One of our goals in our career is to break out and do all types of music, if possible. We love all types of music. . . . We would love to, maybe one day if it's possible, do a gospel album. Or maybe a country album or a classical album. We just love music." When speaking of the future, the members of the group are also quick to call on God: "There are always going to be different forks in the road," Wanya said. "It's just a matter of choosing which dream to follow. You have to look through your dreams and follow them in the right frame of mind with the Lord behind you. That's not just important for us, it's important for everybody."

MAJOR INFLUENCES

All the members of Boyz II Men quickly credit their families and God as the most influential forces in their lives. Musically they cite a range of influences, from listening to gospel at church, to the Motown sound from the 1960s and the Philadelphia sound from the 1970s, including groups like the Temptations, the Four Tops, the Isley Brothers, the Blue Notes, and the O'Jays.

Their most important musical influence, though, is the group they call "the epitome of harmony," the modern gospel group Take 6. "Their blend was just so good that vocally that's who we pattern ourselves after," Nathan confirms. "We dissect Take 6," Michael said, "to see how their vocal parts go, how they switch up, how they find six-part harmony in a song where it's hard to find six-part harmony."

HOME AND FAMILY

The members of Boyz II Men all still live in the Philadelphia area, and all still live at home with their families. None have yet married. They are so busy with their commitments to the group, they say, that they don't even have time for serious relationships.

HOBBIES AND OTHER INTERESTS

The members of Boyz II Men have been so busy touring for the past few years that they have had little free time for any outside interests. They enjoy watching basketball, and they play in charity games to support various organizations. In particular, they have supported Big Brothers and Big Sisters and have visited with sick children.

RECORDINGS

Cooleyhighharmony, 1991
Christmas Interpretations, 1993
II, 1994

HONORS AND AWARDS

Grammy Awards: 1991, for Best R & B Group Vocal Performance, for *Cooleyhighharmony*; 1992, for Best R & B Group Vocal Performance, for "End of the Road"; 1994, for Best R & B Group Vocal Performance, for "I'll Make Love to You"; 1994, for Best R & B Album, for *II*
Image Awards (NAACP): 1992, for Best New Recording Artist; 1994, for Outstanding Vocal Group
American Music Awards: 1992, for Favorite New Soul/R & B Artist; 1993, for Favorite Soul/R & B Group and Favorite Pop/Rock Single, for "End of the Road"; 1995 (3 awards), Favorite Pop/Rock Single and Favorite Soul/R & B Single, for "I'll Make Love to You," and Favorite Soul/ R & B Group
Soul Train Awards: 1992, for Best New R & B/Soul Artist; 1993 (3 awards), for Best R & B Single by a Group, for "Please Don't Go," Best R & B Song, for "End of the Road," and Best Music Video, for "End of the Road"; 1995 (3 awards), for Best R & B Group, Best R & B Album, for *II*, and Best R & B Single, for "I'll Make Love to You"

FURTHER READING

BOOKS

Boyz II Men: Us II You, 1995

PERIODICALS

Boston Globe, Jan. 17, 1992, p.81
Ebony Man, June 1995, p.64
Interview, Aug. 1995, p.70
Jet, Aug. 7, 1995, p.36

New York Times, Oct. 9, 1994, Sec. II, p.38
New Yorker, Aug. 21 & 28, 1995, p.54
Newsday, Sep. 6, 1994, Part II, p.B4
Parade, Oct. 11, 1992, p.20
Philadelphia Magazine, Aug. 1992, p.29
Philadelphia Daily News, Aug. 14, 1991, p.39
Philadelphia Inquirer, Sep. 1, 1991, p.H1; Sep. 6, 1992, p.H1; Aug. 28, 1994, p.G1
Rolling Stone, Mar. 5, 1992, p.21
USA Weekend, Feb. 19-21, 1993, p.4
Washington Post, Apr. 19, 1992, p.G1

ADDRESS

Davis, Bane Associates Inc.
1899 "L" Street NW
Suite 500
Washington, D.C. 20036

Brandy 1979-
American Singer and Actress
Pop Singer and Star of the TV Sitcom "Moesha"

BIRTH

Brandy Norwood was born on February 11, 1979, in McComb, Mississippi. Her father, Willie Norwood, Sr., is a church choir director who also acts as his daughter's vocal coach. Her mother, Sonja Norwood, worked for H&R Block, the tax preparation firm. Now she manages her daughter's singing and acting career. Brandy's brother, Willie Jr., is two years younger. He has a successful career of his own as a television actor and aspiring recording artist.

YOUTH

Willie and Sonja Norwood moved the family from Mississippi to the Los Angeles suburb of Carson City when Brandy was four years old. She was already a singer, having performed her first solo, "Jesus Loves Me," in church at the age of two. Willie Sr. encouraged both of his children to sing with the church choir that he directed, making sure that they always stood in the front where they could be featured as soloists. This early exposure to gospel music had a profound influence on the development of Brandy's singing style.

Brandy was performing in talent shows by the time she was 11 and landed her first record deal at age 14. But her parents kept a close eye on her, refusing to let her date until she was older and making sure that the songs she sang were appropriate for someone her age. Other teenagers might have been tempted to rebel, but Brandy knew that her parents were only trying to prevent her from growing up too fast. Despite the fact that the family has lived in the Los Angeles area for the past 13 years, Brandy's mother states proudly that her daughter has been raised "Southern style."

Brandy credits her mother with encouraging her to pursue her dream of being a singer. "My mom told me that if I was going to listen to all the people who told me I would never make it, I wouldn't realize my dream. If I really wanted it, I had to get my life together and work at being the best I could be."

EARLY MEMORIES

When Brandy was 10 years old, she went to see the legendary Little Richard perform at the Los Angeles Forum. When he invited some members of the audience to come up and dance with him, Brandy bounded onto the stage without a moment's hesitation. But once she was up there, she completely forgot that Little Richard was the star of the show. Instead, she walked to the edge of the stage and started blowing kisses to the audience. Her mother remembers feeling embarrassed. But for Brandy, it was a moment she would never forget. She pretended that she was the one all those people had come to see.

FIRST JOBS

As a 12-year-old, Brandy auditioned for record label talent scouts as part of a three-girl group. Although the trio never landed a record contract, Brandy ended up with a job working as a backup singer for a new group known as Immature. At the same time, she decided to try acting and landed several roles in commercials. After a couple of years with Immature, Brandy was ready to begin working on solo material. But she'd just been hired to play Danesha on ABC's 1993 television sitcom, "Thea." So she had to confine her work in the recording studio to weekends.

"Thea" lasted only one season, but Brandy gained valuable experience by being on the show. "It helped me to be focused," she explains. "I got to be in front of cameras." When she found out the show was being canceled, Brandy was relieved because it meant that she could get back to what she regarded as her real vocation: singing.

EDUCATION

Brandy was a freshman at Hollywood High School in Los Angeles when her singing career took off. She dropped out and hired a private tutor, who works with her for about three hours a day. Brandy says she prefers tutoring because of the one-on-one attention she receives. Her favorite subjects are math and driver's ed.

Now 17, Brandy has every intention of finishing high school. If her singing career falls through, she says she'll go to college, study law, and become "the next Johnnie Cochran," referring to the prominent African-American lawyer who successfully defended O. J. Simpson.

CAREER HIGHLIGHTS

Brandy signed her first record deal with Atlantic Records when she was 14. She worked for eight months putting together her first album, *Brandy*, which she describes as being "very young, positive, soulful, and pop." Her first album was a hit. It quickly went "triple platinum," which means that it sold more than three million copies, and it made Brandy a star. Two of the singles from her album, "I Wanna Be Down" and "Baby," also went platinum, selling more than a million copies each. A third single, "Brokenhearted," has already gone gold, selling half a million copies, and "Best Friend" achieved Top Ten status on the R&B (rhythm and blues) charts.

In addition to her own album, Brandy's voice can be heard on the soundtrack for two feature-length movies, *Batman Forever* and *Waiting to Exhale*. She also sang Michael Jackson's hit song, "Rock With You," for Quincy Jones's album, *Q's Jook Joint*. Most of her songs are a combination of hip-hop and R&B, but her voice has a sincere, emotional quality that reminds people of classic soul music. She's better with ballads than any other young singer recording today, reviewers agree. Her ability to shift from a throaty purr to soft fluttery vocals gives many listeners the impression that she is 10 years older. "I learned a lot about the power of singing by singing praises in church," Brandy adds.

Brandy's new TV show "Moesha," a half-hour comedy on UPN (United Paramount Network), premiered in January 1996. Brandy plays an African-American teenager growing up in Los Angeles. Moesha Mitchell comes from a tightly-knit, middle-class family in which she is accustomed to acting as the woman of the house. But when her father marries a teacher at her high school, Moesha is forced to adjust to a new stepmother. Moesha is a responsible young woman and an excellent student who is still very interested in clothes and boys. In fact, she's so much like the real-life Brandy Norwood that Brandy feels entirely comfortable playing herself in the role.

Although the demands of taping a weekly show have forced her to put her singing career on hold, Brandy plans to return to the recording studio as soon as possible to complete her second album. Does she resent this interruption in her booming career as a recording artist? Not this time. Brandy realizes that the opportunity to do a regular weekly television show is a rare one for a young singer, and that the exposure will prove valuable.

Whether she's singing on MTV or appearing in "Moesha," Brandy cultivates an image that she hopes will be a positive influence on other girls her age. She never wears clothes that are too baggy or too tight. She wears her hair in finely-braided "dreads" that show pride in her African-American heritage. She won't accept movie roles that include swearing, and she avoids promoting sex or violence in any form.

Richard Nash, Senior Vice President of Black Music for Atlantic Records, praises Brandy's response to her sudden fame. "With all that's been hap-pening to her, she's been able to cope with it and remain very humble. Also, she listens well and communicates very intelligently, something that's important in this business."

HOME AND FAMILY

Brandy still lives with her parents, although they've recently moved to the San Fernando Valley so that her mother can have her dream house and Brandy can be closer to the "Moesha" set. She considers her younger brother Willie her best friend. In fact, it was Brandy who gave Willie's career a boost when she took him along to meet her agent. Just like his older sister, Willie is now working on TV and has completed a solo album.

What's it like to have your parents as managers? "Sometimes I get irritated with them," Brandy says, "especially when I want to go places and I can't." But despite her parents' strict supervision—her mother must still approve the lyrics of any song she sings and won't let her wear anything "inappropriate" for a girl her age—Brandy knows that she can attribute much of her commercial success to her parents' support and involvement. Even though her parents gave her permission to date when she turned 16, her busy professional life has left no time for a serious boyfriend. She also admits that it's difficult to know whether the boys who want to date her are interested in her as a person or just want to be seen with her because she's a celebrity.

Brandy's music reflects her stable family background. "Best Friend," her hit single, is about her relationship with her younger brother. "Give Me You" is an expression of her deep religious faith. And in "I Dedicate (Part I)," she pays tribute to her family and the artists who have inspired her.

MAJOR INFLUENCES

When Brandy was learning how to control her own singing voice, she often listened to the music of Aretha Franklin and Stevie Wonder. But since the age of about seven, her idol has been Whitney Houston. The two finally met when Brandy hosted Nickelodeon's Kids' Choice Awards, and Houston herself referred to Brandy as "the next Whitney Houston." Later, Brandy was asked to do a song ("Sitting Up in My Room") for the sound-track of Houston's hit movie, *Waiting to Exhale*.

Houston warned Brandy that being a singer involved a great deal of hard work, and that she would probably be tired and frustrated much of the time. "I've gotten tired," Brandy admits, "but I haven't been frustrated yet."

HOBBIES AND OTHER INTERESTS

When she's not rehearsing or touring, Brandy likes to shop (usually at Urban Outfitters and Contempo Casuals), sleep late, and hang out with her younger brother, whom she describes as "overprotective." When she listens to music, her favorites are Soundgarden, Metallica, Snoop Doggy Dogg, Toni Braxton, and of course Whitney Houston.

Brandy speaks regularly at high schools for Black Entertainment Television's "Back to School" program. She is also an ambassador for the Sabriya Castle of Fun Foundation, which provides outreach activities for hospital-ized children and teenagers. She is an active supporter of the National Council of Negro Women, the Black Family Reunion, the Brotherhood Crusade, and RAINN (Rape Abuse, Incest National Network). She recently took part in an all-star benefit concert at New York City's Madison Square Garden to benefit Urban Aid/LIFEBeat.

Right now Brandy and her mother are putting together a nonprofit organization for underprivileged children who show promise in the arts. Her commitment to social causes has set her apart from some other teenage stars. "I may be young," she says, "but I can already see that you only get out of life what you put in, and music and TV aren't everything."

HONORS AND AWARDS

Billboard Video Awards: 1995, for "I Wanna Be Down" and "Baby"
Billboard Awards: 1995, for Best New Artist, R&B, and Best R&B Female
Soul Train's "Lady of Soul" Awards: 1995, for Best R&B Single, Solo and R&B/Soul Song of the Year for "I Wanna Be Down"; Best R&B/Soul New Artist; R&B/Soul Album of the Year; Best New Artist of the Year

FURTHER READING

Daily News of Los Angeles, Dec. 31, 1995, Women Section p.W1
Ebony, Feb. 1995, p.128
Miami Herald, Jan. 23, 1996, Living Section, p.C1
Orlando Sentinel, Jul. 23, 1995, Arts & Entertainment Section, p.Fl
People, Nov. 21, 1994, p.99
Rolling Stone, Apr. 6, 1995, p.32
Seventeen, Apr. 1995, p.158
USA Today, Feb. 14, 1995, Life Section, p.D6

ADDRESS

"Moesha"
UPN
11800 Wilshire Blvd.
Los Angeles, CA 90025

OBITUARY

Ron Brown 1941-1996
American Political Leader and
Cabinet Member
Secretary of the U.S. Department
of Commerce

BIRTH

Ronald Harmon Brown was born on August 1, 1941. He was born
in Washington, D.C., where his parents, William H. Brown and
Gloria Osborne Carter Brown, had attended Howard University.
He was their only child.

YOUTH

Ron Brown had an interesting and unusual childhood. When he was young, his family moved to Harlem, an all-black section of New York City, where his father became manager of the Hotel Theresa. At that time, Harlem was different from what it is today. There was poverty, to be sure, but very little crime or drugs. In the segregated era of Brown's childhood, Harlem was the largest African-American community in the United States. It was also a cultural mecca for blacks, attracting writers, artists, sports stars, musicians, singers, and other entertainers. Many notable stars performed at the famed Apollo Theater, which was right across the street from the Hotel Theresa. At that time, Jim Crow laws prevailed, segregating the races and restricting the facilities that African-Americans could use. Even top black stars couldn't stay in New York's fancy hotels for whites. So Harlem's Hotel Theresa became the finest hotel in New York for African-Americans, attracting the performers from the Apollo, as well as politicians, doctors, lawyers, sports heroes, and others.

It was in this fabled environment that Ron Brown grew up. He and his parents lived at the hotel, just down the hall from singer Dinah Washington. Brown grew accustomed to the glamorous and wealthy lifestyle of the hotel guests. Billie Holliday, Duke Ellington, Count Basie, and Billy Eckstine would all come over after their shows at the Apollo. Brown met politician Adam Clayton Powell, writer Ralph Ellison, actor Paul Robeson, baseball star Jackie Robinson, and boxers Sugar Ray Robinson and the great Joe Louis, known as the Brown Bomber, who gave Ron a pair of his boxing gloves. In fact, it was Louis who put a stop to Ron's great money-making scheme: he would pester the hotel's famous guests for autographs and then sell them to his friends for five dollars each. Brown's favorite hangout at the hotel was up on the roof, where he played basketball on a makeshift court, watching the streetcorner orators and hustlers down below.

But Brown's early experiences were not limited to that neighborhood in Harlem. His parents, who were both college graduates, believed strongly in the importance of education. They sent their son to several private and public predominately white schools outside of Harlem. Brown developed the ability to move gracefully between different worlds and to function comfortably in all-white settings. These qualities, observers say, combined with his unshakable self-confidence, poise, ambition, and irrepressible good spirits, served him well in later years. For Brown, these early experiences helped him to feel comfortable in every environment.

EDUCATION

Brown attended several schools growing up. He started out at the exclusive Hunter College Elementary School on the upper east side, where he was the only black student in his class. He then attended two private college prep schools on the upper west side, Walden School and Rhodes School. Brown also attended White Plains High School for a time.

In 1958, Brown enrolled at Middlebury College, a predominately white liberal-arts college in Middlebury, Vermont. Like many of his classmates, he pledge a fraternity there, Sigma Phi Epsilon. Brown didn't realize, when he first pledged, that the fraternity was restricted to whites. Then members of the fraternity's national organization tried to talk him into accepting house privileges rather than full membership. Brown refused. The Middlebury chapter then invited him to join despite the national group's restrictions, and Brown became the first black accepted into a fraternity at the college. But the national organization revoked the group's charter, essentially kicking the Middlebury chapter out of the national fraternity. The college responded by banning racial restrictions at all the school's fraternities.

While in college, Brown joined the U.S. Army's ROTC (Reserve Officers' Training Corps) to help pay for school. His parents wanted him to be a doctor, and he started out in the pre-med program at Middlebury. But an unfortunate experience with organic chemistry forced him to switch majors; as he later joked, "Organic chemistry turned me into a political-science major." Brown earned his bachelor's degree (B.A.) from Middlebury in 1962. After a stint in the army, it took him several years of working and going to school at night before he earned his law degree (J.D.) in 1970 from St. John's University School of Law in New York.

MILITARY SERVICE

In 1962, after graduating from Middlebury, Brown joined the army to fulfill his ROTC commitment. He started out in training at Fort Eustis, Virginia. A recently commissioned second lieutenant, he and his bride, Alma, were en route to their new home when they were refused service at a restaurant in Virginia. Brown had had so little experience with racism that he didn't recognize it even then. After training in Virginia, he served first in West Germany, where he supervised a staff of 60 German civilians in charge of logistics. Promoted to captain, he was sent to Korea as commandant of an elite training school that taught Korean soldiers how to work with Americans. In the army, Brown later said, "I learned to be comfortable taking command." He completed his tour of service and left Korea in 1966.

CAREER HIGHLIGHTS

In a distinguished career that spanned some 30 years, Brown rarely focused directly on the issue of race, preferring to let his accomplishments speak for themselves. But still, he achieved a series of notable "firsts": he was the first African-American to be named chief counsel to the Senate

Judiciary Committee, the first to make partner at his influential Washington law firm, the first to be elected chairman of a major national political party, and the first to be named Secretary of the U.S. Department of Commerce. In all these roles, he was known for his skills in leadership, in making deals, and in building bridges between people.

THE NATIONAL URBAN LEAGUE

Brown started his career back in New York, where he had grown up. He returned there after leaving the army and was hired in 1967 by the National Urban League, a respected national civil-rights organization. He worked there for the next 12 years. He started out doing welfare casework and running job training programs. At night, he studied law at St. John's University School of Law, where one of his professors was Mario Cuomo, later governor of New York and a powerful figure in the Democratic party. After receiving his law degree in 1970, Brown continued to work for the National Urban League, earning a series of promotions there. He made his first foray into Democratic Party politics in 1971, when he was elected district leader of the Democratic party in Mount Vernon, New York (just outside New York City). One of his colleagues from that time recalled that Brown "had a knack that he could sit down with anybody and reason with them." Already he was demonstrating the skills in conciliation that would serve him so well later in life.

In 1973, Brown moved to Washington, D.C., where he held a variety of positions with the National Urban League, including chief spokesman, vice-president for Washington operations, general counsel, and deputy executive director, the second-highest post in the organization. By 1979, though, he was ready for a change. He had spent his entire professional career working for an organization that focused on issues for African-Americans, and he was eager to try something new. As he later said, "One of the reasons I was anxious to leave the Urban League was [that] I was tired of being limited by a small pond. . . . You know, I was an expert on all things black."

So in 1979, Brown went to work for Senator Edward (Teddy) Kennedy, who was then running for the Democratic nomination for president in the 1980 election. Brown managed his presidential campaign in California. Although Kennedy lost in the race nationwide, he won in California. In August 1980 he offered Brown a job as chief counsel of the Senate Judiciary Committee, which Kennedy then chaired. Brown was the first African-American to hold that position. But just three months later, after the November elections, the Democratic party lost their majority in the Senate, thereby losing control of the Judiciary Committee. Brown moved to a position as staff director and general counsel of Kennedy's Senate staff.

BECOMING A CORPORATE LAWYER-LOBBYIST

In mid-1981, Brown left his Senate staff position to become a partner in a prominent Washington legal firm, Patton, Boggs & Blow, considered one of the capital's most influential lobbying firms. The first black ever named a partner there, Brown worked as both a lawyer and a lobbyist. On behalf of his clients he would meet with various government personnel, from legislators on Capitol Hill to regulators in government agencies, hoping to influence them to make decisions that would benefit his clients. Brown was good at it. "He has a deft touch on Capitol Hill, just like he has on a basketball court," according to Clifford Alexander, a fellow Washington lawyer and a basketball partner of Brown's. "He makes his opinions clear in a way that seem logical and fair, and he never boxes people into a corner. His approach is designed to get the job done."

With Patton, Boggs & Blow, Brown represented Sony, Toshiba, American Express, and the government of Haiti, among others. This last client, in particular, became controversial later because of the corrupt, dictatorial regime of Jean-Claude Duvalier, the leader of Haiti. At the law firm, Brown became known as a rainmaker, someone who can bring in new clients and revenue. His position as a partner paid a generous salary, the first time Brown had been well-compensated. He soon became known for his expensive clothing and other accouterments of a wealthy lifestyle. This period in his life would later come under close scrutiny amid reports of financial and ethical wrongdoings.

While working for Patton, Boggs & Blow, Brown also served in several political positions. He was the deputy chairman of the Democratic National Committee for three years, from 1982 to 1985. And in 1988 Brown served as Jesse Jackson's manager at the Democratic National Convention.

While making a strong bid for the 1988 Democratic nomination, Jackson had asked Brown to manage his presidential campaign. He resisted Jackson's entreaties until the very end, after Michael Dukakis had already clinched the nomination. Only then did Brown come on board. Both Dukakis and Jackson had strong views about various rules and political issues facing the Democrats, and the convention seemed headed for a battle. Brown's amiable style and consensus-building skills reconciled the Dukakis and Jackson camps and ensured a smooth national convention.

CHAIRMAN OF THE DEMOCRATIC NATIONAL COMMITTEE

Brown next set his sights on becoming the chairman of the Democratic National Committee, a position that is elected by the members of that committee. There were many who strongly opposed him. The Democratic party had been struggling in recent years, losing middle-class white voters to the Republicans during President Ronald Reagan's years. These voters believed that the Democrats were becoming too liberal. Southern voters, in particular, had deserted the Democratic party, and recapturing their support was considered crucial for the party's future success. Brown was seen as the worst possible candidate for party chair because he was supported by minorities and the labor movement and because he had strong ties to such liberals as Edward Kennedy, Mario Cuomo, and Jesse Jackson. The issue of race, also, was a subtext to these discussions, as many wondered whether a black chairman could lure Southern whites back to the party.

His detractors were soon proved wrong. When Brown won the position in 1989, becoming the first black ever to lead a major American political party, he said this in his acceptance speech. "Let me speak frankly. I did not run on the basis of race, but I will not run away from it. I am proud of who I am and I am proud of this party, for we are truly America's last best hope to bridge the divisions of race, region, religion, and ethnicity." He went on to promise that "the story of my chairmanship will not be about race. It will be about the races we win in the next four years."

As party chair, Brown proved to be adept at raising money, at working closely with fellow Democrats in state legislatures and in Washington, at crafting a consistent message, at helping others to solve problems and reconcile differences, and at reinvigorating and unifying a demoralized party. "He was one of the few politicians who could do all that had to be done," according to Eleanor Holmes Norton, the delegate to Congress from Washington, D.C. "He was a master strategist, extraordinary fundraiser, unparalleled spokesperson, and [he] had an uncanny knowledge of policy. Usually people have only one or two of those skills. He was a renaissance man of politics." Most importantly, Brown earned credit for winning elections: many observers praise Brown for recruiting the political team and engineering the strategy that helped Bill Clinton win the presidency in 1992.

SECRETARY OF COMMERCE

After the election, President Bill Clinton chose Ron Brown to be his Secretary of Commerce. As such, Brown served as one of the President's advisors on the Cabinet and also ran the Department of Commerce. A huge bureaucracy, the Commerce Department includes over 100 governmental programs. This diverse group includes weather forecasting, patent administration, high-tech research, and the Census Bureau, in addition to many business-related programs that foster economic development both at home and abroad.

Brown was widely regarded as a great Commerce Secretary. His department had been considered a bit of a backwater, not the most important or influential political role in the administration. With his skill at self-promotion, his flamboyant self-confidence, and his bottom-line emphasis on making deals, Brown changed all that. Determined to create a partnership between business and government, he transformed the department into a strong advocate for U.S. businesses overseas. For Brown, helping U.S. businesses win contracts would ultimately mean the creation of new jobs for Americans, which would strengthen our country. He also believed that economic growth would strengthen our trading partners as well, helping to foster peace, stability, and democracy. Brown called these efforts "commercial diplomacy," which he considered just as important as the usual political diplomacy. "Economic growth is the single most effective path to political stability," he said in 1993.

At the Commerce Department, Brown set up a "war room," where staffers kept track of foreign contracts and helped U.S. firms bid on them. One example that shows the efforts Brown put into helping American business was his work with the Raytheon Company of Massachusetts. Raytheon made a bid on a $1.4 billion radar contract with the government of Brazil. Brown organized a huge campaign to help Raytheon land the contract. He orchestrated a letter-writing campaign to Brazilian ministers from key U.S. governmental personnel, including members of the EPA, the FAA, and Congress. He asked President Clinton to call the prime minister of Brazil to voice his support for Raytheon. Brown made several trips to Brazil himself to lobby in person. He also lined up a financing package from the U.S. Export-Import Bank. Ultimately, with the help of the Commerce Department, Raytheon won the contract.

Personal visits to foreign lands were Brown's most effective bargaining tool. He worked hard to connect American business people with top government officials overseas, to battle red tape, and to convince foreign governments of the importance of business deals to the U.S. government. He would travel overseas on trade missions with the top officers, or CEOs (chief executive officers), of several U.S. companies. By his presence, he would show foreign officials the U.S. government's strong support for the mission. "There is no question," he once said, "that when that plane lands on runways around the world bearing the letters 'The United States of America,' and I come down the steps with a string of CEOs behind me, it conveys the power of this nation to turn commerce into the infrastructure of democracy."

This tactic, which was tremendously successful in winning foreign business for U.S. companies, won widespread accolades from American business leaders. As a top executive from General Electric Company said, "[Brown] succeeded in making of the Commerce Department what a lot of us really wanted it to be, namely a major advocate for American business in both international policy issues and international transactions." As the *New Yorker* explained, "Brown used his Cabinet authority to stimulate American exports . . . by taking a personal interest in helping to broker foreign deals for American companies—small and medium-sized business as well as corporate giants. His efforts paid off in the form of scores of billions of dollars' worth of aircraft, telecommunications, and high technology contracts. . . ." These contracts, according to the *New Republic*, "didn't just enrich individual firms but sustained entire industries." Brown was widely credited with winning more foreign business for U.S. companies than any previous Commerce Secretary.

Despite his successes, Brown also had his critics, and his tenure as Commerce Secretary was often controversial. Some objected to his overseas missions, saying that Brown ignored important human-rights issues with foreign governments in his quest for the deal. Others objected to his management of the Commerce Department on financial grounds, criticizing his refusal to make cutbacks in the department's large staff and faulting what they called excessively high expenses for his overseas trips. Still others charged Brown with favoritism and misuse of power, claiming that he often awarded the highly coveted seats on his overseas trade missions to executives who made sizeable contributions to the Democratic Party.

There were also serious questions about Brown's financial dealings. In 1993, the Federal Bureau of Investigation (FBI) reviewed charges that he had solicited a $700,000 bribe from someone promoting trade with Vietnam. Brown was cleared of those charges. There was also a series of allegations about financial impropriety related to his personal business interests. While none of these issues was ever proved, they led to recurring questions about his ethics. At the time of his death, Brown was under investigation by an independent counsel, who was reviewing allegations that he had used his public office for private gain. The key issue was whether he had violated any laws when he earned more than $300,000 in a business deal.

BROWN'S DEATH

In April 1996, Brown and a group of American executives traveled on a trade mission to Bosnia, charged with devising a plan to rebuild that war-torn nation. On April 3, 1996, his plane crashed into the side of a mountain outside Dubrovnik, on the Adriatic coast of Croatia. All 35 people on board died in the crash. Although the cause of the crash is not definitively known, several factors probably contributed, including poor weather, faulty and outdated instrumentation, lapses in safety procedures, and inadequate training of the crew.

In Washington, response to the accident was swift and heartfelt. As word swept through the capital, a spring day turned grim and tears flowed. The outpouring of grief was widespread and profound. President Clinton offered these words of consolation to the many friends who mourned Brown's loss. "He came on like a force of nature," Clinton said. "Ron Brown walked and ran and flew through life. And he was a magnificent life force. And those of use who loved him will always be grateful for his friendship and his warmth."

MARRIAGE AND FAMILY

Brown made an unusual impression on his future wife, Alma Arrington, on their first date. At the end of the evening, on the car ride from Greenwich Village to her home in Brooklyn, Brown fell asleep. As soon as he woke up, he started planning their next date. "There was always something different about him," she once said. "He was more mature than the other boys and sure of himself." Ron and Alma were married on August 11, 1962. They had two children, Michael and Tracey, who are both now attorneys. The Browns made their home in a four-bedroom townhouse in northwest Washington, D.C.

HONORS AND AWARDS

American Jurisprudence Award for Outstanding Achievement in
    Jurisprudence
Award for Outstanding Scholastic Achievement in Poverty Law

FURTHER READING

BOOKS

Who's Who in America, 1996
Who's Who in American Politics, 1995-1996
Who's Who among Black Americans, 1994-1995
World Book Encyclopedia, 1996

PERIODICALS

Current Biography Yearbook 1989
Ebony, May 1989, p.36; June 1996, p.28
GQ, July 1989, p.142

Jet, Apr. 22, 1996, p.4

New York Times, Apr. 12, 1994, p.A14; Apr. 4, 1996, pp.A1, A6, A7, and A8; Apr. 5, 1996, p.13; Apr. 10, 1996, p.A10; Apr. 11, 1996, p.C19

New York Times Magazine, Dec. 3, 1989, p.44

New Yorker, Apr. 15, 1996, p.9

Newsweek, Apr. 15, 1996, p.44

People, Jan. 18, 1993, p.49; Apr. 15, 1996, p.69

Time, Jan. 30, 1989, p.56; Apr. 15, 1996, pp.68 and 72

Washington Post, Dec. 25, 1994, p.H1; Apr. 4, 1996, p.A1

Mariah Carey 1970-
American Singer
Top Female Recording Artist

BIRTH

Mariah Carey was born on March 27, 1970, in New York City. She is the youngest of three children of Patricia Hickey and Alfred Roy Carey. Her father, who is of African-American and Venezuelan descent, was an aeronautical engineer. Her mother, the daughter of Irish immigrants, was a singer with the New York City Opera and a vocal coach. Her brother, Morgan, ten years older than Mariah, became a fitness trainer and band manager. Her sister, Alison, nine years older, became a homemaker. Mariah's mother named her after a favorite song from the Broadway musical *Paint Your Wagon*, "They Call the Wind Mariah."

YOUTH

Many aspects of Carey's childhood were difficult. Her parents divorced when she was three years old, partly due to the pressures they faced as an interracial couple in the 1960s. For example, she never knew her relatives on her mother's side of the family because they refused to speak to her mother after she married a black man. The Careys were also subjected to taunts and threats in their neighborhood, and Mariah remembers their dog being poisoned and their car being set on fire by intolerant and hateful people.

Shortly after her parents' divorce, Mariah's sister went to live with their father, while Mariah and her brother stayed with their mother. They did not have much money, so her mother often worked three jobs to make ends meet. They also moved around a lot, following job leads or staying with friends when times were tough. In fact, Mariah recalls that she had lived in 13 different places by the time she was 10 years old, when she and her mother finally settled in Huntington, New York, on Long Island.

Though her childhood was sometimes lonely, Carey says that her unusual upbringing also made her independent: "I've never thought of myself as a kid. When I was little, my mother used to say I was six going on 35. I was always around adults. I felt like I grew up on my own. I had a single parent. She was kind of working so I was by myself. I was always a little bit more mature than my friends . . . . I've been pretty self-reliant for a long time."

The now-glamorous singing star claims that she felt like an ugly duckling growing up. "My mom was sort of a left-over hippie. She wasn't the type of mom who dressed their girl's hair in little curly bows," Carey recalls. "At one point when I was 12, I tried to lighten [my hair] and it came out orange. And I didn't know that you were supposed to pluck your eyebrows, so I shaved them and they were uneven. So for a while I didn't have them."

Carey also had some problems coming to terms with her racial identity, which sometimes made her the object of unkind remarks at school. "It's been difficult for me, moving around so much, having to grow up by myself, basically on my own, my parents divorced. And I always felt kind of different from everyone else in my neighborhoods. I was a different person—ethnically. And sometimes that can be a problem," she admits. "You really have to look inside yourself and find your own inner strength, and say, I'm proud of what I am and who I am, and I'm just going to be myself."

CHOOSING A CAREER

Carey loved music from an early age and started singing at the age of four. Her mother gave her voice lessons, but she did not push her to follow in her footsteps and take up opera singing. Instead, she simply encouraged her daughter to develop her talent and let her find her own musical direction. Mariah recalls singing and listening to music constantly during her childhood: "I remember always wanting to be next to the radio and singing. I had to be dragged away from the radio to be put to sleep. And whenever I was down, I would sing to feel better. It seems I've always known this is what I wanted to do. There was like no choice." Her brother and sister enjoyed listening to music, too, and their love of the Motown sound and rhythm-and-blues music rubbed off on her. Sometimes she accompanied her paternal grandmother, who is black, to a Baptist church, where she grew to love gospel music. By the time Carey was 13 she had begun writing her own songs.

EDUCATION

Because she was driven to pursue a singing career, Carey did not apply herself to her studies during her school years. Her principal at Harborfields High School, John Garvey, tried to convince her of the importance of education, but he admits that "You could talk to her until you were blue in the face and it didn't do any good . . . . She'd let you know it just wasn't important in her life because she was going to be a rock star. She was fully convinced it was going to happen. Nothing was going to stand in her way."

Moving around so much prevented her from developing many close friendships, so Carey was able to devote all of her spare time to pursuing her dream. She used the vocal training skills taught to her by her mother, practicing scales and vocalizing to develop her range and strength. During high school she met Ben Margulies, who was a musician friend of her brother, and began collaborating with him in writing songs. They really clicked as a songwriting duo, as Carey remembers. Later, they would go on to great success together.

Carey often went to New York City to work on a demo tape of her singing, and she sometimes returned home late at night, even on school nights. As a result, she was often late for school and was never better than a mediocre student. She graduated from Harborfield High School in 1987.

FIRST JOBS

Immediately after graduating, Carey set out on her own, hoping to make her mark in the music business. "I packed up my stuffed animals and my posters and tapes, and I moved into the city," she explains. The struggling singer slept on a mattress on the floor in a tiny apartment in Manhattan, which she shared with two or three other aspiring performers. To make ends meet, she took various jobs as a waitress, coat-check girl, and hostess at restaurants. She also spent long hours in the recording studio writing songs, working on her demo tape, and singing backup for other artists. Carey gave her demo tape to numerous record-company representatives, but she did not have a big-name agent, and her work failed to attract attention. Her busy schedule and her determination to put her singing career first caused her to be fired from about 20 waitressing jobs within a year. Money was so tight during this time that Carey claims she sometimes made a single box of macaroni-and-cheese dinner last for a whole week.

CAREER HIGHLIGHTS

Carey's big break came in November 1988, about a year after she had moved to the city. At the time, she was singing backup for a rhythm-and-blues singer named Brenda K. Starr. The two women became friends, and Starr invited Carey to a Columbia Records party, where she could try to make recording-industry contacts. There Carey met Tommy Mottola, the president of Sony Music Entertainment (parent company of Columbia), and she gave him a copy of her demo tape. Since aspiring singers approached him all the time, Mottola accepted the tape unenthusiastically and soon left the party. In a turn of events that is now legendary, Mottola played the tape in his limousine on his way home and was so impressed that he instructed his driver to return to the party so he could find the young singer, but Carey had already left. Since her phone number was not on the tape, it took him two days to track her down through Starr's agent. "When I heard and saw Mariah, there was absolutely no doubt she was in every way destined for stardom," Mottola explains.

Within a few weeks, Carey had signed a contract with Columbia Records. The label had been looking for a female star to compete with such artists as Whitney Houston, Madonna, and Janet Jackson, and Mottola was convinced that Carey fit the bill. In fact, the company launched her career with one of the most expensive promotional campaigns ever for an unknown singer. Even before her first album was released, Columbia sent Carey to perform live at the National Association of Recording Merchandisers convention, where the people who decide what records to buy for retail stores are introduced to new talent. She also gained exposure on national television by singing "America the Beautiful" before the first game of the NBA championship series in 1990 and by appearing on the "Arsenio Hall Show" and the "Tonight Show."

ALBUMS MEET WITH PHENOMENAL SUCCESS

When Carey's first album, *Mariah Carey,* was released in 1990, it made her an overnight success. The album eventually sold 12 million copies worldwide, set a record by spawning four consecutive number-one singles, and earned Carey two Grammy Awards and three Soul Train Awards.

Though the album contained a few up-tempo songs, it primarily featured ballads about hardship and heartache. "A lot of those songs were written when I was kind of struggling, before I had a record deal," Carey notes. "It was a harrowing emotional time in my life. I was doing odd jobs and going toward this goal. They weren't necessarily all about relationships, but they were about things happening in my life." Carey wrote or co-wrote all the songs on the album, and she also played a role in its production— though not as large a role as she would have liked. Mottola had hand-picked several prominent producers to work with her, and she felt she should do as they said since this was her first effort.

Even though *Mariah Carey* was a huge popular success, the reaction of music critics was mixed. Some critics found her lyrics immature and her sound too similar to other pop divas, but others appreciated the amazing versatility of her voice. "Most singers are limited to a range of an octave or two," one critic explained. "But through years of training—for example, singing scales every day for 20 minutes at a stretch since the time she could walk—Carey has gradually increased the flexibility of her vocal cords." On her first album she displayed an incredible five-octave range, from deep, resonating bass notes to clear, piercing high notes.

Carey's second album, *Emotions,* released in 1991, was only slightly less successful, selling seven million copies and yielding her fifth consecutive number-one single. This time she handled most of the album's production herself and corrected what she saw as over-production on her initial effort. "You don't need to have five different synth parts on something," she explains. "Just put the most effective part on there, and let the vocals shine through." Carey drew upon the soul and rhythm-and-blues music of her childhood for inspiration in writing the songs for her second album. "*Emotions* has a little bit of an older-type vibe, a Motown feel," she says. "There's a lot more of me on this album. I let myself go a lot more. I tried to sing from deep inside myself."

Critics generally considered *Emotions* to be a more mature effort than her debut album. Carey drew special praise for her song "The Wind," in which she added lyrics about personal loss to an old blues instrumental. "There's a lot of messed-up things happening in the world—AIDS and everything else," she notes. "Actually, I never knew someone my age who died until a friend that I grew up with was recently killed in a drunk-driving accident. So I was kind of inspired by that, because it was the first time it was really real to me. When you're young, you don't really think of that. You think you're invincible."

In 1992 Carey released an extended-play live recording called *Mariah Carey—MTV Unplugged.* This record sold five million copies and generated another number-one single, her version of the Jackson Five hit "I'll Be There." Her next album, *Music Box,* appeared in 1993. This album featured two more number-one singles, "Dreamlover" and "Hero." "I like to try to give positive messages, if I can, in my music whenever I can . . . like with the songs 'Make It Happen' and 'Hero.' I do this because there is a lot of negativity out there and a lot of people are singing about how screwed up the world is, and I don't think that everybody wants to hear about that all the time," Carey says. "I wrote the song for a lot of kids who don't have someone who's supportive of them. All they have is someone who's trying to knock their dreams down." Many young people find "Hero" inspirational, and it has become a popular song played at high-school graduation ceremonies.

In 1994 Carey released an album of holiday favorites, *Merry Christmas*. Her 1995 album, *Daydream*, marked a bit of a departure for the singer. With an upbeat tempo and more of a street sound than her earlier work, it features collaborations with Boyz II Men and Babyface. A *Time* magazine reviewer called it "a refreshingly understated piece of work and her best album yet. Her vocals are strong and serenely passionate. Her lyrics . . . are smarter, and her rhymes more artful and flowing." A *Boston Globe* critic added that "the breadth of the music is startling, from traditional R&B to edgy hip-hop." The first single from the album, "Fantasy," became the first song by a female artist to debut at number one on the charts, and Carey received a Grammy nomination for "One Sweet Day," her duet with

Boyz II Men—thus continuing her unbroken string of recording successes.

PERFORMING IN PUBLIC

Unlike most other successful artists, Carey did not initially support her albums with concert tours. Before she was discovered, Carey had always preferred working in recording studios to performing in clubs, so she did not have much experience playing before an audience. "I know I have to go out and perform eventually," she said after the release of her second album. "It's hard for me because I'm not a ham. You have to be dynamic and showy, and that's not second nature for me. I didn't get the chance to work

my way up from clubs. And all of a sudden, I was on 'Arsenio Hall.' It's scary . . . . I don't think many people learn about performing by going in front of millions of people like that."

After the phenomenal success of her first two albums, music critics and fans began to pressure Carey to perform live, but she insisted on waiting until she was ready. "I've wanted to wait so that when I do go on tour, people aren't disappointed. I want to give a good show. And I want to feel confident I can," she explains. Carey gained a great deal of confidence following her appearance on "MTV Unplugged" in 1992. Calling it a "milestone" in her career, she says, "I felt comfortable after the first song, and something really clicked in my head. It's like I broke through this barrier of not being afraid anymore." The success of this performance, and the resulting live album, significantly improved her credibility as a live performer.

Still, Carey waited until November 1993 to launch her first world concert tour, following the release of her fourth album. Her first show, in Miami, was a bit rocky, and critics complained about Carey's "opening-night jitters" and the elaborate set that "looked oddly like an industrial church." Carey managed to shake off the criticism and make a few key adjustments before her second show, however, and her performance in Boston got rave reviews. A *Boston Globe* reviewer called it "a spectacular performance" and said she "bowled over the crowd with a confidence that grew before their very eyes." Carey says that a new philosophy on performing led to her success: "I've learned that I don't have to be anything but who I am. And the people who are my fans, that's all they want from me. Anybody else who's not into me, they're never going to really be into me. I can't focus on them. I have to focus on giving something back to the people who have supported me since the beginning."

DEALING WITH FAME

Carey's rise to stardom came very quickly. Since releasing her first album in 1990, she has sold a total of 65 million records worldwide, making her the biggest-selling female recording artist of the 1990s. She is the only person in the history of the *Billboard* charts to have their first nine singles make the top five. Carey admits that it can sometimes be difficult coping with fame: "It gets a little weird emotionally. Because there's no one I grew up with—and no one in my family—who can really relate to what I'm going through. It's hard for anybody to understand how it feels. But it's great. I've wanted it all my life."

Carey soon found that fame made her the target of criticism. For example, some people resented her quick ascent to stardom and claimed that she had not paid her dues. "Sometimes people don't look at you like you're a person when you're in the public eye. They don't think that your feelings can be hurt," Carey states. "But when people say I haven't paid my dues or whatever, they don't know a thing about my life or about me. Just because I'm young and everything has happened so quickly is no reason to assume I've just been lucky. I've condensed so much hard work into a short period of time. My whole life hasn't been this incredible fairy tale. Yes, I'm very thankful, but I've worked for it." Her work ethic is reflected in her many songs about fulfilling dreams through hard work and perseverance.

MAJOR INFLUENCES

Carey lists among her greatest influences the gospel music of Edwin Hawkins, the Clark Sisters, and Shirley Caesar. Even today, she says, "I get up and go to bed listening to gospel music." She also drew inspiration from the soul music of Gladys Knight, Al Green, Aretha Franklin, and Stevie Wonder. One of her prize possessions is an answering-machine tape on which Wonder sings "Happy Birthday" to her.

MARRIAGE AND FAMILY

Carey married Tommy Mottola—the record-company executive who discovered her—on June 5, 1993. They fell in love while working together on Carey's first album. Their $500,000 wedding in New York City was attended by 300 guests, including Bruce Springsteen, Barbra Streisand, Robert De Niro, Billy Joel, Gloria Estefan, and other show-business stars. Carey wore a white, off-the-shoulder Vera Wang gown with a 27-foot-long train.

Despite the fairy-tale nature of her wedding, Carey says that she never expected to get married. "I grew up never thinking about getting married," she explains. "Most of my friends' parents seemed so unhappy. It tainted my view. I decided I wanted to be a person in my own right, not an extension of someone else. Now I realize if two people really love each other, it's about being bonded, not being in power." Carey and Mottola have a country estate in upstate New York, which they share with two Persian cats, a Jack Russell terrier, two Doberman pinschers, and five horses. Carey says that they plan to have children, but not for several years. Mottola has two teenage children from his previous marriage.

The marriage aroused some talk in the press because Mottola is 20 years older than Carey, and because he was involved in a messy divorce during the time that they were rumored to be dating. Some people also accused Carey of "marrying the boss to get ahead," and claimed that Mottola may have promoted her career so vigorously because they were involved romantically. Carey reacts strongly to such criticism. "He is my husband and he does a lot for me, but he does a lot for every artist on the label who he believes in," she explains. "The truth is you can't make people go into a store and buy an album. The music has to do that."

HOBBIES AND OTHER INTERESTS

Carey donates much time and money to the Fresh Air Fund, an organization that pays for inner-city children to go to summer camp or to visit
families in rural areas. It also provides the children with information about
career possibilities and helps them gain self-esteem and set goals for their
futures. Carey pledged $1 million to the fund in 1995, which she planned
to raise by giving benefit concerts. The Fresh Air Fund renamed its camp
after her, and Carey entertains and inspires the children during several
annual visits to "Camp Mariah."

SELECTED CREDITS

RECORDINGS

Mariah Carey, 1990
Emotions, 1991
MTV Unplugged, 1992
Music Box, 1993
Merry Christmas, 1994
Daydream, 1995

VIDEO COLLECTIONS

Mariah Carey—The First Vision, 1991
Mariah Carey—"MTV Unplugged," 1992
Mariah Carey, 1993
Fantasy—Mariah Carey at Madison Square Garden, 1995

HONORS AND AWARDS

Grammy Awards: 1991 (two), for Best New Artist and Best Pop Vocal
    Performance—Female
Rolling Stone Readers' Pick Music Awards: 1991, for Best New Female Singer
Soul Train Awards: 1991 (three), for Best New Artist, Best Album—Female,
    and Best Single—Female

FURTHER READING

BOOKS

Nickson, Chris. *Mariah Carey: Her Story,* 1995

PERIODICALS

Billboard, May 15, 1993, p.90; Nov. 20, 1993, p.20
Boston Globe, Oct. 4, 1991, p.49; Aug. 31, 1993, p.41; Nov. 4, 1993, p.13;
    Dec. 4, 1994, p.B16; Oct. 1, 1995, p.57
Chicago Tribune, Aug. 16, 1990, p.10; Nov. 26, 1995; Nov. 29, 1995, p.3
Current Biography Yearbook 1992

Ebony, Mar. 1991, p.54; April 1994, p.55

Jet, Jan. 24, 1994, p.52

Miami Herald, July 8, 1990, p.1H

New York, Sep. 23, 1991, p.84

New York Times, June 13, 1990, p.C12; Apr. 14, 1991, p.B28; Oct. 8, 1995, Section II, p.34

People, June 21, 1993, p.79; Nov. 22, 1993, p.82

Seventeen, Apr. 1994, p.132

Teen, July 1993, p.60

Time, Sep. 25, 1995, p.75

TV Guide, Nov. 13, 1993, p.22

USA Today, July 10, 1990, p.D4; Sep. 17, 1991, p.D1; Feb. 17, 1993, p.D14; Oct. 27, 199 3, p.D1

ADDRESS

Mariah Carey Fan Club
P.O. Box 679
Branford, CT 06405

Jim Carrey 1962-
Canadian Comedian and Actor
Star of the Hit Films *Ace Ventura, The Mask,*
Dumb and Dumber, and *Batman Forever*

BIRTH

James Eugene Carrey was born on January 17, 1962, in Newmarket, Ontario, a suburb about 50 miles from Toronto. He was the youngest of four children born to Kathleen and Percy Carrey. Jim's father had hoped to become a musician but abandoned this idea and became an accountant in order to provide a steady income for his family. In fact, Percy Carrey sold his saxophone to pay for medical expenses incurred during his wife's first pregnancy, thereby giving up his dream of becoming a musician.

YOUTH

From a very young age, Jim showed a knack for entertaining others. His sister Pat notes that "he always made faces instead of eating. He'd make us all laugh, and Mom would get mad because he wouldn't eat and he got really skinny." As Carrey grew older, he performed for his family and friends. "I used to put on all kinds of shows at home," he says. "It was sick, really sick. Every time there was a new person in the house, it was time for me to do the Jim Carrey show. I'd fall down stairs and then go back up and do it in slow motion. Stuff like that. It became nuts after a while." Carrey confesses to keeping his tap shoes handy in case his parents needed a laugh. He especially enjoyed performing in order to cheer up his mother, who was often sick as he was growing up.

According to Carrey, his mother suffered from real and imagined ailments. "Oh, my mother had everything under the sun," he says. "She was a child of alcoholics, and she had a lot of problems as far as, like, the illnesses were her medals. That's all she talked about. It was desensitizing." But when his mother was "really sick, really in pain—I used to come into the bedroom in my underwear and do my praying mantis impression."

EDUCATION

Carrey excelled in grade school, but from his teachers' standpoint there was a downside to his aptitude as a student. "Jim finishes his work first, then bothers the other students," he remembers having read on a school report. His seventh-grade teacher, however, found a way to keep him from disrupting the class—he allowed Carrey to perform for classmates during the last 15 minutes of the day if he behaved during class time. This early exposure to performing for an audience gave him the opportunity to develop skills as an impersonator. Throughout his years as a student, he did wide-ranging impressions of animals—such as dinosaurs and praying mantises—and celebrities—such as actor John Wayne. "Until I was in junior high school," he admits, "I didn't know how to make friends. Then I found out that the things I did at home to entertain people also cracked up everyone at school. I started acting goofy and everyone wanted to hang out with me. Acting goofy became my entire motivation for living."

Life for the Carreys changed drastically when Jim was in high school. His father was laid off from his accounting job, and all the members of the family—with the exception of Jim's oldest sister, who lived away from home by that time—were forced to work as janitors in a wheel-rim factory. Carrey was devastated by the fact that his father had lost his job, and he occasionally took his frustrations out on his employers at the plant. He notes: "I was 15, pushing this sweeper down the . . . hallway of executive offices of people I don't respect in any way because they're, you know, oppressing my father. I'd bury my arm in the wall, then I'd go through hours of elaborate conniving to come up with an alibi of how the sweeper went insane."

A full day of classes followed by eight hours of custodial work eventually took its toll. Carrey, whose schoolwork had been suffering, made the decision to drop out of high school. It was not a popular decision with Carrey's parents, but he felt that the move was necessary to maintain his sanity. The family eventually quit their jobs, and outside the factory they grew closer and happier. But it still took them time to recover financially. In fact, they lived for a time in a Volkswagen camper van and in a tent on Jim's oldest sister's lawn. Such adversity provided Carrey with a healthy sense of perspective concerning his eventual success. "I've gone through periods where I look at street guys and I know that's me," he says. "I know how they got there."

CAREER HIGHLIGHTS

EARLY CAREER

Jim received his first opportunity to appear on stage at the age of 15, when his father signed him up to perform at Yuk Yuk's, a well-known Toronto comedy club. That performance was not a springboard to immediate success, however, which Carrey attributed partly to the yellow polyester suit that his mother made him wear. "That evening was the most awful experience of my life," he admits.

Over the course of the next several years, Carrey was offered more opportunities to perform. He established a stage presence and perfected some of the best impressions on the comedy circuit. Actor Bruce Dern, Muppet Kermit the Frog, and singer Cher were among the personalities that Carrey impersonated. He developed the ability to slip from one character to another fluidly, and he began to improvise conversations between entertainers Frank Sinatra and Sammy Davis, Jr., and between aging actors Katharine Hepburn and Henry Fonda. He often put the people that he portrayed into humorous situations. For example, early routines featured him as Indian pacifist leader Gandhi during a hunger strike secretly eating potato salad, and as actor Jimmy Stewart—well-known for portrayals of optimistic characters in films—acting hopeful in advance of an imminent nuclear attack. In addition to matching voices, Carrey also copied the behaviors and facial features of celebrities. He benefitted from having spent hours as a teenager in front of a mirror stretching his facial features in order to achieve desired effects.

Carrey's success continued to grow, and he was soon able to make a living as a comedian. He went from making about a hundred dollars a night to making what he describes as "killer dough." He moved his parents to

Toronto, lived with them, and drove himself to clubs at night to perform. In February 1981, when Carrey was 19, his career received a boost from an article on the front page of the entertainment section of the *Toronto Star* by revered critic Bruce Blackadar. Blackadar gave high praise to Carrey, comparing watching him perform to seeing famed comedian-director Woody Allen's early performances in New York City's Greenwich Village.

Carrey came to the United States in 1981 and developed a following in Los Angeles through frequent appearances at clubs like the Comedy Store. "I could have stayed up in Canada and made a real good living doing stand-up, but I always had people going 'You're too good to stay here, you gotta go to L.A., go to L.A., go to L.A.' When I finally did it was a real hard decision, but the main thing was knowing my father, who was a really good musician, never made the move and it dwindled and faded and he became an accountant. I wasn't going to let that happen to me," he declares.

In the United States, Carrey wowed audiences with his dead-on impersonations and his ability to improvise routines based on audience suggestions. Colleague Damon Wayans, with whom Carrey would later appear on the television comedy series "In Living Color," notes that comedians dreaded having to follow Carrey on the stage during those early U.S. performances. NBC Entertainment president Brandon Tartikoff recognized the young comedian's promise after seeing him perform at the

Comedy Store, and in 1984 Carrey was offered the role of Skip Tarkenton, an animator, on the TV sit-com "The Duck Factory." Allan Burns, who had served as producer for such legendary television shows as "Mary Tyler Moore" and "Lou Grant," was named executive producer of the program, and the production company responsible for the show invested more than half a million dollars in each episode. With the lead role in a prime-time series, Carrey was able to move his parents to the United States, and they lived with him in his Los Angeles apartment.

CAREER TRANSFORMED

At the same time that Carrey was realizing success in the United States, he decided to overhaul his act. He felt that he was limiting himself by doing a routine that was too slick. "I was putting out something that I didn't want to become known for," he reveals. "I wanted to be myself, to create some things that had never been done before, rather than constantly sitting waiting for the next famous person whom I could impersonate. That held nothing for me. It was a slow realization, but at one point I just said 'never again.'" Several of his fellow comedians were shocked by this decision and advised him against changing his act. Carrey, however, was confident that he could transform his career and remain successful. "I knew in my heart that I could do it, but the only way to prove that I could do it was to just cut it off completely for a while. I just figured, if I cut my right arm off, sooner or later I'll learn to write with my left hand." Carrey took his new act on the road and served as an opening act for established comedian Rodney Dangerfield. He also opened for Linda Ronstadt and generated rumors when he and the older singer were linked romantically.

Carrey suffered a setback when "The Duck Factory" failed. Most of the material for the show had been written before he joined the cast, and Carrey found himself locked into a standard situation-comedy role. Although he received praise from some critics for his work, the show came to the end of its run after 13 episodes. The pressures of having his parents live with him also became overwhelming, especially when further acting jobs dried up. He had nightmares in which he saw himself killing his mother, and he painted angry pictures, including one entitled "Waiting to Die" that showed his father with a gun and a stopwatch. He notes that his behavior expressed "anger toward my parents. I resented them for the responsibility of taking care of them since I was 17. I resented them because there had always been a lot of pressure on me to be the star, to save their lives, to buy them the big house with the pillars—like Elvis, you know? And it came to a head. I had no money. I had no jobs." He sent his parents back to Canada but continued to provide them with money until he himself no longer had any.

Carrey stopped performing on stage and spent several years pondering his next move. The period was marked by depression and inactivity. "You lay on your bed and the thing that you think about most is, 'What is it about me that's special or different? What's my thing?' I would struggle with that, trying to define myself," Carrey remarks of that period. Eventually he recovered professionally. Acting classes contributed to roles in a handful of movies, including the romantic comedy *Peggy Sue Got Married* and the vampire film *Once Bitten*.

RETURN TO THE STAGE

When Carrey returned to stand-up comedy in 1987, he was a changed performer. Judd Apatow, a former stand-up comic, notes: "He would go on stage and ramble like a madman. Some of it was hilarious, and other parts of it wouldn't work at all, but [the performances] would be so daring or so odd that I couldn't get enough of it. If it bombed, he would sit on the floor, and he would supposedly be talking to his wife: .'Yeah, honey, pretty soon we're going to be on Easy Street.' And then he would just start crying." Reactions to his antics were mixed, depending on the night. One night Carrey would squeeze himself into a baby grand piano on stage and remain there throughout the evening with his legs hanging out from under the cover while others performed; another night he would wriggle around the stage like a worm for extended periods of time. Carrey recalls that when he got heckled on stage during his experimental period—and occasionally he provoked the heckling intentionally—he could "either be the most entertaining person that you've ever seen or your worst enemy. I'm like a rat—when you back me into a corner, man, I . . . lunge."

Carrey eventually acknowledged that his stand-up act would benefit if he committed some of the material that he developed during this period to memory. "I realized there is virtue in telling good stories more than once," he remarks. Even though the development of a more established routine made him more marketable to audiences, Carrey maintained a strong element of risk-taking in his act, and even as he began to gain more opportunities in television and in film, he continued to perform on stage. Performing live offered challenges that were different than those offered by television or movie work. "Standing up in front of 3,000 people, you're forced to come up with something. You force yourself out on a limb that way," he says.

TELEVISION WORK LEADS TO FILM ROLES

In 1989 Carrey played one of three aliens in the comedy *Earth Girls Are Easy*. Fellow alien Damon Wayans recommended him for a part on "In Living Color," a television series that was the brainchild of Damon's brother

Keenan Ivory Wayans. The audition that followed was a success, and Carrey—who had been overlooked during a tryout for the skit-based television program "Saturday Night Live"—found himself on a similar program where he could showcase his talent for physical comedy. Over the course of the four years (1990-94) that Carrey was associated with the program, he developed such popular characters as Vera de Milo, a grotesque musclewoman with a steroids habit, and Fire Marshal Bill, a masochistic safety "expert" with an inclination for maiming himself while pointing out the world's hazards.

Due in part to the success of "In Living Color," Carrey was cast as the title character in the 1994 movie *Ace Ventura: Pet Detective,* a role that had been offered to more established feature film stars, such as Rick Moranis. The script had initially been shown to Carrey two years prior to its filming, but he passed on the role until he was given the opportunity to help rewrite the script. Once filming began, director Tom Shadyac gave Carrey free reign to play the character with as much over-the-top outrageousness and reckless abandon as he felt necessary. As filming progressed, Shadyac admits that the film "would either make or destroy our careers. But Jim and I were in agreement that if we were going to light a stink bomb, let's make it a very unique stink bomb."

The movie, which featured Carrey trying to track down the kidnappers of Snowflake (the Miami Dolphins football team's mascot), received negative reviews. Carrey was unnerved by the bad press and wondered if he had indeed made a mistake in working on the film. The movie earned more than 10 million dollars during its opening weekend, however, on its way to grossing more than 70 million dollars before going to video. Carrey sneaked into a theater full of moviegoers early in its run and was overwhelmed by the audience response. The success of the film was attributed, in part, to younger audiences—viewers of "In Living Color"—who flocked to movie theaters to

watch Carrey's antics, which included him demolishing a package while impersonating a delivery person and playing football while dressed as a ballerina.

Upon finishing *Ace Ventura*, Carrey starred in *The Mask* (1994). He played Stanley Ipkiss, a meek bank clerk who is transformed into a living cartoon character when he puts on an ancient mask. On days that he performed as The Mask, Carrey spent four hours in a chair getting made up with green face paint. Additionally, experts at Industrial Light and Magic provided special effects that animated his features in certain scenes. But according to Carrey, director Chuck Russell "knew it would be pointless to bury my face under green gunk. The idea was to make the audience unsure of where my crazy facial expressions leave off and the special effects begin." In the film, The Mask has the ability to change his shape, charm beautiful women, and deflect gunfire. The movie allowed Carrey to demonstrate his ability to sing and dance in a salsa-flavored musical number, "Cuban Pete"—one of the highlights of the film. For Carrey, the film was also significant because it allowed him room to develop Stanley Ipkiss's character, which he admits to having patterned somewhat after his father. "I didn't only want to make The Mask interesting and wild. I wanted Stanley to be entertaining, too . . . . I wanted him to be a real guy," he reveals.

Carrey's success at the box office ensured him of higher pay, and he received seven million dollars for his role in *Dumb and Dumber* (1994), in which he and Jeff Daniels played two imbecile brothers. Although signing such a contract was a lifelong goal for Carrey, he maintained his perspective concerning the increase in pay. "It's just like the stock market, and I happen to be the hot stock of the moment," he states. "The movie business is all based on this illusion of heat. I don't think about the money stuff when I'm working. The business side is almost like this weird hobby for me. It's like looking at a Monopoly board and saying, 'Sure, I'll buy a hotel on Boardwalk.'" With his money, Carrey bought a multi-million dollar home in a wealthy section of Los Angeles and a vintage model Ford Thunderbird.

Following *Dumb and Dumber*, Carrey co-starred as the Riddler in *Batman Forever* (1995), the third in a series of films featuring the comic-book superhero. The role, which had reputedly been offered to popular comedian and actor Robin Williams, gave Carrey another opportunity to develop a character—a computer expert who is driven over the edge when his genius goes unnoticed by his boss, Bruce Wayne. He becomes the Riddler, a villain who must be stopped by the Batman, Bruce Wayne's alter-ego. After *Batman Forever*, Carrey starred in *Ace Ventura: When Nature Calls* (1995), returning to the role that launched his successful film career.

Carrey earned five million dollars for the Riddler role and a reported eight million dollars for his appearance in the *Ace Ventura* sequel. Even so, few were prepared when he signed a contract earning him 20 million dollars for playing the title character in *The Cable Guy.* Although the dramatic pay increase worried some people in the film industry who feared that many actors would demand salaries in that line, Carrey believed such pay was justified considering the returns on his films. His high salary fulfilled a prophecy that he had made during the time when he was struggling to redefine his career in the late 1980s. At that time he had written himself a check, postdated Thanksgiving 1995, awarding himself 10 million dollars for "Acting Services Rendered." The check was buried with Carrey's father, who died of cancer in 1994. Though his father lived to see the first *Ace Ventura* movie and *The Mask*, his mother was not as fortunate. Regularly ill throughout her later life, she passed away in 1991, before Carrey realized success in the movies.

Carrey was happy that success had finally come to him after he had spent more than 15 years paying his dues. While he watched colleagues like Robin Williams and Sam Kinison gain opportunities, he remained patient. "If it happened when I was 20 or 21, I would have gone insane. I wouldn't have felt like I deserved it. I would have self-destructed," he admits. As his career progresses, he hopes to broaden his repertoire by taking on dramatic roles. He remarks that audiences "know I do funny characters, but it's the tip of the iceberg. Not everybody gets to show the whole iceberg, you know? I believe I have a shot at it." Regardless of the roles that he plays or the money that he makes, Carrey has no desire to change his professional approach to acting. "To me, it's always been about work," he says. "Even if I have $40 billion in the bank, if I don't feel that I did a good job that day, I'm a basket case. I'm linked to my work in a probably extremely unhealthy way. It's too important to me."

MARRIAGE AND FAMILY

On March 28, 1987, Carrey married Melissa Womer, who waited tables at the Comedy Store and knew him from his early days performing at the club. He and his wife had a daughter, Jane. However, his relationship with his wife began to suffer during the filming of *Ace Ventura*. Melissa Womer says, "The day he first walked on that set as Mr. Carrey, he decided he wanted to enjoy success from the perspective of a single man." About his role in the failure of the marriage, Carrey notes: "Living with me this last couple years is like living with an astronaut—it's not the most rewarding experience. It's like, I just came back from the moon, don't ask me to take the garbage out. I can relax, but not at the prescribed times, necessarily, and when you're married, you've got to have time for this and that and it's just . . . impossible."

Carrey ultimately filed for divorce. This began a bitter series of legal proceedings that were widely reported in the press as the couple tried to divide their financial assets. Carrey regularly spends time with his daughter now that the couple has divorced.

During the filming of *Dumb and Dumber*, Carrey developed a relationship with co-star Lauren Holly, who was also just coming off of a divorce. "He said to me, 'I would like to be your girlfriend. Would you be my girlfriend?'" Holly says. "What girl on the planet could refuse when someone says that?" Both realized the potential dangers of becoming involved with one another, considering their busy schedules and their position in the public eye, but their relationship has survived. Though Carrey expresses genuine happiness about his relationship with Holly, he also admits to feeling some reluctance to make a commitment, given his experience with marriage: "I hate it when I see people go on talk shows, and they just married the supermodel of the century, and they are like 'This is it, absolutely.' That to me is arrogant in the face of nature. It'd be an incredibly wonderful thing if I end up being, like, 80 years old, and me and Lauren are heading out having a great old time. But as soon as you say you *know*, the universe will prove you wrong."

MAJOR INFLUENCES

Carrey counts among his role models Jonathan Winters, Dick Van Dyke, and Jackie Gleason, comedic actors from whom he learned while watching television as a child. "Jackie was funny to me because he was dysfunctional. That seemed more honest and real. Sometimes you have to cry before you laugh," Carrey says. Film stars Peter Sellers, whom Carrey tried to emulate during the filming of *Ace Ventura: Pet Detective*, as well as Jimmy Stewart, also figure significantly as role models. One of his goals, in fact, is to make a movie that could hold its own against Stewart's film *Mr. Smith Goes to Washington*, which Carrey regards as brilliant.

HOBBIES AND OTHER INTERESTS

While growing up, Carrey developed an artistic side. He drew caricatures of his teachers in class and lost himself in art projects at home. He continues to enjoy painting and sculpting as an adult. As a child, he also played hockey; now, he often plays tennis on his home courts in Los Angeles.

CREDITS

MOVIES

Finders, Keepers, 1984
Once Bitten, 1985
Peggy Sue Got Married, 1986

The Dead Pool, 1988
Earth Girls Are Easy, 1989
Pink Cadillac, 1989
High Strung, 1991
Ace Ventura: Pet Detective, 1993 (also writer, with others)
The Mask, 1994
Dumb and Dumber, 1994
Batman Forever, 1995
Ace Ventura 2: When Nature Calls, 1995
The Cable Guy, 1996

TV

"The Duck Factory," 1984
"Mike Hammer: Murder Takes All," 1989
"In Living Color," 1990-1994
"Tom Arnold: The Naked Truth," 1991
"Jim Carrey's Unnatural Act," 1991
"Doing Time on Maple Drive," 1992
"Comic Relief V," 1992
"The Comedy Store's 20th Birthday," 1993
"A Tribute to Sam Kinison, 1993

HONORS AND AWARDS

Blockbuster Entertainment Awards: 1995, for Favorite Actor—Comedy,
   Theatrical and Video, and Favorite Male Newcomer
Received Star on "Hollywood Walk of Fame": 1994

FURTHER READING

PERIODICALS

Chatelaine, Dec. 1985, p.110
Current Biography, Feb. 1996
Entertainment Weekly, Aug. 5, 1994, p.16
Esquire, Dec. 1995, p.98
GQ, Aug. 1994, p.82
Montreal Gazette, July 24, 1994, p.F1
Newsweek, July 25, 1994, p.50; June 26, 1995, p.49
Rolling Stone, July 13-27, 1995, p.70
Saturday Night, June 1993, p.42
Seventeen, Sep. 1994, p.157
USA Today, July 26, 1994, p.D1
Vancouver Sun, July 22, 1994, p.C1

ADDRESS

United Talent Agency
9560 Wilshire Blvd., 5th Floor
Beverly Hills, CA 90212

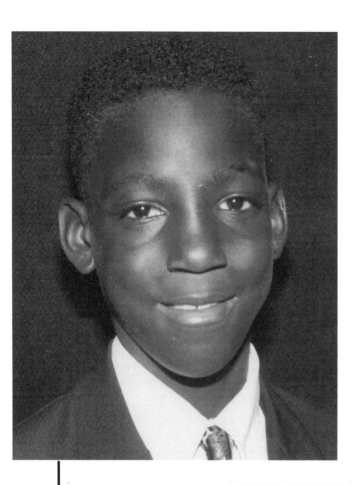

BRIEF ENTRY

Larry Champagne III 1985-
American Student Who Stopped a
Runaway School Bus

EARLY LIFE

Lawrence (Larry) Champagne III was born April 17, 1985, in St. Louis, Missouri. His mom is Dawn Little and his stepfather is Jesse Little. Dawn and Larry's dad, Lawrence Champagne, Jr., divorced several years ago. Larry was still close to his dad, who was stabbed to death just three weeks before Larry became a hero in his community. Larry has a brother, Jerrick, a sister, Clementa, and a step-brother, Eric. Larry is in the fifth grade at Bellerive Elementary School in the St. Louis suburb of Creve Cour, Missouri.

MAJOR ACCOMPLISHMENT

On October 3, 1995, Larry was riding the bus to school in St. Louis. They were speeding down a busy freeway when the bus driver, Ernestine Blackman, slumped over in her seat. She had had a stroke and was unconscious. The bus began to swerve out of control, and it hit the guard rails on the side of the highway. Some of the kids on the bus began to cry. "I thought we were going to die," remembers Larry. "The bus started swaying side to side and hit the guardrail twice. That made everyone fall and hit the window. I thought we were going to crash."

Larry ran to the front of the bus, put his foot on the brake, and grabbed the steering wheel. The bus came to a stop. They were hit from behind by a truck, but the 20 students on the bus survived. Ambulances arrived to take the bus driver and five children who had slight injuries to the hospital. Another school bus arrived to take Larry and his classmates to school.

When they got to school, the students thanked Larry for saving their lives. But Larry didn't want to make a big deal of it.

Despite Larry's attitude, he became the center of attention in St. Louis, and in the country, too. He appeared on all the major network news programs and met a lot of famous people, including Tom Brokaw and Katie Couric of NBC, Jay Leno, and the Reverend Jesse Jackson. A New York deli even named a sandwich after him, the Larry Champagne Hero. Larry's community started a college fund for him and an automotive school in Denver gave him a scholarship. He and his family were also treated to a vacation at Disneyland and Universal Studios. In a real surprise, TV sportscaster John Madden named Larry the MVP of his All-Madden pro football team for 1995. Larry, who would love to play pro football when he grows up, said, "I can't believe it. It's amazing," when he received news of the honor.

Larry is a rather reluctant hero. He thinks that his family should take some of the credit for his actions. "My grandmother always tells me to be confident and to do what's right," he says. He also honors his grandfather, who taught him how to use a brake pedal. And Larry feels his dad was a real hero. "He helped other people, always tried to do the right thing," says Larry. "I think my dad would be proud of me."

FURTHER READING

Chicago Tribune, Jan. 30, 1996, Kidnews Section, p.7
Jet, Oct. 23, 1995, p.32
People, Oct. 23, 1995, p.108
Scholastic News, Nov. 17, 1995, p.2

St. Louis Post Dispatch, Oct. 4, 1995, p.A1; Oct. 6, 1995, p.C1; Oct. 12, 1995, p.A1

ADDRESS

Parkway School District
455 North Woods Mill Rd.
Chesterfield, MO 63017

Christo 1935-
Bulgarian-Born American Environmental Artist
Creator of "Wrap" Art

BIRTH

The artist who calls himself Christo was born Christo Vladimirov Javacheff on June 13, 1935, in Gabrovo, Bulgaria. He was the son of Vladimir Javacheff, a business executive, and Tzveta (Dimitrova) Javacheff. Christo's older brother, Anani, became an actor, and his younger brother, Stephen, is a chemist.

YOUTH

Christo's early youth took place during a devastating time in European history. During World War II (1939-45), Bulgaria's king sided with Germany but refused to help fight Germany's enemy, the Soviet Union (now split into Russia and other countries), because Russia had helped Bulgaria in the past. German Nazis occupied Bulgaria, and young Christo witnessed firsthand the horrors of war: airplane bombings, bodies in the streets, Nazi tanks rolling toward Bulgaria's neighbor the Soviet Union, and Soviet soldiers retaking Bulgaria. In 1944, as the war began to go against Germany, the Bulgarian monarchy was overthrown, and Bulgarian Communists, supported by the Soviet Union, took control of the country. Along with other countries in Eastern Europe, Bulgaria became a Soviet satellite country, and Bulgaria's economic and political systems were dominated by the Soviet Union.

Christo had seen firsthand the horrors of war, but peace brought a new kind of turmoil. His father's business was taken over by the new Communist government, and life became very different. The family was no longer in the upper class because there was no upper class.

EDUCATION

Despite the upheavals in Bulgaria, Christo's artistic talents were recognized. He studied painting, sculpture, and stage design at the Fine Arts Academy in Bulgaria's capital, Sofia, from 1952 to 1956. It was a time when the heavy hand of Stalinism (the harsh policies of Soviet leader Joseph Stalin) was felt throughout the satellite countries of Eastern Europe. At that time, the repressive and controlling Communist government in the Soviet Union banned all forms of opposition. To advance the cause of Communism, artists were expected to promote "Socialist Realism." This doctrine proclaimed that the purpose of literature and art was to educate audiences to the wonders of socialist society and to promote Communist party doctrine. Artistic freedom was stifled. In order to keep his place at the academy, Christo became a propaganda artist. He painted quotations from Stalin and Lenin (the first Soviet leader) on the sides of cliffs. For him, as for many, life under Communism was hard and monotonous, and he dreamed of freedom.

In 1956, Christo went to Prague, Czechoslovakia, to study and work in experimental theater, but the turmoil of war again intruded. Across the border in Hungary, Soviet troops brutally crushed a Hungarian uprising seeking more freedom. Life in neighboring Czechoslovakia became harder as the government watched closely to make sure there was no Czech uprising. A doctor friend invited Christo to escape to the West with the doctor's family in a freight car supposedly carrying medical supplies. Christo took the opportunity, and with his fellow stowaways, he arrived in Vienna, Austria, a free man. He studied at the Vienna Fine Arts Academy and then briefly in Geneva, Switzerland, before making his way to Paris, France, in 1957.

There, Christo made a new start as an artist. He quickly found a home among the French artists experimenting with "new realism," the European equivalent of American pop art. On both sides of the Atlantic Ocean, artists adopted familiar products—such as Andy Warhol's *Campbell's Soup Cans*—to create witty commentary on Western commercialism.

MARRIAGE AND FAMILY

While Christo was gradually developing his artistic skills, he still had to pay the rent. To earn a small income, he painted portraits of high-born members of society. One of his models was a lovely Parisian woman, Jeanne-Claude de Guillebon, daughter of a prominent French general. It was not long before they fell in love, but her parents did not approve. "You've chosen a starving artist?" asked her mother, who then tried to have Christo sent out of the country by the government. But Jeanne-Claude was a strong-willed young woman determined to have her way. She and Christo married on November 28, 1959, and Jeanne-Claude became the business manager of her husband's art career. In fact, in recent years many have considered Jeanne-Claude to be a full partner in her husband's work. They have one son, Cyril, born in 1960.

In 1964, Christo and his family moved to New York City. There, he wasted no time trying to become known. He abandoned his last name and joined the list of such celebrities as Cher, Madonna, and Liberace, for whom one name is enough. Like many Europeans first arriving in the United States, he was overwhelmed with its size and scope. It inspired him to ideas of art on a grand scale.

CAREER HIGHLIGHTS

Christo's career has been a series of monumental projects. Some have won worldwide attention, while others have had less impact on the art world and the public. All of his projects, however, have been imaginative and fresh approaches to familiar or ordinary objects.

CHRISTO'S "WRAP" ART

Christo's novel contribution to the art world was wrapping. In his mind, wrapping an object in fabric makes it more mysterious, somehow more beautiful—in other words, as an artist conceals, he or she somehow reveals. People cover their bodies in clothing every day and no one thinks it odd, he reasoned. By covering ordinary objects, an artist adds rather than detracts from the object. Critics said it brought to mind the perception of the German architect Ludwig Mies Van der Rohe, who said, referring to art and architecture, "Less is more."

To create his art, Christo uses bright-colored fabric, plastic, and metal over and around huge objects and through large spaces. Sometimes he uses the natural landscape, and sometimes a building or other human construction is the centerpiece of his project. Museums, islands, valleys, bridges, and pastures have all been used. Christo's theory is that by "packaging" buildings and nature, he is giving people a new and interesting way to appreciate everyday things. One European woman said that she doubted that his work was art until she saw it for the first time: "It gave me a widening of my soul, a widening of my perception. It added something to me."

Some call Christo a performance artist. Others call him an environmental artist because the environment is his canvas. Another suggestion is that Christo is the "Wrap Artist"—"wrap" as in gift wrapping because, in a sense, Christo considers his art free gifts to the public. No one is ever charged to see them. He finances his works by selling sketches, plans, and scenes of his projects.

Christo's art is always dismantled after a few weeks. Unlike painters or sculptors who create masterpieces for generations to come, Christo's work is temporary. It is "performed" only once. There is no sign of it afterward except what is recorded in photographs, stories, or movies. "Christo is an established master," according to David Bourdon in *Harper's Bazaar*, "of the short-lived extravaganza." As Christo once told California college students, "it is from naivete and arrogance that we build things in gold, stone, with a very childish idea that we will be remembered forever."

GETTING STARTED

In 1969, Christo undertook his first big project in the United States. He packaged the Museum of Contemporary Art in Chicago with 62 pieces of brown tarpaulin tied together with two miles of rope. Young people in particular liked it. Said a Chicago museum spokesperson: "Since Christo wrapped us up, young people have been coming in and sitting down to talk as if the museum were a park."

Christo took on bigger and bigger projects. That same year, at a cost of about $120,000, he wrapped one million square feet of rocky Australian coastline near Sydney with fabric bound with 36 miles of rope. Christo's art view was "the bigger the better."

VALLEY CURTAIN

Also in 1969, Christo spent the summer as artist-in-residence at the Aspen Center of Contemporary Art in Colorado. The majesty of the Rocky Mountains intrigued him. He decided the Rockies would be the stage for his next creation, *Valley Curtain*, which would consume the next three years of his life. Christo hired a surveyor, rented a jeep, and scouted the rugged landscapes. Finally, 70 miles west of Aspen, in a tiny town called Rifle, he found the mountain vista he was seeking: Rifle Gap, a high yet narrow valley of vertical sandstone cliffs. His plan was to erect a huge, vivid orange nylon "curtain" across the ravine with an arch cut from the bottom for the passage of motor vehicles. It was an enormous under-taking. It took three years just to obtain permission to begin the actual work. The residents of Rifle thought Christo's plan odd, but they agreed to it because of the tourist money it would bring to their otherwise isolated town. Environmentalists claimed that the project would endanger wild animals, but a biologist from the University of Colorado reassured them that the wildlife would survive. Finally, Colorado's highway officials feared that the entire curtain would crash onto the road below. Christo hired independent engineers, who gave assurance that the plan was structurally sound, but he was still required to take out a $1.5 million insurance policy in case of damages. The entire project would cost Christo about $850,000, which he raised by selling plans and models for *Valley Curtain*. Now he could begin.

Christo hired the best heavy-engineering company in the area to string four thick steel cables across the ravine and lock them into concrete blocks. From these cables were suspended 200,000 square feet of orange nylon plastic weighing 8,000 tons. But the first effort failed. During its construc-tion, the curtain went up and soon came down. On October 9, 1971, a gust of wind tore it from its moorings, and it fell onto the rocks below.

In August 1972, with new equipment in place, Christo gave the order to unfurl the bright orange *Valley Curtain II*. It was a remarkable sight. Reporters and television crews from all over the world were there. So were art critics, tourists, and most of the people who lived in the tiny town of Rifle. The Maysles Brothers, experimental filmmakers, were there also and later made a *Valley Curtain* documentary.

Christo planned his *Valley Curtain* to stand for a month, but the very next day, a freak sandstorm ripped it to shreds, sending orange fragments far away into the hills. Disappointed, Christo turned east. He wrapped a wall in Rome and the oceanfront off Newport, Rhode Island. He was also planning his next extravaganza—*Running Fence*, which would consume the next three years.

RUNNING FENCE

Christo envisioned *Running Fence* as an expanse of white nylon fabric 18 feet high and stretching 24 miles from the rolling hills north of San Francisco down to the sea. It would wind across vineyards, farms, ranges, and roads. After raising $2 million, Christo sought permission from 59 landowners and 15 government bodies. He testified at 17 public hearings and 3 California Supreme Court sessions. He had to overcome sneers from local artists who regarded *Running Fence* as a publicity stunt. Finally, after filing a 450-page Environmental Impact Statement and personally persuading every last resident, he won permission and began work.

It took six months to erect the 2,000 panels of nylon strung on steel cables between steel poles. The work was done by professional engineers, helped by college students. By September 1976, it was up, and it was a hit. Californians loved it; they came by the thousands to see Mother Nature's new clothes. So did art critics. Marina Vaizey of the *New Republic* wrote, "*Running Fence* in some uncanny way is not only a piece of sculpture . . . but itself sculpts the land, and is in turn sculpted by the wind and light. It intensifies the characteristics, physical and emotional, of the way in which we apprehend the meeting points of man and his landscape." After a month, the fence was dismantled and the parts given to the owners of the land it crossed.

Christo's next performance was to wrap six-and-a-half million square feet of pink cloth around 11 small islands in Biscayne Bay in Miami, Florida, in 1983. From the air and sea, the islands looked like pink lily pads floating on the blue sea. *Surrounded Islands*, according to art critics, was exuberant, gaudy, witty, and surprisingly beautiful. Two years later, after 10 years of negotiation with the French, Christo flew to Paris, France, to wrap the Pont Neuf, a 17th-century bridge over the Seine River. "It's like [Claude] Monet painting the cathedral at Rennes," Christo said at the time. "He gave his own impression of it. That's what I'm doing with the Pont

Neuf—interpreting it for 14 days and then giving it back to the people of Paris in its original form."

UMBRELLAS

One of Christo's most ambitious projects was *Umbrellas*. His plan was to erect hundreds of large umbrellas in both coastal California and coastal Japan. Opened simultaneously on opposite sides of the Pacific, *Umbrellas* symbolized the linkage between East and West. As usual, it was an enormous undertaking. Engineers had to be consulted, contracts had to be drawn, and $26 million had to be raised. Permission had to be won from dozens of government agencies and hundreds of landowners. Californians were skeptical but were at least familiar with Christo's *Running Fence.* Japanese landowners thought it peculiar but saw no harm, especially since they seemed charmed by Christo's personality. A Japanese woman's observation was typical. "We did not understand the meaning of it at all, but it sounded interesting, and we wanted to cooperate, so why not?"

Christo believed that the Japanese grasped his idea quicker than the Californians: "To the Japanese mind, art is not only a painting on a wall or a bronze sculpture, but also a flower arrangement and stones in a garden. This is not the same with the cowboys of the West. The Japanese sensitivity to beauty and art is much broader." Christo regarded the personal negotiations as part of the artistic process. Having dialogues with people, he has said, is another form of art. Japanese bureaucracy was another story. It took four years of lobbying before the government of Tokyo gave its approval, after officials insisted that the umbrellas first be tested in a wind tunnel.

Now it was time to get busy. Christo contracted for 1,760 yellow umbrellas in California and 1,340 blue umbrellas in Japan. All stood 20 feet tall, sported 8-sided canopies 28 feet wide, and flew from aluminum poles set in heavy concrete bases. The plastic fabric was almost transparent so they could be perceived, Christo said, as "luminous, shimmering flowers." Finally, on a sunny morning in October 1991, all was ready. The umbrellas in each country were opened. For artist and onlookers, it was rewarding. Almost 2 million people came to see *Umbrellas* in California and Japan. Many have regarded it as a once-in-a-lifetime experience that they will never forget.

Three weeks after the exhibit's debut, there was a tragic accident at the California site. A strong gust of wind uprooted an umbrella. Although weighing 500 pounds, the umbrella lifted off like a rocket and hit 33-year-old Lori Keevil-Matthews of Camarillo, California, crushing her to death against a boulder. She and her husband had come especially to see Christo's *Umbrellas*. Demoralized, Christo ordered the entire California project shut down out of respect to Keevil-Matthews's memory and asked

Japan to do the same. During the disassembly in Japan, 51-year-old Masaaki Nakamura was electrocuted when the boom of his crane touched a high-voltage power line. A critic for the *New York Times* wrote that the "project . . . Christo once called 'a symphony in two parts' became a tragedy in two acts." Commenting later on the deaths, Christo suggested that art, like life, has dangers. "My works are not artificial but of the real world. And for me, the real world involves everything: risk, danger, beauty, energy. . . . This project demonstrated that anything is possible because it is part of reality."

WRAPPED REICHSTAG

Christo planned his next major project in Berlin, Germany. Christo wanted to wrap the historic Reichstag, Germany's parliament building. The decision to wrap the building was controversial and hard won. German Chancellor Helmut Kohl echoed the opinions of many of his fellow Germans when he said that such a vital national symbol should not be the subject of an experiment. But Christo successfully argued that if artists can paint God, "I cannot believe any politician in his right mind thinks the Reichstag is more important than God." After over 20 years of lobbying, he won permission in 1994. The project would use one million square feet of custom-made, silver polypropylene fabric, enough to cover 14 football fields, sewn with 800 miles of special thread, and tied with 17,000 yards, or 9½ miles, of blue rope.

Many commentators described *Wrapped Reichstag* not only as art but as a symbol of the social and political changes in Germany. For Germans, whose nation has just recently been reunited after the end of the Cold War, the Reichstag had a special meaning. Completed in 1894, it was the country's first house of parliament. The Reichstag became the symbol of democracy in a nation that lived through the rise of the Nazis under Adolph Hitler, the devastating impact of World War II, and the division of Germany into two parts, one of which was dominated by the Soviet Union.

"If some viewers saw the *Wrapped Reichstag* as the celebration of reunification and renewal," David Galloway wrote in *Art in America*, "for the vast majority it was no more and no less than the occasion for a Volksfest [people's festival] unprecedented in German history." During the two weeks in June and July of 1995 that *Wrapped Reichstag* was on display, more than five million people saw the transformed parliament. A carnival-like atmosphere developed on the grounds around the building, as it attracted assorted jugglers, mimes, musicians, fire-eaters, and political activists. But most members of the large and cheerful crowds had simply come to gaze in awe at the classically elegant form of the finished work.

FUTURE PLANS

Recently, Christo has been at work on several projects. For years he wanted to create a piece of public art in New York City, where he lives. He has made several proposals, but all have been turned down. One such proposal was called the "Gates" project. Christo planned to install 11,000 steel arches along the 25 miles of paths in Central Park. The 15-foot-high arches would hold streaming golden-colored banners. "New York is the city of displaced people, of refugees like us," Christo says. "We wanted to do a project with that feeling of openness, that airy feeling, which is so exhilarating." The city of New York rejected the proposal back in 1981. But Christo waited over 20 years to get permission to wrap the Reichstag, and he hasn't given up on his hometown yet.

Since 1992, he has also been at work on a new project in the western United States. Called "Over the River," this proposed installation would include woven fabric panels, suspended by wire cables, that would hang above a winding river. Successive panels would follow the course of the river over about five miles. Six different sites in the west are being considered, in the states of Idaho, Wyoming, Colorado, and New Mexico.

THE IMPACT OF CHRISTO

Art professionals have widely differing opinions on Christo's work. Some say he only does one kind of art and that he is not a particularly significant artist. "It's a type of art, but it's not important art," said Thomas

Hoving, former director of the Metropolitan Museum of Art in New York City. "It's not something that I, anyway, would want to take to a desert island with me for the rest of my life. I'd like to have somebody who probed the depths of human nature and revealed something about the human condition."

But revelations of that sort may not be his objective. Christo seems content to make people happy. For many people, his work brings smiles and appreciation. They say his style and whimsy are a welcome breath of fresh air amid the stuffiness of much of formal art. One woman who visited the *Umbrellas* project in California remarked, "You could walk out and everyone was having picnics under the umbrellas and walking around smiling. They would be extremely kind and courteous to each other. I think it brought out the best in them."

HONORS AND AWARDS

Cassandra Award (William and Noma Copley Foundation): 1966
Colorado Award for Engineering Excellence: 1973
Royal Danish Academy of Art Award (Denmark): 1979
Skowhegan Award for Process and Environment: 1979
Liberty Award, Ellis Island Medal of Honor: 1986
Kaiser Ring Award (West Germany): 1987

FURTHER READING

BOOKS

Alloway, Lawrence. *Christo,* 1969
Bourdon, David. *Christo,* 1972
Contemporary Artists, 1996
Encyclopedia Britannica, 1995
Tomkins, Calvin. *The Scene: Reports on Post-Modern Art,* 1976
Who's Who in America, 1996
Who's Who in American Art, 1995-96

PERIODICALS

Art in America, Mar. 1992, p.100; Nov. 1995, p.86
Current Biography Yearbook 1977
Harper's Magazine, Feb. 1996, p.58
Life, Sep. 6, 1968, p.65
Los Angeles Times, Apr. 23, 1991, p.F1; Oct. 6, 1991, Calendar, p.3; Oct. 7, 1991, p.A3; Oct. 24, 1991, p.E1
New York Times, July 22, 1987, p.C17; Nov. 12, 1991, p.C13; Jan. 7, 1993, p.C13; July 3, 1995, p.20

New York Times Magazine, Mar. 31, 1996, p.26
Newsweek, June 22, 1981, p.14; July 3, 1995, p.34
People, Nov. 11, 1991, p.145
Wall Street Journal, June 26, 1995, p.A10

ADDRESS

Harry N. Abrams, Inc.
110 East 59th Street
New York, NY 10022

Chelsea Clinton   1980-
American Daughter of the President of
the United States

BIRTH

Chelsea Clinton was born February 27, 1980, in Little Rock, Arkansas, to Bill and Hillary Clinton. At the time Chelsea was born, her father was the governor of Arkansas, and her mother was an attorney. Now, of course, Bill Clinton is the President of the United States, and Hillary Clinton is the First Lady. Chelsea has no brothers or sisters.

Chelsea was named for a famous song of the late 1960s, "Chelsea Morning," written by Joni Mitchell. It was a song her parents loved.

83

EDUCATION

Growing up in Little Rock, Chelsea attended the local public schools. Chelsea is an excellent student, and she skipped third grade while in Arkansas. Her last public school there was Mann Magnet Junior High, a magnet school specializing in math and science. After her father was elected president and the family moved to Washington, Chelsea enrolled at a private school, the Sidwell Friends School. The decision was somewhat controversial in the press, because the Clintons, who are advocates of quality public education, had decided to send their daughter to a private school. Also, the other students at Sidwell had to make changes in their own routines because of the security measures necessary for a president's daughter. But everything turned out alright. "Once she got on campus, we realized she was just a kid like the rest of us," said one of her middle school classmates. "The Secret Service watches her outside, not in class. She's friendly, nice to everybody, she can be funny, and she's very bright for her age."

LIFE IN THE WHITE HOUSE

Chelsea Clinton was 12 when her father won the 1992 presidential election. According to accounts in the press, when she first found out her dad had won, she cried. She was a bit overwhelmed by what life would be like for the next four years. She called Amy Carter, daughter of former President Jimmy Carter, who was nine when her dad won the office.

Chelsea's parents have made the decision to shield her from the press and public as much as possible. They want to protect her from the cruelty of the press and the over-exposed life of political figures and their families. When the family first arrived in Washington, some of the press focused on her adolescent gawkiness and braces, and some comedians, notably those on "Saturday Night Live," made fun of the way she looked. It was a cruel way to enter the world of national public life, but Chelsea seems to have weathered the worst.

In the spring of 1995, Chelsea accompanied her mother on a trip to India, Pakistan, Sri Lanka, and Nepal. Chelsea enjoyed the trip, and the press noted that she had become a "poised and mature" young lady.

FUTURE PLANS

After high school, Chelsea will almost certainly go to college, but where and what she'll study aren't known now. In 1993, she told Scholastic Update that she might like to be an aeronautical engineer someday, a job that would require her excellent math and science skills.

In the near future, Chelsea, who turned 16 in February 1996, has received a driver's license and is looking forward to doing some driving. In fact, on her birthday, she received three free cars from various organizations in the U.S. Her parents returned them all. Her dad has a '68 Mustang she likes, which he keeps back in Arkansas. But the president isn't so sure that's the car for Chelsea. "I have my 1986 Oldsmobile Cutlass, and I told her one day that when she had a driver's license, she was free to drive it," says Bill Clinton. "She just rolled her eyes."

HOBBIES AND OTHER INTERESTS

Chelsea has studied ballet for years. In 1993, after taking classes at the Washington School of Ballet, she danced in the Washington Ballet's annual performance of *The Nutcracker*. Chelsea also enjoys sports and plays on the softball, soccer, and field hockey teams at Sidwell Friends.

Chelsea even babysits. Last year, she took part in the Sidwell Friends fundraiser by advertising a free night of babysitting to the highest bidder. She raised several thousand dollars for the school.

And although it isn't easy being a normal teenager as the daughter of the President of the United States, Chelsea recently started dating, according to her mother. She has also gone out with a group of friends—five girls and five boys—to the local Planet Hollywood for a late snack. The Secret Service agents who protect Chelsea sat at the next table while the teenagers enjoyed their evening, and Chelsea was home by midnight.

FURTHER READING

Baltimore Sun, Feb. 8, 1995, p D1
Family Circle, June 28, 1994, p.91
New Yorker, May 10, 1993, p.38
Newsweek, Jan. 18, 1993, p.53
Parents, May 1994, p.22
People, Sep. 21, 1992, p.120; Nov. 29, 1993, p.70
Philadelphia Inquirer, Apr. 4, 1995, p.A2
San Jose Mercury News, June 15, 1995, p.A4
Scholastic Update, Jan. 15, 1995, p.15
Time, Dec. 20, 1993, p.75
Washington Post, Feb. 27, 1996, p.D1

ADDRESS

The White House
1600 Pennsylvania Avenue
Washington, D.C. 20500

INTERNET SITE

The White House offers students information on the U.S. government and the White House on a Web site called "White House for Kids." The address is:

http://www1.whitehouse.gov/WH/Kids/Html/kidsHome.html

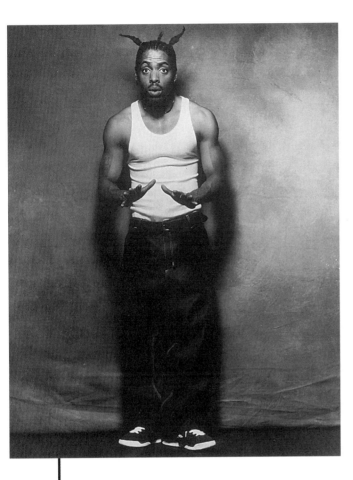

Coolio 1963-
American Rap Artist
Creator of "Gangsta's Paradise"

BIRTH

Artis Ivey, Jr., known to his fans simply as Coolio, was born in Los Angeles, California, on August 1, 1963. His mother worked in a factory, and his father was a carpenter. He has one older sister, Venita.

YOUTH

It is difficult to pin down precisely the details of Coolio's biography. Accounts of his early years differ on the dates and the duration of some events. But the general outlines of his life are clear.

Coolio and his family started out in South Central Los Angeles, one of the toughest areas in the country. His parents split up when he was very young, perhaps as young as two. His father moved north, to San Jose, while Coolio and his sister stayed in Los Angeles with their mother and her new husband, a postal worker. Artis had asthma when he was young—he still does today—and he was also small for his age. He used to get picked on a lot by the neighborhood kids.

The family moved to Compton, an industrial city south of LA, when Coolio was about eight. There, they lived about a block away from a library. "I lived in that library, man," Coolio says. "I read every kid's book they had in there." For a while, life in Compton was good. His parents had good jobs, and they were able to afford a decent house and visits to the beach and Disneyland. The Matterhorn, he says now, was his favorite ride.

After a while, though, their lives started to fall apart. By the time Coolio was about 11, his mom and stepfather were arguing all the time. One time, in the middle of a fight, she grabbed a gun and shot him in the arm. That ended the marriage. Pretty soon, she quit going to work. Some accounts say that she started to drink; others say she took drugs. Either way, the family was falling fast, sinking into poverty. With no money for food and no parental discipline, Coolio started a life of petty thievery, shoplifting at stores and breaking into people's cars and houses.

EDUCATION

The good and the bad times of Coolio's home life were reflected in his school life as well. At first, he was an excellent student, with good grades strengthened by his love of reading. "I used to walk to school with my nose buried in a book," he recalls. One of the top students in his class, he earned straight-As when he was young. "I was in all these special classes for gifted students and they used to take us to the museum," he recalls with pride. But there was a downside, too. Smaller than his classmates, he was getting beaten up all the time. "I got picked on. Kids used to chase me home from school," he now says.

By the time he reached junior high he'd had enough. "By eighth grade, I started messing up," he says. "I was tired of playing the victim, so I started carrying knives to school and playing the crazy role . . . doing things to gain respect in the street." By tenth grade he was skipping classes all the time, too embarrassed to go to school in his shabby clothes. All his years of straight-As, his hopes that he might even get into Harvard, were over.

His family life had deteriorated by this time, and so had his neighborhood. Much of Compton was overrun by gangs. In his neighborhood, the Crips ruled. He says he never actually joined the gang, was never officially inducted, but he hung out with gang members and wore their colors, trying to fit in. "I started acting crazy: bring a knife to school, hit you on the head with a bottle, whatever." As the gangs became more violent, though, he started pulling away. "I was running with these cats that were straight killers," he says, not boasting at all. "I saw them rob this guy on the street and beat him to death with a hammer. . . . I saw that, and said to myself, 'This ain't me. This is not the type of person I am.'"

LIFE ON THE STREETS

It took him a couple years, though, before he was able to break free of that life. Some time around the age of 20, he did a favor for a friend and tried to cash a money order that the friend had stolen. He was caught by the police, arrested, and sent to jail. His jail time has been reported as anywhere from six to ten months. After leaving prison, his life didn't improve much. He was hanging out, stealing, and doing drugs.

By 1985, when he was about 22, Coolio was addicted to crack cocaine. He had been smoking marijuana cigarettes laced with crack. Pretty soon, he graduated to smoking rock, or straight crack. His longest job was at the Los Angeles International Airport. He worked there for about two years, first as a screening technician, checking people for weapons before they boarded the planes. He later transferred to luggage duty so he could steal unclaimed suitcases. He worked in several other jobs, including fast-food restaurants like Taco Bell and Jack-in-the-Box, always looking for ways to steal from his employer, trying to get enough money to pay for the drugs that were ruling his life.

"I was out of control . . . I can look back on those times and make myself cry," Coolio says now. After one bad night he decided to quit. "One day, after being up [all night], I just kind of flipped. I walked past the mirror and I didn't like what I saw. I was looking bad and I started talking to myself: 'You're stupid. You need to cut this out. You're going to have to leave this. You're going to get your [life] together.' I just psyched myself out."

By 1987, Coolio quit doing cocaine. To escape the temptations in his neighborhood, he moved up to San Jose to stay with his father. Then he joined the California Department of Forestry and trained as a fire fighter in Sacramento. "I wasn't looking for a career, I was looking for a way to clean up—a way to escape the drug thing," he explains. "It was going to kill me and I knew I had to stop." Coolio joined an elite 15-member crew that fought forest fires. "Fire fighting is the hardest physical labor known to man," he now says, "but it was the only way to focus my mind away from drugs. It was like being on a football team. I was totally fulfilled. Doing the shifts, working out, running every day, eating three squares, sleeping. It was regimented . . . like a boot camp but it was what I needed." Coolio was part of a firebreak team. Fire fighters use a variety of ways to put out a fire; in one of them, a firebreak, a crew clears all the burnable materials from an area just past the fire's reach to prevent it from spreading. As he explains it, "You're looking to cut a firebreak ten feet wide and a mile long . . . and the one thing you ain't got is time. The chain saw goes in first to cut the big [pieces]. You move in with axes with holes in them to smooth and loosen the topsoil. You've got to get down to bare earth, remove all the combustibles." He spent almost two years as a fire fighter, and when he was done, he had successfully kicked crack.

CHOOSING A CAREER

It took Coolio over 15 years to get his career as a rap artist off the ground. When he was just starting out, rap music was still new. Rap had originated in New York City in the mid-1970s and then traveled west, to Southern California. Compton, where Coolio grew up, later became the birthplace of "gangsta rap," with such local talents as N.W.A., Dr. Dre, and Snoop Doggy Dogg.

Coolio was first introduced to rap music by some neighbors who had moved to Compton from Brooklyn, New York. He got started as a rapper back in 1979. At the time, he was still in high school—in fact, the first time he ever rapped in public was at a high-school dance when he was in 11th grade. He got his nickname, a reference to singer Julio Iglesias, when he and a friend were hanging out and joking around in the early 1980s. "It was a snapping session," Coolio recalls. "I had on this Western shirt, and was playing some goofy song with a little guitar, and my homeboy asked me, 'Who do you think you are, Coolio Iglesias?' They called me that and it stuck." Sometime between 1983 and 1985 he became one of the first LA rappers to record when he made a 12" single, "Watcha Gonna Do," on a private label. It turned into a hit around Los Angeles, and Coolio thought he was going to be a star. "I got big-headed. I envisioned myself buying all these houses and cars and flyin' around having my own jet. When it didn't happen I was crushed." Coolio was just starting to make a name for himself around LA—until his drug problems interrupted his career.

After finishing his stint as a fire fighter in the late 1980s, Coolio returned to the Los Angeles area and immersed himself in the music business. He spent the next five years or so paying his dues and trying to make a name for himself in rap. He rapped at house parties, skating rinks, and anyplace else that would hire him. He joined a number of local groups including WC and the MAAD Circle. Their greatest success came in 1991 when they released an album, *Ain't a Damn Thing Changed*, that sold 150,000 copies. At about that time he hooked up with DJ Wino, who is still his partner. But times were still very tough, and he was broke a lot. He even ended up on welfare, as he later recounted in the song "County Line."

CAREER HIGHLIGHTS

Coolio finally got his big break in 1993. He took a demo tape to Paul Stewart, a manager known for discovering other LA rap acts. "Coolio came to me with a demo and I really liked the song," Stewart says. "I looked at him more as a West Coast street artist who didn't have any pretensions. He could talk about being on a welfare line or smoking crack without any shame. He had a very intense life." Stewart passed the demo tape on to Tommy Boy Records, which signed Coolio to a recording contract.

IT TAKES A THIEF

Coolio's first big release came in 1994. *It Takes a Thief*, according to James T. Jones in *USA Today*, "mixes hard-core themes with tongue-in-cheek attitude and funky, unflinching rhythms." Coolio himself has called the songs autobiographical, saying that many describe scenes from his life—like stealing, in the title track "It Takes a Thief," being on welfare, in "County Line," being broke and hungry, in "Can-o-Corn," and doing drugs, in "N Da Closet." Despite the often grim subject matter, many of the songs also show a wry and witty sense of humor. The album went platinum, selling over one million copies.

One of the album's greatest strengths, listeners agreed, was the hit song "Fantastic Voyage." The tune was based on the 1981 funk hit of the same name by Lakeside, while the lyrics were inspired by the Staples Singers' classic song, "I'll Take You There." The utopian party anthem "Fantastic Voyage" reached the Top 10 and was nominated for many awards. Part of its popularity was surely due to its crossover theme, in which Coolio dreams of a place where "It really don't matter if you're white or black." Its multicultural beach party video, which received constant airplay on MTV, also helped move it to the top of the charts.

GANGSTA'S PARADISE

Coolio went on to even greater success with his next release,

Gangsta's Paradise (1995). "If *It Takes a Thief* was an autobiography of Coolio's childhood days of hustling and drug addiction," *Rolling Stone* reporter Mark Kemp wrote, "*Gangsta's Paradise* is more like a collection of parables for the 'hood: instructions, dedications, and a smattering of adventure stories tossed in purely for amusement." Several of the tunes offer updates of old standards, including "Too Hot," from the Kool & the Gang classic, "Cruisin'," from the old standard by Smoky Robinson, and "A Thing Goin' On," from Billy Paul's "Me and Mrs. Jones."

In recent times, a lot of rap music has come under attack. Critics say that the vulgar lyrics degrade women, glorify violence, and debase human life. Gangsta rap, in particular, has been criticized by politicians, educators, and others for the brutal depictions of urban life. "Gangsta rap, a style of hip-hop that combines ferocious funk rhythms with explicit rhymes about life in the ghetto war zone," according to *Chicago Tribune* critic Greg Kot, "is typically portrayed as music that glorifies a culture of death and depravity, a selfish pursuit of pleasure and power. It is seldom regarded as a portrait of conflicted youth, lured by the security and promise of easy money offered by gang life, and dejected by the dwindling prospects for a future outside the ghetto." This second view, though, is exactly that taken by Coolio in *Gangsta's Paradise*. With this recording, he changed the street tone of his earlier raps, replacing it, instead, with cautionary message raps. He decried violence, advocated safe sex, extolled fatherhood, and praised strong black women, always with a funky R & B beat.

Probably the best example of this new approach is the hit song "Gangsta's Paradise," which appeared both on his album of the same name and on the soundtrack for the film *Dangerous Minds*. The song, which pairs Coolio with singer L.V., features a lush string section, a strong bass line, and powerful lyrics. "Coolio's 'Gangsta's Paradise' [is] a sumptuously orchestrated hip-hop epic from gangbanger country, Compton, California. It is one of the biggest hits of the year . . . and also among the unlikeliest, a voice of compassion from the heart of an African-American holocaust," Greg Kot wrote movingly. "In the soaring, heartbreaking chorus, delivered by singer L.V., the song asks, 'Tell my why are we so blind to see / that the ones we hurt are you and me?' Even as the song acknowledges the brutality of the streets, it prays for a way out." Coolio himself has expressed surprise at its success. "My song is depressing as hell," he says. "I had no idea that it would be so successful. It shows you what's on the minds of people in the world today. They have no hope, and they found hope in that song. It's a spiritual, straight up. That's why people's grandmothers can relate to it. Everybody likes spirituals."

"Gangsta's Paradise" spent four weeks in July in the No. 1 spot on the charts, selling more than 2 million copies and becoming the best-selling song in 1995. While winning a Grammy Award and an American Music

Award for best rap performance, it was also the first hard-core rap single ever nominated for the Grammy Award for song of the year. It catapulted both Coolio's album and the movie soundtrack to the top of the charts.

Coolio has often said that he's interested in acting, and he got his chance in *Phat Beach* (1996), a film that has been described as "a big, fun, beach party for urban teenagers." The rapper played himself in a memorable party sequence. He has also appeared in several commercials, including one for Reebok Black Tops, and he hopes to do more acting as well. "I'd love to be a Klingon with a talking part in 'Star Trek,'" Coolio says. "That would be so dope."

MARRIAGE AND FAMILY

Coolio lives with his fiance, DJ Josefa Salinas, in a mostly African-American neighborhood in Los Angeles. Although he is unmarried, Coolio has six children—three daughters, two sons, a stepdaughter, plus a new baby on the way—by several different mothers.

FAVORITE BOOKS

Coolio still loves to read, just as he did as a child. Back then, he loved the Great Brain series about a boy genius by John D. Fitzgerald. Today, his favorite books are the Pern fantasy novels by Anne McCaffrey. "I think it's her compassion," he says of the books' appeal. "Plus I like the idea of speaking to dragons telepathically." Coolio has said that he would like to write fantasy novels when he retires from the music business.

CREDITS

RECORDINGS

It Takes a Thief, 1994
Gangsta's Paradise, 1995

FILMS

Phat Beach, 1996

HONORS AND AWARDS

American Music Awards: 1996, Favorite Rap—Hip Hop Artist, for "Gangsta's Paradise"
Grammy Award: 1996, Best Solo Rap Performance, for "Gangsta's Paradise"

FURTHER READING

PERIODICALS

Details, Mar. 1996, p.140
Los Angeles Times, Feb. 25, 1996, Calendar Section, p.6

People, Jan. 29, 1996, p.51
Rolling Stone, Sep. 22, 1994, p.37; Dec. 14, 1995, p.33
Spin, Mar. 1996, p.86
Us, May 1996, p.78

ADDRESS

Tommy Boy Music, Inc.
902 Broadway
New York, NY 10010

Coolio Fan Club
11 Loraine Street, #5B
Brooklyn, NY 11231

WORLD WIDE WEB ADDRESS

http://www.sonicnet.com/sonicore/chat/bios/biocoolio.html

Bob Dole   1923-
American Politician
U.S. Senator from Kansas
Senate Majority Leader and
Republican Candidate for U.S. President

BIRTH

Robert Joseph (Bob) Dole, the leading Republican presidential contender for the 1996 elections, was born July 22, 1923, in the farming and oil community of Russell, Kansas. His parents were Doran Ray and Bina (Talbot) Dole. The family also included Bob's older sister Gloria and younger siblings Kenneth and Norma Jean.

YOUTH

Bob Dole grew up during a wrenching time in American history. The Great Depression of the 1930s and the Dust Bowl poverty in Kansas, a prairie state, made every day a struggle. The term "Dust Bowl" describes regions of the Great Plains of the western United States and Canada. The area earned that name when enormous windstorms beginning in 1934 swept across grasslands already parched from over-grazing and over-plowing. The devastating winds carried away what was left of the precious topsoil, leaving the earth too barren to be farmed. Years passed before nature replenished the plains. In the meantime, many families endured extreme poverty and suffering.

The Dole family coped with these harsh financial circumstances during their children's developing years. One year, they were forced to earn money by renting out their modest bungalow to oil riggers. The six Doles lived in makeshift quarters in the basement of their house. All told, the family situation was an accurate reflection of the marginal living circumstances for many Americans in the 1930s.

Dole spent his boyhood much like other rural kids growing up during the Depression. His parents worked long hours to make ends meet and expected their children to help with household chores and to work odd jobs after school. Doran ran an egg and cream distribution center in the early years and later managed a grain elevator. Bina drove an old car around Russell County selling Singer sewing machines in the outlying farm areas. The kids helped out too. As a young boy, Bob peddled newspapers. By the time he was in high school, he held a regular evening job as a soda jerk at Dawson's drugstore, where his salary was two dollars a week and all the ice cream he could eat.

If work was a given in Dole's teen years, so too was his enthusiasm for sports and physical fitness. "I wanted to be like Charles Atlas," he says of his long-ago obsession with body-building. (Atlas was a famous body-builder once proclaimed the World's Most Perfectly Developed Man.) "Tall and husky," according to a sketch in *Current Biography,* "Dole was a natural athlete and a sports and fitness enthusiast, working out constantly with homemade weights and competing fiercely in basketball, football, and track." Even today in his early 70s, Dole still exudes a vibrant physical presence.

EARLY MEMORIES

Dole's memories from childhood are of two rather stern parents. He has been quoted as saying that he received a weekly spanking from his mother, adding "No good reason—just must be Saturday." Those recollections of strict discipline were reinforced several years ago by brother Kenny (now deceased), who told *New York Times* reporters that Doran Dole "never asked you to do something twice," implying that parental decisions were *not* to be questioned.

EDUCATION—HIGH SCHOOL AND EARLY COLLEGE

Growing up, Bob Dole attended the local public schools. At Russell High School, he was a member of the National Honor Society and a top athlete—he ran the 880 in track, played end on the football team, and was the school's first basketball player to shoot one-handed. He was popular and well-liked, although he was shy with girls. Dole graduated from Russell High School in 1941. Planning to become a physician, he accepted a personal college loan from a local banker to attend the University of Kansas. The first in his family to go to college, he began undergraduate study in pre-med at the University of Kansas in Lawrence, about 200 miles from home. He enlisted in the U.S. Army in December 1942, but finished his sophomore year before being called to active duty in June 1943.

WORLD WAR II SERVICE AND A DEVASTATING INJURY

Dole took basic training in the summer of 1943 at Camp Barkley in Texas, and then was sent to train as an engineer at the Army Specialized Training Program in Brooklyn, New York. After further training as an anti-tank gunner in Louisiana and Kentucky, he was accepted into officer candidate school at Fort Benning, Georgia. Commissioned a second lieutenant in the autumn of 1944, Dole shipped out to Italy. He soon joined the 85th Regiment of America's legendary Tenth Mountain Division, created to combat the possibility of a German attack in winter in the mountainous northeastern United States. "Typical Army," he recalls. "I was not a skier. I am not a mountain climber. I came from the plains of Kansas and wound up in the mountain division." At that time, the need for fighting men was such that the elite Tenth was forced to lower its stringent requirements, and Dole was assigned to take over the platoon of a fallen officer. He was only 21.

On April 14, 1945, just three weeks before the war ended in Europe, Dole was struck by an exploding shell as he led an assault on a German machinegun nest in the hills above the Po Valley, south of Bologna. He had just scrambled out of a ravine to rescue his downed radioman, not realizing that the soldier was dead. Then Dole was hit. The blast shattered his right shoulder, fractured vertebrae in his neck and spine, and embedded metal shards throughout his upper body. "I lay face down in the dirt," he later wrote. "Unable to see or to move my arms, I thought they were missing. In fact they were stretched out above my head, until [Dole's rescuer, Sergeant Frank Carafa] made his way across 40 yards of scarred earth to drag me to safety and cross them over my chest." After that, he blacked out.

In shock and semi-conscious, Dole lay on the battlefield for a full day before he could be moved out. He was sent first to an Italian evacuation hospital for emergency surgery on his shoulder. They stabilized his condition, then two days later shipped him to a military facility in Casablanca, Morocco. There, the full extent of his injuries were discovered for the first time: not only were his shoulder and arm hurt, but a vertebrae in his spine was hit too. Dole was paralyzed. Placed in a body cast, he was shipped in June 1945 to a hospital in Florida, and then to one in Topeka, Kansas. His mother, Bina Dole, rented an apartment in Topeka to stay with Bob. Complications soon arose. Still in a body cast, he was running a fever of 108°, and Dole lost a kidney to raging infection.

In November 1945, Dole was moved to Percy Jones Hospital in Battle Creek, Michigan, where he spent almost two years fighting his way through physical therapy. There, he suffered a pulmonary blockage, a blood clot in his lungs that threatened to kill him. His mother was already there; his father rode several hundred miles by train. As Dole told "60 Minutes" in 1993, "He had to stand all the way on the train, the trains were so crowded. He got up there—his ankles were swollen. But he made it." In later years, the memory would move Dole to tears. Unable to remove the blood clot, the doctors offered one last chance, with the drug streptomycin, a powerful antibiotic that was still in experimental form. It worked.

Rehabilitation would take 39 months in all. It took phenomenal courage, willpower, resourcefulness, and dedication. His doctors believed Dole would never walk again. The once-strong athlete had lost 70 pounds. At first, he had to be fed, bathed, and dressed by others. Even when he was ready to resume some semblance of normal life, his right hand and arm remained essentially useless, stuck at a $90°$ angle across his chest. He was forced to learn to write and to button his clothes with a left hand that had little feeling.

When Dole returned to Russell, people in his hometown wanted to help. They set up a collection box at Dawson's drugstore, where Dole had worked as a boy. People tossed in quarters and dollar bills, and ultimately collected $1800. With that money, Dole began a final round of surgery in 1947, totaling seven separate operations, to increase the mobility in his right arm. With the help of his surgeon, the late Dr. Hampar Kelikian, Dole began to understand and accept that he would remain disabled for life. It was time to move on. "[One] day you get up and say, Okay, let's get outta here. Let's start thinking about the future instead of the past and maybe Bob Dole can do something else."

MAJOR INFLUENCES

Dole's agonizing struggle toward physical rehabilitation proved to be the greatest influence on his future life. He credits Dr. Kelikian with urging him to accept a situation that he could not change, and to start over. "[Dr. Kelikian] said, in effect, 'You've got to grow up,'" recalls the senator. "'You're not going to be like you were.'" It was then that Dole's driving ambition was rekindled.

RETURN TO CIVILIAN LIFE AND COLLEGE

After rehabilitation, Dole was ready to return to college. He knew he wouldn't be able to fulfill his dream of a medical career, so he chose law instead. He studied for one year at the University of Arizona on the GI Bill, a 1944 law that provides educational and other benefits for veterans of the U.S. armed services. He then transferred after a year to Washburn University in Topeka, Kansas, where he was awarded *both* an A.B. and an LL.B. (Bachelor of Arts and Bachelor of Law degree), summa cum laude, in 1952. He passed the bar examination that same year, and soon opened a practice in his hometown.

CAREER HIGHLIGHTS

While Dole was still in law school, he first ventured into public service. His background was not Republican; the senior Doles were New Deal Democrats who had endorsed government programs set up in the 1930s to battle the desperate conditions of the Depression. Yet Bob Dole discovered that the majority of voters in his district were Republicans, so he ran for and won a term in the Kansas state legislature as a member of that party.

After his two-year legislative stint, Dole served throughout most of the 1950s as Russell County Attorney. He then decided to broaden his base to the national level. He was elected to the U.S. House of Representatives in 1960 in a relatively easy campaign, but the primary race had been marred by a whispering campaign about his opponent's alleged drinking problem. Dole denied any part in the dirty politics of that nominating process, but it was a sour note that heralded what a *New York Times* story would later describe as a "bitterness that has plagued his political career."

The young congressman from Kansas was solidly conservative during his eight years in the House. He opposed most of the federal aid programs of the John Kennedy and Lyndon Johnson administrations, among them Medicare. Dole did break rank with his party, however, to favor aid to agriculture, the hungry, and the handicapped, drawing on his own experiences. He also cast consenting votes for the 1964 Civil Rights Act and the 1965 Voting Rights Act.

THE UNITED STATES SENATE

Dole was elected to the U.S. Senate in 1968. There, he developed a reputation as a blunt-talking, fiercely partisan defender of Republican policies.

His acerbic tongue savaged opponents of then-President Richard Nixon, and "even some Republicans considered him a brash upstart," notes a sketch in *Current Biography Yearbook.* Although a staunch Republican, he was pragmatic as well, and his skills as a negotiator on many prickly issues came to be appreciated by both parties. One particular bipartisan cause was his work with former Senator George McGovern on the food-stamp program. It was an ironic twist of political expediency. The nutrition program was strongly backed by Dole's Kansas farm constituency. The two senators were able to work together despite Dole's earlier attacks on McGovern when he was a Democratic presidential candidate. Throughout his long career in the Senate, Dole often has repeated such contradictions of his conservative stance with centrist leanings. "I may not be totally predictable," he admits, adding reflectively, "I'm not certain that's all bad."

In 1974, the Watergate scandal forced the resignation of President Nixon, and Gerald Ford became president. Watergate still burned in the minds of the voting public when Ford chose Bob Dole as his running mate in his 1976 campaign for the presidency. Ford needed a fighter, but his choice of Dole to be his vice president is still believed to be a large part of their 1976 loss to Democratic contender Jimmy Carter. Dole's campaign style was bitter, abrasive, aggressive, caustic, sarcastic, and mean-spirited, and this reputation has followed him ever since. His stinging jabs at the opposition intensified his image as the nominee's "hatchet man," a label that was pinned on him some years earlier by a Republican colleague, Senator William Saxbe of Ohio.

Long remembered from the 1976 campaign was a remark by Dole during a public debate. He said that the wars of the 20th century—World Wars I and II, Korea, and Vietnam—were "Democrat wars," and also said that "if we added up the killed and wounded in Democrat wars in this century, it would be about 1.6 million Americans, enough to fill the city of Detroit." His comment deeply offended and angered many, and there was an immediate furor. Some say that it cost Ford and Dole the election. Dole returned to the Senate to immerse himself in legislative detail and tactics that continued to mark his growing visibility.

REACHING FOR THE WHITE HOUSE

In 1980, Dole made his first bid for the Republican nomination for president. He made a dismal showing in the important New Hampshire primaries, and he quickly withdrew from the race. Ronald Reagan became the party nominee and won the election in a landslide that fall. Dole returned to the Senate, this time as chairman of the Senate Finance Committee. Most of his work during the next decade would be concentrated on tax-related issues. During his presidency, Reagan conceived sweeping changes in the U.S. tax system. But although the president can propose such changes, it is the Congress that must pass the laws that make it happen. Dole didn't support many of the president's proposals, but he pushed the new tax bills through the Congress and got them passed. Dole's handling of budget issues during this period has been described as masterful.

In 1984, when the Republicans won the majority of seats in the Senate, he succeeded the retiring Howard Baker as Majority Leader, only to surrender that powerful post two years later when elections returned the Democrats to congressional power. Dole's prestige grew within his own party, however, with his resourceful handling of the 1986-87 Iran-Contra scandal. The Reagan administration was charged with secretly selling arms to Iran and unlawfully diverting the profits to the Contra rebels of Nicaragua. Dole quickly stepped up to be a spokesman for the administration, urging President Reagan to cooperate with investigators and to appoint a special prosecutor. Dole was earning a reputation as "the master of compromise," even though he often compromised his own positions, political observers said.

Dole launched a second bid for the presidency at the end of Reagan's second term in 1988. His main rival for the nomination was Vice President George Bush. For a brief time, Dole was favored in the caucuses and primaries. But when he angrily told Bush on national TV news to "stop lying about my record," he appeared truculent and belligerent. Again, the iron-willed Kansan, reluctant as ever to delegate authority, followed his own mismanaged and disaster-prone agenda. He became mired in the "personality [that had] always been the real problem underlying his candidacy," suggested an article in *Time* magazine. Dole blew a 20 point lead in the polls, and Bush went on the win the Republican nomination and the 1988 presidential election.

In 1991, Dole was diagnosed with prostate cancer. He was successfully treated with surgery; the doctors believe they got it all. He has had no recurrences since then.

In 1992, Bush failed to win a second term, and Bill Clinton was elected president with the promise of a new tomorrow. But Dole was still a figure to be reckoned with. It was he who stayed focused on holding the conservative line against the administration's proposed and widely challenged reforms. "I always say gridlock is a good thing. If you're on the other side of the issue, you better hope there are people up there defending your interest," Dole said about his efforts to block Clinton proposals. "All this talk about gridlock is a joke. That's what the Founding Fathers had in mind when they created the Senate and said we could debate forever."

Mid-term congressional elections in 1994 changed the balance of power in favor of the Republicans, who took control of the Senate and the House of Representatives. Dole became Senate Majority Leader, a post he still holds today. The Republican Party created the "Contract with America," a 10-point legislative plan that addressed such issues as balancing the budget, limiting taxes, creating crime-fighting measures, overhauling the welfare system, increasing defense funding, and setting term limits for members of Congress. The plan was brought before the American public by the Speaker of the House, Newt Gingrich. The "Contract with America" elevated Dole to an even higher level of public recognition as he engineered party initiatives through Senate debate.

A THIRD PRESIDENTIAL BID AND THE AGE ISSUE

As Dole prepares to mount his third presidential challenge in the 1996 election, certain criticisms from the past have resurfaced. One is the issue of his age. He is 72 years old and would be 73 upon assuming office, if he won the Republican nomination and the general election in 1996. He would be the oldest man ever inaugurated, and four years older than Ronald Reagan when he became president. Nevertheless, Dole's mental sharpness and his robust good health seem to allay fears about his ability to carry out presidential responsibilities.

Another issue is the steadfastness of his political beliefs. As the consummate Senate insider, Dole has been well known for years for his pragmatism and his ability to compromise. In the current political climate in the Republican party, he has been shrewdly hedging his bets. He has courted conservative hard-liners with budget-slashing and right-wing social pronouncements, while at the same time hinting at compromise to appeal to more moderate elements of his party. While some call this compromising, others call it waffling.

Additionally, the issue of his attitude has resurfaced, with commentators concerned about the bitter and mean-spirited remarks from the past. Dole claims to have learned from the failures of his last bid. This time around, he sports a softer image—more comfortable, more at ease. Yet, David Shribman of the *Boston Globe* suggests that "there is no new Bob Dole. There's just the same old Bob Dole, and if it strikes you that there is something new about him, it may be because advisers are telling him to smile more, to keep his chin up so that he doesn't look so menacing."

At this point, Dole dominates the Republican field of contenders, among them the ultra-conservative Senator Phil Gramm of Texas, and commentator-columnist Pat Buchanan. Since Colin Powell, the popular former chairman of the Joint Chiefs of Staff, decided in November 1995 not to pursue the nomination, Dole's position has been measurably strengthened. Experience and leadership may be the most important factors in his favor. The challenges he has faced in Congress over the past 35 years serve to underscore his place as a true survivor. In his 1994 biography of the senator, Jake Thomas points out that "Dole has been at the heart, often as protagonist, of the great upheavals of the last half-century—World War II, the Cold War, the 1960s civil rights and student-protest turbulence, Vietnam, Watergate, the Iran-Contra scandal, the Persian Gulf War, and the menace of the expanding federal deficit." As the last World War II hopeful for a shot at the presidency, Dole is readying himself for the rigors of still another campaign.

MARRIAGE AND FAMILY

Dole has been married twice. His first wife was the former Phyllis Holden. They met toward the end of his rehabilitation period at Percy Jones Hospital. She was an occupational therapist there, although she worked in a different department and never treated Dole. According to the *New York Times*, "She had worked with so many disabled men that she didn't consider him handicapped." They started dating, fell in love, and got married three months later, in June 1948. They had one daughter, Robin, who is now grown. They divorced in 1972.

Dole's second wife is the former Elizabeth Hanford. Their marriage on December 6, 1975, created a powerful union of two of the capital's most politically ambitious figures. Now president of the American Red Cross, Elizabeth Dole twice served as a U.S. Cabinet member, as Secretary of the Departments of Transportation and Labor under Presidents Reagan and Bush. The Doles live in a Watergate duplex apartment with Leader, a miniature schnauzer that was a gift to Bob from his wife in 1984, the first time he won the coveted majority-leader post. They own a condominium at Bal Harbor, Florida, but, with his constituency in Kansas, the senator maintains his childhood home in Russell as his legal residence.

HOBBIES AND OTHER INTERESTS

Relaxation is almost a foreign concept to Bob Dole. A former staffer calls him a "perpetual-motion machine," and Dole confirms his workaholic nature by acknowledging his and his wife's common interests: "(A) we like to work, (B) we like to work, and (c) we like to work." A friend once described the couple for a *People* magazine writer as "total public-service junkies."

Dole is neither particularly interested in spectator sports, nor is he known to indulge in hobbies. His television habits are mainly confined to watching news and public-interest programs. He is, in fact, a frequent guest himself on the CBS "Face the Nation" panel and on NBC's "Meet the Press." When his and Elizabeth's grueling schedules permit, they enjoy a video or an occasional TV show in the evening. Sunday is the day they nearly always spend together, at church and at brunch afterward with daughter Robin or with close friends.

Even that simple weekend ritual may suffer, though, while the Doles concentrate on the senator's campaign. Elizabeth Dole has taken a one-year leave of absence from her high-profile job, stating that, even if her husband attains the presidency, she will return to her career.

Senator Dole stays in excellent physical condition through a daily treadmill workout and a careful diet, both of which help to compensate for the loss of the mobility that was so much a part of his youth. His only noticeable handicap is indicated by the trademark pen or roll of paper he clenches to remind others not to reach for his damaged hand in greeting.

WRITINGS

The Doles: Unlimited Partners, 1988 (with Elizabeth Dole and Richard Norton Smith)

HONORS AND AWARDS

Bronze Star with oak cluster: 1945, for heroic battlefield service
Purple Hearts (two): 1945, for wounds suffered in action
Horatio Alger Award (Horatio Alger Association of Distinguished Americans): 1988

FURTHER READING

BOOKS

Bob Dole: The U.S. Senator Who Was Severely Wounded in World War II, 1995 (young adult)
Dole, Bob, and Elizabeth Hanford Dole. *The Doles: Unlimited Partners,* 1988 (with Richard Norton Smith)
Thomas, Jake H. *Bob Dole: The Republicans' Man For All Seasons,* 1994
Who's Who in America, 1996

PERIODICALS

Boston Globe Magazine, June 11, 1995, p.13
Current Biography Yearbook 1987
Esquire, Apr. 1995, p.65
New Republic, Oct. 3, 1994, p.10
New York Times, Feb. 19, 1995, p.A32; June 8, 1995, p.A28
New York Times Biographical Service, Nov. 1987, p.1155
New York Times Magazine, Mar. 5, 1995, p.33
Newsweek, Nov. 16, 1987, p.66; Feb. 22, 1988, p.16; Feb. 13, 1995, p.30;
  Apr. 24, 1995, p.32; June 12, 1995, p.28
People, May 11, 1992, p.119; Dec. 13, 1993, p.121
Rolling Stone, Sep. 30, 1993, p.35
Wall Street Journal, Apr. 6, 1995, p.A1; June 15, 1995, p.A12

ADDRESS

U.S. Senate
141 Hart Senate Building
Washington, DC 20510-1601

David Duchovny 1960-
American Actor
Star of "The X-Files"

BIRTH

David William Duchovny (Doo-CUV-nee) was born on August 7, 1960, in New York City and grew up in Manhattan. His parents are Amram, a writer and a publicist for the American Jewish Committee, and Scottish-born Margaret, the administrator of an elementary school in Manhattan. He has an older brother, Daniel, and a younger sister, Laurie.

YOUTH

Because he was so quiet when he was a child, Duchovny's older brother Daniel used to tell people that he was retarded. "They would speak very loudly and slowly to me, and that just made me more shy." But he was not so quiet that he didn't get into some rowdy mischief once in a while. His younger sister Laurie remembers that in order to scare her, David and a friend would put stockings on their heads and chase her around the house wielding kitchen tools.

EARLY MEMORIES

His parents divorced when he was 11, and Duchovny took it very hard. His father left, and his mother had to make the transition from being a homemaker to a working single mother. He believes it caused him to repress his feelings in order to maintain his good student/good athlete "hero" image for the family. When he discovered acting later in life it was like finding an emotional release valve. "It became a technique of survival not to feel things too deeply. I was always supposed to be the one who didn't have any problems," he recalls. "And when I got to act, it was like all of a sudden I could have problems."

EDUCATION

His first on-stage experience occurred in the fifth grade, when Duchovny played one of the Three Wise Men in a school Christmas play. Later, on a scholarship, he attended Collegiate Prep, a prestigious private school in Manhattan, where he also played basketball and baseball. His high school years were marked by high academic and athletic achievement, but Duchovny dated rarely.

Duchovny went on to attend Princeton University, where he majored in English literature and earned his bachelor's degree in 1982. While there he also played baseball and, for one year, basketball on the school's team.

He decided to pursue an academic career and continued studying English literature at Yale University, which he attended on a Mellon fellowship. At this point in his life, Duchovny was following the track toward becoming a college professor. He earned a master's degree in English literature from Yale University and took classes toward his Ph.D.

During graduate school, he divided his time between teaching undergraduate courses and proceeding with his own degree requirements. He remembers reading constantly in preparation for his oral exams: "the day before, my head felt heavy . . . I remember thinking, 'I'll never be this smart again'." He got as far as planning his dissertation, which was to be on "Magic and Technology in Contemporary Poetry and Prose."

But he was also growing interested in writing scripts, something his father had also done a bit of. He took to hanging out with students from Yale's drama school.

CHOOSING A CAREER

As his interest in theater grew, Duchovny decided that he should get some acting experience in order to nurture his growth as a screenwriter. So he took an acting class at Yale, and in 1987 was persuaded to try out for a spot in a beer commercial. He got the job. That year he realized that he didn't want to continue his academic career. "I enjoyed reading, I enjoyed writing. It was pretty much because I hadn't found anything that moved me, and this was something I could do and I liked in a tepid kind of a way as a career." He says that it was never really a decision he made, but something that just happened; seemingly, acting was the thing that moved him, giving him an outlet he hadn't really had before: "I had grown up in a very controlled academic environment. But here people were saying, 'Yes, it's good to scream, it's good to cry.'"

FIRST JOBS

So he moved to New York and endured a couple of dry difficult years before his career began to take off with some parts in off-Broadway plays and, eventually, small movie roles. Duchovny won minor parts in movies like *Working Girl* (1988), *Don't Tell Mom the Babysitter's Dead* (1991), *The Rapture* (1991), *Chaplin* (1992), *Kalifornia* (1993), and *Beethoven* (1992). He played a wicked yuppie businessman in the latter, and says of that experience, "Saint Bernard saliva is sticky and nasty. If you can imagine bad-smelling maple sap, that's what it's like to work with that dog."

His TV career began in 1990 on "Twin Peaks"—in what happened to be its final season. On that show he had his first experience playing an FBI agent. Later, he appeared in the *Showtime* series "The Red Shoe Diaries."

CAREER HIGHLIGHTS

"THE X-FILES"

"The X-Files" debuted on Fox Television in 1993. By the show's second season in 1994, it had gone from being a cult favorite to a mainstream hit, and the stars have reportedly agreed to do the show for five more years.

Reminiscent of earlier TV shows like "The Twilight Zone" and "Outer Limits," "The X-Files" treats viewers to stories of the paranormal—but tries always to do so within the reach of "extreme scientific possibility." Duchovny plays Agent Fox Mulder to co-star Gillian Anderson's Agent Dana Scully. Every Friday night, the two FBI agents explore such bizarre mysteries as UFOs and alien abductions, psychic phenomena, secret government experiments run amok, ghosts and evil spirits, marauding computers, and genetically mutated beings of all kinds, ranging in form from insect to human.

As Duchovny puts it, the show "aims at the point where physics and metaphysics meet, where science and poetry come together. We take the real world and put imagined things in it. We're not science fiction and we're not cops-and-robbers. We have one foot in each."

Mulder is known as "Spooky" Mulder by other agents for his interest in strange phenomena; the character refers to himself as "the FBI's most unwanted." Mulder has a sign hanging in his office that reads "I want to believe."

According to "X-Files" producer Chris Carter, Duchovny seemed almost made for the role of Mulder: "I wrote these characters who were very serious, who were very real. When David came in a few years ago [to audition], he was very deadpan, very minimalist in his approach to acting. And so it worked for the character of Fox Mulder." Carter adds that Duchovny "is also one of the funniest people you'll ever meet." It should cause no surprise then that the tie he wore to his audition was covered with pink pigs.

One of the most captivating elements of the show is the riveting relationship between the lead characters. Many of the show's fans like to speculate on a possible romantic relationship developing between the two. One crew member notes that "the way Mulder and Scully are on-screen is the way David and Gillian are in person. They help each other, they respect each other." However, Duchovny reports that he and his co-star "don't hang

out. We are very wary of the fact that at any moment the other can turn into a psychotic human being because of the demands that are put on us, the 16-hour days."

The days are long and rigorous on the "X-Files" set, where the crew and actors often work late into the night. He and co-star Anderson enjoy breaking up the monotony of the long work days with various pranks, like the time they sprayed the crew with a fire extinguisher that happened to be on the set.

SUCCESS AND FAME

Duchovny is becoming as known for his understated acting style as he is for playing Mulder. Early on in his career, he remembers, people were saying, "'He doesn't seem to be doing anything.' And now, if somebody says that to me, I say, 'Well, thank you!'" He admires Marlon Brando as an actor because "I always feel he's showing me that it's painful . . . to act. The best actors have an air of failure even at the height of their success."

Although Duchovny misses his anonymity, stardom does seem to have its high points. As he told a *TV Guide* reporter, one day on the "X-Files" set a crew member came up to him and said that Robin Williams wanted to meet him. "As I was turning, I said, 'No, he wouldn't.' And he was *standing right there*. And he goes, 'Oh, yes, he would!'"

Another perk was a trip to the real FBI headquarters. The show is popular with real-life FBI agents, and they invited Duchovny and Anderson to visit the FBI in Washington, D.C., and its training center at Quantico, Virginia. Duchovny was interested in learning how authentic his portrayal is. Agents fed both actors with tips on FBI protocol, like never show your ID with your gun hand and never enter a dark building with no backup help waiting outside.

Although his mother was not thrilled with his choice to leave academics for acting, his father seems to have a sense of humor about it all. Duchovny says that "when I was six years old, I told my father I wanted to be a bathtub. So now he always calls me and he goes, 'So, still a failure, huh?'"

HOME AND FAMILY

Most of the time, home is a trailer in Vancouver, British Columbia, where the "X-Files" is filmed. He shares quarters with his dog, a Border collie mix named Blue—an allusion to the Bob Dylan song, "Tangled Up in Blue." He also has a place in Malibu, California.

Duchovny would eventually like to get married and have a few children, but for now he just tries to see his girlfriend, actress Perrey Reeves, whenever his frantic schedule allows. They met in 1993 at an L.A. clothing store. She has since played a vampire in an "X-Files" episode.

HOBBIES AND OTHER INTERESTS

A vegetarian, Duchovny has many interests—yoga, acupuncture, squash, swimming. He's an avid reader and especially enjoys novels by Norman Mailer, Thomas Pynchon, and Elmore Leonard. He writes poetry and has read his work at poetry readings in L.A. clubs. Poets who have inspired him include John Ashbery, Wallace Stevens, and John Berryman. And the taste for screenwriting that brought him into acting has not disappeared; he has contributed some story lines to the "X-Files."

Unlike Mulder, Duchovny is not obsessed with UFOs, but he thinks that "there may be something out there. . . . To me, it would be more amazing to say: There is going to be one little planet in this vast universe that has life on it, and nobody else can sustain life. That, to me, seems ridiculous."

SELECTED CREDITS

TELEVISION

"Twin Peaks," 1990-91
"The X-Files," 1993-

FILMS

Working Girl, 1988
Don't Tell Mom the Babysitter's Dead, 1991
The Rapture, 1991
Chaplin, 1992
Beethoven, 1992
Kalifornia, 1993

FURTHER READING

BOOKS

Genge, N. E. *The Unofficial X-Files Companion*, 1995
Lowry, Brian. *The Official Guide to the X-Files*, 1995

PERIODICALS

Akron Beacon Journal, July 27, 1993, p.C13
Chicago Tribune, Jan. 27, 1995, Tempo section, p. 3
Cosmopolitan, Oct. 1995, p.144
Details, Oct. 1995, p.121
Entertainment Weekly, Mar. 18, 1994, p.58; Dec. 2, 1994, p.32; Sep. 29, 1995, p.20; Dec. 22, 1995, p.12; Dec. 29, 1995, p.30
Miami Herald, Mar. 18, 1994, p.F7
Newsweek, Dec. 5, 1994, p.66
New York Times, Mar. 26, 1995, section II, p.37
People, Apr. 25, 1994, p.59; Oct. 9, 1995, p.72; Nov. 13, 1995, p.49
St. Paul Pioneer Press, July 10, 1994, TV section, p.3
Seventeen, Dec. 1995, p.66
TV Guide, Jan. 15, 1994, p.20; July 2, 1994, p.8; Mar. 11, 1995, p.8
Us, May 1995, p.80
USA Today, Sep. 1, 1995, p.3D
Vancouver Sun, Aug. 23, 1993, p.C1

ADDRESS

David Duchovny
"The X-Files"
P.O. Box 900
Beverly Hills, CA 90213

INTERNET SITES

On-line "X-Files" fans, known as "X-Philes," meet on the Usenet group on the Internet at these 2 sites:
alt.tv.x-files
alt.tv.x-files.creative

The David Duchovny Estrogen Brigade is on the Internet at:
http://www.egr.uh.edu/~escco/DDEB.html

The official Fox "X-Files" World Wide Web site is at:
http://www.foxnetwork.com/Prime/FoxFaves/xfiles/index.html

Debbi Fields 1956-
American Entrepreneur
Founder of Mrs. Fields Cookies

BIRTH

Debra Jane (Sivyer) Fields, the Mrs. Fields of cookie fame, was born September 18, 1956, in East Oakland, California. She was the youngest of five daughters of Edward and Mary Lucy (Casovia) Sivyer. Edward ("Bud") was a World War II veteran who worked as a welder at the U.S. Naval Base in Alameda, California. Mary was a homemaker for Debbi and her sisters, Linda, Mary, Marlene, and Cathy.

The Sivyers were working-class people whose heritage was an interesting mix of French, Yugoslav, Cherokee, and Czech descent.

The maternal grandparents, ethnic Czechs, had owned a San Francisco restaurant that was destroyed in the devastating earthquake and fire in that city in 1906. They rebuilt, only to fail in business when the Great Depression brought the nation's economy to a halt in the 1930s.

YOUTH

Fields speaks of her years growing up in East Oakland as "a crazy mixture of cooperation and chaos." She describes a bustling household where five girls shared a morning ritual of crowding around the bathroom mirror, spilling into the kitchen for a hearty breakfast, and setting up an assembly line to prepare bag lunches for school. From dawn to bedtime, there was constant activity in the East 27th Street house that had once belonged to Bud Sivyer's parents.

As a child, Debbi always felt left out. Most of her sisters' games called for four players. Since she was the baby of the family, there never seemed to be a place for her. She became "pest-in-residence," she recalls, tagging along "like any little kid" with older siblings, but often being snubbed. Fields believes now that she developed a need for acknowledgment in those early years, which became the underlying reason for her drive to do, and to be, "something special." Her yearning for the spotlight in a close-knit family that treated all members equally set her on a path of making things happen for herself. She became a fiercely independent child, questioning the system at home and at school, and testing the limits as far as she dared.

Home life was loving—and also strict. There were household duties for each girl as she grew old enough to assume them, and special privileges were not an everyday expectation. Phone use was off- limits until the teen years and, even then, was restricted. The Sivyers's neighborhood was in a tough area of Oakland, so their parents made Debbi and her sisters confine their activities to home, school, and church. Fields chafed under the rules and still considers them overly confining. She has warm memories of good times and vacation fun, though, and of her parents' many willing sacrifices. The family's income was modest, but the Sivyer wealth was counted in family and friends, never in money. Fields concedes today that in matters of caregiving, discipline, and finances, her mother "may not [always] have given me what I wanted, but she never once missed giving me what I needed."

EARLY MEMORIES

Bud Sivyer, as a welder, could repair or make almost anything. When Debbi set her heart on having a bicycle that would have strained the family budget, he welded one for her out of spare parts and painted it fire-engine red. Fields vividly recalls zipping down the street on her new wheels, acting like a daredevil to please her father who, she instinctively knew, had always hoped for a son. "I wanted desperately to make my dad happy," she explains. She tells how she became a "hellraiser of a tomboy," even though her reckless antics sent her "poor mother into fits."

EDUCATION

The Sivyer sisters all went to Catholic schools. Unlike the others, Debbi was a reluctant student, bored and distracted most of the time. Her experience at Bishop O'Dowd High School was one of nonconformity. She says that it wasn't that she didn't learn anything in school, "I just never learned what they were trying to teach me." She became a loner, making barely passable grades and growing increasingly unhappy.

When Debbi's parents agreed to let her transfer to public school, she chose Alameda High, far enough away from home that she had to stay with her sister Mary. Her social life brightened considerably at Alameda, even though her grades remained mediocre, and she was elected homecoming queen in her senior year. She graduated in 1974. College was neither an academic or financial option after graduation, but she started working full time. Later, Fields took courses at Los Altos Junior College.

MAJOR INFLUENCES

Fields found focus, and a mentor, at junior college, which she attended for several years in her late teens and early 20s. "There was one teacher at Los Altos, Mr. Applebaum, who saw something in me that no one else had noticed," she reveals in her 1987 autobiography, *One Smart Cookie*. "He adopted me as a special project, and that in itself was a source of motivation. He *believed* in me." Applebaum's encouragement produced a self-confidence in Fields that was evidenced by an upward swing in her grades and a sense of pride, she says, that she had never known before.

FIRST JOBS

Debbi had started working when she was a teenager. The longing for nice things—skis and other luxuries—had Debbi out scouting for jobs as soon as she could wangle permission from her parents. When she was only 13, she started working as a ball girl for the Oakland Athletics professional baseball team, chasing balls along the foul line. She was the first female hired to do that job. She started saving money for the frills that her parents didn't provide. A succession of part-time jobs followed. She worked at Mervyn's department store during high school, winning recognition there for her enthusiasm and energy, and then took a job as a performer at Marine World. She started out as a water skier, then moved up to cavorting with the dolphins.

After graduating from high school in 1974, Fields packed up her old Volkswagen and took off for Lake Tahoe, a resort town on the California-Nevada border. She was hoping to find enough odd jobs to keep her fed and sheltered and to purchase tickets for the ski lifts. She worked briefly as a nanny for a family with five children, then headed home again to Oakland, still looking for a direction for her boundless energy.

CHOOSING A CAREER

Fields had been the family cookie-maker as a teenager. She would experiment with the famous old Toll House chocolate-chip cookie recipe by using her spending money to buy butter instead of margarine to make the taste richer and more flavorful. Each of the Sivyer girls had a kitchen specialty, but no one dreamed then that Debbi's would one day grow into a successful enterprise. Shortly after her marriage to financial whiz Randy Fields in 1975 when she was 18, Debbi was looking around for a way to earn her own money. Her delicious cookies were such a hit with Randy's friends and associates that she decided to open a store to sell them.

Everyone except Debbi's husband thought it was a "dumb idea," wrote Barbara Mahany a few years ago in the *Chicago Tribune.* "Even the banker who gave the Fieldses their first loan . . . took Mr. Fields aside and whispered conspiratorially that when business went under, the loss of a $50,000 down payment would be 'a terrific tax shelter.'" Mahany further observes, "That was 15 years, 741 stores, and 5,000 employees ago."

CAREER HIGHLIGHTS

The cookie operation opened in 1977 in Palo Alto, California, as Mrs. Fields Chocolate Chippery, a lighthearted description for her product. As for using the name Mrs. Fields (no apostrophe), Debbi and Randy never realized that most customers would expect an old-fashioned, grandmotherly baking lady; they would have been startled to know that the Mrs. Fields behind the cookie was a 21-year-old. The first day in her marketplace storefront might have discouraged a less determined owner. Fields had to lure customers to her counter by passing out free samples of her cookies in the mall. When the give-aways were gone from her tray, she returned to the store to bake a fresh batch, and the aroma wafting through the doorway soon had customers drifting in to buy.

That first day's sales were a meager $50, barely covering her bet with Randy that her cookies would sell; the next few days saw a rise in proceeds, and the hopes of the young entrepreneur started to rise also. Business increased so rapidly that she had to hire help. From the beginning, quality customer service was one of her first concerns. She insisted that all her staff cater to customer demand with the prompt, helpful service that has been a hallmark of her business for almost 20 years. She wanted Mrs. Fields stores to be fun and friendly places to work and shop.

In little more than a year after her "grand opening," a second store was added, this time in Pier 39, a new San Francisco mall. Soon afterward came a third, and more were on the drawing board. By 1981, the number of stores had reached 14. Randy developed a computerized management system that allowed the company to maintain centralized control. The system analyzed sales store-by-store on an hourly basis. It provided information to the store manager and the central office to chart baking demands, to plan personnel needs, and to keep track of sales.

Sales rocketed in the 1980s. They were opening 70 new stores a year, and the company grew to nearly 800 stores. Fields soon faced a problem common to those who start successful businesses. As her stores became more successful, she needed better business and management systems to oversee finances, personnel, equipment, inventory, etc. Fields needed more than her instincts to handle the burgeoning business. "She was compelled to bring in others: store managers, area sales managers, regional directors of operations," says a *Working Woman* feature. "Randy was drawn in as the financial specialist, handling real-estate purchasing and corporate development. Fields took the company public in 1986 . . . to position it for international growth."

BUSINESS PROBLEMS DEVELOP

Yet problems developed in the late 1980s. A downturn in the nation's economy meant less traffic in malls, which resulted in fewer customers at Mrs. Fields stores willing to pay for the luxury of an expensive cookie. In addition, the company had expanded so rapidly that it began to experience serious money problems because of its large debt; in 1988 alone, Mrs. Fields Cookies posted a $19 million net loss for the year, and 97 stores had to be closed. A shift in strategy, which added a new level of middle management to handle the staggering details of the $150 million business, brought about a brief respite, but in the 1990s loan debts again threatened to strangle the company.

The company's financial problems derived, according to some experts, from its business philosophy. Fields was determined to do everything herself. She is a perfectionist with a hands-on approach, a business philosophy that has backfired. That approach became unworkable as the company grew. In addition, she was reluctant from the beginning to relinquish any control by franchising or licensing, in which an individual purchases the rights to set up and run a store using the company's name and products. Fields has defended that stance by saying "I always feared that independent franchisees might substitute product or sacrifice quality," which are the defining aspects of the empire she built from scratch.

But all that changed in 1993. She was forced to reorganize, surrendering to her lenders nearly 80 percent of her company in exchange for their writing off $94 million in debt. Although Fields remains the largest individual stockholder (11 percent), she no longer has control of day-to-day operations of Mrs. Fields Cookies, the company that she started. She gave up her position as President and Chief Executive Officer (CEO). Instead she now reports to a new CEO; her current responsibilities include public relations, new product development, and quality control. In addition to her work for the company, Debbi Fields recently added writing to her repertoire. She penned an autobiography in 1987 and published two cookbooks in the 1990s. She also hosts a new cable show called "Hospitality," which offers tips on entertaining.

MARRIAGE AND FAMILY

Debra Sivyer first met Randall Keith Fields at the Denver airport where she was waiting for a flight home after a skiing trip. They were an unlikely pair—he was 28 and she was 18; he was a Phi Beta Kappa economist with his own investment company and she was still looking for focus in her life. Yet, their casual meeting soon led to romance and marriage. They married on September 21, 1975, initially against the better judgment of both sets of parents, and have spent the ensuing years raising a family and building a business. Since the Mrs. Fields corporate offices moved in 1981 from Palo Alto, California, to Utah, the Fields family has lived on a ranch near Park City, Utah. The couple has five children, all girls: Jessica, Jenessa, Jennifer, Ashley, and McKenzie.

CREDITS

BOOKS

One Smart Cookie, 1987 (with Alan Furst)
100 Recipes From the Kitchen of Debbi Fields, 1992
The Mrs. Fields ''I Love Chocolate Cookbook'': *100 Easy and Irresistible Recipes*, 1994

TELEVISION

"Hospitality," Food Network, 1995-

FURTHER READING

BOOKS

Aronoff, Craig E., and John L. Ward. *Contemporary Entrepreneurs: Profiles of Entrepreneurs and the Businesses They Started*, 1992
Fields, Debbi, and Alan Furst. *One Smart Cookie*, 1987
Ingham, John M., and Lynn B. Feldman. *Contemporary American Business Leaders*, 1990
Spiesman, Harriet. *Debbi Fields: The Cookie Lady*, 1992 (juvenile)

PERIODICALS

Chicago Tribune, Mar. 26, 1987, Food Guide, p.1; June 8, 1992, Tempo, p.1
Good Housekeeping, Aug. 1983, p.44
Inc., July 1984, p.38; Oct. 1987, p.65;
Los Angeles Times, Sep. 4, 1986, Business section, p.1
Parents' Magazine, Sep. 1986, p.71
People, Mar. 23, 1981, p.102
Success, Sep. 1993, p.64
Working Woman, Jan. 1992, p.42; July 1993, p.9

ADDRESS

Mrs. Fields Cookies
333 Main Street
Park City, Utah 84060

BRIEF ENTRY

Chris Galeczka 1981-
American Student and Winner of the
1995 National Geography Bee

EARLY YEARS

Chris Galeczka was born September 2, 1981, in Sterling Heights, Michigan. His parents are Elizabeth and Edward Galeczka. Elizabeth is a medical transcription supervisor and Edward makes engines at an auto plant in suburban Detroit. Chris is the oldest of three children. The family lives in Sterling Heights, Michigan.

120

MAJOR ACCOMPLISHMENTS

THE NATIONAL GEOGRAPHY BEE

The National Geography Bee is sponsored by the National Geographic Society and Chrysler Corporation. The competition is open to students across the U.S. in grades five through eight. Six million kids try out every year for the award, which carries a $25,000 scholarship and a chance to compete on the international level.

Chris first competed in the National Geographic Bee in 1994, when he made it to the final group of six finalists. The following year, he also made it to the finals, which took place in Washington, D.C., in June 1995. The final question, given to Chris by moderator Alex Trebek of "Jeopardy!," was: "Pashto and Dari are the official languages of which mountainous, landlocked country in central Asia?" Chris wrote down "Afghanistan." He was right! "It's kind of nice," Chris said of his win.

In addition to his scholarship, Chris also won a 10-day trip to anywhere in the U.S. He chose the Mall of America in Minneapolis, Minnesota. "It looks like it's 20 times the size of St. Peter's" (a famous cathedral in Rome), he said of his decision. He and his family enjoyed their trip to the Mall in the summer of 1995.

After the trip, Chris competed in the International Geography Bee, held at Disney World in Orlando, Florida, in late July of 1995, where, unfortunately, he failed to place in the finals.

Chris says that learning is easy for him, because he has a great memory. "I don't study much," he says. "I just absorb anything that comes in." Chris's mom, Elizabeth, says that her son "likes to dream about other countries." And he's not scared of competition. "It's a hobby of his," says Elizabeth Galeczka. "He likes being up in front of other children and being quizzed." His dad, Edward, notes that Chris was "in the encyclopedia books constantly and the atlases." And while Chris says he is not a voracious reader, he has read *National Geographic* for five years. "Lots of the questions come from the magazine," he says of the Geography Bee. "So if you read that, you know a lot of the stuff." He is also a regular reader of the *World Almanac*, magazines, and newspapers.

Chris is now a ninth grader at Henry Ford II High School in Sterling Heights, Michigan. He would like to be president some day. He would also like to appear on "Jeopardy!" He loves to travel and also enjoys snowmobiling and playing in the high school band.

FURTHER READING

Arizona Republic, June 1, 1995, p. A2
Cincinnati Post, June 1, 1995, pA3

Detroit Free Press, June 1, 1995, p.A1
Seattle Times, June 1, 1995, p.A6

ADDRESS

The National Geographic Society
1600 M Street, NW
Washington, DC 20036-3208

OBITUARY

Jerry Garcia   1942-1995
American Musician
Lead Guitarist and Singer for the
Grateful Dead

BIRTH

Jerome John Garcia, the beloved long-time leader of the Grateful
Dead, was born on August 1, 1942, in San Francisco, California.
His father, Jose Ramon Garcia, known as Joe, was a musician and
later a bar owner, and his mother, Ruth Marie (Clifford) Garcia,
was a nurse who also worked in the bar. They had two children:
Clifford (called Tiff), who was named after his mother's family,

and Jerry, five years younger, who was named after the Broadway composer Jerome Kern, one of his father's favorites.

Jose Garcia, Jerry's father, was just a teenager when he and his family immigrated in 1919 to San Francisco from La Coruna, Spain. The Garcias were a well-to-do family who supported Jose's desire to become a professional musician. He played clarinet and other reed instruments in small jazz bands before becoming the leader of his own big band ensemble. But soon after he and Ruth married in 1934, he lost his livelihood as a musician. It was the Great Depression, and many people were out of work. The musicians' union made a rule that each member could work no more than five nights a week, to spread the available work around a little bit. Jose Garcia broke that rule. He was ousted from the union, which meant that he could no longer play in any venue that hired union musicians. That ended his musical career. He began bartending and soon bought the Four Hundred Club, a bar located across from the Sailors' Union of the Pacific. Sailors from the merchant marines often filled the bar, telling exciting stories of their travels to exotic lands in the Far East.

YOUTH

Jerry Garcia was born about five years after his father bought the Four Hundred Club. From the beginning, Jerry's life was filled with music: his father's nighttime lullabies on the clarinet, his mother's opera recordings, and his grandmother's country and bluegrass music. His mother played piano, also, and she encouraged Jerry to learn. He took lessons for about eight years, but he never learned to read music. He would fake his way through each lesson, learning the piece by ear.

When Garcia would reminisce about his childhood, certain events would always stand out. The first occurred when he was about four. His family took a trip to the Santa Cruz mountains, and he and his older brother were outside chopping wood. Jerry would set up the piece of wood, pull his hand away, and then Tiff would swing the ax. By accident, Tiff cut off part of the middle finger of Jerry's right hand. At the time, he was probably in shock; it didn't even hurt. The worst part, Jerry would say, came later, when they took off the bandages and he finally realized that his finger was gone. "But after that it was OK," Garcia explained, "because as a kid, if you have a few little things that make you different, it's a good score. So I got a lot of mileage out of having a missing finger when I was a kid."

A tragic event occurred the following year. In the spring of 1948, when Jerry was five, he and his family took a camping trip. His father waded out into the river to go fly-fishing. While Jerry was watching, Jose Garcia slipped and was swept away by the current. He drowned. As Garcia recalled, "We were on vacation, and I was there on shore. I actually watched him go under. It was horrible. I was just a little kid, and I didn't really understand what was going on, but then, of course, my life changed. It was one of those things that afflicted my childhood." It proved to be extremely traumatic for him. "I couldn't even stand to hear about it until I was 10 or 11," he also said. "I didn't start to get over it till then, maybe because of the way it affected my mother."

Ruth Garcia, who had stayed home taking care of the children up to that point, had to start working in the bar to support her family. Working and taking care of the kids proved to be too much, and she sent Jerry to live with her parents for the next five years. They lived in the Excelsior District of San Francisco, a tough blue- collar neighborhood. Both his grandparents worked every day, and Garcia was left on his own a lot. "I think that probably ruined me for everything," he later said. "It made me what I am today. I mean, they were great people, but they were both working and grandparently and had no stomach for discipline." He would wander around the neighborhood, stopping in at his mother's bar to listen to the sailors' stories. But he was also asthmatic and often sickly, and he spent a lot of time at home reading comic books and science fiction novels.

When Jerry Garcia was 10, his mother married Wally Matusiewicz. With his help at the bar, Ruth was able to bring Jerry back home from his grandparents' house. By this point, Ruth Garcia was becoming concerned about Jerry's behavior, sure that her younger son was becoming a hoodlum. So Ruth, Wally, and the two boys moved out of San Francisco to Menlo Park, a quiet suburb near Stanford University on the Peninsula south of San Francisco.

EDUCATION

Throughout his years in school, Garcia was, for the most part, an unremarkable student. He excelled in those classes that involved reading or art, but he was an undisciplined student who usually refused to do his homework.

Garcia often told stories about two teachers who inspired and fostered his creative and intellectual independence. One was his third-grade teacher, Miss Simon. She valued his creativity, encouraged him to paint, draw, and sculpt, and helped him develop what would become a life-long love of art. Another important influence was his seventh-grade teacher, Dwight Johnson. He was an iconoclastic, rebellious figure who drove an old MG sports car and a Black Shadow motorcycle. As Garcia later explained, "When we went down to the Peninsula, I fell in with a teacher who turned me on to the intellectual world. He said, 'Here, read this.' It was [George Orwell's novel] 1984 when I was 11 or 12 . . . that was when I was turning on, so to speak, or became aware of a world that was other than the thing you got in school, that you got in the movies and all that; something very different." It was Johnson who showed Garcia that there was a whole other world, full of art and music and ideas, that he had yet to explore.

After three years in Menlo Park, the family moved back to San Francisco. There Garcia attended Denman Junior High School, a tough school where he had to join a gang to survive. "Either you were a hoodlum or you were a puddle on the sidewalk. I was part of a big gang, a nonaffiliated gang. . . . It was a state of war, and I didn't last long in that. I spent a lot of time in Mission Emergency Hospital on weekends, holding my lip together, or my eye, because some guy had hit me with a board." After Denman, Garcia attended Balboa High School, another rough school. But by this time he was leading a double life—high school during the week, and art classes on the weekend at the California School of Fine Arts (now the San Francisco Institute) in the North Beach section of the city. At that time, the Beatnik movement was just getting started and was centered in North Beach. Garcia, "a high-school kid and wannabe Beatnik," hung out at coffeehouses and listened to poetry readings by the Beat poets Lawrence Ferlinghetti, Kenneth Rexroth, and Allen Ginsberg.

GETTING INVOLVED WITH MUSIC

Garcia was a teenager at what proved to be a pivotal time—when rock and roll was just appearing on the scene. Rock music took the rhythm and blues sound from black music and adapted it for the white mainstream audience. Garcia's brother Tiff introduced him to rhythm and blues and early rock, played by guys like Chuck Berry, Eddie Cochran, Buddy Holly, and Bo Diddley. In addition, Jerry started listening to both jazz and blues at art school parties.

Garcia became determined to play rock and roll. He tried on the piano, but he really wanted an electric guitar. He asked for one for his birthday, but his mom got him an accordion instead. He ranted and raved, in his words, and she finally relented and returned it. He went to a pawnshop and got a Danelectro guitar with a small Fender amplifier. "I started banging away on it without having the slightest idea of . . . *anything*. I didn't know how to tune it up, I had no idea. My stepfather tuned it in some kind of weird way, like an open chord. I thought: 'Well, that's the way it's tuned. OK.' I played it that way for about a year before I finally ran into some kid at school who actually could play a little. He showed me a few basic chords, and that was it. I never took any lessons. I don't even think there was anybody teaching around the Bay area. I mean electric guitar was like from *Mars*, you know. You didn't *see* 'em even."

By this time, Garcia had completely lost interest in high school. He was constantly getting into trouble, and his mother was getting concerned. In hopes of keeping Jerry out of trouble, the family moved again, to

Cazadero, a small resort town in Sonoma County that was deserted most of the year. He attended Analy High School in Sebastapol, riding 30 miles there by bus. But the move had no effect on his attitude about school—he hated it there. "I couldn't stand high school. . . . I was involved in more complex ideas. I started reading [the German philosophers] Schopenhauer, Heidegger, and Kant when I was in seventh grade. After that, school was silly. I couldn't relate to it. Not only that, I was a teenager, so I had an attitude. I kept saying, 'Why should I be doing these dumb things?' So I failed school as a matter of defiance." Garcia dropped out of high school at the end of his junior year.

Next, at age 17, Garcia decided to enlist in the U.S. Army. He was stationed on a base in San Francisco, where he started to get serious about music. He spent a lot of time on base playing acoustic guitar and five-string banjo. He taught himself to play by listening to records, slowing them down with his finger, and then learning the music note by note. But he also kept skipping out and going AWOL (absent without leave), a serious offense in the military. He spent about nine months in the army before being discharged in 1960. "They didn't say I was pathologically anti-authoritarian, but I guess that was out of kindness."

FIRST BANDS

Garcia spent the next few years bumming around. For a time, he returned to art classes at the California School of Fine Arts. He also started playing at folk-music clubs around Stanford University in Palo Alto, just south of San Francisco, often crashing with friends. At one point he was living out of his car in a parking lot where he met Robert Hunter, who became the principal lyricist for the Grateful Dead. Then in 1961 Garcia was a passenger in a serious car crash in which another passenger, one of his friends, was killed. The accident forced Garcia to take stock of his life and helped him to focus on his passion for music. He began playing traditional folk ballads and bluegrass music with renewed energy. He started teaching guitar lessons at a local shop and performing evening gigs at small clubs in the area. At first, Garcia teamed up with a variety of area musicians, often forming a new band every few weeks. Then in 1963 he formed Mother McCree's Uptown Jug Champions, an acoustic jug band that featured such instruments as banjo, washtub, jug, guitar, harmonica, washboard, and kazoo. The band, which played folk, blues, and country music, also featured two later members of the Grateful Dead, Bob Weir on rhythm guitar and Ron "Pigpen" McKernan on harmonica, organ, and vocals.

In 1964, Garcia was inspired by the Beatles' first appearance on "The Ed Sullivan Show," a group that changed the face of rock music in this country. According to Garcia, "The Beatles took rock music into a new realm

127

and raised it to an art form. Dylan, too—he's a genius. It wasn't long before the jug band became an electric band, 'The Warlocks.'" With the addition of Bill Kreutzman on drums and Phil Lesh on bass guitar, they were now a rock and roll band. They started out playing at a pizza parlor. Fans responded so well that they were soon appearing six nights a week in local nightclubs, playing covers of pop songs and some free-form works. Soon after, the band was forced to change its name when they discovered that another band was playing as the Warlocks. As the story goes, Garcia opened the dictionary and pointed at random to the term "grateful dead," which the *New York Times* defines as "a type of British folk ballad in which a human being helps a ghost find peace."

CAREER HIGHLIGHTS

The band soon reached what would prove to be a turning point. In 1965, they were invited to play at the Acid Tests run by author Ken Kesey. Both Kesey and Garcia's friend Robert Hunter had volunteered to participate in tests the U.S. Government was running on LSD (lysergic acid diethylamide), also known as acid. At the Veterans Hospital in Menlo Park, the government was testing the mind control properties of the drug to see if it was suitable to use against the country's enemies. Soon, Kesey and friends were taking LSD for other purposes as well. At the time, LSD was legal. Many people didn't recognize the harmful properties of the drug. They believed that a psychedelic acid trip would reveal truths about the universe and would expand their minds.

THE ACID TESTS

With a loose-knit group known as the Merry Pranksters, Kesey began holding what he called Acid Tests. They set up huge parties, invited hundreds of people, added psychedelic light shows and wild music by the Grateful Dead, and then provided acid to all involved. The intent was a total participatory experience in which the Merry Pranksters, the band, and the audience were all equally involved. According to Mikal Gilmore in the *Rolling Stone*, "The Acid Tests were meant to be acts of cultural, spiritual, and psychic revolt, and their importance to the development of the Grateful Dead cannot be overestimated. . . . [The] Acid Tests became the model for what would shortly become known as the Grateful Dead trip. In the years that followed, the Dead would never really forsake the philosophy of the Acid Tests. Right until the end, the band would encourage its audience to be involved with the music and the sense of fellowship that came from and fueled the music."

While the Acid Tests were short-lived, lasting for only a few years in the mid 1960s, the participatory free-for-all spirit that they created lived on in the Grateful Dead. They started out by playing concerts locally. By 1966 they were living in the Haight Ashbury district of San Francisco, the center of hippie culture, giving free concerts out in the street. Their distinctive style, which fused bluegrass, rhythm and blues, country, and folk music with rock, could be heard at all the counterculture happenings of the late 1960s—the Acid Tests in the mid 1960s, the Human Be-In in 1967, the Monterey Pop Festival in 1967, Woodstock and Altamont in 1969, and Watkins Glen in 1973. The Grateful Dead retained the same personnel for over 20 years, with a few exceptions: Ron "Pigpen" McKernan died in 1973 of alcohol-induced cirrhosis of the liver; his successor, Keith Godchaux, died in a car crash in 1980; and his successor, Brent Mydland, died of a morphine and cocaine overdose in 1990. Recently, the line-up of the Grateful Dead included Garcia and Bob Weir on guitar, Phil Lesh on bass, Bill Kreutzmann and Mickey Hart on drums, and Vince Welnick on keyboards, with Robert Hunter continuing to collaborate on song writing.

The band released many records over the years, but only a few are considered representative of their best work: *Live Dead* (1969), *Aoxomoxoa* (1969), *Workingman's Dead* (1970), *American Beauty* (1970), *Europe '72* (1972), *Blues for Allah* (1975), and *In the Dark* (1987), which produced their only Top 10 single, "Touch of Gray." The archival live recordings *One from the Vault* (1991), *Two from the Vault* (1992), and *Dick's Picks Vol. 1* and *Vol. 2* (1993, 1995), are also widely praised. Throughout the years, some of their

best-known songs include "Dark Star," "Truckin'," "Casey Jones," "Uncle John's Band," "Sugar Magnolia," and "Friend of the Devil." But overall, the Grateful Dead became best known for their live performances.

THE GRATEFUL DEAD IN CONCERT

For almost 30 years, the Grateful Dead toured steadily and routinely sold out their shows. Long, freeform events, their concerts featured both original material and covers of other bands' songs. The Grateful Dead never wrote a set list; they never played a song the same way twice. Each live event was made up as they went along. They decided what to play once they got on stage, started the song, and then improvised extensively. Each song became a long, unstructured piece in which the band members would listen to and respond to each other. In *Captain Trips: A Biography of Jerry Garcia,* Sandy Troy described it like this: "Garcia, as lead guitarist, would often develop melodic themes in the middle of jams, taking the music in a new direction. This improvisational style of playing became the Dead's trademark. . . . It was an avant-garde approach to music more akin to jazz than rock 'n' roll. It was unusual for a rock band to take this approach, but Garcia and the others weren't inclined to stay with the safe, the tried-and-true. More than anything else—more than the symbols, more than the psychedelics, more than the caravans of supporters—this penchant for innovation was how Garcia and the Grateful Dead made their mark in the music world."

As Garcia once explained, "When we get onstage, what we really want to happen is, we want to be transformed from ordinary players into extraordinary ones, like forces of a larger consciousness. And the audience wants to be transformed from whatever ordinary reality they may be in to something that enlarges them. So maybe it's that notion of transformation, a seat-of-the-pants shamanism, that has something to do with why the Grateful Dead keep pulling them in." It was this approach, in fact, that made them so popular with their fans. And Grateful Dead fans, known as Deadheads, are devoted fans, as Mikal Gilmore explained in *Rolling Stone.* "From the late 1960s to the mid-1990s, the Grateful Dead enjoyed a union with their audience that was unrivaled and unshakable. Indeed the Dead and their followers formed the only self-sustained, ongoing fellowship that pop music has ever produced—a commonwealth that lasted more than a quarter-century."

They established that fellowship back in 1971, when the band added a message to the liner notes of their *Grateful Dead* album. "Dead freaks unite," it began, and asked fans to send in their addresses. From that, the Dead built up a mailing list that they used to notify fans of their upcoming events; they set up a hot line to keep fans up to date; and more recently, fans have been able to track the band's activities on-line. The result was a huge group of informed and devoted fans. In addition, the Dead allowed fans to tape their concerts for free, a rarity in this commercial age, and Deadheads would trade tapes of their favorites and dispute which were the best performances. Many would follow the band from city to city, from concert to concert, enjoying the incredible music, the vibrant, ecstatic dancing, and the counterculture lifestyle on tour. Part of the appeal of traveling with the Dead was the sense of adventure, as Garcia once explained. "It's an adventure you can still have in America. . . . You can't hop the freights anymore, but you can chase the Grateful Dead around. You can have all your tires blow out in some weird town in the Midwest, and you can get hell from strangers. You can have something that lasts throughout your life as adventures, the times you took chances. I think that's essential in anybody's life, and it's harder and harder to do."

Many fans considered Garcia the leader of the Grateful Dead. They enjoyed his reedy singing voice, his distinctive, bell-like guitar tones, and the songs that he co-wrote, which constitute about half of the Dead's original material. Yet for some, Jerry Garcia was more than just a musician. Many fans treated him as an icon, as the embodiment of the utopian and idealistic spirit of the 1960s. Garcia vehemently objected to this personal adulation, repeatedly asking that people just listen to the music.

In addition to his work with the Grateful Dead, Garcia worked with others as well, both as a producer and a performer. Outside the Dead, he enjoyed exploring the musical styles that so influenced the band's music. At various times, he played jazz-rock with keyboardist Merl Saunders and bluegrass with the group Old and in the Way; he also collaborated with keyboardist Howard Wales and mandolinist David Grisman.

MOUNTING HEALTH PROBLEMS

Dedicated Dead fans began to notice signs of Garcia's health problems in the 1980s. Both his singing and his guitar playing sounded uninspired. In fact, Garcia had developed a serious addiction to both heroin and cocaine. In January 1985, the band members told Garcia that he would either have to quit using drugs or quit the band. Later that month, he was arrested in San Francisco for possession of heroin and cocaine. The courts allowed him to enter a drug-treatment program instead of a prison. In addition to his problems with drugs, Garcia was overweight and diabetic, a dangerous combination. In 1986, he fell into a diabetic coma, brought on by years of abusing his body with drugs and food. He came out of the coma after several days, feeling in his words "a little scrambled." It took him several months to completely recover and to relearn how to play guitar. In 1992, he collapsed from exhaustion, forcing the Dead to cancel their fall tour. He committed himself to recovery and started a diet and exercise plan.

For a while, his new plan seemed to work: he lost 60 pounds, showed renewed strength and energy, and seemed more focused on stage. In July 1994, though, he checked into the Betty Ford Center in California, apparently still trying to overcome his heroin addiction. He left after about two weeks; he didn't want to spend his birthday in a clinic. About a week later, he checked into another clinic, Serenity Knolls. In the early morning of August 9, 1995, an employee there found Garcia dead in his room. He was 53. His wife later said that he died with a smile on his face. An autopsy report revealed that he had used heroin a few days prior to his death, but the heroin didn't cause his death. Instead, the report found that Garcia died from natural causes—a heart attack brought on by arteriosclerosis, or hardening of the arteries.

The response to Garcia's death was overwhelming. A private funeral for family and friends was held just north of San Francisco, but his fans found their own ways to mark his passing. Candlelight vigils and memorial services were held throughout the country, from California to New York and in between. In San Francisco, a tie-died Dead flag flew at half mast at City Hall, attracting many fans to a massive memorial service for 25,000 in Golden Gate Park and to an informal vigil in Haight Ashbury, where the band had started out in the 1960s. Others offered their reminiscences on the Internet and other on-line services. Fans of all ages and all walks of life mourned his death, from Dead Heads in tie dye to such high profile fans as Vice President Al Gore and his wife, Tipper Gore, novelist Ken Kesey, musicians Bob Dylan and Bruce Hornsby, former NBA star Bill Walton, Governor William Weld from Massachusetts, and Senator Patrick Leahy from Vermont.

LEGACY

Tributes to Garcia poured in following his death. "His achievements," Mikal Gilmore wrote in *Rolling Stone,* "were enormous. He helped inspire and nurture a community that in some form or another has survived for 30 years and may even outlast his death; he co-wrote a fine collection of songs about America's myths, pleasures, and troubles; and as the Grateful Dead's most familiar and endearing member, he accomplished something that no other rock star ever has: He attracted an active following that has only grown larger in size and devotion with each passing decade, from the 1960s to the 1990s. You would have to look to the careers of people like Louis Armstrong, Duke Ellington, Count Basie, Miles Davis, and Charles Mingus to find the equivalent of Garcia's musical longevity and growth in the history of American bandleaders."

"When Jerry Garcia died," Greg Kot wrote in the *Chicago Tribune,* "he left behind a body of work as wide-ranging and adventurous as that of any rock musician, rooted in the melodic and lyrical conceits of bluegrass and the blues, yet informed by jazz improvisation and avant-garde experimentation. Nonetheless, Garcia the musician often was obscured by Garcia the symbol of counterculture independence. . . . [Throughout] his life Garcia was doing exactly what he wanted to do: Playing music, unfettered by the commercial demands of the record business."

And finally, Bob Dylan offered this tribute to Garcia: "There's no way to measure his greatness or magnitude as a person or a player. I don't think eulogizing will do him justice. He was that great—much more than a superb musician with an uncanny ear and dexterity. . . . He really had no equal. To me he wasn't only a musician and friend, he was more like a big brother who taught me more than he'll ever know. There are a lot of spaces and advances between the Carter family, Buddy Holly, and, say, Ornette Colemen, a lot of universes, but he filled them all without being a member of any school. His playing was moody, awesome, sophisticated, hypnotic, and subtle. There's no way to convey the loss."

The Grateful Dead announced on December 8, 1995, that the group was breaking up. They decided that, in the wake of Garcia's death, "the long, strange trip of the uniquely wonderful beast known as the Grateful Dead is over."

MARRIAGE AND FAMILY

Garcia was married three times. His first wife was Sarah Ruppenthal, a musician, whom he met in the early 1960s in Palo Alto. They performed locally for a short time as the acoustic duo Jerry and Sarah. Married in May 1963, they had one daughter, Heather. When they split up in 1966, Sarah took custody of Heather.

Garcia was then involved with Carolyn Adams, known as Mountain Girl, who later became his second wife. Garcia and Mountain Girl, who was one of the Merry Pranksters, had a long-term, on-again off-again relationship. They lived together for several years and had two daughters, Annabelle and Theresa. They split up in 1975, came together and apart several times, and actually married only in 1981. By 1987, though, their relationship fell apart when he became involved with one of his fans, Manasha Matheson, and Garcia and Mountain Girl divorced. Matheson became Garcia's companion, and they had a daughter, Keelin. Their relationship broke up by 1992.

In 1993 he became involved with Deborah Koons, an independent filmmaker whom he had dated in the mid 1970s. They married on February 14, 1994. Many of his friends credit Koons with encouraging his attempts to develop a healthier lifestyle.

HOBBIES AND OTHER INTERESTS

Garcia enjoyed a wide range of artistic pursuits. He liked to draw, paint, and design a variety of items, including wet suits and men's ties. He even did some interior design, creating Jerry Garcia Suites at several hotels in which he designed all the furnishings.

In recent years, Garcia's favorite pastime was probably scuba diving. A certified diver, he had made more than 500 dives since taking up the sport in 1988. He particularly enjoyed the waters off the Kona coast in Hawaii.

RECORDINGS

WITH THE GRATEFUL DEAD

Grateful Dead, 1967
Anthem of the Sun, 1968
Aoxomoxoa, 1969
Live/Dead, 1970
Workingman's Dead, 1970
American Beauty, 1970
The Grateful Dead, 1971
Europe '72, 1972
Bear's Choice, 1973
Wake of the Flood, 1973
Best of the Grateful Dead—Skeletons from the Closet, 1974
Grateful Dead from the Mars Hotel, 1974
Blues for Allah, 1975
Steal Your Face, 1976
Terrapin Station, 1977
Shakedown Street, 1978
Dead Reckoning, 1981
Dead Set, 1981
In the Dark, 1987
Built to Last, 1989
Without a Net, 1990
One from the Vault, 1991
Two from the Vault, 1992
Dick's Picks, Vol. 1, 1993
Dick's Picks, Vol. 2, 1995

SOLO AND WITH OTHERS

Hooteroll, 1971
Garcia, 1972
Merl Saunders, Jerry Garcia, John Kahn, Billo Vitt: Live at the Keystone, 1973
Cats Under the Stars, 1978
Run for the Roses, 1982
Jerry Garcia Band, 1991
Jerry Garcia--David Grisman, 1991
Not for Kids Only, 1993

HONORS AND AWARDS

Rock and Roll Hall of Fame: 1994, with the Grateful Dead

FURTHER READING

BOOKS

Troy, Sandy. *Captain Trips: A Biography of Jerry Garcia,* 1995
Who's Who in America 1995

PERIODICALS

Chicago Tribune, Aug. 10, 1995, News section, p.1; Aug. 13, 1995, Arts
 section, p.12
Current Biography Yearbook 1990
New York Times, Aug. 10, 1995, p.A1, C.18
New Yorker, Oct. 11, 1993, p.96
Newsweek, Aug. 21, 1995, p.46
People, Sep./Oct. 1995 (special tribute issue)
Rolling Stone, Oct. 31, 1991, p.37; Sep. 2, 1993, p.42; Sep. 21, 1995, p.44
 (and many related articles)
San Francisco Chronicle, Aug. 10, 1995, p.A1
San Francisco Examiner, Aug. 9, 1995, p.A1
San Jose Mercury News, Aug. 9, 1995, p.A1
Time, Aug. 21, 1995, p.60

Jennie Garth   1972-
American Actress
Stars as Kelly on "Beverly Hills, 90210"

BIRTH

Jennie Garth was born on April 3, 1972, in Urbana, Illinois. Her parents were John Garth, a school administrator, and Carolyn Garth, a former teacher and real estate agent. Both John and Carolyn had been married before, and they each had three children from their first marriage. Jennie, the youngest of the family, was their only child together. Jennie has four older sisters, Lisa, Cammie, Wendy, and Lynn, and two older brothers, Johnny and Chuck. Jennie, her mom has said, "was the adhesive that joined the two families together."

YOUTH

Garth remembers a happy childhood. "I was treated like a little princess," she now says. She spent her early years on a 25-acre horse farm outside Urbana. She was a tomboy, preferring to work out in the barn rather than play inside with dolls. But she also loved to perform, even when she was very young. "[She] was always the little entertainer," her mother recalls. "She would stand in front of this sliding glass door where she could see her reflection and sing and dance to music on TV." When Garth was 13, her father had triple-bypass heart surgery, and his doctors recommended a move to a warmer climate. The family moved to Phoenix, Arizona.

EDUCATION

Garth attended the local public schools in Urbana and Phoenix. As a teenager, she took dance lessons and did some modeling for catalogs. But she never really expected it to lead anywhere. She assumed, at that point, that she'd grow up to live in a Midwestern farm community. "I just thought I'd go to college and get a teaching degree for dance and have my own studio," Garth says. "But my life took a turn."

When she was 15, Garth entered the Cinderella Scholarship Pageant. She ended up taking fourth place in the statewide event. A talent scout suggested acting lessons, and then recommended that she quit high school and move to California to become a professional actress. She took his advice. In her junior year, she dropped out of high school and moved to Hollywood. Her mother went along as chaperone, leaving her father and the other kids in Arizona. Garth later took the GED exam and earned a high-school equivalency diploma.

FIRST JOBS

Garth arrived in California at about age 16, hoping to become an actress. As her mother, Carolyn, now admits, "My friends thought I was crazy. But I knew if anyone could do this, Jennie could. She has always been this magical person who could make anything she wanted happen."

At first, though, it didn't seem that way. Carolyn worked in part-time jobs and drove her daughter to auditions and acting classes. For a while, nothing came through. After their first two months in California, John Garth, Jennie's father, had a serious heart attack and had to undergo four operations in 48 hours. Carolyn Garth flew back to Phoenix to be with him. Jennie commuted between Phoenix and Los Angeles, visiting her father and helping out at home on the weekends and returning to Los Angeles to look for work during the week. It was a difficult time for all.

Then her luck started to change. She won guest shots on several TV series, including "Growing Pains." She also appeared in a couple of TV movies, including *Just Perfect* and *Teen Angel Returns*, where she met Jason Priestley. Then only four months after moving to Los Angeles, she earned her first recurring role, opposite Barbara Eden on the short-lived series "A Brand New Life." Put up against "60 Minutes," Garth's new show only lasted 6 episodes.

CAREER HIGHLIGHTS

Her luck was about to change, though. In spring 1990, the Fox network announced that it was creating a new show about high school life in Beverly Hills and was beginning casting young actors for the roles. Garth auditioned five times before winning the role of Kelly.

"BEVERLY HILLS, 90210"

"Beverly Hills, 90210" has evolved greatly since its debut in the fall of 1990. In the early days, the show revolved around Brenda (played by Shannen Doherty) and Brandon (Jason Priestley), their parents, Jim and Cindy Walsh (James Eckhouse and Carol Potter), and their friends at West Beverly High, including Kelly Taylor (played by Garth), Dylan McKay (Luke Perry), Donna Martin (Tori Spelling), Steve Sanders (Ian Ziering), David Silver (Brian Austin Green), and Andrea Zuckerman (Gabrielle Carteris); more recent additions to the gang include Valerie Malone (Tiffani-Amber Thiessen) and Clare Arnold (Kathleen Robertson). Within this framework, the series tackled a variety of issues, including teen sexuality, peer pressure, drug and alcohol use, eating disorders, date rape, teen pregnancy, and divorce. But over the years, the characters matured from high school to college, and some of the actors left the show. Shannen Doherty was the first to go, at the end of the 1993-94 season, amid rumors that she was fired for being chronically late to the set and difficult to work with. Carol Potter, James Eckhouse, and Gabrielle Carteris left at the end of the 1994-95 season, and Luke Perry, creator of everybody's favorite bad boy, Dylan McKay, left the following year.

Garth has stayed with the series since its debut in 1990. But the character of Kelly has evolved a great deal during that time. At the beginning of the series Kelly was rather shallow, superficial, frivolous, and one-dimensional. The most popular girl in school, Kelly was the stereotype of a rich blonde in her BMW, concerned only with boys, hair, clothes, and being cool. But her character proved to be appealing—she was an immediate trend-setter with the show's devoted fans. Garth was so convincing as Kelly, in fact, that the actress was often confused with the character that she played. Many were surprised to read press reports that described Garth as pleasant, down-to-earth, and unaffected in person.

As the series progressed, though, Kelly's true character was gradually revealed. Viewers saw her deal with her alcoholic and drug-addicted mother and her absent father, lending depth and credibility to her character. Still, over the years some of her exploits have been pretty wild, like joining a cult, getting burned in a fire, becoming a magazine-cover model, and, of course, getting involved with Dylan, Brandon, and just about every male on the series, making good and bad choices in her romantic life. With her most recent love interest, the artist Colin (Jason Wiles), she got hooked on cocaine and alienated her old friends with her drug-related stunts. Long-time viewers are confident, though, that Kelly can pull through this latest trauma.

In addition to her work on "Beverly Hills, 90210," Garth has kept herself busy with additional projects. She made a workout video, "Body in Progress," that has won praise for its sensible advice and safe and effective workout. She has also made several TV movies, jumping into a new project each time her regular series has gone on vacation. Her past movies include *Star* (1993), based on the best-selling Danielle Steel novel, in which she played a sweet farm girl who grows up to become a music and film star; *Lies of the Heart: The Story of Laurie Kellogg* (1994), a fact-based film in which Garth played a woman who was convicted of killing her abusive husband; and *Without Consent* (1994), in which she played a rebellious teenager committed to a mental institution by her parents. For *Without Consent*, Garth was both the star and the executive producer, in her first time working behind the camera. In her most recent film, the thriller

Falling for You (1995), she played a New Yorker who is being stalked by a serial killer.

For the future, Garth has signed a contract with ABC to produce and star in movies. "If all I do for the rest of my life is make TV movies about issues that help people, that'll make me happy," she once said. But she has also expressed an interest in doing feature films, hoping to have a long career in acting. As Garth explains here, "I don't think I want to do another series. What I'd really like to do is make movies. I admire Jessica Lange, the kind of movies she's made. I intend to be around for a while. I'm going to have a family. I'm in no hurry."

MARRIAGE AND FAMILY

Garth met her husband, musician Dan Clark, in April 1991. She first saw him at a coffeehouse, performing with his band; later she went to a party and saw him again. They began to date, and were engaged in December 1991. They were married in April 1994 in a private, heavily-guarded ceremony in Beverly Hills, California. Currently, they live near Los Angeles.

HOBBIES AND OTHER INTERESTS

Garth likes exercising and going out to clubs to listen to music, particularly her husband's band. A vegetarian, she supports animal-rights causes, including People for the Ethical Treatment of Animals, and enjoys spending time with her animals.

CREDITS

"Beverly Hills, 90210," 1990-
Star, 1993
Lies of the Heart: The Story of Laurie Kellogg, 1994
Without Consent, 1994
Falling for You, 1995

FURTHER READING

PERIODICALS

Entertainment Weekly, Sep. 23, 1994, p.22
People, Aug. 9, 1991, p.80; May 11, 1992, p.81
Rolling Stone, Aug. 8, 1991, p.81; Feb. 20, 1992, p.22
Sassy, Apr. 1993, p.44
Teen, Dec. 1992, p.16
TV Guide, Apr. 8, 1995, p.12

ADDRESS

James/Levy/Jacobson
3500 West Olive Avenue, Suite 920
Burbank, CA 91505

BRIEF ENTRY

Wendy Guey 1983-
American Winner of the 1996 National
Spelling Bee

EARLY YEARS

Wendy Guey (pronounced "gway") was born on September 29, 1983, in Boston, Massachusetts. Her father is Ching Guey, who holds a doctorate in physics from Massachusetts Institute of Technology (MIT) and works as an engineer with Florida Power and Light Company. Her mother, Susan Guey, teaches Chinese, which Wendy also speaks. Ching and Susan Guey immigrated to the United States from Taiwan 14 years ago, and English is their second language. In addition to Wendy, the Gueys have two other daughters: Emily, who is now 14 and is an accomplished speller herself, and Lynne, who is six. They live in Palm Beach Gardens, Florida.

MAJOR ACCOMPLISHMENTS

THE NATIONAL SPELLING BEE

The National Spelling Bee is sponsored by the Scripps Howard media organization. Spellers can compete through the eighth grade. Each year, regional contests include more than nine million students from the United States, Mexico, Guam, Puerto Rico, the Virgin Islands, and Defense Department schools. Over 200 winners of these regional contests go on to compete in the national championships. In all these events, each participant is given a word to spell. With a correct spelling, the student advances to the next round; with an incorrect spelling, the student is eliminated from the spelling bee. Participants are given lengthy lists of practice words that are used in the first few rounds of the spelling bee; after that, the words are unfamiliar and difficult.

It took Wendy Guey four years of practice to win the National Spelling Bee. In 1993, at age nine, she started out as a fourth grader at Dwight D. Eisenhower Elementary School in Lake Park, Florida. After winning at the regional level, she went on to the National Spelling Bee, which

takes place each year in late May and early June. She made it to the 11th round, when she incorrectly spelled "meiosis" (which means "a type of cell division used in reproduction"). Guey tied for fourth place, becoming the youngest person ever to make it into the finals. She actually laughed when she left the stage after her mistake; she said later that "I just felt really good after beating eighth graders." In 1994, she won the regional contest again and returned to the National Spelling Bee. But that year, she was knocked out in the 10th round by misspelling "farouche" ("shy" or "lacking in social graces"). She tied for ninth place that year. In 1995, both Wendy and her sister Emily made it into the National Spelling Bee, becoming the first siblings ever to compete together. Emily was eliminated in the fourth round and Wendy was eliminated in the fifth round, when she misspelled "mycetophagous" ("feeding on fungi").

The following year would be Wendy's big success. A seventh grader at Palm Beach County School of the Arts, Wendy was 12 years old when she won the regional competition for the fourth straight year. Along with 246 other finalists, she went on to the championships in May 1996 in Washington, D.C. The final rounds would be broadcast live on television, on ESPN2. The going got really tough by round nine, when the field was narrowed down to just three finalists. The last few rounds were exciting but difficult. In round nine, Wendy misspelled "lacertilian" ("related to a lizard") and left the stage in defeat. But then the other two remaining spellers also made mistakes. Under contest rules, when all the spellers in a round miss their words, they all get another chance. In round 10, one girl was eliminated, and then in the following round, both Wendy and her sole remaining competitor made mistakes. When they returned for round 12, Wendy correctly spelled "lisle" ("a type of thread"), while the other girl misspelled "cervicorn" ("branching out like antlers"). Wendy then correctly spelled her final word, "vivisepulture" ("burying alive"), and won the contest.

As the first-place winner of the 1996 National Spelling Bee, Wendy won the trophy and $5,000. Reporters crowded around with questions. What were her plans now that the contest was over? "To relax," Wendy said. And what would she do with the prize money? "Spend it." Did she have any suggestions for other kids who wanted to be champion spellers? "Study hard. And never let older kids make you feel smaller," she advised.

After winning the National Spelling Bee, Wendy was treated like a champion. At school, she was greeted with flowers, balloons, and a fanfare by the brass ensemble. The principal declared Wendy Guey Day, and she was crowned Queen (Spelling) Bee. She made several TV appearances, including some spelling practice with Jay Leno on "The Tonight Show." And Leno's staff treated her to a trip to Disneyland and Universal Studios—to make up for missing her school trip to Universal Studios in Florida.

143

According to her parents and her teachers, Wendy became such a good speller because she likes to read so much. She has learned to spell a lot of new words just by coming across them in books. But she worked hard on her spelling, too, practicing her word lists and studying the dictionary for about an hour every day. In addition to reading and practicing spelling, Wendy takes music lessons and plays violin and piano.

FURTHER READING

PERIODICALS

Palm Beach Post, Apr. 8, 1993, p.B1; June 8, 1993, p.B1; June 1, 1996, p.B1; June 4, 1996,p.B1
Sun Sentinel, May 31, 1996, p.A1; June 4, 1996, p.B1

ADDRESS

Scripps Howard National Spelling Bee
P.O. Box 5380
Cincinnati, OH 45201

WORLD WIDE WEB ADDRESS

http://www.spellingbee.com

Tom Hanks   1956-
American Actor
Star of *Splash, Big, Philadelphia, Forrest Gump, Apollo 13,* and *Toy Story*

BIRTH

Thomas Hanks was born on July 9, 1956, in Concord, California. His parents were Amos Hanks, a cook in a restaurant, and Janet Hanks, a waitress. Tom Hanks has three siblings: Larry and Sandra, both older than Tom, and younger brother Jim.

YOUTH

The Hanks family moved often when Tom was a child, as Amos moved from one restaurant job to the next. The defining event in his childhood came when he was five. In 1961, his parents split up. One night, Amos Hanks had each of the three older kids, including Tom, pack a suitcase and a couple of toys. They loaded up the car and left, with their dad, in the middle of the night. In the beginning, it was very tough on Hanks. "I was only five when we first started moving around. I just felt lonely; I felt abandoned, in the dark. 'How come no one's telling me?' No one is telling you the why, just the what: 'Pack your bags, get the stuff you want and put it in the back of the station wagon.'" Tom's younger brother, Jim, stayed behind with his mother. The parents split the kids up, Tom would later say, because neither had enough money to take care of them all. After that Tom never lived with his mother again, and saw her only occasionally.

From that point on, Hanks's youth was quite tumultuous, and the details on his family life are sketchy. His father was soon remarried, to a woman in Reno, Nevada, with many children of her own. "There were these extremely large dinners," Hanks recalls. "You could get lost in the shuffle or you could be a loudmouth. I chose the latter route. My apprenticeship years, I call them." But that marriage failed after two years, and Amos married again, to a woman with three children; they remain married today. Tom's mother, also, remarried several times. Throughout his young years, Hanks's family moved often, every six months or so, for Amos's work, mostly around northern California. "By the time I was ten years old," Hanks once said, "I had a mother and two stepmothers, I'd lived in ten different houses and five different cities, sometimes with siblings, sometimes without. In hindsight, I realize this was an absolutely hideous time for both of my parents."

With his father's third marriage, the new blended family settled in Oakland, California. It proved to be a difficult adjustment. Because their father often worked nights, Tom and his brother and sister had gotten used to being on their own and taking care of themselves. They enjoyed their independence. They didn't react well to their new stepmother telling them what to do.

EDUCATION

Hanks attended at least five elementary schools, by his count. He was always the new kid in school—shy, but also the class clown, using humor to deal with the discomfort of being new. But Hanks disputes the assumption that these early years had a traumatic effect on him, saying that with time he came to enjoy moving often. And, in fact, it ultimately helped make him the comic actor he is today. "I loved being the new guy in class. It was a new classroom, they had different books—'Oooh, they're using *these* pencils!' The class-clownish-type thing was a defense mechanism, but I was pretty good at making people laugh. If the adrenaline rush that comes with performing is addictive, I got it at an early age. I could make kids laugh standing in line for handball. And it would perk me up. *That's where I learned timing.*"

Hanks attended Bret Harte Junior High School and Skyline High School in Oakland. He ran track and played soccer; for a time he was active in a church youth group. Then he signed up for the drama class, and it changed his life. In his words, "I tried out for the plays, and got into them, and had more fun than I could possibly imagine. It was an incredible group of people, some of whom are still my friends. I got into this eclectic group that was kind of rootless and cliqueless." Especially important to him was his drama teacher, Rawley Farnsworth, whose name he would invoke when he won his first Oscar. Voted Male Class Cutup in his senior year, Hanks graduated from Skyline High School in 1974.

ENTRANCED BY THE THEATER

Hanks then enrolled at Chabot College, a junior college in nearby Hayward, California. During his second year there he took a theater course that required reading dramas and then seeing them in live performance. "The turning point for me was *The Iceman Cometh* [by Eugene O'Neill]. I literally could not wait to finish the play—I read the last pages curled up on the front steps of my house. Then I went to see it at the Berkeley Repertory Theater—150 seats, three-quarter staging. You were right on top of the stage, transported back to the Lower East Side of New York. This was the most magical thing that had ever happened to me. For four hours, nobody moved in the audience. It was incredible. I came out of the theater enthralled with what those people had done that night. Four hours of concentration. I had never seen that anywhere else. Not on the basketball court. Certainly not in the hotel where I was working as a bellboy. And I wanted to do something in the theater, something as immediate and personal as that."

"It was the turning point of my life," Hanks also said. "The awesome power of the play, the performances, everything and everyone was so intense— something inside of me just clicked. By the end of the night, I had a goal in life."

"I developed an instant respect for everyone involved, not just the actors, but the director, stage crew, lighting people, set designers—everyone who could work together to bring an audience a new sense of awareness. That's what really got to me."

"Even though I call this my turning point, and I did end up an actor, I have to stress that because of the performance I didn't decide to become an actor. It was so much more than that. I didn't care what I did—build sets, string lights, paint props, or act—the main thing was to somehow be a part of this life. I knew it would make me happy."

After that, Hanks enrolled in the theater arts program at California State University in Sacramento. He took acting classes there and also worked behind the scenes on a number of productions, working as a stage manager and as a carpenter, designing and painting sets, and hanging lights. A pivotal move came when he auditioned for and won a role in *The Cherry Orchard* by Anton Chekhov. It was being staged by guest director Vincent Dowling, then the artistic director of the Great Lakes Shakespeare Festival in Lakewood, Ohio (near Cleveland). Dowling offered an internship at the Festival to Hanks and several other students, including Samantha Lewes, later Hanks's first wife. Hanks officially dropped out of college in 1977.

FIRST JOBS

From 1977 to 1979, Hanks spent three summers at the Great Lakes Shakespeare Festival, learning all aspects of stagecraft under the tutelage of Vincent Dowling. It was a repertory company, with the actors appearing in different roles in six different plays that would alternate throughout the season. It was a tremendous advantage, Hanks says, to learn the art of acting through the works of Shakespeare: "It was like learning to play the violin on a Stradivarius. This wasn't just singing, dancing. . . . I had to be the best—this was the Bard. It automatically gave me a professional attitude. You had to be disciplined. You had to do your homework." In addition, he spent some of the winter months working as an associate technical director at a community theater back in Sacramento.

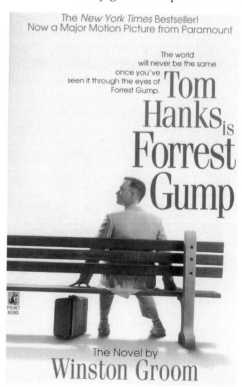

The *New York Times* Bestseller!
Now a Major Motion Picture from Paramount

The world will never be the same once you've seen it through the eyes of Forrest Gump.

Tom Hanks is Forrest Gump

The Novel by
Winston Groom

After his second season with the Great Lakes Shakespeare Festival, Hanks decided to try his luck in New York City. He and Lewes, who was then pregnant with their first child, moved to the city in 1978. They returned to Ohio that next summer, for Hanks's last season with the Great Lakes Shakespeare Festival, and then settled in New York. There, Hanks collected unemployment to support his wife and new baby and set out to become an actor. He joined the Riverside Shakespeare Company as an unpaid actor and also started making the rounds looking for work. He did some small parts on stage and won his first film role—a bit part as a student in a slasher film called *He Knows You're Alone* (1980). His luck changed when he attended a cattle call audition by ABC television looking for the network stars of tomorrow. He so impressed the judges that he was called back for further auditions and soon won a role on a new TV sitcom. With that, Hanks was on his way.

CAREER HIGHLIGHTS

Along with actor Peter Scolari, Hanks won a co-starring role on the new series "Bosom Buddies" on ABC. Hanks and Scolari teamed up to play two young advertising executives in New York who are unable to find an apartment. They end up dressing up as women to get a place in an inexpensive all-female hotel, and many of the jokes derived from that premise. "Bosom Buddies" ran for two seasons, from 1980 through 1982. Many critics were unenthusiastic and audiences were largely indifferent, but the series eventually won a cult following in syndication. Hanks went on to bit parts on several series ("Happy Days," "Family Ties") before his first big hit.

SPLASH

In *Splash* (1984), Hanks played Allen Bauer, a produce manager who falls in love with a mermaid, played by Daryl Hannah. It was the first of many roles featuring Hanks as a romantic lead in a rather novel form—as an ordinary guy unexpectedly thrust into an extraordinary situation. In this case, he played an average guy who falls in love with an average mermaid. For Hanks, this first leading film role turned him into a movie star. He remembers what he expected as *Splash* first opened in theaters in 1984: "I didn't think it would be a stinker, maybe a little cartoonish, but the first weekend I get a call: 'Six million bucks at the box office.' You're in your first big film. It's beyond my comprehension. That's a lot of money. You can't get it much better, right outta the box. It's perfect."

Since *Splash*, Hanks has been very prolific, appearing in 20 films in just over 10 years. He was especially prolific at the beginning of his career, often appearing in two movies per year. And yet his career has been very uneven. Many of his early films were less than successful, although critics often commented on the quality of Hanks's performances in what were otherwise undistinguished films. Still, a few of these movies, in particular, stand out.

After *Splash*, Hanks appeared in a series of unsuccessful films—*Bachelor Party, The Man with One Red Shoe, Volunteers,* and *The Money Pit*—before co-starring in *Nothing in Common* (1986). He played David Basner, a young,

149

successful advertising executive who is witty, charming, and slick. All that changes, though, when he has to deal with a family crisis—the break-up of his parents, played by Eva Marie Saint and Jackie Gleason, and his father's illness. Critics applauded Hanks's depiction of the character's transformation from selfish and immature to sensitive, giving, and mature.

BIG

After appearing in the box-office flops *Every Time We Say Goodbye* and *Dragnet*, Hanks's next hit was *Big* (1988). In this breakthrough film, he played Josh Baskin. Humiliated about his small size in front of a girl he likes, 12-year-old Josh (played by young actor David Moscow) wishes that he could be big. Overnight, his wish comes true. He wakes up to find himself in an adult's body, as played by Hanks. The role presented a real challenge for Hanks, to learn to act and to move and to play like a 12-year-old kid again. For help, he watched David Moscow, the actor who played the young version of Josh. The movie was a huge success, with audiences and critics alike raving about his very physical performance as an awkward and gawky adolescent. Hanks's convincing, touching, and delightful performance won him his first Academy Award nomination.

After *Big, Punchline* (1988) followed just four months later, showing the range of his talent. Co-starring with Sally Field, Hanks played Steven Gold, an edgy and ambitious stand-up comedian. He was roundly praised for

the depth of emotion—anger, sadness, neediness, and rage—that he brought to the role. As David Ansen said of his performance, "His acting has wit, velocity, relaxation, and the extraordinary physical dexterity he demonstrated in *Big*. This guy may give you the creeps, but he holds you spellbound."

A series of box-office misses followed, including *The 'Burbs*, *Turner & Hooch*, and *Joe Versus the Volcano*. That series was capped off by *Bonfire of the Vanities* (1991), a recreation of the novel by Tom Wolfe that was drubbed by critics and audiences alike. After that film Hanks took about a two-year break from acting. Since his return, critics have applauded the maturity and depth of his recent performances. He's broken the mold of his earlier guy-next-door persona, moving from light comedy pieces to sensitive roles in more dramatic films. The result has been an unbroken series of critical successes and box-office smashes.

RECENT FILMS

The first of these films was *A League of Their Own* (1992). Hanks played Jimmy Dugan, a down-on-his-luck, washed-up, alcoholic baseball manager for a women's professional team during World War II. This supporting role represented a real change for Hanks, helping him break out of the confines of his usual leading man role. He went on to the box-office smash *Sleepless in Seattle* (1993). Hanks played Sam Baldwin, a lonely widower still grieving after his wife's death, whose son uses a radio call-in show to help him find a new love, played by Meg Ryan. While the movie was certainly a romantic comedy, Hanks brought to the widower's grief a new maturity and depth of feeling.

Those qualities were especially evident in his next film, *Philadelphia* (1993). Hanks played Andrew Beckett, a high-powered lawyer and homosexual who contracts AIDS, Acquired Immuno-Deficiency Syndrome. When Beckett is fired for having AIDS, he sues his law firm for discrimination with the help of a lawyer played by Denzel Washington. As explained by David Ansen in *Newsweek*, "[Homophobia] is what *Philadelphia* is about—not a disease, but a climate of intolerance that turns a disease into a stigma." The movie was praised for forthrightly addressing such issues as intolerance, homophobia, AIDS, and death. These difficult issues were more acceptable for many viewers, according to critics, because Hanks is so charming and well-liked. Indeed, Hanks was widely praised for his moving and affecting performance and for his courage for taking on this tough dramatic role despite the social stigma still attached to AIDS. For his performance as Andrew Beckett, Hanks won the Academy Award for Best Actor. At the awards ceremony, he gave a moving tribute to those who have died from AIDS and thanked two people from his high school years who had influenced him, his drama teacher, Rawley Farnsworth, and his former classmate, John Gilkerson, both gay.

After *Philadelphia,* Hanks next went on to *Forrest Gump* (1994), based on the novel by William Groom, which tells the life story of a man with limited intelligence. Despite his limitations, Gump becomes a football star, a Vietnam War hero, a champion table-tennis player, a shrimp boat captain, and a marathon runner. He meets John F. Kennedy, George Wallace, John Lennon, Lyndon B. Johnson, and Elvis Presley (through the miracle of computer technology, which inserted Hanks's image into film footage from the past). Through Gump, we see American history from the 1950s through the 1980s. It was, for many, a film filled with nostalgia for our shared past and hope for our future. And Hanks's inspiring acting won him his second Academy Award for Best Actor—his second in two years.

After *Forrest Gump,* Hanks went on to explore another piece of our history in *Apollo 13* (1995). The movie is an accurate recreation of a true story. It tells what happened during the 1970 voyage of Apollo 13, a spacecraft that was designed to travel to the moon. Hanks played Jim Lovell, the NASA astronaut who was the commander of that mission. During the voyage, in real life and as recreated in the film, a serious defect in the ship resulted in a significant loss of power. For several days, Americans remained glued to their televisions, worrying and wondering what would happen. It took all the ingenuity of the astronauts and the NASA team on earth to devise a way to bring that ship, and the men inside, home safely. The movie's depiction of their terrifying voyage through space, interspersed with frantic scenes from Mission Control and tearful scenes from their frightened families at home, is riveting and thrilling. And Hanks, as mission commander Jim Lovell, is commanding and charismatic. For a space junkie like Tom Hanks, the movie was a real thrill to film—particularly the weightless sequences, filmed on a KC-135 jet, known as the "Vomit Comet," because it produces the weightlessness of space and the nausea that can accompany it. (See entry on Jim Lovell in this issue of *Biography Today.*)

TOY STORY

Hanks's most recent project is *Toy Story* (1995), the first full-length animated film to be completely generated by computers. The three-dimensional effect of the computer imagery, in particular, has won raves. *Toy Story* is about the toys in one boy's bedroom, and how they come to life when he's not around. Hanks provided the voice for Woody, a cowboy who is the boy's favorite and the toys' leader until the arrival of Buzz Lightyear, a space-age action figure voiced by Tim Allen. The story is clever, the dialogue is inventive, the graphics are outstanding, and the technology is a marvel, but it is the acting that gives life to the film.

Hanks is currently at work on his next project, *That Thing You Do!* In this film, in which Hanks is the writer, director, and star, he plays the manager of a rock band in Erie, Pennsylvania, in 1964. *That Thing You Do!* is scheduled for release in 1996.

MARRIAGE AND FAMILY

Hanks met his first wife, actress Samantha Lewes, while they were both students at California State University. They married in 1978, as they moved to New York. They had two children, a son and a daughter. Hanks and Lewes separated in about 1985 and finalized their divorce about a year later. The children remained with their mother, with long visits to their father on vacations.

Hanks and his second wife, actress Rita Wilson, first met when she appeared on his early sitcom "Bosom Buddies." They hooked up again several years later when they co-starred in the movie *Volunteers*. At that point, he was in the process of splitting up with his first wife. Soon afterward Hanks and Wilson started dating, and they married on April 30, 1988. They have one son, Chester, and Wilson is currently pregnant with their second child.

CREDITS

TELEVISION

"Bosom Buddies," 1980-82 (TV series)
Rona Jaffe's Mazes and Monsters, 1981 (TV movie)

FILMS

He Knows You're Alone, 1980
Splash, 1984
Bachelor Party, 1984
The Man with One Red Shoe, 1985
Volunteers, 1985
The Money Pit, 1986

Nothing in Common, 1986
Every Time We Say Goodbye, 1986
Dragnet, 1987
Big, 1988
Punchline, 1988
The 'Burbs, 1989
Turner & Hooch, 1989
Joe Versus the Volcano, 1990
Bonfire of the Vanities, 1991
Radio Flyer, 1992 (narrator)
A League of Their Own, 1992
Sleepless in Seattle, 1993
Philadelphia, 1993
Forrest Gump, 1994
Apollo 13, 1995
Toy Story, 1995 (voice of Woody)

HONORS AND AWARDS

Golden Apple for Outstanding News Impact (Hollywood Women's Press Club): 1988 (tied with Keven Costner) and 1994

American Comedy Award: 1989, for Funniest Lead Actor in a Motion Picture, for *Big*

Golden Globe Award: 1989, for Best Actor—Musical/Comedy, for *Big;* 1994, for Best Actor—Drama, for *Philadelphia*

Academy Award (Academy of Motion Pictures Arts and Sciences): 1994, for Best Actor, for *Philadelphia;* 1995, for Best Actor, for *Forrest Gump*

Silver Bear Award, Berlinale Prize (Berlin International Film Festival): 1994, for Best Actor, for *Philadelphia*

The Actor Award (Screen Actors Guild): 1995, for Best Performance by a Male Actor in a Leading Role, for *Forrest Gump*

Man of the Year (Harvard University's Hasty Pudding Theater Club): 1995

FURTHER READING

BOOKS

Trakin, Roy. *Tom Hanks: Journey to Stardom,* 1995
Wallner, Rosemary. *Tom Hanks: Academy Award-Winning Actor,* 1994 (juvenile)
Who's Who in America, 1996

PERIODICALS

American Film, Apr. 1990, p.20
Cosmopolitan, Mar. 1987, p.224
Current Biography Yearbook 1989
Entertainment Weekly, July 9, 1993, p.14

Esquire, Dec. 1993, p.74
Good Housekeeping, May 1989, p.168
GQ, Jan. 1988, p.136; June 1995, p.160
Interview, Mar. 1994, p.112
Maclean's, July 11, 1994, p.52
Newsweek, Sep. 26, 1988, p.56
Rolling Stone, June 30, 1988, p.38
Time, July 11, 1994, p.58
Vanity Fair, June 1994, p.98

ADDRESS

PMK Inc.
1776 Broadway, 8th Floor
New York, NY 10019

OBITUARY

Alison Hargreaves   1962-1995
British Mountain Climber
First Woman to Climb Mt. Everest without
Using Oxygen or Porters

BIRTH

Alison Hargreaves was born on February 17, 1962, in Belper,
England. Her father, John, was a scientist and her mother, Joyce,
was a teacher. Alison was the Hargreaves's middle child; she had
a brother and a sister.

YOUTH

Alison's father remembers her showing an early interest in climbing mountains. Because their town was located near the Peak District National Park, hill-walking was a popular family pastime. The vacations they spent there instilled in Alison a love of the mountains and their rough, wild landscape. "When she was about nine years old," he recalls, "we went climbing on Ben Nevis, the highest mountain in Britain. Suddenly she dashed ahead of us, and we got quite worried. We found her sitting quite happily about 500 feet higher up."

Alison first tried rock-climbing at the age of 13. Rock climbing is different from mountain climbing in that it requires specialized equipment—ropes, picks, etc.—and usually the climber is attempting to scale a vertical face of sheer rock. By the time Hargreaves was 14, she was traveling all over Britain in search of more challenging rock faces. Eventually she was ready for winter climbing in the Scottish Highlands.

EDUCATION

As a student at Belper High School, Alison was encouraged to pursue climbing by one of her teachers, Hillary Collins—the wife of a well-known mountaineer who later died while climbing Mount Everest, the world's highest mountain. Collins made all of her students spend a morning rock-climbing, although few of them enjoyed it as much as Hargreaves did.

Although both of her parents and her sister had studied mathematics at Oxford University, Hargreaves decided she didn't want to go to college. Instead, she left school at the age of 18 to set up an outdoor equipment business with her boyfriend, Jim Ballard, an amateur rock-climber who was 16 years older. Her parents weren't happy with her decision, but Hargreaves was determined to make enough money to support her career as a professional climber.

MARRIAGE AND FAMILY

Ballard quickly realized that Hargreaves's talent for climbing far exceeded his own. He was happy to run the business while Alison spent as much time as she could climbing. By the time she was 21, Hargreaves was running for two hours a day up the steep hillsides of the Peak District to build up her stamina.

Hargreaves and Ballard were married in 1988. Their son, Tom, was born later that year. Hargreaves was five-and-a-half months pregnant with her second child when she became the first British woman to climb the north face of the Eiger, in Switzerland. The Eiger is part of the Alps, a large mountain system in south-central Europe that runs through Switzerland and along the borders of France, Italy, Germany, Austria, and Slovenia.

After the Eiger, Hargreaves took a break until her second child, Kate, was born in 1991. But she always kept herself in peak physical condition by climbing the Scottish mountains near her home.

To her dismay, Hargreaves's career as a mountaineer forced her to spend long periods of time away from her children. She was often torn about leaving them, even though her husband was happy to stay behind and take care of them.

CAREER HIGHLIGHTS

In 1993, Hargreaves and Ballard sold their home and the business to finance a trip to the Alps. They lived in an old Land Rover so that Hargreaves could spend all of her time climbing. That summer she became the first person of either sex to climb, in one season, all six north faces of the Alps: the Eiger, Matterhorn, Dru, Badile, Grandes Jorasses, and Cima Grande mountains. The north faces are the steepest, most challenging faces in the range. The book she wrote about her experience, *A Hard Day's Summer,* was not a big financial success. But the feat won her the respect of climbers all over the world because she had done it alone, with no partner to hold the rope in case of a fall. When she returned to Britain, Hargreaves moved her family to Spean Bridge, Scotland, so she could be closer to the mountains and continue her training.

At this point in her career, Hargreaves turned her attention to the Himalayas, a huge mountain range in southwest Asia that runs through parts of Pakistan, India, Tibet, Nepal, Bhutan, and China. This is where the world's three highest mountain peaks are located: Mount Everest (29,028 feet), K2 (28,244 feet), and Kanchenjunga (28,169 feet). In 1993, Rebecca Stephens had been the first British woman to reach the top of Mt. Everest. But she had carried oxygen with her—something most climbers are forced to do because at altitudes above 26,000 feet, there is only one-quarter of the oxygen found at sea level. Breathing becomes very difficult. Stephens had also reached the summit by the traditional South Col route. Hargreaves decided to make it more difficult for herself by not carrying supplemental oxygen and by following the more hazardous North Ridge route. Two other British climbers, George Mallory and Sandy Irvine, had died while trying to reach the summit using this route in 1924. In fact, only one solo climber, Reinhold Messner from Italy, had succeeded in reaching the summit without oxygen via the North Ridge. But Hargreaves refused to be discouraged. Having already conquered the six north faces of the Alps on her own, her goal now was to climb the world's three highest mountains without oxygen or porters to carry her equipment, beginning with Mt. Everest.

THE ASSAULT ON EVEREST

Hargreaves made her first attempt to climb Mt. Everest in October 1994. She turned back just a short distance from the peak because her fingers and toes were going numb, and she didn't want to risk losing them to frostbite. Many people felt that her decision showed her commitment to safety and survival.

She tried again in May 1995, this time carrying all of her own equipment up the North Ridge route and reaching the summit without the aid of oxygen. She was so overcome with emotion when she saw the summit within her reach that she burst into tears. Later Hargreaves said that climbing Everest had brought her the happiest day of her life. On her way up, however, she'd passed the frozen corpses of two other climbers who hadn't been as lucky. She laid a red silk flower on the peak of the mountain in their memory.

When Hargreaves returned to Britain, she was famous. That was fortunate, because her climbing had become the family's sole source of income. Her husband was responsible not only for taking care of the children while she was gone, but for negotiating contracts, lining up speaking engagements, and finding sponsors who would cover the cost of her next climb.

K2: THE "SAVAGE MOUNTAIN"

Only a few weeks after she returned from Everest, Hargreaves set out for K2, the world's second high-est mountain and technically the most difficult to climb. Although Everest is about 780 feet higher, K2 is steeper, and it has a reputation for being subject to sudden, severe storms. The first British climbers to reach the summit of K2 were Alan Rouse and Julie Tullis, but both died on their way down as they tried to survive 90 mile-per-hour winds and blinding snow. By 1986, in fact, as many people had died on K2 as had reached the top—a track record that even Everest couldn't match.

Hargreaves arrived at the K2 Base Camp on June 25, 1995, with Alan Hinkes, another British climber. They were still together at Camp 2, but they were climbing at different rates and Hargreaves decided to team up with a 34-year-old American climber, Rob Slater. Hinkes ended up taking advantage of a break in the weather and going to the summit alone on July 17. He spent some time with Hargreaves on his way down and later described her as being "in good sprits and determined to stay and do the climb."

Hargreaves spent the next couple of weeks trudging up and down between the lower camps, testing her equipment and getting her body accustomed to the altitude. On the morning of August 13, she finally left for the summit with Slater, Lorenzo Ortas and Pepe Garcas (both Spanish), and Bruce Grant, a New Zealander. A number of other climbers—including Peter Hillary, son of Sir Edmund Hillary, the first man to conquer Mt. Everest—turned back because they didn't like the looks of the weather.

Hargreaves and Slater radioed that they'd reached the summit at 6:00 p.m. But soon after, it is believed that they were engulfed by one of the violent storms that have given K2 its reputation as "the savage mountain." All that is known for sure is that Hargreaves and five companions died on their way down. Experienced climbers suspect that they were actually blown off the mountain by 100 mile-per-hour winds as they moved across the Death Throat—a steep snowy slope near the peak.

Ortas and Garcas were later rescued by helicopter and said that they saw Hargreaves's body—which they were able to identify by the color of her jacket—about 5,000 feet from the summit. Because of the dangerous conditions, there are no plans to retrieve her body.

THE CONTROVERSY

Hargreaves's death provoked a great deal of discussion over whether the mother of two young children had a right to pursue such a dangerous sport. Many saw this as a double standard because no one was challenging the rights of the *fathers* who had died under similar circumstances. Others, though, accused Hargreaves of putting her own needs above those of her children. In her own mind, there was no such conflict. "By climbing I can give my children 100 percent rather than be a frustrated mother at home," she once explained. Her radio message from the top of Mt. Everest to Kate and Tom back in Scotland summed up her feelings perfectly: "I'm on top of the world and I love you dearly."

There was also speculation at the time of her death that Hargreaves, in her frustration over the continuing bad weather and her eagerness to get back home to her children, may have urged the others to try for the summit rather than turning back when Hillary did. Jim Ballard, her husband, insists that she was too experienced to underestimate the dangers posed by the weather. Yet other climbers wonder whether the lack of oxygen might have affected her judgment.

Ballard's response to her death provoked even more controversy. Instead of appearing before the television cameras heartbroken and clutching his weeping children, he dealt calmly with the reporters who came to his house and urged Tom and Kate to smile for the cameras. He seemed unshaken in his belief that his wife had died the way she would have chosen to, quoting her favorite Tibetan proverb: "It is better to have lived one day as a tiger than one thousand years as a sheep."

Jim Ballard wanted his children to see "their mother's last mountain." In October 1995, Ballard tried to take the children to the K2 Base Camp, where they planned to lay a plaque in honor of Hargreaves. But the mission had to be abandoned when the doctor who accompanied the family became ill. The group returned to England. Ballard was again a figure of controversy in the press. He was criticized for putting his children at risk because of the danger of the climb, but he replied that, "I fulfilled my promise to my children."

Ballard now plans to write Hargreaves's biography and oversee the production of a film about her life. Using the diaries of her Mt. Everest expedition, he hopes to create an archive that will help Tom and Kate remember what their mother was like.

WRITINGS

A Hard Day's Summer, 1994

FURTHER READING

BOOKS

Hargreaves, Alison. *A Hard Day's Summer,* 1994

PERIODICALS

Independent (London), May 21, 1995, Britain Section, p.11; Aug. 18, 1995, News Section, p.3; Aug. 19, 1995, Features Section, p.11; Aug. 21, 1995, Gazette Section, p.14; Oct. 16, 1995, News Section, p.5
People, Sep. 4, 1995, p. 69
Times of London, May 15, 1995, Home News Section; May 28, 1995, Home News Section; Aug. 18, 1995, Homes News Section; Aug. 20, 1995, Features Section; Aug. 21, 1995, Features Section; Sep. 3, 1995, Features Section; Sep. 24, 1995, Home News Section; Oct. 15, 1995, Home News Section.

OTHER

"All Things Considered," Transcript from May 22, 1995, National Public Radio

Sir Edmund Hillary 1919-
New Zealander Mountaineer and Explorer
First Person to Reach the Top of Mount Everest

BIRTH

Edmund Percival Hillary was born in Auckland, New Zealand, on July 20, 1919. He was the son of Percival Augustus Hillary, a newspaper editor and apiarist (beekeeper), and Gertrude Clark Hillary. Hillary described his parents as "very worthy people with strong ideals." He also had a younger brother, W. F. Hillary, who was known as Rex.

YOUTH

Though Hillary was shy as a boy, he had an active imagination. He loved to read adventure stories and then pretend that he was the hero. "There was a phase when I was the 'fastest gun in the West,' another when I explored the Antarctic. I would walk for hours with my mind drifting to all these things," he explained. Surprisingly, Hillary was not a natural athlete. One journalist described him as a "bright but gawky child . . . his extremities huge and clumsy."

Hillary had a stubborn streak that sometimes got him into trouble as a boy, but later helped him to achieve great things as an explorer. He described one of the standoffs he had with his stern father: "He was a very good gardener and had grown a successful grapevine. One very good year there was a good crop and one outstanding bunch of grapes. The bunch mysteriously disappeared. My father was convinced that I was the culprit. He took me to the woodshed and more or less tried to beat a confession out of me. But I wouldn't admit to it. He finally became exhausted. I never admitted it. I can't remember if I did or didn't take the grapes. I just know I wouldn't give up."

EDUCATION

After attending a small primary school near his family's farm, Hillary was sent to Auckland Grammar School in the city at the age of eleven—two years younger than average. "Physically small and inexperienced, unaccustomed to mixing socially with anyone outside my own family, I descended on the world of the big city and found it a terrifying experience," Hillary recalled. Within the next few years, however, he grew rapidly— four to five inches per year—until he was taller than most of his classmates.

In 1935, Hillary saved his money and went away on a ski weekend with some friends. This was the first time he had ever been in the mountains, and he was captivated by the experience. From then on he escaped to the mountains whenever he could to go skiing, hiking, or climbing. He reached his first summit—on 7,500-foot Mount Oliver in New Zealand—a few years later. "It wasn't a difficult mountain by any manner or means, but making it through the snow to the ridge, then along the ridge and up to the summit, really captured me," Hillary recalled. "It was then that I resolved I was going to do a lot more mountains." For a time Hillary spent two seasons a year in New Zealand's Southern Alps working on his technique and ice-climbing skills. Before long, he was a talented mountaineer ready to face new challenges.

EARLY JOBS

All during his childhood Hillary helped out in his father's apiary, or beekeeping business. He quit college after two years in order to work with his father full-time. "It was a good life—a life of open air and sun and hard physical work," he explained. It also left Hillary free to pursue other interests in the winter, when the bees hibernated. In 1946, Hillary and his brother, Rex, took over the business themselves. "We were in partnership as professional apiarists, beekeepers, with 1,600 hives," Hillary noted. "It's just another farming activity . . . except that it can be a slightly debatable sort of activity in New Zealand. The weather can make it a bit of a gamble." Hillary remained involved in this business at least part-time until 1959, when he became too busy with his other activities.

In 1939, Hillary enlisted in the Royal New Zealand Air Force. During World War II, he served as a navigator with a patrol squadron in the South Pacific. Though he was wounded in battle, he was determined to make a full recovery so that he could continue mountain climbing.

CAREER HIGHLIGHTS

THE CONQUEST OF MOUNT EVEREST

At 29,028 feet, or nearly six miles high, Mount Everest is the highest point on Earth. It is located in the Himalayas of southern Asia, on the border between Nepal and Tibet. Local people call it Chomolungma, which means "Goddess Mother of the World." People from all over the world wanted to climb Mount Everest when Tibet opened its borders to foreigners in 1920. The most famous attempt during the early years occurred in 1924, when British educators George Mallory and Andrew Irvine were seen nearing the summit before they disappeared in some fog and were never heard from again.

By 1950, 11 teams had tried to climb the mountain from the Tibetan side, and 15 lives had been lost. Then Chinese Communists conquered Tibet and reinstated travel restrictions, so future attempts had to be made from the unfamiliar Nepalese side. In 1951, England sent a team led by Eric Shipton to explore the area and find a new route up the mountain. An expert climber by this time, Hillary became a member of this successful expedition. The Royal Geographic Society then started planning to send a well-organized and fully supplied team to conquer Mount Everest using Shipton's route.

Hillary was invited to join the expedition, which was led by Colonel John Hunt. They spent the next two years training in the Scottish highlands and in the European Alps. In March 1953, they went to Nepal to continue practicing on the frozen lower slopes of Mount Everest itself. By the time the group began its attempt the following month, it included 20 of the best climbers in the British Commonwealth, over 350 Nepalese porters carrying 10,000 pounds of food and equipment, and 36 Sherpa guides. The Sherpas are a Himalayan people who make their living as yak-herders and potato-growers. Since they are familiar with the mountains and used to living at high altitudes, they were valuable guides for Western explorers in the region.

On their way to the top, the expedition established nine different base camps. The final camp was at 27,900 feet, just 1,100 feet from the summit. The first two-man team sent by Colonel Hunt failed to reach the top, but they brought back useful information for the next team—Hillary and a 38-year-old Sherpa named Tenzing Norgay. The night before they made their attempt at reaching the summit, the two men huddled together in their small tent as it was battered by high winds. In the morning, which turned out to be bright and clear, Hillary had to thaw his boots over their small stove.

They left the camp at 6:30 A.M. and moved slowly upward, sometimes having to rest after every three steps due to the lack of oxygen at such a high elevation. Along the way, they nearly met with disaster when Hillary broke through an ice bridge and fell into a crevasse. He would have fallen thousands of feet to his death if it had not been for Norgay, who quickly tied off Hillary's climbing rope and pulled him back up. Later, the valve of Norgay's oxygen tank froze and he could not breathe. Hillary managed to work the valve open, thus returning the favor for his partner. "I experienced fear on many occasions," Hillary admitted. "I often thought, 'What the heck am I doing here when I could be on the beach?' But I always considered fear to be a stimulating factor. It makes you perform beyond what you thought was physically possible."

As they neared the summit, Hillary and Norgay suddenly found a 40-foot rock wall blocking their path. "To climb the rock step direct would have been very difficult," Hillary noted. "Then I noticed a crack hanging over the Kangshung face. Oh, I suppose it was two feet wide. I crawled inside and wriggled and jammed my way to the top of the 40-foot step. When I reached that top, I knew we were going to get to the summit. I could see the ridge." Since then, this part of Mount Everest has been known as "Hillary's step."

On May 29, 1953, at 11:30 A.M., Hillary and Norgay became the first people ever to stand at the top of the world. Upon reaching the summit of Mount Everest, Hillary said, "I had two feelings. A considerable sense of satisfaction, and surprise. I found it hard to accept." His partner, though, was not quite as reserved in celebrating their accomplishment. "I went to shake his hand, but Sherpas are more emotional. Tenzing threw his arms around my shoulders and hugged me. So I threw my arms around his shoulders. We had a nice little hug on top of the mountain. I'm not really a very demonstrative person. But I quite enjoyed that," Hillary recalled. They took a few pictures to prove they had made it, then planted British and Nepalese flags on the summit. But they only had enough oxygen to enjoy their success for about 15 minutes before they had to make the difficult journey back down.

DEALING WITH FAME

"I was very surprised at the media and public response after our ascent of Everest," Hillary recalled. "I thought it might be worth an interview or two, but I really didn't have any idea at all as to the impact." In fact, Hillary's accomplishment captured the attention of the entire world, and the quiet, unassuming man instantly became an international hero. People in England were particularly excited about his feat. Although Hillary was a New Zealander, his success in climbing Mount Everest was considered a triumph for England because New Zealand was part of the British Commonwealth. "For weeks I moved in a completely different world, drifting through a succession of parties, official functions, a State banquet and a Buckingham Palace garden party. My diet seemed to be largely smoked Scotch salmon and champagne. I started waking every morning with a mild hangover," he noted. "It was rather entertaining for a while." In July 1953, Hillary received England's highest honor when he was knighted by Queen Elizabeth II.

One aspect of the media attention that Hillary found disconcerting was the extreme interest in learning who had actually set foot on the summit first—he or Norgay. As a matter of national pride, people in England hoped that Hillary had reached the top first, while people in the Himalayan region felt it was important for Norgay to have reached the summit first.

"Philosophically we reached the top together. We were a team," Hillary stated. "I never really thought of it in terms of who got there first. We were absolutely amazed to be asked that back in Kathmandu." Although it eventually came out that Hillary had reached the summit a few steps ahead of Norgay, they kept this secret between themselves for many years.

Hillary and Norgay remained friends for over 30 years, until Norgay's death in 1986. Their relationship became especially close later in Norgay's life, when the Sherpa's command of English improved. "When we climbed Everest, we could discuss which ridge to use or the weather conditions," Hillary noted. "But it wasn't until a few years ago that we could have a discussion on subjects like the philosophy of the Sherpas, our families, or the changes taking place in mountaineering."

FURTHER ADVENTURES

In the years since his successful ascent of Mount Everest, Hillary has not simply sat back to enjoy his fame. Instead, he has taken part in several other exciting adventures. "Climbing Everest had the greatest effect on my life as far as the public and media impact were concerned. But I don't regard it by any means the greatest experience I've had," Hillary explained. "For me, my trip to the South Pole and expedition up the Ganges River were equally as challenging."

The South Pole excursion began in 1957, when Hillary was asked to establish supply depots for British explorer Vivian Fuchs, who was attempting to cross Antarctica from the other direction. After setting up the depots, Hillary continued on to the South Pole on a specially designed tractor, reaching it several days ahead of Fuchs on January 3, 1958. He thus became only the second person to reach the South Pole overland, and the first to do so using a vehicle. Hillary then waited for Fuchs and led the expedition back over the route he had taken. "There were similarities between that expedition and Everest in that we were dealing with snow and ice and intense cold," Hillary recalled. "But on a mountain like Everest, the danger is more immediate. Avalanches, crevasses, sudden storms, falling down steep slopes. In Antarctica we were having to travel for long, long periods, months, always with the possibility we'd break through into a crevasse area and our tractors—and us—would go to the bottom. We were an awful long way from anyone and anything. So there were prolonged periods of tension." Hillary later described this adventure in two books, *The Crossing of Antarctica* and *No Latitude for Error.*

In 1961, Hillary took part in another Mount Everest expedition. This one was devised to study the effects of high altitude on humans and to search for the legendary abominable snowman. The people of the Himalayas had long told stories about a large, hairy creature known as the *yeti*, but Hillary could not find anyone who had actually seen it. His team set out to accomplish a scientific exploration of whether such a creature existed. Although Hillary did find some huge, strangely shaped footprints in the snow, he ultimately discovered that "if you follow the footprints far enough they always turn out to be the prints of a very ordinary animal. The sun melts them so they spread out and look huge."

In 1977, Hillary set out on another adventure to find the source of the Ganges, the sacred river of India. His large party went up the river in jet boats as far as they could, then continued on foot into the heart of the Himalayas. Although some members of the expedition succeeded in reaching the source of the Ganges, Hillary himself had to be helicoptered down from 15,500 feet, after suffering from severe altitude sickness.

ONGOING CONCERN ABOUT THE HIMALAYAN REGION

In the years since his historic conquest of Mount Everest, Hillary has been able to use the public's considerable interest in him to raise money to improve the lives of people in the Himalayan region. His help was desperately needed: each person in Nepal earns an average of $180 per year, making it one of the poorest countries in the world. In addition, hundreds of children under the age of five die each day due to preventable or curable diseases. "I built very happy relationships with the local people. I saw they needed help," Hillary explained. "I just accepted that I had to do something, and so I have, for 35 years. It's not calculated. It's just my upbringing and the impact of my parents. Mind you, I've got to like it. And I have benefitted as much as they have."

In 1961, thanks to a grant from the World Book Encyclopedia, Hillary established the Himalayan Trust. Since then, the trust has built many schools and hospitals in the valleys surrounding Mount Everest. By 1979, he was spending three or four months each year giving speeches, raising money, and overseeing the work of the trust. He has also been very active in the Sir Edmund Hillary Foundation, which was established in 1972. The foundation has raised hundreds of thousands of dollars each year to build roads, health clinics, and other public works for the Sherpas of Solu-Khumbu. Hillary explained that his many adventures, "good fun though they have been . . . are less important to me now than the projects we are undertaking" on behalf of the Himalayan people. "The building of hospitals, schools, bridges . . . these are the things I think that I am always going to remember." In recognition of his work, Hillary was named New Zealand's high commissioner to India and Bangladesh, and its ambassador to Nepal.

VIEWS ON THE POPULARITY OF EVEREST

Besides helping the people of the Himalayas, Hillary has frequently spoken out about the damage done to the area's environment by increasing numbers of "adventure tourists." Since Hillary's initial climb, thousands of people have attempted to reach the summit of Mount Everest. Unfortunately, "the vast number of expeditions to Mount Everest has resulted in making it the world's highest garbage dump," according to Hillary. The base camps have become littered with plastic bags, tin cans, human waste, discarded mountaineering gear, and other trash. "I must admit, when we went to Everest in 1953 we heaved our rubbish around with the best of them," he admitted. "In those days hardly anyone had even heard of conservation." To limit the ecological degradation of Mount Everest, Hillary once suggested that the Nepalese government close the mountain to climbers for a period of three to five years. However, he realized that this would be nearly impossible, since Nepal has come to depend on the revenue generated by Everest expeditions.

Hillary has also expressed concern about the safety of inexperienced people attempting to summit Mount Everest. Though more than 600 people have reached the peak since Hillary, well over 100 have died trying. In recent years, people with a sense of adventure have been able to pay experienced guides to help them climb the mountain. "Everest, unfortunately, is largely becoming a commercial, money-making opportunity," Hillary noted. "If you are reasonably fit and have $35,000, you can be conducted to the top of the world." Climbers nowadays are equipped with satellite telephones and Internet access, which makes the mountain seem accessible to anyone. On one day in May 1992, 32 people stood on the summit of Mount Everest. Hillary, who described the summit as about the size of a couple of desktops, commented that "I would not have liked to have been jostling for position on the summit of Everest with 30 other people."

Despite advanced equipment and proven routes, however, climbing Mount Everest is still extremely dangerous. In fact, climbers today often encounter the dead bodies of earlier adventurers on the slopes, since shifting snow and changing weather conditions make it nearly impossible to retrieve them. One of the worst disasters in recent memory occurred in May 1996, when eight climbers were killed in a sudden blizzard near the summit. "I have a feeling that people have been getting just a little bit too casual with Mount Everest," Hillary noted after the tragedy. "This incident will bring them to regard it rather more seriously."

"The spirit of adventure is more widely present now than when I was young. The trouble is, the grand things have been done," Hillary stated. However, he does not believe that this should prevent people from creating their own adventures and exploring their own abilities. "You may have very modest mountaineering ambitions, and maybe modest physical ability. But whatever abilities you have, you can climb a nice little peak and reach the summit and feel the same sense of achievement as a hotshot climber clambering up the last slopes of Everest," he said.

MARRIAGE AND FAMILY

Hillary married Louise Rose, a musician and the daughter of the president of the New Zealand Alpine Club, on September 3, 1953. They eventually had three children: Peter, Sarah, and Belinda. On March 31, 1975, Louise and Belinda, who was then 15, were killed in a plane crash near Kathmandu, Nepal. They had been flying to meet Hillary for a school dedication ceremony. "It was extremely difficult for me," Hillary confided. "But ultimately I made the determination to keep doing the projects I'd been doing with my family. That way, at least life became worth living again."

For 20 years Hillary and his wife were close friends with Peter and June Mulgrew. Then Peter, who was Hillary's frequent climbing partner, was killed in a plane crash in Antarctica in 1979. Following this tragedy, Hillary and June found comfort in each other's company. "We were a foursome for 20 years, then each of us was suddenly widowed. So I suppose it was only natural we came together," Mulgrew noted. The couple were married in December 1989. Hillary and his wife maintain a home and a seaside cottage outside Auckland, New Zealand. Hillary has filled their home with Tibetan and Nepalese art—such as rugs, paintings, and furniture—as well as hundreds of books on the Himalayas.

Hillary's daughter Sarah became an art restorer in Auckland. His son Peter became a ski instructor and mountaineer in Melbourne, Australia. Hillary claimed that his son was "a better mountaineer than I probably was." In 1990, Peter succeeded in reaching the summit of Mount Everest on his fourth attempt. In 1995, he averted near disaster on K2, the second-highest mountain in the world. As part of an expedition led by Scottish mountaineer Alison Hargreaves, Peter decided to turn back before reaching the summit. Hargreaves persuaded other members of her party to continue on in questionable weather conditions, and they were all killed. Lately Peter has become involved in his father's fund-raising efforts for the people of Nepal. He has also written several books about mountaineering.

WRITINGS

High Adventure, 1955
East of Everest: An Account of the New Zealand Alpine Club Himalayan Expedition to the Barun Valley in 1954, 1956
Challenge of the Unknown, 1958
The Crossing of Antarctica, 1959 (with Vivian Fuchs)
No Latitude for Error, 1961
High in the Thin Cold Air, 1962 (with Desmond Doig)
Schoolhouse in the Clouds, 1964
Nothing Venture, Nothing Win, 1975
From the Ocean to the Sky: Jet Boating, 1979

Ascent: Two Lives Explored: The Autobiographies of Sir Edmund and Peter Hillary,
   1984
Ecology 2000: The Changing Face of Earth, 1984 (editor)

HONORS AND AWARDS

Knight Commander of the Order of the British Empire: 1953
Order of the Strong Right Arms of the Gurkhas (Nepal): 1953
Royal Institution of Chartered Surveyors (Nepal): 1953
Cullum Medal (American Geographical Society): 1954
Hubbard Medal (National Geographic Society of the United States): 1954
First living person ever selected to appear on New Zealand currency: 1992

FURTHER READING

BOOKS

Davidson, Bob. *Hillary and Tenzing Climb Everest,* 1993 (juvenile)
Fraser, Mary Ann. *On Top of the World: The Conquest of Mount Everest,* 1991
   (juvenile)
Gaffney, Timothy R. *Edmund Hillary: First to Climb Mount Everest,* 1990
   (juvenile)
Hillary, Sir Edmund and Peter. *Ascent: Two Lives Explored: The Auto-
   biographies of Sir Edmund and Peter Hillary,* 1984
Hillary, Peter. *Rimo: Mountain on the Silk Road,* 1992
Hunt, Sir John. *The Conquest of Everest,* 1953
Kramer, S. A. *To the Top! Climbing the World's Highest Mountain,* 1993
   (juvenile)
Norgay, Tenzing. *Tiger of the Snows,* 1955
Rosen, Mike. *The Conquest of Everest,* 1990 (juvenile)
Who's Who in the World, 13th ed.

PERIODICALS

Backpacker, May 1985, p.62
Charlotte Observer, May 23, 1993, p.A2
Current Biography 1954
Los Angeles Times, Apr. 5, 1992, p.A30
Newsweek, Apr. 23, 1979, p.98
Ottawa Citizen, Aug. 11, 1990, p.J1; Nov. 27, 1992, p.D11
People, Nov. 18, 1985, p.107
Time, May 27, 1996, p.36
Toronto Star, Aug. 6, 1990, p.C1; Nov. 22, 1990, p.W9; Nov. 27, 1992, p.C16
Washington Post, July 31, 1979, p.B1; June 27, 1992, p.C1

ADDRESS

278A Remuera Road
Auckland 5, New Zealand

Judith Jamison   1944-
American Dancer and Choreographer
Artistic Director of the Alvin Ailey American
Dance Theater

BIRTH

Judith Jamison (JAM-i-son) was born May 10, 1944, in Philadelphia, Pennsylvania, to Tessie and John Jamison. Judith was the
second child in the family; she has one older brother, John. Tessie
was a teacher and John was a sheet-metal worker. Both parents
were accomplished musicians, and John had wanted to be a concert pianist when he was growing up. But when he married and
had children, he chose instead to become a laborer in order to
earn money for the family.

YOUTH

Jamison grew up in the Germantown section of Philadelphia, next door to her grandparents. She remembers always loving music, and the house was filled with music, from classical music to gospel, including opera on Saturday afternoons, when the family listened to the live radio broadcasts from the Metropolitan Opera in New York.

Jamison's first music teacher was her father, who taught her to play the piano. She remembers his rough, calloused hands and the way they would bring out the beauty of favorite pieces like Beethoven's "Moonlight Sonata." "He played with a complete release of passion that was terribly internal, but very generous at the same time," recalls Jamison. "Here was a man who was really willing to share his vulnerability and his passion through those notes that played on the piano—and then work from nine to five with drills and nails and hammers."

Jamison took formal piano and violin lessons as a young child, and she sang in the choir of the Mother Bethel African Methodist Episcopal Church in Philadelphia, the oldest black church in America. The church was an important part of her life growing up, and she remembers loving the pageantry of church rituals. "I saw what the spirit could do," she says, "what something that was intangible could do and how it could change your life."

Judith was active—she loved to move. "As a child, I thought I wanted to be a pilot or drive something that had a powerful engine—like a train or a plane or an aircraft carrier. I have always been one of those people who know exactly what they want." Through dance, she was able to combine the things she loved—movement and ritual, and the sharing of the spirit.

EDUCATION

DANCING

Jamison was a tall, busy child, and her parents started her in ballet classes at the age of six, thinking it would give her grace and channel her tremendous energy. She loved it. She took ballet, jazz, and tap classes, as well as acrobatics, at the Judimar School in Philadelphia, under the watchful eye of Marian Cuyjet. She vividly remembers her first performance, at age six. "I wore a red-checkered shirt, blue jeans, and pink ballet shoes and danced to "I'm an Old Cowhand." She studied at the Judimar School for 11 years, and in that time had the opportunity to work with outstanding guest teachers, including Anthony Tudor, one of the preeminent choreographers of ballet.

SCHOOL

Jamison attended the local public schools in Philadelphia, where she was an excellent student. She graduated from Germantown High School one year early, in 1960. She didn't know what she wanted to do, so on the advice of her family, she accepted a scholarship to Fisk University in Nashville, Tennessee. She spent three semesters at Fisk, where she considered majoring in psychology. But by the time she was 18, Jamison knew she wanted to dance.

She returned to Philadelphia and studied at the Philadelphia Dance Academy (now the University of the Arts). She polished her ballet technique, and for the first time began to study modern dance. Classical and modern dance technique are different in what they demand of a dancer and the way the dancer moves through space. As Jamison herself described it, "Classical dance is usually danced very high in space, on pointe. Modern dancers are very much into the floor." Just as ballet stresses length and height, modern dance is rooted in the ground. The kind of dance Jamison was now studying, based on the concepts of Martha Graham and Lester Horton, works on the concepts of "contraction and release," a method that is characterized by deep bends, angular movements, and broad, swooping turns.

CAREER HIGHLIGHTS

NEW YORK DEBUT

In 1964, while studying in Philadelphia, Jamison was spotted by Agnes de Mille during a master's class. One of the major choreographers of 20th-century dance, De Mille knew talent when she saw it. She was so struck by Jamison's ability that she invited her to perform in the New York debut of her new ballet, *The Four Marys*. So in December 1964, Judith Jamison made her New York debut with the American Ballet Theater in De Mille's new piece. But after *The Four Marys*, no new work came her way. Jamison went to many auditions, but she didn't get parts. She had two things working against her. For one, she was tall for a ballerina, 5'10", at a time when most ballerinas averaged about 5'4". And at that time there were no major ballet companies that had black dancers.

Undaunted, Jamison stayed in the area and made ends meet by doing odd jobs, including running the water flume ride at the New York World's Fair. In 1964, while auditioning for a TV special starring Harry Belafonte, she was spotted by Alvin Ailey, an aspiring young black choreographer, and he asked her to audition for his company. Jamison thought she did a terrible audition, and she left the stage in tears. But three days later, Ailey called to invite her to join his company, the Alvin Ailey American Dance Theater. She accepted immediately. It was a decision that would make her a star, and that would determine her path in the dance world.

ALVIN AILEY AMERICAN DANCE THEATER

Alvin Ailey was a pioneer in the world of modern dance. He had studied with Lester Horton, a major figure in 20th-century modern dance, who had created the first integrated dance company in the U.S. Ailey took over the Horton company on Horton's death in the 1950s. By 1958, he decided he wanted a company of his own. He began to choreograph the ballets for which his company became famous, including works like *Revelations*, set to black spirituals. The themes of Ailey's dances were often drawn from the African American experience and reflected the influence of Broadway dancing and modern technique, expressed with an exuberant physicality. His female dancers were far from the pale, fragile ideal of classical ballet. Jamison recalls that "in Alvin's company, the dancers were full-bodied women. They had breasts and hips and whatever." His lead dancer was "kind of a voluptuous-looking woman, no bean pole, you know." Jamison's

height, strong body, and commanding physical presence made her a natural for the Ailey company; she went on to become its symbol and its star.

Jamison made her debut with the Ailey company in 1965 in *Congo Tango Palace*. At the time she joined, she was one of only 10 dancers in the company. The company was young, vibrant, and often broke. Throughout the 15 years Jamison performed with the company, Ailey was always facing financial problems, and the group disbanded several times due to lack of funds. During these hiatuses, Jamison took the opportunity to perform with other dance companies around the world, including the Harkness Ballet, the Hamburg Ballet, and Maurice Bejart's Ballet of the Twentieth Century.

Jamison always returned to the Ailey company, however, and became his muse and the dancer who embodied the company and the dream of its creator. At first, Ailey wasn't sure how to use Jamison's tremendous potential, "This girl, like a long drink of water," he called her. He also spoke of her as "a terribly powerful dancer, a terribly powerful personality. She challenges and in a way she intimidates the choreography."

Jamison's superb technique and depth of understanding of dance have always set her apart from other dancers. Deborah Jowitt, a dancer, choreographer, and critic, describes her this way: "Movements that other dancers tend to flatten or make rhythmically square look richly three-dimensional and polyrhythmic when she performs them. Jamison doesn't show you steps, she uses them to show you a woman dancing. This ability both to maintain a human dimension and to project superhuman power and radiance is perhaps one of her most impressive skills."

Jamison appeared in Ailey's greatest works, like *Revelations* and *Masekela Lounge*, set to the music of Hugh Masekela and revealing the despair of black people in an oppressive, racist society. In 1971, Ailey created *Cry* for Jamison. He called it his tribute to black women and their suffering throughout history, and dedicated it to "all black women—especially our mothers." When the work begins, it appears to be a lament of servitude and oppression, but it becomes a metaphor for the triumph of the spirit. Jamison and Ailey were so attuned to one another that she remembers that: "*Cry* was created in eight days, and we barely said anything to each other." The work became her signature, and she performed it to enraptured audiences for years.

The Ailey troupe traveled the world, and with them Jamison toured Africa, Russia, France, India, Cuba, Sweden, and Japan. Africa affected her powerfully. "The diversity and beauty of the continent hit me in the face, in the spirit, and in the heart," she recalls in her autobiography, *Dancing Spirit*. "I very much wanted to be identified as being from somewhere on the continent. In Senegal, I was told that I looked like a member of the Peul tribe. My coloring was very much like theirs, as were my facial features. I was tickled when I learned that the Peul were nomadic. It was perfect. *They were gypsies, so was I."*

Jamison also danced with some of the premier male dancers from the world of ballet during her years with Ailey. In the 1970s she was partnered by Russian superstars Mikhail Baryshnikov and Alexander Gudonov.

BROADWAY

In 1980, Jamison decided to leave the Ailey company to perform in the Broadway show *Sophisticated Ladies*. She starred with veteran performer Gregory Hines in a show featuring the music of Duke Ellington that gave her the opportunity to try singing and Broadway dancing. The show was a hit, even though some critics thought the choreography was not enough of a challenge for Jamison.

After two years on Broadway, Jamison was ready for a break. She bought a home in the Connecticut woods and took two years off from performing. During the period she calls her "two-year sleep," Jamison "recuperated. I slept. I walked in the woods. I grew asparagus. I did what normal people do." She also began coaching and teaching at Jacob's Pillow, the summer home of various New York dance ensembles. And she started a small catering business, Jamison's Choice Ltd., out of her home, preparing such favorites as her sweet potato pie, which her friends had raved about for years. But retirement didn't work. "Once you're given the gift, you just can't go off into the sunset," said Jamison. "I felt a compulsion to share this gift."

BECOMING A CHOREOGRAPHER

By 1984, she was back to dancing and ready for a new challenge—choreography. Her first work, *Divining* (1984), was created for Ailey's company. When opening night rolled around, Jamison didn't know what to expect from the critics. She hid in her room until the reviews came out. They were fine. With new confidence in a new field of art, Jamison has gone on to create other dances for the Ailey company and several other troupes, including such works as *Just Call It Dance* (1984), *Time Out* (1986) *Forgotten Time* (1989), and *Rift* (1991).

Jamison also found time to serve on the board of the National Endowment for the Arts for six years, during which she became a national spokesperson for the importance of the arts. The Ailey company had always had a strong outreach program for the black community, and this became even more of a focus in the 1980s. Ailey founded summer camps in New York, Baltimore, and Kansas City where kids can study dancing, creative writing, and the visual arts; Jamison helped to develop, fund, and run them.

THE JAMISON PROJECT

In 1988, Jamison decided to form her own company, the Jamison Project. The group toured the U.S. to acclaim in 1988, but it was short lived. In the spring of 1989, Ailey called Jamison to tell her he was ill and that he wanted her to take over the company. She agreed.

In December 1989, Alvin Ailey died of an AIDS-related blood disease. At his memorial service in New York, attended by more than 5,000 people, Jamison remembered Ailey as her mentor and her "spiritual walker." Several weeks later Jamison accepted the position as the artistic director of the Alvin Ailey American Dance Theater. Recalling her conversation with Ailey before his death, she said, "We had talked about it once, only once, several years ago. I knew it was what I had to do. Alvin nurtured me, took care of me and gave me so much. Now, he's given me this great gift. And I'm going to take care of it."

The Jamison project disbanded, with Jamison taking six of the 12 dancers into the Ailey troupe.

ARTISTIC DIRECTOR

Jamison took the reins of the Ailey company in 1990, a job she says requires her to be "a salesperson, nurse, mother, psychoanalyst, rehearsal director." She has vowed to continue the traditions of this outstanding dance ensemble. "The idea is not to feed the company with my work, but to stay consistent with traditional choreographers, with the fresh ideas that come out of the mouths of babes, and to pay tribute to the works of Ailey and the treasure that is the foremost repertory company in the world." She isn't intimidated by the thought of being Ailey's successor: "I don't feel I'm standing in anyone's shoes. I'm standing on Alvin's shoulders. The horizons become broader." She has directed the company in several anniversary performances, including one celebrating the troupe's 35th birthday in 1993, for which she created the work *Hymn*. The 1995 season opened in New York in December 1995 with a revival of *Revelations*, also in its 35th year.

Of her own legacy to dance, Jamison says that what she strove for, and what she looks for in her dancers, is vulnerability. "There is no place else but the stage for me where you can be that vulnerable. There's an honesty there that does not exist in the real world. What I hope people remember about my dancing is not that my legs went high or that I turned three or five times. I hope they remember a spiritualness about what they saw."

One of Jamison's goals is to expand the outreach program begun by Ailey, especially to children in poor areas. "Very much on my mind is not to miss out on the opportunity to stimulate young audiences that are not used to concert dance, and to help them understand that concert dance is a reflection of themselves, an identifiable part of their lives."

ADVICE TO YOUNG DANCERS

"Don't let what your body does define what you can do. Think of movement as much bigger than what your body says you're limited to. Your hand can go into the depths of your heart and pull out what you need to communicate with another person. Dance is bigger than the physical body. Think bigger than that. When you extend your arm, it doesn't stop at the end of your fingers, because you're dancing bigger than that; you're dancing spirit."

MARRIAGE AND FAMILY

Jamison was married from 1972 to 1974 to Miguel Godreau, a former Ailey dancer. Jamison prefers not to talk about the relationship even now. She has not remarried.

HOBBIES AND OTHER INTERESTS

Even though her catering business is now a part of the past, Jamison still loves to cook, especially for friends. She says that if she could invite three people in all of history to dinner, they would be "Nelson Mandela, Maya Angelou, and Alvin Ailey."

HONORS AND AWARDS

Dance Magazine Award: 1972
Key to the City of New York: 1976
Distinguished Service Award (Mayor of New York City): 1982
Distinguished Service Award (Harvard University): 1982
Spirit of Achievement Award (Yeshiva University, Albert Einstein College
   of Medicine): 1992

SELECTED WORKS

Divining, 1984
Just Call It Dance, 1984
Mefistofele, 1987
With Us, 1988
Forgotten Time, 1989
Rift, 1990
Hymn, 1993

WRITINGS

Dancing Spirit, 1993 (with Howard Kaplan)

FURTHER READING

BOOKS

Charlotte, Susan. *Creativity: Conversations with 28 Who Excel,* 1993
Jamison, Judith, with Howard Kaplan. *Dancing Spirit,* 1993
Who's Who in America 1995
Who's Who of American Women 1995-96

PERIODICALS

Boston Globe, Feb. 3, 1985, p.A1; Dec. 2, 1989, p.C11; Mar. 15, 1991, p.C41
Chicago Tribune, Jul. 19, 1987, Section: Home, p.3
Current Biography Yearbook 1973
Dance Magazine, Aug. 1990, p.12; Nov. 1993, p.50, 130; Dec. 1993, p.28
Ebony, Dec. 1990, p.132
Essence, Sep. 1981, p.12
Los Angeles Times, Mar. 2, 1995, Section: Calendar, p.7
Jet, July 16, 1981, p.56

Ms., Nov./Dec. 1991, p.80
New York Times Biographical Service, July 1976, p.1740
Newsweek, Sep. 18, 1989, p.80
Philadelphia Inquirer, Oct. 26, 1984, p.C5; Feb. 9, 1985, p.D1; Aug. 9, 1987, p.D1; Nov. 9, 1988, p.E8; Dec. 21, 1989, p.D3
Washington Post, Apr. 20, 1995, p.D1

ADDRESS

Alvin Ailey American Dance Theater
211 W. 61st St.
New York, NY 10023

OBITUARY

Barbara Jordan   1936-1996
American Legislator, Orator, Educator, and Civil-Rights Advocate

BIRTH

Barbara Charline Jordan was born on February 21, 1936, in Houston, Texas. Her father, Benjamin Jordan, was a warehouse clerk and later, after 1949, a Baptist minister; her mother, Arlyne (Patten) Jordan, was a homemaker and a popular and eloquent speaker at their church. Barbara had two older sisters, Bennie and Rose Mary.

YOUTH

Jordan faced many challenges as a black female growing up in the South in the early 20th century. At that point, the South was still completely segregated under what were called "Jim Crow" laws. These laws forced the segregation of the races and created "separate but equal" facilities—housing, schools, restaurants, movie theaters, bathrooms, drinking fountains, and more—for blacks and whites. In reality, the separate facilities for blacks were pitifully inadequate. They served as a constant reminder to African-Americans that they were considered inferior, second-class citizens, hated and feared by whites.

Jordan grew up in a poor, all-black neighborhood in Houston. "We were poor, but so was everyone around us, so we did not notice it," she later recalled. "We were never hungry, and we always had a place to stay." Despite the difficulties the family faced, Benjamin and Arlyne Jordan had high expectations for their daughters. They taught the girls to value education and hard work, to excel in school, to practice self-discipline, and to treat themselves and others with dignity and respect. Benjamin Jordan had high standards for his three daughters. He was strict with the girls, and they learned to comply with their father's discipline with complete obedience and self-control.

But it was also a loving and happy household. In the Jordan family, their lives were filled with religion and music. Faith was central to their lives. They attended church services every Sunday at the Good Hope Missionary Baptist Church, where Benjamin Jordan later became the minister. The family's religious practices forbade dancing, playing cards, reading novels, and going to the movies, which was rough on the girls growing up. But they all enjoyed music. The parents were both accomplished singers and pianists, and the girls all took piano lessons, too—until Barbara rebelled one day, refusing to continue the long hours of practicing. Her defiance angered her father. He told her that the only good jobs for black women were teaching music, and asked her what she planned to do. "I don't know," she told him, "but I'll manage somehow."

And in fact she did manage, of course, to become known for her oratorical skills, which were emphasized in her family early on. Her mother and father were both talented speakers. They shared their love of language and taught her to choose her words precisely and to speak with perfect diction. In addition, Jordan learned from the cadenced speech of her minister and other accomplished speakers at church. Early on, she learned how to use public speaking to inform, to persuade, and to move an audience.

MAJOR INFLUENCES

Jordan once offered the follow comments when asked who had been her role models when she was growing up: "Most of my teachers, because they helped me develop a heightened sense of self-esteem. My parents, because they worked hard and instilled in me the idea that anything I wanted to get, I had to exercise some effort to get it. And my maternal grandfather, who was a very strong influence in my life."

EARLY MEMORIES

Some of Barbara Jordan's happiest childhood hours were spent visiting her grandfather, John Ed Patten, after church on Sundays. After they ate, the rest of the family would leave, and Barbara would stay with her grandfather. Patten had had a very difficult life. As a young man he had owned a shop, until one day he was robbed. Patten grabbed his gun and chased the thief. But the police saw him running with a gun, and they started chasing him. The police shot him in the hand, and he accidentally shot a white police officer. He was charged with assault with intent to murder, sent to trial, convicted of the crime, and sentenced to prison. Although the whole thing was a mistake—he had not intended to shoot the officer—his appeals were useless in a legal system that favored whites. He spent almost 10 years in prison before being pardoned by the governor.

Years later, when Jordan was a young girl, Grandpa Patten was a junk man. He would go out in a wagon pulled by two mules and collect the junk that people would put out for him—newspapers, metal scraps, old rags—which he would then sell by the pound. Jordan loved the special times they spent together. In their many talks, he made her memorize an important message: "Just remember the world is not a playground, but a schoolroom. Life is not a holiday, but an education. One eternal lesson for us all: to teach us how better we should love."

EDUCATION

Jordan attended the all-black public schools in segregated Houston. Always a good student, she imposed high standards on herself. If she earned all A's on her report card with just one B, she would feel disappointed. She attended Phillis Wheatley High School, named after a poet who was the first African-American and the first American woman to publish a book of poems. At Wheatley High, Jordan started out by worrying more about her social life than her studies, concentrating on fitting in. With time, though, she started thinking ahead to college and became more serious about her schoolwork. She got involved in school clubs, became president of the honor society, and joined the debate team.

It was in high school that Jordan decided on her future career. The school held a Career Day, where people from different professions would come and talk about their work. Each professional served both as inspiration and role model for the students. For Jordan, it proved to be a pivotal moment. She heard a speech by Edith Sampson, a Chicago lawyer and future judge. Impressed by this talented and self-confident black woman, Jordan decided that she, too, would become a lawyer—even though she wasn't exactly sure what that was.

By the end of high school, she was already training the voice and the oratorical skills that would win her so much later acclaim. She won a variety of awards for debate at the local, regional, and district levels. As a senior, she won two state contests, earning a trip to Chicago for the national competition. She took first place there, winning a $200 scholarship for college. She also won the Julius Levy Oratorical Contest Award and was chosen "Girl of the Year," an award for the most outstanding black student at her high school, by the national black sorority Zeta Phi Beta. In 1952, Jordan graduated from Phillis Wheatley High School in the top five percent of her class.

COLLEGE AND LAW SCHOOL

Jordan went on to attend Texas Southern University, an all-black school in Houston. There, she majored in government and joined a sorority. She also joined the debate team, which proved to be a seminal experience in her future training. The team would pile into the coach's car and drive all over the U.S. to take part in competitions. For this group of blacks, driving through the South was often the toughest part of the trip. Here Otis King, one of her teammates, recalls those days: "There was strict segregation in the South at that time, so we had to travel from place to place based on where we could stay. We spent long stretches in the car because there was nowhere to stay in between. We would buy food at grocery stores and eat in the car unless we found a black-run restaurant or a restaurant that would serve blacks around through the back. Occasionally, we would find a place where blacks were allowed to come in the back door and sit and eat in the kitchen. You had to plan for food and even plan ahead to locate service stations where blacks could use rest rooms." Arriving in the North was an eye-opening experience, to discover that they could walk in the front door of any restaurant or hotel and be treated just like white people. The team's finest moment came when a debate competition against the team from Harvard University ended in a tie. For a team from a small, Southern black college, that was a tremendous accomplishment. In 1956, Jordan graduated *magna cum laude* (with great distinction) with a B.A. (bachelor of arts) degree from Texas Southern University.

From there, she went on to Boston University Law School. She planned to use her training as a lawyer to fight the segregation she had endured throughout her life. But law school proved to be very tough. For the first year she felt completely out of her depth. Her undergraduate studies had not prepared her for the type of reasoning that law school required. She felt that the education and training she had received at a "separate but equal" black school had been inferior to that received by the white students around her. Jordan worried that she wouldn't make it—that she would have to tell her parents that she'd failed. But she studied almost around the clock, sleeping only a few hours a night, and pulled it off. Boston University seemed free of the racial prejudice that she had known throughout her life. Prejudice against women was common, though, and female students were often ignored or patronized. But she didn't let that stand in her way. Jordan graduated from Boston University Law School in 1959, receiving her LL.B. (bachelor of laws) degree. She passed the bar examination in Massachusetts and Texas, earning the right to practice law.

FIRST JOBS

After law school, Jordan planned to set up a law practice in Boston, deciding that she wanted to live in an integrated community. She remained in Boston for the first summer after finishing school. But after three years in the North, she was ready to go home. Jordan returned to Houston and moved back home with her parents. She set up a private law practice in her parents' kitchen, handling legal problems mostly for poor people in her neighborhood. From 1959 to 1966, she also worked as an administrative assistant to a county judge to supplement her income.

In 1960, Jordan had her first experience with politics. She volunteered to help out in John F. Kennedy's presidential campaign. "They put me to work licking stamps and addressing envelopes," she later recalled. "One night we went out to a church to enlist Negro voters, and the woman who was supposed to speak didn't show up. I volunteered to speak in her place and right after that, they took me off licking and addressing." All the years spent learning to give speeches was starting to pay off. In that election, she proved to be highly effective in organizing a get-out-the-vote campaign that brought Houston's black voters to the polls. At the same time, she started to make a name for herself in the legal community. She became active in several legal organizations and in the Democratic party. In 1962 and 1964, Jordan ran for a seat in the Texas House of Representatives, but lost both times. Her luck, though, was about to change.

CAREER HIGHLIGHTS

THE TEXAS SENATE

The year 1966 saw what would be the first of many firsts in the career of Barbara Jordan. The previous year, the legislative districts in the Houston area had been reapportioned. A new, predominately black district was created to reflect accurately the local population. In 1966, Jordan ran for the new state senate seat and won by a two-to-one margin. She was the first woman ever elected to the Texas Senate, and the first black elected since 1883. She was reelected to her seat for a four-year term in 1968.

In the Texas Senate, Jordan quickly became known for certain key qualities. Honesty, integrity, independence, an incisive intellect, and an authoritative air were the hallmarks of her approach to politics, and to life. Known for her eloquent speech, Jordan's deep, rich voice and precise enunciation lent an air of certain truth to her pronouncements. But Jordan was also a pragmatic politician, one who learned early all the rules—and the tricks—of parliamentary procedure. She also stood ready to compromise, while staying true to her philosophy: "You yield on matters which are peripheral while protecting the central core." Texas legislators were surprised to learn that she could outmaneuver them on their own turf, and she quickly earned their admiration. Even those who disagreed with her viewpoints respected her integrity and her political acumen. These qualities, political observers agree, marked her entire political career.

Fellow Texan Molly Ivins, a columnist and political commentator, recently recalled those early days. "Let me tell you what it was like for Barbara Jordan when she joined the Texas Senate. One of her colleagues always referred to her as 'the nigger mammy washerwoman.' Others treated her with the condescending courtliness then deemed appropriate for Southern gentlemen in the presence of a lady. Even her admirers were inadvertently cruel. It was considered a great joke in those days to bring your racist friends into the Senate gallery, listen to their appalled 'Who is THAT?' when they first saw Jordan, and then enjoy their stupefaction when she rose to speak. She always did sound like God."

During her six years in the Texas Senate, Jordan worked to reform welfare, pass minimum wage laws, fight racial discrimination in hiring and housing, create tax laws that were fair to the poor, and defeat a bill that would have made it more difficult for people to register to vote. It was during this time that she began to forge a relationship with fellow Texan Lyndon B. Johnson, U.S. president from 1963 to 1968, who later turned to her for advice and helped her in her political career. In 1972, near the end of her term in the Texas Senate, she was elected president pro tem of the Texas Legislature. As such, she would fill in as governor if both the governor and lieutenant governor were out of the state at the same time. That occurred on June 10, 1972, and Jordan was named governor for the day. It was the first time in U.S. history that a black person was governor, even for only a day. Her father, who had been ill, lived just long enough to see his daughter sworn in as governor. He suffered a stroke later that day and died the next morning.

THE U.S. HOUSE OF REPRESENTATIVES

In 1972, Jordan was elected to the United States House of Representatives. Along with Andrew Young of Georgia, who was also elected that year,

Jordan was the first black to serve in Congress since 1901; she was the first black woman ever to do so. Yet Jordan rarely emphasized her race in her legislative efforts. She considered herself the representative for all the people in her district in Texas, not just for blacks, and she resisted calls that she support a specifically black agenda.

After her election, Jordan turned to former President Lyndon B. Johnson for advice on what committee assignment she should request. In the U.S. House, the 22 committees do much of the work to write and review legislation in their area of concern. For members of Congress, the committee assignment greatly affects the types of issues in which they will be involved in pending legislation. Johnson pulled some strings and helped her get assigned to her first choice, the Judiciary Committee. At the time, neither he nor Jordan knew how important that would become.

Jordan was reelected to the U.S. Congress in 1974 and 1976. During her six years there, she had a solidly liberal record. She worked on legislation that challenged price fixing by manufacturers, increased the minimum wage, extended Social Security to homemakers, provided legal aid for the poor, increased school funding, expanded the school lunch program, protected the environment, and required that federal funds be used in a nondiscriminatory fashion. But by far, Jordan was best known for her work on the Judiciary Committee during the Watergate proceedings in 1974.

WATERGATE

The term "Watergate" describes a series of political scandals involving President Richard M. Nixon just before and during his second term in office. In 1972, before the presidential election later that year, police in Washington, D.C., caught five men trying to break into the headquarters of the Democratic National Committee, the main organization of the Democratic party. These offices were housed in the Watergate building complex. During their trial on burglary charges, these men and their accomplices were found to have ties to the reelection campaign of President Nixon, a Republican. A series of coverups was revealed that eventually implicated the president himself and his closest aides, transforming the affair into a huge political scandal and a national trauma. People were reluctant to believe that the president of the United States had been aware of a criminal act, either before or after the fact, and had not informed the authorities. Instead, it seemed, he had tried to cover the whole thing up. A tape recorder in the president's office had recorded conversations there, and many believed that the tapes would finally determine what the president knew, and when he knew it. Nixon refused to turn these tapes over to the authorities investigating the cover up, although he was ultimately forced to do so. Nixon's actions created a crisis of confidence amongst Americans, the majority of whom believed that their president had been involved in a massive, illegal cover up.

In response, the U.S. House of Representatives launched an impeachment investigation against the president. "Impeachment" is the term used when the legislature formally accuses an elected official of misconduct. Under the U.S. Constitution, which delineates these laws, the House of Representatives is empowered to impeach the president. The members of the House Judiciary Committee start the investigation. If they find that there are grounds for impeachment, they send the matter to the full House of Representatives. If the House votes to impeach the president, the matter would be sent to the Senate for a trial. If the president was found guilty there, he would have to leave office. By early 1974, the House of Representatives enjoined its Judiciary Committee to begin impeachment proceedings.

As part of the Judiciary Committee, Jordan was involved in the investigation of President Nixon for his role in Watergate. Still a relative newcomer to the legislature, Jordan would be one of 38 Committee members charged with evaluating the evidence in the possible impeachment of the president. After reviewing the evidence, the Committee would make public its findings. Each member of the Committee would give a 15-minute speech on national TV, clarifying his or her position to the American people.

Jordan spoke to a rapt national audience on July 25, 1974. In deep, majestic, resonant tones, she expressed her unshakable faith in the Constitution and our nation's body of laws. She spoke with eloquence and authority and intelligence to an audience that was absolutely spellbound by her passionate conviction. "She was," in the words of political activist Ann Lewis, "the voice of moral authority." Rather than review specific charges against the president, she spoke in broad terms about the ideas, explaining the Constitutional issues to the American people. She expressed anger and outrage at the idea that elected officials had betrayed the public trust. She articulated what many

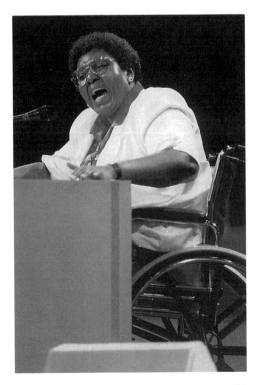

Americans felt. The nation was in the middle of a crisis, and people had lost confidence in their leaders. Many who had once trusted their political leaders now felt only doubt and suspicion. People responded immediately to her speech, which catapulted Jordan to national prominence. Here is part of the speech that had such a big impact on the nation.

> "We the people"—it is a very eloquent beginning. But when the Constitution of the United States was completed on the 17th of September in 1787, I was not included in that "We the people." I felt for many years that somehow George Washington and Alexander Hamilton just left me out by mistake. But through the process of amendment, interpretation, and court decision, I have finally been included in "We the people."

> Today I am an inquisitor. I believe hyperbole would not be fictional and would not overstate the solemnness that I feel right now. My faith in the Constitution is whole. It is complete. It is total. I am not going to sit here and be an idle spectator in the diminution, the subversion, the destruction of the Constitution.

Following these opening remarks, Jordan went on to argue forcefully and convincingly that the evidence against Nixon was so compelling that the House should vote to impeach him. After outlining her case against the President, she concluded with these words.

> Has the President committed offenses and planned and directed and acquiesced in a course of conduct which the Constitution will not tolerate? That is the question. We know that. We should now forthwith proceed to answer the question. It is reason and not passion which must guide our deliberations, guide our debate, guide our decision.

The speech made Barbara Jordan a hero to the American public, who deluged her with letters voicing their support. Along with the majority of the Judiciary Committee, Jordan voted to impeach Nixon on three separate counts. The matter was turned over to the full House. But on August 8, 1974, before the House could vote, President Richard Nixon resigned, in disgrace. Vice President Gerald Ford became President. Many people expected that Nixon would soon be brought to trial, but President Ford pardoned Nixon for any crimes he might have committed in office. While some were glad, feeling that it was time for the nation to move on, others, including Jordan, were frustrated and angry that Nixon's complicity was never fully examined and his guilt or innocence established.

Following Watergate, Jordan continued her work as a legislator, albeit in a less public way. She next came to national attention in 1976, when she was one of two keynote speakers at the Democratic National Convention that selected Jimmy Carter to be the Democratic presidential nominee.

She was the first black woman ever to give the keynote speech. That night, she followed senator and former astronaut John Glenn, whose speech failed to quiet the crowd or even get their attention.

In contrast, Jordan electrified the convention hall, and the TV viewing audience, with her emotional appeal for unity, using her own life as an example. After mentioning the history of the Democratic party's nominating convention, Jordan continued, "[There] is something different about tonight. There is something special about tonight. What is different? What is special? I, *Barbara Jordan*, am a keynote speaker. . . . A lot of years [have] passed since 1832 [when the first Democratic party convention was held], and during that time it would have been most unusual for any national political party to ask that a Barbara Jordan deliver a keynote address . . . but tonight here I am. And I feel, notwithstanding the past, that my presence here is one additional bit of evidence that the American Dream need not forever be deferred."

She concluded that night with the following: "Now, I began this speech by commenting to you on the uniqueness of a Barbara Jordan making the keynote address. Well, I am going to close my speech by quoting a Republican president, and I ask that as you listen to these words of Abraham Lincoln, you relate them to the concept of a national community in which every last one of us participates: 'As I would not be a *slave*, so I would not be a *master*. This expresses my idea of democracy. Whatever differs from this, to the extent of the difference, is no democracy.'" The crowd loved it. Once again, Jordan had proven herself able to speak for the American people.

RETIREMENT AND TEACHING

In December 1977, Jordan announced that she would not run for office again the following year. Intensely private, she refused to divulge her reasons, but there was speculation at the time that it was either because of a growing sense of disillusionment with the political process or because of a medical problem that seemed to be affecting her mobility (she declined to discuss it at the time, but later revealed it was multiple sclerosis). She retired from Congress and from political life at the end of her term in 1978. Returning to Texas the following year, she accepted a teaching position at the Lyndon B. Johnson School of Public Affairs at the University of Texas (Austin). Her courses in policy development and political values and ethics were so well-attended that the university instituted a student lottery for admission. In 1982, she was appointed to the university's Lyndon B. Johnson Centennial Chair in National Policy. During her tenure at the university, she also served as Special Counsel on Ethics for Texas Governor Ann Richards and as Chair of the U.S. Commission on Immigration Reform for President Bill Clinton. In 1994, capping a lifetime of public service, Jordan was awarded the Presidential Medal of Honor. The citation, given to her by President Clinton, sums up Jordan's philosophy: "Guided by an unshakeable faith in the Constitution, she insists that it is the sacred duty of those who hold power to govern ethically and to preserve the rule of law."

HEALTH PROBLEMS

Jordan's health had declined over the years. Suffering from the effects of multiple sclerosis, a chronic and debilitating disease of the neuromuscular system, she used a wheel chair and a walker to get around. In 1988, she had a serious setback when she blacked out while swimming in her backyard pool. Her housemate found her face down and unconscious in the water, and pulled her out of the pool. She was revived by paramedics and made a full recovery, although doctors were never able to explain why she lost consciousness. In recent years Jordan also suffered from leukemia, a form of cancer that affects the blood. Barbara Jordan died of viral pneumonia, which had developed as a complication of leukemia, on January 17, 1996, in Austin, Texas.

JORDAN'S LEGACY

At her funeral, President Bill Clinton delivered a eulogy that evoked Jordan's spirit and her significance to many Americans. "Through the sheer force of the truth, she spoke. With the poetry of her words and the power of her voice, Barbara always stirred our national conscience. She did it as a legislator, a member of Congress, a teacher, a citizen.

"Perhaps more than anything else in the last years, for those of us who had the privilege of being around her, she did it in the incredible grace and good humor and dignity with which she bore her physical misfortunes. No matter what, there was always the dignity. When Barbara Jordan talked, we listened. . . .

"Barbara Jordan's life was a monument to the three great threads that run constantly throughout the fabric of American history—our love of liberty, our belief in progress, our search for common ground. Wherever she could and whenever she stood to speak, she jolted the nation's attention with her artful and articulate defense of the Constitution, the American Dream, and the common heritage and destiny we share, whether we like it or not. . . .

"She also did all she could as a lawmaker and as a teacher to give future generations of Americans for all time to come equal standing under that Constitution. That's what she was doing when God called her home."

ON DISABILITY

In 1992, Jordan had this to say about the effect of physical disability on her life. "My legs don't work like other people's because of multiple sclerosis, but I discovered quite early that no one was asking me to walk or run or dance. I discovered that my physical impairment did not diminish my thinking or the quality of my mind. And it did not impact on my capacity to talk.

"I assessed the physical limitations and the things that still worked. I felt I should treat the limitations as irrelevant and refuse to let them be an impediment."

HOME AND FAMILY

Jordan decided early on not to marry or have children; she felt that she had dedicated her life to politics and that she could not effectively divide her time between a family and a political career. She once said, "Politics is . . . almost totally consuming. A good marriage requires that one attend to it and not treat it as another hobby." Except for her years in Washington, she made her home in Texas. At the time of her death, Jordan lived in a spacious ranch-style home in Austin.

HOBBIES AND OTHER INTERESTS

In her spare time, Jordan enjoyed singing and playing guitar. She could often be found cheering the Lady Longhorns, the women's basketball team at the University of Texas. Along with several others, she founded People for the American Way, an organization created to counteract the influence of the religious right.

WRITINGS

Barbara Jordan: A Self-Portrait, 1979 (with Shelby Hearon)

HONORS AND AWARDS

Eleanor Roosevelt Humanities Award: 1984
Best Living Orator (International Platform Association): 1984
Charles Evans Hughes Gold Medal (NCCJ): 1987
Harry S Truman Public Service Award (Harry S Truman Scholarship Foundation): 1990
National Women's Hall of Fame: 1990
National Civil Rights Museum Freedom Award: 1992
Springarn Award (NAACP): 1992
Nelson Mandela Health and Human Rights Award: 1993
Presidential Medal of Freedom: 1994

FURTHER READING

BOOKS

Biographical Dictionary of Black Americans, 1992
Blue, Rose, and Corinne Naden. *Barbara Jordan*, 1992 (juvenile)
Encyclopedia Britannica, 1992
Hardy, Gayle J. *American Women Civil Rights Activists: Bibliographies of 68 Leaders, 1825 1992*, 1993
Haskins, James. *Barbara Jordan*, 1977 (juvenile)
Johnson, Linda Carlson. *Barbara Jordan: Congresswoman*, 1990 (juvenile)
Jordan, Barbara, and Shelby Hearon. *Barbara Jordan: A Self-Portrait*, 1979
Notable Black American Women, 1992
Roberts, Naurice. *Barbara Jordan: The Great Lady from Texas*, 1984 (juvenile)
Who's Who in America 1996
Who's Who of American Women 1995-1996
World Book Encyclopedia, 1994

PERIODICALS

Current Biography Yearbook 1974; 1993
Jet, Feb. 5, 1996, p.54
New York Times, Jan. 18, 1996, p.A1; Jan. 19, 1996, p.A28; Jan. 21, 1996, p.A18
Washington Post, Jan. 18, 1996, p.A1 and C1; Jan. 21, 1996, p.A3

Annie Leibovitz 1949-
American Photographer
Famed for Her Photographs of Rock Stars
and Other Celebrities

BIRTH

Anna-Lou Leibovitz (known as "Annie" since childhood) was born on October 2, 1949, in Waterbury, Connecticut. Her father, Sam Leibovitz, was a lieutenant colonel in the United States Air Force, and her mother, Marilyn Leibovitz, was a modern-dance teacher who had studied and performed with the renowned Martha Graham dance company. Annie was the third of their six children: Susan, Howard, Annie, Paula, Philip, and Barbara.

YOUTH

The Leibovitz family moved around frequently during Annie's childhood as her father was stationed at different air force bases both in the United States and overseas. These included Fort Worth, Texas; Biloxi, Mississippi; various posts in Alaska and Colorado; and Clark Air Force Base in the Philippines. Annie and her brothers and sisters were "military brats"—with parents in the armed forces, these children moved frequently and learned to adjust quickly to new homes, schools, and friends. As such, they were all very close and looked out for each other. "We protected ourselves against the world," Annie remembers. Wherever the family was living, she liked taking dance classes, and when there was no dance teacher available, her mother would start a class herself. Annie also learned to play the guitar a little and liked singing folk songs.

EDUCATION

Leibovitz received her elementary education at many different schools because her family was always on the move. She graduated in 1966 from Northwood High School in Silver Spring, Maryland. In 1967, she enrolled at the San Francisco Art Institute in California to study painting. She also took a night course in photography and soon left her painting studies to concentrate on photography. During her junior year, she went to Israel for a work-study program on a *kibbutz* (a communal farming community). She returned to college, but before finishing, she was hired in 1970 as a photographer by *Rolling Stone* magazine.

CHOOSING A CAREER

Leibovitz became interested in photography while still young. Her mother, Marilyn, was always taking snapshots of the family, and Annie enjoyed thumbing through photo albums containing hundreds of pictures taken during their travels over the years. She bought her first camera while visiting her father in the Philippines in 1968 and took some memorable photographs of Filipinos with American soldiers from Clark Air Force Base. The next year, while on a work-study program in Israel, she took pictures of archaeological excavations of the ruins of King Solomon's temple. On her return from Israel to San Francisco in 1970, she took some shots of an antiwar demonstration, including one of the noted Beat poet Allen Ginsberg. Leibovitz did not think much of these photos herself, but her boyfriend at the time, a newspaper photographer, urged her to show them to *Rolling Stone* magazine, then based in San Francisco. To her surprise, the editors were greatly impressed, signed her up on the spot, and sent her right out on assignment to shoot concert photos of Grace Slick, then lead singer of the rock group Jefferson Airplane. Leibovitz's career was off to a quick start.

CAREER HIGHLIGHTS

Leibovitz spent the next 13 years working as a photographer for *Rolling Stone* magazine. Starting in 1970 as a staff photographer, she was soon in New York City doing a photo session with John Lennon of the Beatles and was thrilled to see her portrait of him appear on the magazine's cover. For the next couple of years, she traveled around the country taking pictures of blues, rock, country, and jazz performers on tour or at home. These early assignments included Tammy Wynette, Gregg and Duane Allman, Joan Baez, Alice Cooper, Ray Charles, and the Grateful Dead. Instead of glamorizing them, Leibovitz preferred to shoot her famous subjects as just plain people. One noteworthy photograph from this time is her portrait of Dixieland jazz trumpeter Louis "Satchmo" Armstrong. Other assignments included taking photos of inmates at Soledad Prison in California being visited by their wives, children, or girlfriends on Christmas Day; the launching of *Apollo 17* (the last moon shot) at Cape Kennedy, Florida; and coverage of Richard M. Nixon's departure from the White House following his resignation from the presidency. By 1973, Annie Leibovitz had become *Rolling Stone* magazine's chief photographer.

ON TOUR WITH THE ROLLING STONES

In 1975, the British rock group the Rolling Stones hired Leibovitz to be its official photographer on a six-week concert tour across the United States. This proved to be one of the most difficult, challenging, and even dangerous experiences in her life. Her objective, as a photojournalist, was to obtain intimate, revealing, candid photographs of her subjects. She followed the tried-and-true photojournalist's approach of staying as close as possible to the story and people involved, to make sure that she didn't miss any opportunity for a shot. As a result, Leibovitz got *too* close and actually became part of the reckless, angry, drug-ridden side of the rock world. She eventually became very afraid of what was happening to her. She remembers, "It seemed romantic at the time, and in the long run it got sort of ugly. . . . I told myself if I was going to survive this that I was never to let the camera go. I kept it on my body the whole time; to me it was my armor." Leibovitz's work saved her. One particular photo she took of lead performer Mick Jagger captured the twisted atmosphere of that tour. It showed his wrist and forearm with a deep, almost foot-long gash in it caused by smashing his fist through a glass window. It was freshly sewn together with surgical stitches. From then on, Leibovitz began to maintain a distance between herself and her subjects.

CELEBRITY PHOTOS

After that tour, and all during *Rolling Stone* magazine's move to New York City the following year, Leibovitz's attitude toward her photography and her working methods began to change. From the mid-1970s to the early 1980s, she was on the road shooting entertainment celebrities on assignment. She traveled all over the world for *Rolling Stone* and also sometimes for *Life, Time, Newsweek, Vogue, Esquire,* and *Ms.* magazines. Previously, Leibovitz had documented her famous subjects' off-guard, random moments as ordinary people. She took candid black-and-white shots using natural light. Now, she switched to producing carefully posed, studio-lit photographs in bright, often garish colors, accentuating her subjects' public images and celebrity status.

The result was a wildly successful series of daring and original images of pop-culture figures, often posed nude or in other unconventional ways, both humorous and outrageous. Among the best known of these photos are Leibovitz's studies of actress Meryl Streep in white clown makeup; actor Clint Eastwood standing in a dusty Western set, trussed up in ropes; comic Steve Martin wearing a light tuxedo painted over with black stripes; fashion model Lauren Hutton buried in mud; singer-actress Bette Midler smothered in roses; and perhaps the most sensational and ultimately tragic of them all, a shot of a nude John Lennon, curled like an infant around his fully dressed wife, Yoko Ono. Lennon was murdered only a few hours after this photo was taken. With such photos, according to *American Photographer* magazine, Leibovitz established herself as "the most resourceful and influential portraitist of her generation."

In 1983, an exhibition of 60 of Leibovitz's celebrity photographs opened at the Sidney Janis Gallery in New York City and then toured both the United States and Europe. In an introduction to the book that went along with the exhibit, *Annie Leibovitz: Photographs,* journalist Tom Wolfe wrote admiringly that he thought none of the famous people Leibovitz had portrayed "will impress the reader half as much as the antic eye of their portraitist." Indeed, because of her photos, Annie Leibovitz became a celebrity herself.

VANITY FAIR

After 13 years with *Rolling Stone,* Leibovitz was ready for a change, so she accepted an offer in 1983 to become chief photographer of the contemporary lifestyle magazine *Vanity Fair.* "One of the reasons that I went to *Vanity Fair,*" she said, "was that I knew I would have a broader range of subjects—writers, dancers, artists, and musicians. And I wanted to learn about glamour." She had outgrown her identity, in her own words, as "the bad girl coming from the rock and roll magazine." As a result, her photographs became more sophisticated and polished than ever, and her working methods changed once again. In the past, a photo shoot was simply between Leibovitz and her subject. Now, agents, publicists, hairstylists, and makeup artists, plus a staff of assistants, accompanied Leibovitz in the studio or on the road.

Even with creative input from others, her *Vanity Fair* pictures still had the unique Annie Leibovitz flair and excitement. Among the famous shots of this time were actress Whoopi Goldberg in a bathtub of milk; jazz great Miles Davis in bed dressed in polka-dot pajamas, with his trumpet and rose-colored glasses at his side; actor Arnold Schwarzenegger chomping on a cigar, wearing just boots and riding pants, astride a white horse; the Reverend Al Sharpton, his hair up in curlers, seated under a hair dryer in a beauty salon; and then-married actors Roseanne and Tom Arnold mud-wrestling. Quieter character studies, many in black and white, included such figures as actor Christopher Walken, basketball star Magic Johnson, religious leader the Dalai Lama, writers Susan Sontag and Peter Mattheissen, and Czech playwright and political leader Vaclav Havel.

Leibovitz's celebrity photographs have proven to be very appealing. By glamorizing celebrities, her work fulfills a typical function of photography, according to critic Andy Grundberg of the Friends of Photography center. "But she does it in a more self-aware way than we've been used to. She exaggerates the distinctive characteristics of their public images in a way that's funny and deflating." In the *New York Times*, critic Roberta Smith also explained Leibovitz's emphasis on celebrities' public images. "Ms. Leibovitz's pictures are only as interesting as the achievements or public persona of her subjects, whether she is doing editorial or advertising work. . . . [It's] hard to imagine a photographer better suited to chronicle the deep glitz of the 1980s than Ms. Leibovitz. Psychic revelation on the order of [Alfred] Stieglitz or [Diane] Arbus is not her strength. But if she rarely penetrates beneath the surface of her subjects, she does heighten or subtly parody our sense of their public persona."

RECENT WORK

Looking to branch out from her work with *Vanity Fair*, Leibovitz began doing commercial advertising in the late 1980s and early 1990s for Honda automobiles, Arrow shirts, Rose's Lime Juice, The Gap, American Express, and other large corporate clients. She also took on an extensive, two-year advertising campaign for the 1996 Summer Olympics in Atlanta, Georgia.

On the more personal, serious, and artistic side of her work as a photographer, she set time aside in 1990 to shoot the White Oak Dance Project collaboration between ballet star Mikhail Baryshnikov and modern dancer Mark Morris. Of this project—done in black-and-white, and much different from her glitzy fashion and commercial advertising styles—Leibovitz said, "I was doing work that was not necessarily to be published, so it was really shooting from the soul." She also took photographs of HIV-positive people in San Francisco. In 1992, together with writer Susan Sontag, Leibovitz visited the war-torn city of Sarajevo in Bosnia. One day while Leibovitz was driving through the city streets, a mortar

199

shell exploded right next to her car. It hit a young boy on a bicycle; he died in her car on the way to the hospital. Leibovitz's photograph of the fallen bike and the blood-smeared pavement is an unforgettable image.

CRITICAL REACTIONS

In 1991, a retrospective museum exhibit of Leibovitz's work was held at the National Portrait Gallery in Washington, D.C., and then at the International Center of Photography in New York City. She is one of only two living photographers ever to be so honored in the National Gallery. Willis Hartshorn, co-curator of the exhibition, summed up Leibovitz's 20 years of achievement by saying, "I think the thing that's most important about Annie is that her work really has come to speak for a generation of popular culture and celebrity."

But her photographs have not always been so well-received, and at times they have even caused a good deal of controversy. According to some, her focus on fame and glitter, while striking on the surface, is merely shallow and superficial. "It is a media phenomenon that illuminates neither people nor the way we live," critic Max Kozloff insists. Leibovitz herself does not fully deny this kind of criticism but points out truthfully, "Sometimes I enjoy just photographing the surface because I think it can be as revealing as going to the heart of the matter."

Leibovitz's photograph of Arnold Schwarzenegger

Writing in *New Statesman* magazine, Marina Benjamin aptly summarized opposing views of the photographer's work. Benjamin divides Leibovitz's reviewers into two camps, supporters and detractors, and then describes the viewpoints of each. "According to the former [camp], Leibovitz can do no wrong; her vision is unique, her wit unsurpassed, her ability to elicit a rare honesty from her celebrity subjects unparalleled. According to the latter [camp], her work is overcooked and one-dimensional, her vision as vacuous and superficial as the glitterati among whom she cavorts. Both groups agree on one thing: Leibovitz is difficult, a perfectionist with a fiery temper and a tendency to slave-drive her assistants. . . . My own suspicion," Benjamin continues, "is that there are two Annie Leibovitzes. One is a photographer of feeling whose inspiration is born of experience, and who has an uncanny knack for cutting through America's candy-floss self-image; the other, a hard-nosed professional with an affinity for kitsch, whose best intentions have been sacrificed on the altar of Mammon [material wealth] for the sake of ad-world exigencies." These two Annie Leibovitzes, according to Benjamin, are the intense but understated early artist whose work perfectly captured the social climate of the 1970s, and the later photographer of often overly slick, one-dimensional celebrity portraits known for their "self-conscious sophistication."

One of Leibovitz's most controversial shots was her photograph of the nude and then-pregnant actress Demi Moore for the August 1991 cover of *Vanity Fair*. It caused an uproar, both for and against the cover. Some national supermarket chains went so far as to remove the issue from their shelves, while many readers all over the country stoutly defended the photograph. Leibovitz responded to this hubbub by saying, "I thought it was a glamorous, sensational cover of Demi pregnant. It turns out to be an important photograph for women. There's a Western taboo about a woman being pregnant, even to the point where women are made to think they're not beautiful."

Leibovitz resents the habit of critics and the media to pin labels on her or her work. She points out, "When I was at *Rolling Stone*, people called me a 'rock photographer'. When I was at *Vanity Fair*, people called me a 'celebrity photographer'. And when I started doing the American Express campaign, people called me an 'advertising photographer'." But in her own mind, she states simply, "I'm just a photographer. I've always been a photographer." Looking over the span of her career up to now and her future, Leibovitz adds, "I feel there's a lot of work to be done."

MAJOR INFLUENCES

Leibovitz cites several different important influences on her work. First and foremost, her mother's snapshots of the family had the earliest and most lasting effect on her photography. "That personal closeness I certainly have incorporated in my portrait work today," she states. She cites a similar influence from the French photographer Jacques Henri Lartigue, who is famous the world over for his moving pictures of family and friends. She also admires another internationally renowned French photographer, Henri Cartier Bresson, whose keen eye captured poignant moments of life in plain, uncropped compositions. Leibovitz met and interviewed Bresson in France in 1976.

The example of other female photographers, iuncluding Diane Arbus, Nan Goldin, and Margaret Bourke-White, also encouraged Leibovitz in her early career. Susan Sontag, author of the book *On Photography*, stimulated her to think more deeply about the art form. Finally, Leibovitz acknowledges a great debt to the late designer Bea Feitler, a friend and co-worker for seven years at *Rolling Stone*. Feitler showed her that to learn and improve, Leibovitz had to look critically at her old work. When she did that, she says, "I suddenly realized what it was I was doing . . . the style. For the first time I had an identity about my work."

HOME AND FAMILY

Annie Leibovitz lives on the Upper East Side of New York City, in a Fifth Avenue apartment that has high ceilings and windows and a great view of Central Park. During the summers, she spends time at her home on Long Island, New York. Her apartment, which she describes as "just a book room and a couch room," is filled with volumes on photography. All sorts of photographs, including many of her friends and family, hang on the walls or are scattered among her things. Her 1991 book of photos was dedicated to all her brothers and sisters. Leibovitz is unmarried, and she admits that she is far too busy to have much of a personal life.

HOBBIES AND OTHER INTERESTS

Leibovitz enjoys exercise and likes to go to health spas when she has the chance. She finds her photography work so varied, interesting, and ful-filling in itself that she does not have very many other absorbing interests. If asked what she does in her spare time, she replies, "Get ready for my next shoot."

SELECTED WORKS

Annie Leibovitz, Photographs, 1983
Photographs, Annie Leibovitz, 1970-1990, 1991

HONORS AND AWARDS

Clio Award in Advertising: 1988
Infinity Award (National Center of Photography): 1990
Person of the Week (ABC Nightly News): August 1992

FURTHER READING

BOOKS

Marcus, Adrianne. *The Photojournalist: Mary Ellen Mark & Annie Leibovitz,*
   1974
Who's Who in America, 1996
Who's Who in American Art, 1995-96

PERIODICALS

American Photographer, Jan. 1984, p.38
ARTnews, Mar. 1992, p.90
Chicago Tribune, Mar. 13, 1992, p.86
Current Biography Yearbook 1991
Life, Apr. 1994, p.46
Los Angeles Times, Oct. 30, 1991, p.E1
New Statesman, Mar. 4, 1994, p.35
New York, Mar. 14, 1988, p.24
New York Times, July 25, 1991, p.C15; Sep. 8, 1991, Section 2, p.43
New York Woman, Sep. 1988, p.100
People, Nov. 18, 1991, p.31
Vanity Fair, Sep. 1991, p.204; Dec. 1993, pp.16, 145
Washington Post, Apr. 19, 1991, p.D1

ADDRESS

Jim Moffat Art and Commerce
108 West 18th Street
New York, NY 10011

Carl Lewis 1961-
American Track and Field Athlete
Winner of Nine Olympic Gold Medals in
Four Consecutive Olympics

BIRTH

Frederick Carlton Lewis was born in Birmingham, Alabama, on July 1, 1961. Both of his parents were successful collegiate athletes. His mother, Evelyn (Lawler) Lewis, traveled with an American contingent to compete as a hurdler in the Pan-American Games in 1951. His father, Bill Lewis, excelled in football and track at Tuskegee University, where he and Evelyn met. Later, both took jobs as teachers in Willingboro, New Jersey. Carl was the third of four children in the Lewis family, which also included older brothers Mack and Cleve and younger sister Carol.

YOUTH

As a boy, Carl didn't show much promise as an athlete. His sister Carol, who is two years younger than Carl and shares a close bond with him, performed better in competition early on. But Carl showed unusual determination to excel in track and field. He measured out distances in his backyard and began long jumping against his sister. In 1968, when Carl was seven years old, he was inspired by Bob Beamon's accomplishment of jumping 29 feet, 2½ inches in the Mexico City Olympics. Mexico City is 7,525 feet above sea level, however, and the thinner air probably contributed to the record-breaking jump, because the air would give less resistance to the jumper than air at a lower altitude.

Since both of their parents were outstanding athletes, Carl and his siblings were encouraged, but not pushed, to participate in sports. "A lot of parents want their kids to do something, like play tennis. A kid may be good at it, but he rebels. He wants to make his own decision," Carl's brother Cleve noted. "What they did was expose us to a lot of things and let us make out own decisions. We were all raised independent," his sister Carol added.

The Lewis children grew up in Willingboro, New Jersey, a suburb of Philadelphia, Pennsylvania, where their parents taught high school. Evelyn also founded the Willingboro Track Club for young athletes in the area. Without a great deal of funding, the Lewises could not afford professional-looking uniforms. The team wore white shirts with the letters WTC stenciled on them. "We got cutouts for the letters and sprayed blue paint on the shirts, and they wore whatever shorts they had. We didn't have warm-ups or anything like that," Evelyn Lewis recalled. From its humble beginnings, the club grew rapidly through the 1970s. The Lewis parents eventually had nearly 300 athletes competing for them as members of the club.

Lewis began running with the club at the age of eight, which provided him with many chances to participate in meets. At the age of 12, at a track event in Philadelphia, he met Jesse Owens, an Olympic champion to whom Lewis would ultimately be linked throughout his career. Owens recommended that the other youngsters in attendance look to the "spunky" Lewis as an example as they set their goals. It appeared that Owens's advice might have been misguided, however, since Lewis's performances at that point were mediocre. "Carl used to come home from meets and say, 'Name the brand of track shoe and I'll tell you how many spikes it has,'" his father remembered. "He knew. He was always looking at the back of all those different track shoes when he ran."

EDUCATION

HIGH SCHOOL

Lewis attended Kennedy High School for his first two years, and then transferred to Willingboro High School. This move was partly due to his poor performance in a relay event at an important track meet for Kennedy. Lewis made the mistake of wearing the wrong spikes for the event, and he failed to hold a lead that his teammates had built up during the race. Afterward, he received stern lectures from the other relay runners about his performance. Lewis then decided to transfer to a new school and devote himself entirely to his sport.

During and following his sophomore year in high school at Kennedy, Lewis went through a growth spurt that helped him approach his current height of about six feet, three inches. For a time he had to walk on crutches to alleviate the pain caused by such rapid growth. The added size allowed Lewis to compete with other athletes.

By the time he enrolled at Willingboro, Lewis had improved tremendously. Almost immediately he became a standout in both the 100-yard dash and what would become his signature event, the long jump. At first, the coaches were reluctant to allow him to compete in both events, fearing that practicing so much might harm his physical development. So Lewis made a deal with his coaches. If he could jump more than 25 feet and run 100 yards in less than 9.5 seconds, they would let him decide the events in which he wanted to compete.

Lewis had aspired to reach a long jump distance of 25 feet since the beginning of his high-school track career. He even wore a jacket with the number 25 on it, advertising the goal toward which he strove. Lewis first achieved that goal at the 1978 junior national championships in Memphis, Tennessee, when he was just 17. He ran the 100 meters in 9.3 seconds and leapt a remarkable 25 feet, 9 inches. After that, the coaches let him pick his own events. As a senior, Lewis developed into one of the top five long jumpers in the entire world, and by the time he graduated, he was considered the top-ranked prospect for track and field in the country.

COLLEGE

In 1979 Lewis entered the University of Houston on an athletic scholarship. He majored in communications there, but he devoted as much attention to athletics as he did to academics. In fact, his decision to attend the University of Houston was based, in large part, on the opportunity to work with Tom Tellez, a nationally respected coach who might help him improve his long jump technique. Tellez advised Lewis to increase the length of his approach run from less than 150 feet to more than 160 feet. The extra distance allowed him to build up his speed to approximately 27 miles per hour en route to the jump pit. Lewis also learned to employ a "hitch kick" as he launched himself into the air, pedaling his arms and legs to maintain his balance and to lengthen his jump. "What I do is totally unnatural. I leave the board going almost forward. Most people go up and look beautiful in the air, but they come straight down. When I'm in the air, I rotate forward, and I have to fight to keep my balance or I'll fall flat on my face. That's why I use a hitch kick to swing my balance backward," Lewis explained. "My best attribute is my balance in the air. I was always a terrible basketball shooter, but I could double and triple pump in the air because I had balance."

During practices Tellez broke the jump into coachable elements, forcing Lewis to focus on isolated aspects of the exercise. One session would focus entirely on the approach, for example, with Lewis putting forth only enough effort during the jump to avoid injury. Another session would be devoted entirely to the hitch kick. The desired end result was the combination of all of these isolated elements into a perfect jump. Lewis's desire to learn and improve aided the coach's efforts. "Carl is interested in the why of things," Tellez related. "He's always asking 'How can I be better?' He thinks about what he has to do to jump far and run fast. His antennae are always out. I say something, he does it, and it's locked in. Teaching, you keep trying to punch the right button. With Carl, you punch one button and—boom—he's got it. With other kids you've got to punch 11 or 12 buttons to get them to the same place. Carl is a great athlete, opening himself up completely and always to you. He never closes his mind to anything."

After only a year under Tellez's guidance, Lewis earned a spot on the 1980 United States Olympic Team in the long jump. Unfortunately, President Jimmy Carter decided to boycott the 1980 Olympics in Moscow to protest the Soviet invasion of Afghanistan. Along with many other American athletes, Carl and his sister Carol—who had qualified for the women's long jump—were thus prevented from competing.

Despite this disappointment, Lewis continued to compete in the many other national and international track and field meets that are held each year. In 1981, he became the first competitor to win both a track event and a field event in the National Collegiate Athletic Association (NCAA) Indoor Championships when he was victorious in both the 100 meters and the long jump. Through 1981 and 1982, Lewis repeated the feat on more than one occasion in major meets. In the long jump he regularly broke 28 feet; in the 100 meters he consistently crossed the finish line in under 10 seconds. For his efforts in 1981, Lewis received the Sullivan Award, presented by the Amateur Athletic Union to the best amateur athlete of the year. Comparisons between Lewis and Jesse Owens became more frequent.

In the fall of his junior year at Houston, Lewis skipped a history exam, which ultimately resulted in his being declared academically ineligible to participate in sports. He then began running as a member of California's Santa Monica Track Club. Under the auspices of the new association, he jumped 30 feet at a meet in Indianapolis. This jump, which was not aided by altitude, would have shattered Beamon's record had it been deemed legal. The jump was disallowed, however, when an official claimed that Lewis fouled by crossing the line before launching himself. Others disagreed with the official, though, and the call proved controversial. Lewis went on to win three gold medals at the Helsinki world championships in 1983. He also finished first in three events at the Athletics Congress Outdoor Championships.

CAREER HIGHLIGHTS

Earning a living, for most Olympic athletes, is very difficult. And Carl Lewis, at first, was no exception. Top professional athletes in certain sports can earn tremendous sums, but for many others, in sports like gymnastics, swimming, and track and field, there is no hope for a career in a professional league with big salaries. It is even more difficult for amateur athletes. In the past, amateurs were not allowed to receive any pay for their sport. This was a real hardship for the athletes, trying to hold down a job to earn a living and still make time for training. Over the years, the governing bodies for different sports have created different rules defining what constituted amateur status. In track and field, changes were made in 1981 and 1985 that gradually loosened the rules to allow athletes to be paid for competing and for endorsing products.

Lewis came of age as an athlete during this period of transition, while the rules governing eligibility for amateurs were changing. Over the years, he has been able to take advantage of these changing rules to ensure a decent living standard. Even as a college student, he attracted attention from companies eager to take advantage of his celebrity to promote their products. Although the rules at that time forbade the practice of offering shoe contracts to amateurs, Lewis was still able to earn thousands of dollars for wearing Nike shoes. Before committing to Nike, he had received money and equipment from other shoe companies in less lucrative—but nonetheless unauthorized—arrangements.

Lewis has always felt strongly, for himself and others, about the importance of earning a good living while training. Throughout his career, he has looked with disdain at the term "amateurism," knowing that athletes who spend much of their time competing can be prevented from cashing in on their success if they are subject to the rules of governing bodies. "Amateurism is the strongest form of discrimination in sports because it discriminates against the poor," he stated. "If we want sports to go back to the wealthy, let's make it amateur again." Lewis has actively fought for the rights of the athletes competing in his sport and has pushed for the ruling bodies of track and field to promote it more aggressively.

1984 OLYMPICS

By 1984, Lewis was the focus of intense media attention. At the 1984 Millrose Games in Madison Square Garden, New York, Lewis set a world indoor record in the long jump of 28 feet, 10¼ inches, equaling his personal best. Many were eager to see what he would accomplish at the Olympics, to be held in Los Angeles that year. But by that point, he was receiving almost as much attention for his activities off the field. He recorded a song, "Going for the Gold," which he co-wrote in anticipation of the Olympics. During the pre-Olympic buildup, his manager, Joe Douglas, added to the hype by declaring that Lewis's earning potential following the games would be on par with singer Michael Jackson. "There are going to be some absolutely unheard-of things coming from me," Lewis predicted at the start of the games. Such statements, coupled with his aloof behavior, earned Lewis a reputation for being arrogant, egotistical, calculating, and overly concerned with his image. This reputation has plagued him ever since.

Lewis qualified for the long jump and the 100- and 200-meter runs and was picked to be a member of the 4 x 100-meter relay team. His entry in four events drew inevitable comparisons with Owens, who won four track-and-field gold medals in 1936. Lewis captured his first gold in the 100 meters with a time of 9.99 seconds. But he disappointed some fans and caused the media to question his motives when he grabbed an American flag from an onlooker and paraded around the track with it. Combined with Douglas's earlier remarks, the victory lap made it seem as if Lewis's motives had more to do with promoting himself than representing his country.

In the long jump, Lewis leapt 28 feet, ¼ inch in his first attempt. After a foul on his second jump, he declined to try again, passing on what could have been four more attempts. Though his initial mark was good enough to win a second gold medal, many spectators felt deprived. They had hoped to see Lewis achieve a more spectacular, possibly record-breaking jump. He went on to win the 200 meters with an Olympic record time of 19.8 seconds. He finished the 1984 Olympics by winning his fourth gold medal when the American team won the 4 x 100-meter relay.

Instead of raking in endorsements based on his performance, however, Lewis actually lost the sponsorship of one of his major patrons, Nike. The company felt that Lewis had lost some of his marketability due to the image he created outside of competition. In addition, an endorsement offer from a major soft-drink company—which he could have signed prior to the Olympics—was retracted. Lewis "became so big and so hyped that the bandwagon became unappealing before people even started jumping on it," according to sports agent Brad Hunt. "I don't think the sporting press, and that's where your image starts, wanted the Olympic hero to be Michael Jackson. They wanted the Olympic hero to be Jesse Owens, who up until that time was the symbol of Olympia, the man who did it for the glory of the country and the thrill of participation. The press still laps that up." Lewis began to resent the expectations placed on him, particularly the comparisons to Owens. "They started comparing me as a person to Jesse Owens," he stated. "I was supposed to be humble and nice and say, "Thank you for coming out," and be totally accessible. I'm not supposed to be able to speak clearly, and decipher what's going on in the media. I'm supposed to be the typical amateur who's 22 and scared to death and can't believe he won the Olympics."

With limited financial opportunities in the United States, Lewis went overseas to earn money with endorsements and appearances in track meets. In Europe, he commonly received anywhere from $50,000 to $100,000 per appearance. In Japan, he promoted shoes, sports drinks, and film. In theory, Lewis's status as an "amateur" allowed him to withdraw only $7,200 in so-called training expenses from a personal trust fund set up by the track and field governing body. But like many other "amateur"

athletes, he was able to bend the rules. The money he earned allowed him to adopt a comfortable lifestyle and to purchase several expensive cars, an extensive wardrobe, and high-priced furnishings for his home in a wealthy part of Houston.

1988 OLYMPICS

In the mid-1980s, Lewis entered into a rivalry with Ben Johnson, a Canadian athlete who often ran head to head against Lewis in the 100 meters. When Johnson defeated him at the 1987 World Championships in Rome, Lewis alluded to the probability that some competitors in the sport were using performance-enhancing drugs. At the 1988 Olympics in Seoul, South Korea, Johnson again beat Lewis in the event. But Johnson tested positive for steroids, and Lewis was handed the gold medal and the world record that Johnson had claimed in the event. Along with the long jump, it was one of two gold medals that Lewis won in the games.

The fallout from the discovery of Johnson's steroid use affected the sport. Track and field declined in popularity, as audiences dwindled at the major meets and corporate sponsors withdrew their support. Some felt that Lewis was partly to blame for the negative attention he had brought to the sport. In 1989, Lewis himself was accused of drug use by a competitor, Darrell Robinson, who claimed that Lewis had used performance-enhancing substances in 1982. Lewis later won a defamation suit against Robinson, but the clearing of his name did not make up for the endorsement opportunities lost by the muddying of his reputation. Lewis has always tested clean, and he has fought an ongoing campaign to eliminate drugs from his sport.

A WORLD RECORD

By 1990, Lewis was perceived by many as having lost a step. His long jumps—although still impressive—did not rank with his phenomenal jumps of years past, and his 100-meter races usually resulted in times of over 10 seconds. That was hardly surprising, though. Lewis was almost 30, which is considered old for a sprinter. However, he returned to form the following year and silenced detractors during the World Championships in Tokyo, Japan. Having lost his world record in the 100 meters to Leroy Burrell, who ran it in 9.90 seconds in June 1991, Lewis reclaimed the record by running 100 meters in 9.86 seconds. In doing so, he fulfilled his goal of achieving an undisputed individual world record. Speaking to reporters afterward, Lewis claimed that his father—who died in 1987 and was buried with Carl's first gold medal—played a major role in his accomplishment. "This is a most special time," he noted. "[My father] can't be here with me, but I know he's with me. When there's a clear sky, he's able to see through the clouds. Tonight, he was able to see through the dark, and I was happy I was able to do what I could do."

During the same meet, five days later, Lewis participated in the long jump. Confident that Bob Beamon's mark of 29 feet, 2½ inches would be broken on that night, he set his sights on achieving that goal and then retiring from the long jump. Even though Lewis stayed airborne for more than 29 feet on three of his jumps, it was fellow American Mike Powell who captured the glory. As Lewis recalled, "When I went 29, 2¾ (wind-aided) on my third jump, it was, 'Yeah, that's it. You're putting on a clinic.' Then Mike jumped 29, 4½. No problem. In my mind, I knew I was going to jump farther. No doubt in my mind. It was going to be a great way to go out. Then, I didn't do it."

Lewis's performance at the World Championships put an end to questions about his age. "People ask, 'Why are you still in the sport?' I'm still in it because I enjoy it," he stated. "That's the way it started for me. The middle of my career, the mid-to-late '80s, was for setting up my future. But, now, the money part is straight. I'm set for life. The '90s are for fun." In the early 1990s, Lewis found that the media no longer portrayed him as negatively as they had in the late 1980s."I'm only 30 years old and I've had to deal with more than most people in an entire lifetime," he remarked. "I went through the Olympics and people tried to put me down and tear me down and force me to retire. And for some silly reason I kept on running and ignored them, and now I've made it and I'm reaping the benefits of that perseverance. I'm publicly bigger than I've ever been, and it's a great thing to go through a career and be at this stage and everyone loves you the most." Before the trials for the 1992 Summer Olympics in Barcelona, Spain, Lewis signed an endorsement deal with Panasonic. Despite his many overseas contracts, this was the first lucrative deal for him in the United States since early in his career, and it was a relief for Lewis to finally feel accepted at home. That same year, he was also a member of the Santa Monica Track Club's 4 x 200-meter relay team, which set a world record in the event with a time of 1:19.11.

1992 OLYMPICS

At the 1992 Olympic trials in New Orleans, Lewis disappointed himself and his coach. He failed to qualify for the 100 meters, missed a chance to compete in the 200 meters by .01 seconds, and only made the long jump team by placing second behind Mike Powell. Still, Lewis remained optimistic about his chances in Barcelona. "A lot of people are going: 'Oh, my God. Oh, my God,'" he admitted. "But I've accepted it. I'm not really devastated. That's just the way it is. I can either commit suicide or go to the Olympics and get a gold medal in the long jump." Lewis achieved his goal by beating Mike Powell and earning the gold medal. He also was on the relay team that won gold in the 4 x 100-meter relay.

After the 1992 Olympics, Lewis continued to achieve occasional successes. He suffered tissue damage in his upper back when he was involved in a car accident in February 1993. He rebounded that summer, however, to run the fastest time of the year to that point in the 200 meters. He beat an impressive field of runners, including current world-record holder Michael Johnson, with a time of 19.99 seconds. As his career progressed, Lewis shifted his focus and concentrated more exclusively on major meets. "These meets are a little more sweet now than when you start off," he noted. "Things change as you mature. I've been confronted with the end of my career many times. It makes it special that I work harder than I did before. I haven't decided when to quit. I'm still running well, I guess. And this is no time to go because we're just starting to make real money."

1996 OLYMPICS

At the 1996 Olympic trials, Lewis surprised many people by qualifying for the American team in the long jump event at the age of 35. It took his best jump of the year—27 feet, 2¾ inches—to make the team, and he made it by just an inch. At the Olympics, Lewis looked shaky in the qualifying rounds and in his first two jumps of the finals, but he returned to his old form in his third attempt. Lewis launched into the air, accompanied by the flashes of thousands of cameras in the stands, and came down in first place with his best jump in four years, 27 feet, 10¾ inches. Remarkably, Lewis won the event and earned a ninth career gold medal. His accomplishment of winning gold medals in the same event in four consecutive Olympics matched the record set by discus thrower Al Oerter and prompted many to call him the greatest Olympic athlete in history. Considering his past love-hate relationship with fans, he was gratified to receive a lengthy ovation from spectators in Atlanta in recognition of his achievement. As an added bonus, Lewis's mother actually watched his winning jump; before that point she had always kept her eyes shut during his performances. "I'll be sitting there, but I won't watch [my children] compete, I never do," Evelyn Lewis explained. "I close my eyes and say a little prayer, 'Lord, help them to do their very best.' I hold my breath sometimes, too. If they were milers, I wouldn't survive."

Lewis created yet another Olympic controversy when, after winning the long jump, he lobbied in the media for a chance to earn an unprecedented tenth gold medal as a member of the 4 x 100 relay team. Earlier, Lewis had refused to practice with or try out for the relay team, and his individual time was not fast enough to qualify for the race. Public opinion was decidedly mixed on the issue of whether he should be allowed to compete. Some people hoped to see Lewis win another medal, while others felt it would be unfair for him to replace a lesser-known and more qualified athlete who had worked hard to earn a place on the relay team. The coach finally decided against letting Lewis run, and the issue became irrelevant when the Americans were upset by Canada and had to settle for a silver medal in the event.

FUTURE PLANS

Lewis has discussed plans of becoming a broadcaster after he retires from competition. In fact, he majored in communications when he attended the University of Houston. He has also mentioned the possibility of entering politics. "I am extremely interested in the political scene of today and what's going on," he stated. "I've been through a lot of the things that politicians have to go through in political life, and I've weathered those storms."

HOME AND FAMILY

Lewis is not married, and throughout his career he has had to dismiss rumors that he is a homosexual. To this day, he maintains a close relationship with his mother and his siblings. He lives in a luxurious home in Houston.

MAJOR INFLUENCES

In addition to the man to whom he is most often compared, Jesse Owens, Lewis counts his parents among those who most actively influenced his career in track and field. He has said that before he began achieving success in sports, his parents pushed him to develop his potential. "They would urge me to do drills right after a meet, when I could have been resting or doing something with my friends," he recalled. "And I always had to do extra drills. If Carol was on the track for one hour, I would have to be there for two. Back then, I was never sure why I was being pushed. But now I think I have a pretty good idea. My parents knew how much it hurt me to be the worst [athlete] in the family, knew how much I wanted to succeed, and they spotted some talent in me before anyone else did, myself included. They thought that if they pushed me, they could help me develop that talent."

HOBBIES AND OTHER INTERESTS

With the Santa Monica Track Club, Lewis developed a unique line of sport fashions which sold well in Europe and found a niche in the United States. He is also an avid shopper. "I do like to have things I take pride in. I like to spend money in that sense," he admitted. He has also dabbled in singing and acting.

WRITINGS

Inside Track: My Professional Life in Amateur Track and Field, 1992 (with Jeffrey Marx)

HONORS AND AWARDS

High School All-American, 200 meters and long jump: 1978
NCAA Champion, 100 meters and long jump: 1981
Sullivan Award (Amateur Athletic Union): 1981
World Championships, 100 meters: 1983, first place; 1991, first place
World Championships, long jump: 1983, first place; 1987, first place
World Championships, 4 x 100 meter relay: 1983, first place; 1987, first place; 1991, first place
Olympic Track and Field, 100 meters: 1984, gold medal; 1988, gold medal
Olympic Track and Field, 200 meters: 1984, gold medal; 1988, silver medal

Olympic Track and Field, long jump: 1984, gold medal; 1988, gold medal; 1992, gold medal; 1996, gold medal
Olympic Track and Field, 4 x 100 meter relay: 1984, gold medal; 1992, gold medal
Jesse Owens Award: 1985
World Record, 100 meters: 1991
World Record, 4 x 200 meter relay: 1992

FURTHER READING

BOOKS

Aaseng, Nathan. *Carl Lewis: Legend Chaser,* 1985 (juvenile)
Coffey, Wayne R. *Carl Lewis,* 1993 (juvenile)
Contemporary Black Biography, 1993
Grolier Library of North American Biographies: Athletes, Vol. 2, 1994
Lewis, Carl, and Jeffrey Marx. *Inside Track: My Professional Life in Amateur Track and Field,* 1992
Lincoln Library of Sports Champions, Vol. 8, 1993
Who's Who in America, 1996
Who's Who among Black Americans, 1994

PERIODICALS

Boys' Life, July 1996, p.14
Chicago Tribune, June 10, 1984, p.C1
Current Biography Yearbook 1984
Detroit Free Press, Aug. 3, 1996, p.B1
Los Angeles Times, Apr. 16, 1992, p.C1
New York Times, June 6, 1982, Section 5, p.1; July 22, 1984, Section 5, p.3; July 23, 1990, p.C5; Aug. 26, 1991, p.C1; July 31, 1996, p.B9; Aug. 7, 1996, p.B12
New York Times Magazine, June 17, 1984, p.13; July 19, 1992, p.31
Newsweek, Aug. 10, 1984, p.26; June 17, 1996, p.68; Aug. 12, 1996, p.25
Sporting News, July 30, 1984, p.198; July 24, 1995, p.8
Sports Illustrated, May 30, 1994, p.62; Sep. 19, 1994, p.74; May 8, 1995, p.56; Apr. 15, 1996, p.84; Aug. 5, 1996, p.54
Time, Aug. 12, 1996, p.44

ADDRESS

United States Olympic Committee
One Olympic Place
Colorado Springs, CO 80909

Jim Lovell 1928-
American Former Astronaut and Businessman
Commander of Apollo 13 Mission for NASA

BIRTH

James Arthur Lovell, Jr., was born March 25, 1928, in Cleveland, Ohio. He was the only child of James and Blanche Lovell. The family later moved to Milwaukee, Wisconsin. Jim was 12 when his dad died.

YOUTH

Jim grew up in Milwaukee and showed an early interest in space travel, but not the kind for which he would become famous. Instead, he loved Flash Gordon and Buck Rogers, stars of early sci-fi films featuring adventures in outer space.

When he was just a teenager, Jim began to build model rockets. In high school, he and a friend built a liquid fuel rocket that didn't work. Next, under the advice of his high school chemistry teacher, Lovell developed a solid-fuel rocket, using wood, home-made gunpowder, and glue, with a long stick as a guidance system. It exploded 80 feet in the air.

Jim was also active in the Boy Scouts, and he fulfilled all the requirements for Eagle Scout when he was 17. He remembers that Scouts played an important part in his life after his dad's death. "The scouting movement gave me the masculine companionship so important to a teen-age boy," he recalls.

EDUCATION

Lovell attended the public schools in Milwaukee and graduated from Juneau High School in 1946. His early interest in rockets led him to write several space pioneers to ask for recommendations for a college where he could pursue his interests. They recommended Stanford University or MIT (Massachusetts Institute of Technology), but those schools were far too expensive for Lovell. Instead, he attended the University of Wisconsin for two years, then transferred to the Naval Academy at Annapolis. Lovell graduated from Annapolis in 1952 with a bachelor's degree in science.

CAREER HIGHLIGHTS

THE NAVY

After graduation from Annapolis, Lovell entered the Navy. He served as a test pilot and flight instructor for several years, and in 1958, when President Dwight D. Eisenhower founded NASA (the National Aeronautics and Space Administration), Lovell applied to become an astronaut. He didn't get in on his first try, but in 1961 he reapplied and joined the elite group of test pilots and engineers who pioneered the U.S. space program.

NASA AND THE U.S. SPACE PROGRAM

The modern age of space exploration began in 1957 when the Soviet Union launched Sputnik I, the first unmanned satellite. Both the Soviet Union and the U.S. had the rocket technology necessary to place an orbiting vehicle into space. That technology had been developed as part of weapons delivery systems used in World War II. After the war, the U.S. and the Soviet Union emerged as the two superpowers in the world. These two nations became locked in the conflict known as the Cold War—a war defined not by open warfare, but by escalating hostilities between the two nations and the division of the major world governments into pro-U.S. and pro-Soviet nations. With the Cold War raging, the two superpowers began what was known as the "Arms Race," in which the two nations were engaged in a potentially deadly competition to create ever more powerful weapons. The Arms Race led to the "Space Race," with the goal to be the first nation to land a man on the moon.

Yuri Gagarin, a Soviet cosmonaut, was the first person in space. He made a one-orbit flight on April 12, 1961, aboard the Soviet spacecraft Vostok. Less than a month later, Alan Shepard became the first U.S. astronaut to fly in space, as part of Project Mercury. The main NASA programs in those early years were Mercury, Gemini, and Apollo. Mercury's mission was to gather data on space and the capabilities of the rockets and spacecraft. The purpose of the Gemini missions was to prepare for a landing on the moon. Lovell's early years with NASA were spent on advance work for the Gemini program. As he told *Life* magazine at the time: "We've been getting a good smattering of everything, from celestial mechanics and rocket propulsion to the geology of the moon. In my special assignment, recovery and landing systems, the actual landing on the moon intrigues me most."

GEMINI 7

Lovell's first mission was aboard Gemini 7 in December 1965. With Frank Borman, Lovell flew for 14 days in an orbit around Earth. At that time, it was the longest mission anyone had ever flown in space. During the Gemini 7 mission, Lovell and Borman delicately maneuvered their spacecraft to dock with the Gemini 6 spacecraft, completing the first successful space rendezvous in history.

GEMINI 12

In November 1966 Lovell flew on the last of the Gemini missions, Gemini 12. This time his fellow astronaut was Buzz Aldrin, and the two made a four-day orbit of the Earth. They gathered information for Lovell's next mission, in which NASA astronauts would orbit the moon.

APOLLO 8

In December 1968 Lovell, along with Borman and William Anders, took part in the first manned orbit of the Moon. The orbit took place on Christmas Eve, and members of the crew sent dramatic pictures back to Earth and read passages from the book of Genesis from the Bible. In addition to its scientific importance, the Apollo 8 mission produced one of the modern era's most memorable photographs: a view of the Earth rising over the edge of the moon.

On July 20, 1969, the U.S. won its race against the Soviet Union to put a man on the moon, as Apollo 11 astronaut Neil Armstrong became the first person to land and walk on the moon. Later that year, the crew of Apollo 12 also landed on the moon to continue America's pioneering lunar explorations. Five months later, in April 1970, it was finally Jim Lovell's turn.

APOLLO 13

In a career that spanned eight years and four missions, Lovell logged a total of seven million miles in space, a record in the history of space flight. But he is best remembered for a six-day mission that went terribly wrong and that he, his crew, and NASA's Mission Control in Houston made into one of the great triumphs of teamwork, courage, and technical know-how in the history of space travel.

By the time Apollo 13 blasted off from Cape Canaveral on April 11, 1970, Americans had become rather blase about missions to the moon. The audience that was electrified by the first moonwalk in July 1969 had lost interest by the time Lovell and his crew, Fred Haise and Jack Swigert, attempted to make the third moon landing in history. The Apollo 13 spacecraft lifted off aboard a Saturn rocket that blasted it out of Earth's orbit. The ship that was to take them to the moon was made of three basic parts: the service module, which contained the fuel, oxygen, and pro-pulsion systems; the com-mand module, which was the crew's main base during flight; and the lunar module, which would take them to and from the moon's surface.

For the first day of the mis-sion, everything went accord-ing to plan. The crew broad-cast what they thought was a live interview from space for the TV audience at home. But although the crew didn't know it, the major TV networks opted not to air the show from space—they just didn't think the audience cared to watch.

Then something went terribly, horribly wrong. Fifty-six hours into the mission, the space-craft was rocked by a huge blast. "As soon as I heard the bang, I looked at my co-pilots," Lovell recalled. "Their expressions told me everything. They didn't have a clue. They were as startled as I was. I looked out the window and saw a big cloud of oxygen venting from the ship. That's when I knew we were in serious trouble." He radioed to NASA Mission Control in Houston the now-famous line: "Houston, we've had a problem."

The oxygen tank on the side of the spacecraft had exploded, cutting off the crew's oxygen, electrical power, and propulsion system. Two hundred thousand miles from Earth, the crew of Apollo 13 had to figure out how to get their damaged spacecraft home. Mission Control in Houston immediately went to work to figure out how long the crew could survive in their ship, how much fuel was left to get them back, and how to utilize what resources they had left. First, the crew had to abandon the larger command module and spend the duration of the flight in the tiny lunar module. Created to support two men during a moon landing for a total of 50 hours, the lunar module now had to serve as the main craft for the three astronauts for 90 hours.

They knew the lunar landing had to be scrubbed. They also knew they would need to circle the moon and use the momentum of the moon's gravitational pull—like a slingshot—to send them back to Earth. The crew performed a rocket firing—called a burn—to take them around the moon and head them back toward Earth. They disappeared behind the moon, losing radio contact with Earth. Swigert and Haise took pictures of the lunar surface. "Boys, take a good look at the moon," said Lovell. "It's going to be a long time before anybody gets up here again."

After they were around the moon, the astronauts performed a second rocket firing, and the craft was on target for the return trip. Now, to save all energy possible for the difficult re-entry, all the ship's systems were shut down. The temperature in the module dropped to 38 degrees. It was so cold they couldn't sleep. They were, in Lovell's words, "tired, hungry, wet, cold, and dehydrated." Fred Haise developed an infection. Other problems plagued the crew. Three astronauts in the close quarters of the lunar module had created a toxic level of carbon monoxide; Houston had to improvise a way to vent the gas and keep the oxygen at livable levels.

Meanwhile, Mission Control was working furiously to devise a way to get the batteries in the command module in working order to power the ship's re-entry. After days in the ice cold, the batteries needed to be fired to propel the ship into the Earth's atmosphere. And the command module had to be aligned exactly to the necessary trajectory for re-entry. They needed to reenter the Earth's atmosphere at an altitude of 400,000 feet, and within a narrow corridor only 30 miles in diameter. They had to come in at an angle of six and a half degrees to the Earth's surface. If they erred more than one degree in either direction, the ship would either burn up on re-entry, or bounce back into space. And they had no power to make another attempt.

As they prepared for re-entry Swigert looked out the window and noted that "Earth is whistling in like a high-speed freight train." With 11 hours to go, they fired up the lunar module, whose power they needed to guide them until the command module would take over. They then jettisoned the damaged service module, the site of the explosion. All three astronauts watched as the module floated by. An astonished Lovell radioed to Houston: "There's one whole side of that spacecraft missing."

Despite the cold and the moisture that had formed from space, the batteries worked in the command module when they were fired up. The crew settled into their original seats and braced for reentry. One last disaster was yet to be averted: the crew didn't know if the heat shield that had to protect them from the intense heat of reentry had been damaged in the explosion.

As Apollo 13 sped back to Earth, one billion people watched on television and listened to radio coverage of the event. After ignoring the launch, the people of the world were galvanized by the plight of the crew. The *Christian Science Monitor* wrote that: "Never in recorded history has a journey of such peril been watched and waited-out by almost the entire human race."

During the four-minute reentry, radio contact was lost between Houston and Apollo 13. The world watched and waited as the minutes clicked slowly by. Then, Swigert's voice came in over the radio, and a roar went up at Mission Control and around the world. The crew was safe. They splashed down in the Pacific Ocean and were rescued by a waiting U.S. ship.

Did the crew ever panic during their ordeal? "Certainly we had the impulse," says Lovell, in his characteristic low-key way. "Anybody would. But if we had panicked during Apollo 13, all we would have done is bounce off the walls for 10 minutes. Then we would be right back where we started, with 10 less minutes to figure things out."

And what if they had not been able to get home? "We would have carried on with the mission, operating under a principle called 'downmoding.' You have to keep asking yourself, 'OK, what can we accomplish with what we've got left.' In an eerie image of what could have happened, Lovell relates that, because there was no way to rescue a lunar flight, the crew of Apollo 13 would have continued to orbit the Earth, and "the ship might have been out there longer than the species that launched it."

In retrospect, Lovell calls the flight of Apollo 13 "a successful failure. We proved we could operate in real time to bring a crew home safely after an accident nobody had ever dreamed would happen."

When asked if they were ever afraid during the mission, Lovell explains: "We were all test pilots. And the only thing we could do was to try to get home. The idea of despair never occurred to us, because we were always optimistic we would get home."

RETIREMENT FROM NASA AND A NEW CAREER IN BUSINESS

For Lovell, the true heroes of the Apollo 13 mission were the ground control operatives—the men who were responsible for helping them to return from space alive. He and his fellow Apollo 13 astronauts knew they wanted to put the record of their mission on paper, but time and other commitments got in the way. Fred Haise left the space program in 1979 to pursue a career with the Grummand Corporation. Jack Swigert, after leaving NASA in 1973, entered politics. Shortly after being elected to Congress in 1982, he died of cancer. In 1973, Lovell retired from NASA and moved into private industry, first as president of Fisk Telephone Systems (1977-1981) and then to Centel Corporation, where he served as senior vice president from 1980 until his retirement in 1991.

LOST MOON: THE PERILOUS VOYAGE OF APOLLO 13

With time on his hands for the first time since the Apollo 13 Mission, Lovell was ready to write his version of the events. In 1991 he received a letter from Jeffrey Kluger, an editor with *Discover* magazine and an instructor at New York University, who told him that he wanted to work with Lovell to write the story of Apollo 13. Lovell liked Kluger's proposal and writing style, and the two became co-authors.

Lovell realized that he had to research the story to represent all sides. So he and Kluger spent two years reviewing tapes and transcripts of the mission and interviewing the people involved. The result was the book *Lost Moon: The Perilous Voyage of Apollo 13* (after the success of the movie version, the book was rereleased under the title *Apollo 13*). Published in 1994, the book was a great success, and it drew the attention of TV and film director Ron Howard, whose movie credits include *Splash* and *Cocoon*.

Now a Major Motion Picture from Universal Pictures
A RON HOWARD FILM
Starring

TOM HANKS   KEVIN BACON   BILL PAXTON   GARY SINISE   ED HARRIS

"Houston, we have a problem."

APOLLO 13

JIM LOVELL & JEFFREY KLUGER
Motion Picture Screenplay by
WILLIAM BROYLES, JR. & AL REINERT

APOLLO 13: THE MOVIE

Ron Howard bought the film rights to *Apollo 13* in 1994. From the beginning of the film's creation, Howard was committed to making the movie as authentic as possible. When the movie was released in the summer of 1995, millions of moviegoers all over the world shared the story of the Apollo 13 crew in Howard's vivid recreation of those tense days in April 1970.

The movie was the hit of the summer in 1995. It was a tense, taut, thrilling film, brought to life with a fine ensemble cast that included Tom Hanks as Lovell, Kevin Bacon as Swigert, and Bill Paxton as Haise. Ed Harris played lead flight director Eugene Kranz of Mission Control, and Gary Sinise played Ken Mattingly, the astronaut who was forced to forego the mission just days before the flight because he had been exposed to measles. Kathleen Quinlan played Marilyn Lovell.

Lovell was pleased with the film and delighted with the authenticity Howard and the cast were able to achieve. Of the set recreating Mission Control in Houston, he said, "The instrument panels, the console switches. That's exactly what it looks like." The clothes and haircuts of the characters and the furnishings of the interiors were all meticulously recreated. Even the Lovell's living room of their house in Houston was remade in the sets, and Lovell found it almost spooky to be in a house he'd lived in 25 years ago.

Two-time Academy Award winner Tom Hanks visited with Lovell at his home in Horseshoe Bay, Texas, to research his character. "Hanks is a great guy," says Lovell. "Down to earth, easy to talk to." In the opinion of most who know him, in fact, a lot like Jim Lovell. (For more information on Tom Hanks, please see the entry in this issue of *Biography Today*.)

MARRIAGE AND FAMILY

Jim married his high school sweetheart, Marilyn Gerlach, after he graduated from the Naval Academy. The couple have four children, Barbara, James, Susan, and Jeffrey, and nine grandchildren. Lovell's daughter Susan remembers that her dad didn't make a big deal out of being an astronaut. "I never knew that he had a dangerous kind of job," she remembers. "A lot of dads would get up in the morning and go on a business trip. My dad would get up, go away and go up into space."

Many moviegoers were struck by the authenticity and believability of the scenes involving Lovell's family in the film *Apollo 13*. One scene in particular, in which Marilyn Lovell awakes from a nightmare in which her husband is sucked into space from a lunar module, was based on a dream Marilyn actually had. Marilyn had in fact provided important facts and remembrances of Apollo 13 when her husband was writing his book.

"Those were exciting, marvelous times in our lives," she says." "Jim's book also tells what happened to me and my children during those days. Yes, there were some difficult, anxious times, but I wouldn't want to trade those exciting days. And I always had faith in the program. But now I'm happy we're retired."

HOBBIES AND OTHER INTERESTS

Lovell is retired now, and he and Marilyn travel between homes in Lake Forest, Illinois, and Horseshoe Bay, Texas. He is still physically active and served on the President's Council on Physical Fitness for 11 years. He also still loves to fly. During the filming of *Apollo 13*, he took star Tom Hanks for a ride in his plane, a Baron twin-engine six passenger. "In spaceflight it's always nighttime. In the back seat I had a cutout that simulated the commander's window of the lunar module. It was dark over west Texas. I told Hanks to look out the window to get an idea of what it's like in space. I also wanted to give him the feeling of begin a test pilot. So I did a series of stalls, dives, Dutch rolls and phugoides—an oscillating longitudinal aeronautic maneuver." Hanks handled it well. Lovell recalls that Hanks "did such a good job of researching my life and probing my personality that before he left I had Marilyn take a Polaroid of the two of us sitting on a sofa together. At the bottom I wrote, 'Will the real Jim Lovell please stand up'."

HONORS AND AWARDS

Distinguished Service Award (NASA): 1965
Congressional Medal of Honor (U.S. Congress): 1970
Men of the Year (*Time* Magazine): 1970 (award shared with Fred Haise and Jack Swigert)

WRITINGS

Apollo 13 (previously titled *Lost Moon: The Perilous Voyage of Apollo 13*), 1994 (with Jeffrey Kluger)

FURTHER READING

BOOKS

Lovell, Jim, and Jeffrey Kluger. *Apollo 13* (previously titled *Lost Moon: The Perilous Voyage of Apollo 13*), 1994
Who's Who in America, 1994

PERIODICALS

Chicago Tribune, Apr. 15, 1990, p.B1; Apr. 14, 1991, p.B1; Sep. 22, 1991; Dec. 17, 1993, p.B1; Sep. 11, 1994, p.B1; Nov. 15, 1994, p.A2

Current Biography Yearbook 1969
Daily News of Los Angeles, Oct. 20, 1994, p.L4
Life, Sep. 23, 1963, p.36
New York Times, July 19, 1995, p.B1
Orlando Sentinel, Jan. 6, 1995, p.E1
People, July 24, 1995, p.160
Philadelphia Inquirer, June 11, 1986, p.C4; Mar. 21, 1993, p.A9

ADDRESS

Houghton-Mifflin
215 Park Ave.
New York, NY 10003

OBITUARY

Mickey Mantle   1931-1995
American Professional Baseball Player with
the New York Yankees
Legendary Yankees Centerfielder and
All-Time Sports Hero

BIRTH

Mickey Charles Mantle was born October 20, 1931, in the small
town of Spavinaw, Oklahoma, to Elvin Clark and Lovell (Richardson) Mantle. His father, an avid baseball fan and semipro pitcher
known throughout his life as "Mutt," named his son for Hall of
Fame catcher Mickey Cochrane, who played for the Philadelphia

Athletics and the Detroit Tigers in the 1930s. Mickey was the eldest of the five Mantle children, with twins Ray and Roy, Barbara, and Larry (Butch), 10 years younger than Mickey. Mickey also had a half-brother, Theodore, from Lovell Mantle's earlier marriage.

YOUTH

Mantle always remembered his boyhood as being "all about baseball." His youngest years marked the beginning of a lifelong obsession with the sport. When Mickey was four, the family moved to Commerce, in northeastern Oklahoma near the border of Kansas. Mutt found work there in the zinc and lead mines. Then Mickey's training began in earnest. From that time on, his father groomed him for baseball, whittling down broken bats to fit the small child's grasp. Every night, when he came home from work, Mutt would practice with his son, determined that Mickey would make it to the major leagues and help lift the family out of poverty. His dad "made a playing area (usually against a barn) wherever they lived," wrote Stephen Jay Gould in *Sport*. "[He] converted his son, a natural righty, into a switch-hitter by delaying dinner each night until Mickey had taken enough successful swings from the left side." Teaching the youngster to switch-hit soon became a family project, with Mickey batting right-handed against his father's pitching and left-handed against his grandfather's. Charles Mantle, the granddad and a lefty who had pitched for a mining company team, was eager to help.

As Mickey grew, he played in sandlot games and, eventually, on sponsored teams much like those of today's Little League. He also followed Mutt to semipro games whenever possible, to be there, he once said, as his father's "personal cheering section." There was little money in the family budget for other entertainment besides card games or occasional movies. But in the small town of Commerce during the Depression, such simple pleasures were the norm.

EDUCATION AND THE ROAD TO A CAREER

All of Mantle's school years were spent in Commerce, at Central Grade School and Commerce High School. Academics were never a priority; he lived and breathed only for athletics. By the time he was a teenager, he played sports 12 to 14 hours a day. In high school, he played football and basketball, as well as baseball. One day in football practice during his sophomore year, he was accidentally kicked in the shin. When his leg swelled up as big as a watermelon, Mickey was rushed to the hospital. He had osteomyelitis, a bone disease that results from an infection. When doctors recommended amputation of Mickey's left foot, his frantic mother took him to Crippled Children's Hospital in Oklahoma City for further medical consultation. Ninety injections of penicillin, which had recently emerged as a miracle drug, finally brought the raging infection under control.

It was that frightening experience that sent Mickey back to high school focused on baseball and studies, in that order. He starred as shortstop for his school team. On weekends and during the summer months, he played amateur ball, usually short stop, with the Whiz Kids of Baxter Springs, Kansas. One day in 1948, Tom Greenwade, the scout for the New York Yankees, stopped at the park. Mantle's amazing speed and his skill with the bat—he hit three home runs that day—attracted Greenwade's attention. But Mantle hadn't finished school yet. The night of his high-school graduation in 1949, Greenwade showed up and asked the principal if Mantle could go play baseball instead. Mantle skipped his graduation ceremony, went to the ballpark in Baxter Springs, and hit a couple of home runs. A week later, Mantle was signed by the New York Yankees and sent to the team's Class D farm club in Independence, Missouri. He earned $1,500 for signing with the team. His formal education had come to an end, but that was not unusual for an era when baseball players nearly always went directly from amateur play into the professional leagues.

CAREER HIGHLIGHTS

Within a year, Mickey was promoted to Class C ball with the Yankees' farm club in Joplin, Missouri, where his tremendous batting power made him a sensation. He hit .383 that 1950 season, blasted 26 homers, and batted in 136 runs. Also, he was moved from shortstop to the outfield, a position better suited to his fielding ability. He stayed in condition during the off-season by picking up work in the mines, fully expecting to resume farm-club play. Instead, the Yankees invited him to spring training for the major-league team. His superb performances in training games—hitting .400—encouraged team management to the unprecedented move of skipping a player over two levels of minor-league baseball to offer him a contract with the majors worth $5,400 per year.

First, though, was the question of his draft status. At that time, the United States was involved in the Korean conflict, and healthy young men were required to serve. In spite of his rugged physical appearance, Mantle had been disqualified for military service because of the aftereffects of his osteomyelitis. He would continue to be rejected over the next few years as his playing injuries mounted.

The excited, fresh-faced kid from Oklahoma reported to New York at the start of the 1951 season with a cardboard suitcase under his arm. Baseball was easy for Mickey, but the big city was almost too much for this un-sophisticated country boy to handle. He was scammed almost immediately by a sleazy agent and victimized in a phony insurance scam until, finally, he was rescued from those unsavory contracts by the Yankees' legal staff.

Mantle's first half-season in the majors was a disappointment. He impressed observers, says an early *Current Biography* sketch, "with his speed on the base paths and occasional displays of exceptional power at bat [his first major league home run was a 450-foot drive], but he was generally ineffective against big-league pitching." The club sent Mickey down to Class AAA Kansas City in mid-season after he struck out 52 times in 242 at-bats. He redeemed himself there by hitting .364, and he was recalled in time to join the Yanks for the opening of the 1951 World Series against the New York Giants. A serious injury in the second game, though, ended his contribution to the Yankees' eventual win. He was running through center field when his spikes caught on an underground pipe. He fell and tore the ligaments around his knee, marking the start of his long history of knee problems, broken bones, and surgery.

The 1952 season brought professional accomplishment but, also, profound personal loss. Mutt Mantle, barely 40 years old, succumbed to Hodgkins disease, a form of cancer that had plagued the family through three generations. Grandfather, father, two uncles, and even one of Mick's own young adult sons became its victims. Tragically, the Oklahoma miner who had dedicated so much of his short life into molding a career for his son died before his hopes could be realized. Mantle was devastated. He went on to great fame, but was haunted throughout his life by his father's early death. It was then, he later said, that he started to drink, to escape the

pain. He felt sure that he, too, would die young. The lament of his later years—"If I'd known I was going to live this long, I'd have taken better care of myself"—was his own commentary about the self-destructive lifestyle that eventually sapped his physical and emotional well being.

SEASONS OF GLORY

Joining the New York Yankees in the early 1950s, Mantle became part of probably the best, and the best-loved, team in the history of baseball. And he earned his place on that team once he inherited center field in 1952 after the retirement of the exalted Joe DiMaggio. Mantle electrified baseball with his powerful switch-hitting and dazzling speed—his speed from home plate to first base was clocked at an amazing 3.1 seconds. For 18 years he remained one of the most dominant baseball figures of his time. He played in 2,401 games as a Yankee, "more even than the Iron Man, Lou Gehrig," writes Kent Hannon in *Sport*. "And he hit more home runs in World Series [18] than Babe Ruth." Mantle's total of 536 homers reflect the skill and intensity with which he faced legions of star pitchers. He helped lead the Yankees to 12 American League pennants and seven World Series titles until mounting injuries and his well-documented late-night drinking with teammates Whitey Ford and Billy Martin finally ended his career. At that time, though, the media usually neglected to cover such behavior, and Mantle's crudeness, arrogance, and drunkenness went largely unreported.

The might of his bat, even as he played through pain and with bandages wrapped to his knees, was awesome to see. As veteran baseball writer Roger Kahn said in eulogizing Mickey, "Probably his most famous home run was the 1953 [right-handed] wallop in Washington off Chuck Stubbs, which was calculated at 565 feet. . . . Batting left-handed in Yankee Stadium in 1956, he cracked a line drive that was still rising when it crashed into the facade fixed to the roof of the third deck. The baseball was still climbing at a point 108 feet high and 380 feet distant from home plate." Mickey and his teammates always figured that one to be his best shot. Several years later, though, the Mick smacked a ball into third deck at almost exactly the same spot, and stories still make the rounds about *that* drive and how it could have soared beyond 600 feet had it been unobstructed.

The numbers that Mantle racked up are amazing, and the highlights can never do justice to his incredible career. In 1953, he hit the run that he later called his "greatest thrill," a grand slam against the Dodgers in the fifth game of the World Series, which the Yanks went on to win. In 1954, he batted in 129 RBIs, leading the American league. In 1955, he led the league in home runs (37) and triples (11). Many believe that his greatest season was 1956. That year, he won the Most Valuable Player Award and the Triple Crown, leading the league with 52 home runs, 132 runs batted in, and a .353 batting average. He also won the S. Rae Hickok Belt as the Professional Athlete of the Year. He was chosen MVP again in 1957, hitting .365 with 34 home runs and a league-leading 121 RBIs. He led the league in 1958 with 42 home runs and 127 RBIs, and in 1960 with 40 home runs and 119 RBIs. In 1961, Mantle and Roger Maris, a fellow Yankee, played out their famous duel, trying to beat Babe Ruth's record of 60 home runs in a single season. Maris succeeded with 61 home runs, with Mantle a close second at 54, with 132 RBIs. In 1962, Mantle won his only Golden Glove award and was chosen MVP for the third time.

Mantle's career was fading by the mid-1960s, although the highlights still stand out. In his final World Series in 1964, his 12th, he hit his 18th Series homer, a record. In 1967, he hit his 500th home run. In 1968, he was named to the All-Star team for the 16th—and last—time. On September 20, 1968, he hit his 536th home run, It would be his last. He reluctantly left baseball the following March, his weakened legs no longer able to carry him through another strenuous season. A lifetime of injuries had taken their toll. Three months later, the # 7 uniform he had worn for all but a few rookie months of his career was officially retired in a rousing ceremony at Yankee Stadium. Rare honor was accorded to Mantle again in 1974, when he was unanimously voted into the National Baseball Hall of Fame in the first year of eligibility.

RETIREMENT AND BRIEF SOBRIETY

Following his retirement from baseball, Mantle focused on money-making schemes and promotional ventures. Baseball salaries during his playing days were minuscule compared to today's million-dollar contracts. Mantle's highest annual salary ever was $100,000, and that was at the peak of his stardom and after years of lean compensation for his services. So he had to find another way to support his family. He made public appearances, tried his hand at broadcasting, played corporate golf, owned a small interest in a Manhattan sports

bar that bears his famous name, and, in general, traded on the celebrity of his youth.

Mantle's drinking and arrogant behavior went mostly unreported for decades. His excesses caught up with him at last, and the general public became aware of his drinking problem in the 1980s. In 1994, Mantle checked himself into the Betty Ford Center in California for treatment of alcoholism and, says *People*, "something remarkable happened. . . . Sober, he revealed himself to be truly the warm, self-effacing character who had so often inspired loyalty and love in friends and teammates." He wrote about his experiences in *Sports Illustrated* in April 1994, sharing his own troubles and offering hope to others struggling with alcohol abuse. In particular, he wrote about how painful it had been to lose his father, how afraid he was that he would die young, how disappointed he was with his own inadequacies as a ballplayer, and how sorry he was about his poor relationships with his own sons. It was an intimate and courageous report from an athlete who had spent his entire adult life trying to live up to the public's desire for a hero.

After less than 18 months of sobriety, Mantle's plans for a calmer life were cut short by grave illness. His hospitalization in late May 1995 for severe abdominal pain revealed extensive liver damage, and he received a transplant in June. Donor organs are scarce, and candidates usually have to wait a long time for one to become available. When Mantle received a liver transplant so quickly, many people believed that his celebrity had brought preferential treatment. They were outraged, even though his doctors denied it. His chances for recovery seemed good at first, but undetected cancer had spread aggressively to other organs. Mantle died on August 13, 1995, at Baylor University Medical Center in Dallas.

The depth of feeling for Mantle became clear after his death. Mere numbers could never sum up the career of a man who was, for many people, their greatest sports hero. Marty Noble of the *Sporting News* touchingly remembers the hero worship of his own childhood as he watched Mickey cast his spell on Yankee Stadium. "The feeling was special then, and it's a permanent part of my baseball baggage," he writes. "I mastered long division quickly because I wanted the ability to update Mantle's average after each at-bat. My first *Baseball Encyclopedia* still opens automatically to *his* page." NBC sportscaster Bob Costas, who has carried a Mickey Mantle baseball card in his wallet since he was 12 years old, had this to say: "He seemed like the perfect baseball hero at a time when baseball seemed like the most perfect game. He would have been the first to acknowledge his flaws and regrets. But the last chapter of his life was marked by courage and dignity and at last an understanding and appreciation of what he meant to a generation of baseball fans."

MAJOR INFLUENCE

Mutt Mantle was unquestionably the motivating force in Mickey's life. It was Mutt who inspired and trained and encouraged his son to be a great baseball player. "I did it all for, and because of, my father," Mickey told an interviewer several years ago. "No boy, I think, ever loved his father more than I did. . . . I would do anything to keep him happy." Sadly, the elder Mantle did not live to celebrate the glory years of Mickey's career.

MARRIAGE AND FAMILY

Much the same as his parents had done, Mantle married young. He and his high school sweetheart, Merlyn Louise Johnson, were wed on December 23, 1951, when Mickey was only two months past his 20th birthday. The couple had four sons—Mickey Elvin, David Harold, Billy Giles (named for Billy Martin), and Danny Merle—but Mick and his boys never had close father-son relationships. "I was not a good family man," he admitted after his long-delayed treatment for alcoholism. "When they were growing up I was playing baseball, and after I retired I was too busy being Mickey Mantle."

The soul-searching statement that Mantle published two years ago in *Sports Illustrated* unmasked the deep regret he felt at neglecting his wife and sons. Merlyn and Mickey separated in 1988, yet they maintained a close relationship, spending holidays and anniversaries together as a family. "Even though we didn't live together," she told reporters after his funeral, "he loved me, I loved him."

Three of Mantle's sons survive him. Billy, a victim of Hodgkin's disease in his late teens, died of a heart attack in 1994, at the age of 36, after long years of cancer treatments, alcohol and drug addiction, and heart trouble. David and Danny also abused alcohol, as did both their parents, but the family has gone through counseling and is sober. There are two Mantle granddaughters.

WRITINGS

The Mick, 1987 (with Herb Gluck)
All My Octobers: My Memories of 12 World Series When the Yankees Ruled Baseball, 1994 (with Mickey Herskowitz)
Mickey Mantle: The American Dream Comes to Life, 1994 (with Lewis Early; companion volume to Public Television Videography Program Special)
My Favorite Summer, 1956, 1992 (with Phil Pepe)

HONORS AND AWARDS

American League All-Star Team: 1952-65, 1967-68
Major League All-Star Team (*Sporting News*): 1952, 1956-57

Triple Crown: 1956, for his .353 batting average, 52 home runs, and
130 RBIs
American League Most Valuable Player: 1956, 1957, 1962
Major League Player of the Year (*Sporting News*): 1956
Outstanding American League Player (*Sporting News*): 1956-62
Male Athlete of the Year (*Associated Press*): 1956
S.Rae Hickok Belt: 1956, as Professional Baseball Player of the Year
American League All-Star Team (*Sporting News*): 1961-62
Gold Glove Award (American League): 1962
Uniform (Number 7) retired by New York Yankees: 1968
Baseball Hall of Fame: 1974

FURTHER READING

BOOKS

Gallagher, Mark. *Explosion! Mickey Mantle's Legendary Home Runs,* 1987
Gallagher, Mark, and Neil Gallagher. *Baseball Legends: Mickey Mantle,* 1991
Great Athletes: The Twentieth Century, 1992
Lincoln Library of Sports Champions, 1985
Mantle, Mickey, and Herb Gluck. *The Mick,* 1987
Mantle, Mickey, and Mickey Herskowitz. *All My Octobers: My Memories
of 12 World Series When the Yankees Ruled Baseball,* 1994
Mantle, Mickey, and Lewis Early. *Mickey Mantle: The American Dream
Comes to Life,* 1994 (companion volume to Public Television Videography
Program Special)
Mantle, Mickey, and Phil Pepe. *My Favorite Summer, 1956,* 1992
Who's Who in America 1996

PERIODICALS

Newsweek, June 19, 1995, p.70; Aug. 21, 1995, p.54
New York, Apr. 21, 1990, p.49; Sep. 30, 1991, p.41
New York Times, Jan. 30, 1994, Section VIII, p.5; June 8, 1995, p.B13; June
11, 1995, Section IV, p.5 and Section VIII, p.9; June 25, 1995, Section
VIII, p.9; Aug. 14, 1995, p.A1
People, Aug. 28, 1995, p.76
Sport, Dec. 1986, p.76; Dec. 1993, p.88
Sporting News, Aug. 21, 1995, p.8
Sports Illustrated, Mar. 25, 1985, p.70; Apr. 18, 1994, p.66; June 19, 1995,
p.104; Aug. 21, 1995, p.18
Time, Aug. 21, 1995, p.72

Lynn Margulis 1938-
American Biologist
Proponent of Controversial Theories about
Microbes and Evolution

BIRTH

Lynn Alexander Margulis was born on March 5, 1938, in Chicago, Illinois. She described her father, Morris Alexander, as a "liberated lawyer-turned-businessman." For a time he worked as an assistant state's attorney in Illinois, and later he owned a small company that manufactured plastics. Lynn described her mother, Leone Wise Alexander, as a "glamorous housewife" who sometimes worked as a travel agent. Lynn had three younger sisters in her immediate family. After her parents were divorced and her father remarried, she gained one half-sister and three half-brothers.

YOUTH

As a child, Margulis never sat still for long. She earned spending money by working at several part-time jobs after school, and she also enjoyed reading and writing. "Whether diary entry or essay, jingle or dialogue, if I failed to write on any given day I suffered a sense of deprivation," she stated. Sometimes she wrote plays and acted them out in the base- ment of her Chicago apartment building. Self-confident even in her youth, Margulis always played the starring role herself. She also liked being the director so that she could boss around her younger sisters.

EDUCATION

In 1953, at the age of 15, Margulis found herself bored with her sophomore classes at Hyde Park High School. She also wanted to spend time away from her parents, who were always arguing, and to meet interesting young men. She decided to attend the University of Chicago through an "early entrant" degree program. During her first year there, she met and began dating Carl Sagan, a graduate student in physics who later became a famous astronomer. "He shared with me his keen understanding of the vastness of time and space," Margulis recalled. "More importantly, he was a living example that young people, with all their foibles and fumbling, could direct their energies toward the scientific enterprise."

Although initially Margulis was not sure what kind of career she wanted, she quickly became interested in science at the University of Chicago. "I always claimed I wanted to be "an explorer and a writer," not realizing that those are precisely the two activities of working scientists," she stated. Her professors exposed her to the original writings of great scientists, which encouraged her to think deeply about some of the fundamental questions that lead to scientific discoveries.

In 1957, Margulis graduated from the University of Chicago with a bachelor of arts degree. Later that year she married Sagan, and the couple moved to Wisconsin. Margulis then entered the master's program in zoology and genetics at the University of Wisconsin in Madison, earning her master's degree in 1960. She continued her studies in the doctoral program in genetics at the University of California at Berkeley. In 1963, she and Sagan divorced. Two years later, she earned her doctoral degree from Berkeley and moved back east with her two sons. That same year, she married Thomas N. Margulis, another scientist, with whom she would later have a son and a daughter.

CAREER HIGHLIGHTS

After spending a year doing research at Brandeis University in Waltham, Massachusetts, Margulis joined the faculty of the department of biology at Boston University in 1966. She taught at least two courses there every semester for the next 20 years, earning the title of professor in 1986. In 1988 she moved on to become a distinguished professor at the University of Massachusetts at Amherst.

THE MYSTERY OF THE ORIGIN OF CELLS

In addition to her teaching duties, Margulis conducted research into several large, theoretical areas of biology over the years. Her creative approach toward solving the mysteries of science earned her a reputation as one of the most brilliant yet radical thinkers in the field. Beginning in graduate school, Margulis became fascinated with cell division, or mitosis. Cells multiply by dividing in half, with each half getting an exact duplicate of the parent cell's DNA, or genetic code. Sometimes, though, the new cells contain DNA that is *not* exactly the same as in the parent cell's nucleus. Margulis wanted to know why. At this time, DNA was known to exist only in the nucleus of the cell. Working with two of her professors, Margulis was able to show that there is additional DNA outside of the nucleus, within the cell substance known as cytoplasm. Margulis focused on these stray genes in the cytoplasm when she went on to investigate the origin of complex cells, such as those that make up the human body.

After doing research in the library and the laboratory, Margulis developed a theory to explain both how DNA came to exist outside the nucleus of cells and how this two-part origin of genetic information affected evolution. She started out by working with a "crackpot" theory that had been proposed by other scientists in the early 1900s. They had claimed that millions of years ago, different bacteria living within a cell depended on each other, creating a "symbiotic relationship." A symbiotic relationship is a give-and-take between two living organisms, in which each organism sacrifices something but at the same time benefits from the other's presence. Margulis expanded upon this theory to propose that all complex cells had originated as collections of smaller organisms.

There are only two types of cells comprising all life forms on earth: "prokaryotes," or cells without a nucleus, and "eukaryotes," or cells with a nucleus. In the mid-1960s, the question of how simple, prokaryotic cells had evolved into complex, eukaryotic cells was considered to be one of the major unsolved biological mysteries. Margulis's bold "symbiotic theory" explained this mystery. It stated that small, energy-producing structures called organelles, which live in the cytoplasm of all cells with a nucleus, had evolved from a symbiotic relationship between bacteria, which are single-celled organisms with no nucleus. Under an electron microscope, she was able to see that different types of organelles closely resembled types of bacteria, which supported her view that the organelles in complex cells were descended from ancient bacteria strains. Her theory provided a whole new way of thinking about the evolution of early life forms on earth.

Margulis proposed that several billion years ago, when there was very little oxygen on earth and the only life forms were primitive one-celled organisms, the planet underwent a sudden change in its atmospheric conditions. For some unknown reason, the earth's oxygen supply increased significantly, killing off much of the non-oxygen-breathing bacteria. This change allowed oxygen-breathing bacteria to multiply and invade the much larger non-oxygen-breathing bacteria. Although these two types of bacteria originally fought for survival, they eventually developed a symbiotic relationship. Both bacteria survived, but one was incorporated into the other to create a new type of organism that was better suited to the environment. Over time, the smaller bacteria became the oxygen-breathing structures within plant and animal cells.

Margulis's symbiotic theory differed in important ways from the prevailing theory of evolution developed by Charles Darwin. Darwin said that organisms adapt to their surroundings over time through a series of chance mutations or genetic changes, and that the organisms which are best suited to their environment live to pass on their genetic traits through "natural selection." In contrast, Margulis's theory held that the complexity of all life—including human beings—evolved not through chance mutations, but through symbiotic relationships between different organisms. "These people are trying to claim that natural selection is responsible for the creative novelty one sees in evolution," Margulis stated. "Of course, natural selection may select the symbionts over the individual partners or an animal with one genotype over another. It's an intrinsic part of the evolutionary process. But natural selection is the editor, not the author."

Margulis's explanation for how eukaryotic cells originated and evolved was immediately rejected by the scientific community. Her requests for financial support for her research were denied and the importance of her ideas was not recognized by her peers. In fact, the paper Margulis wrote describing her theory was rejected by 15 scientific journals before it was finally accepted by the *Journal of Theoretical Biology*. Because of her stubborn personality and her personal conviction that she was right, however, Margulis persisted in gathering data to prove her theory. One of the examples of a bacterial symbiotic relationship she found in nature was the carpenter ant. By itself, a carpenter ant could not digest the cellulose that makes up the wood that it eats. To overcome this problem, carpenter ants developed a symbiotic relationship with a certain type of bacteria. The stomachs of all carpenter ants contain this bacteria, which ingests the cellulose and provides the ant with nutrients. "All of us are walking communities of microbes. . . . Every plant and animal on earth today is a symbiont, living in close contact with others," Margulis commented. "Ten percent or more of our body weight is bacterial in its evolutionary origins, and it's just foolish to ignore that."

Meanwhile, a scientist named Kwang Jeon, who was a researcher at the University of Tennessee at Knoxville, accidentally created a real-life example of the evolutionary process that Margulis was trying to prove. During an experiment involving colonies of single-celled organisms called amoebas, bacteria had somehow infected Jeon's colonies. Over a period of five years, the only amoebas to survive were ones that had taken in—that is, consumed, or eaten—the bacteria that had originally made them sick. The new generations of amoebas in Jeon's colonies could not live unless the bacteria were present—an example of "endosymbiosis," in which one life form takes in another life form to the benefit of both.

Thanks to the proof provided by this experiment and many later ones, Margulis's theory gradually gained acceptance within the scientific community. By 1981, her theory even began to appear in biology textbooks. Margulis came to be regarded as "the woman who dared to challenge the scientific establishment." As one critic noted, "She's made people think more than any other figure in contemporary biology, and for many men it is particularly galling that this has been done by a woman." In 1983, Margulis received one of the highest honors in the scientific world when she was elected to the National Academy of Sciences. With this increased recognition of her work came much-sought-after grant money to support her research at Boston University.

THE LOWLY SPIROCHETE IN HUMAN CELLS

One aspect of scientific work that Margulis particularly enjoys is field study. Each year, she travels to the extensive mud flats of Baja California in Mexico to examine the vast colonies of bacteria living there. That thick, squishy mass of mud consists of tens of millions of microorganisms. Scientists believe that these mud flats are similar to the "primordial ooze" that covered the earth three billion years ago, out of which life developed. Margulis strongly believes that the keys to humankind's biological evolution are contained in microorganisms, so she regularly collects specimens in Baja California to help her unravel the mystery.

Margulis's recent research involves a form of bacteria known as a spirochete. Spirochetes are small, spiral-shaped, extremely mobile bacteria with tails. Margulis is attempting to prove that spirochetes are the ancestors of microtubules, which are the structures that move things around within every living cell. "I believe, as do most biologists, that cell hairs—and all sorts of other microtubule-containing structures in living cells and whole animals—all share common ancestry," she explained. Many things in nature—such as lobster antennae, the tiny hairs of the inner ear, and the tails of sperm—look similar in many ways and are "composed of the same set of proteins," according to Margulis. As a result, she has developed a theory that says that microtubules evolved from a symbiotic relationship with spirochetes. Many scientists find this idea farfetched—just like her earlier theories—but such skepticism does not bother Margulis. "There is enormous hostility to the ideas behind the data. Some people resist the concept that the tails of their own sperm evolved from free-living spirochetes," she admitted. "I haven't convinced everybody, and I know it will be a while. There will be tweakings, certain modifications as we learn more, but it doesn't matter what anyone else thinks. I know it's right."

THE GAIA HYPOTHESIS

Margulis entered into yet another scientific controversy when she became one of the most visible supporters of the "Gaia hypothesis." The Gaia hypothesis—named after the Greek goddess of earth—was created by James Lovelock in the mid-1970s, when the National Aeronautics Space Administration (NASA) attempted to find life on Mars. A British chemist and inventor, Lovelock proposed that living organisms act together to regulate the environment of their planet by continuously exchanging gases and other natural products. The essence of the theory holds that life itself controls the nutrients and conditions that enable life to flourish. Margulis and Lovelock worked together to analyze the atmosphere on Mars and concluded that there could be no life there because there are no changes in that planet's gases. If there *were* life forms on Mars, they argued, then there *would* be measurable changes in the gases. When NASA sent a spacecraft to Mars, they discovered that Margulis and Lovelock were right—there was no life on the planet. However, this finding does not prove the Gaia hypothesis.

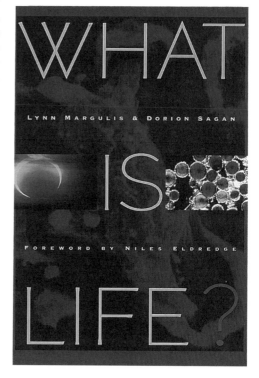

According to the Gaia hypothesis, everything about the earth and its atmosphere—the temperature, level of oxygen, saltiness of the oceans, and formation of rocks and soil— is maintained by the living organisms on the planet. While most scientists agree that there is a continuous interaction between living organisms and the planet they inhabit, the Gaia hypothesis goes further to suggest that the earth somehow adapts to changes in order to continue to support the organisms that live there— almost as if the planet were alive. The Gaia hypothesis has been used, for example, to explain the fact that the earth's average temperatures have changed very little over millions of years even though the intensity of the sun has increased by about 25 percent. There are other possible explanations for the earth's temperature stability, but at this point it is impossible to prove, or disprove, the Gaia hypothesis.

Some people have attempted to use the Gaia hypothesis as an excuse to pollute and harm the environment, figuring that if the hypothesis is correct, then the earth will simply make adjustments to compensate for the pollution. Still others have adopted the hypothesis as a compelling reason to protect the environment, since the earth can be considered a living organism. Margulis feels that these conflicting interpretations of the hypothesis stem from the fact that human beings view themselves as essential to the planet's survival. "People think that the earth is going to die and they have to save it. That's ridiculous," she stated. "If you rid the earth of flowering plants, people would die, period. But the earth was without flowering plants for almost all of its history. There's no doubt that Gaia can compensate for our output of greenhouse gases, but the environment that's left will not be happy for any people." Instead of viewing humans as the most important species on the planet, Margulis believes that the distinction belongs to microorganisms. "Of the 3.5 billion years that life has existed on earth, the entire history of human beings from the cave to the condominium represents less than one-tenth of one percent. . . . Symbiotic microorganisms preceded all animals and all plants by at least one billion years," she commented. "Kill off animals and plants, and the planet will recover. But kill off microbes and in weeks the earth will be just as sterile as the moon."

EDUCATING THE PUBLIC

Despite widespread opposition to many of her views, Margulis has been called "one of the most original and creative biologists of our time." Margulis continues to challenge scientists to look at the world in new ways with her unconventional thinking. One prominent scientist admitted that "When I was an undergraduate, two theories were held up for ridicule, to show how farfetched scientific theories can get. . . . One was the theory of continental drift and the other was the symbiotic theory of the origin of the cell. Neither is laughed at today. The reason that the symbiotic theory is taken seriously is Margulis. She's changed the way we look at the cell." Another of her colleagues claimed that "Every science needs a Lynn Margulis. . . . I think she's often wrong, but most of the people I know think it's important to have her around, because she's wrong in such fruitful ways. I'm sure she's mistaken about Gaia, too. But I must say, she was crashingly right once, and many of us thought she was wrong then, too."

In order to spread the word about her theories, Margulis has written dozens of articles, given public lectures, and appeared on television and in films. Her main message is that human beings represent only a small part of the total of the earth's organisms, and that microorganisms should be given more respect—and further study—as the basis of all life on earth. "What people do when they don't like an idea is they don't confront it head on, because then they'd have to learn something," Margulis noted. "My work more than didn't fit in. It crossed willy-nilly the boundaries that people had spent their lives building up." In 1996, *Smithsonian* magazine asked Margulis and other well-known figures to discuss what historical time period they would most like to visit if they had the opportunity. Recalling a piece of 3,500-million-year-old fossilized algae, called stromatolite, that is on display at the National Museum of Natural History, Margulis commented: "What I wish is to be able, like Alice in Wonderland, to step through the looking glass into that scene and spy on life 3,500 million years ago. With microscopic eyes, I would watch that stromatolite take shape and grow. Did the landscape in Western Australia swell with microbial mats like those from Matanzas, Cuba, today? How many years passed before this layered sample of rock grew to this size? Why and how did it harden? Was oxygen bubbling into the air by then? Was oxygen used up so quickly by respiring microbes that it never had a chance to accumulate in the atmosphere?" Questions such as these promised to keep Margulis busy for years to come.

MARRIAGE AND FAMILY

Margulis has been married and divorced twice. Her first marriage, to Carl Sagan, lasted from 1957 to 1963 and produced two sons, Dorion and Jeremy. In 1965 she married Thomas N. Margulis, a scientist who studies the molecular structure of crystals. They had a son, Zachary, and a daughter, Jennifer, before they were divorced in 1980. Margulis's son Dorion Sagan became an author and has written six books with her.

SELECTED WRITINGS

The Origin of Eukaryotic Cells, 1970 (revised edition published as *Symbiosis in Cell Evolution,* 1981)

Five Kingdoms: An Illustrated Guide to the Phyla of Life on Earth (with Karlene V. Schwarz), 1982

Microcosmos: Four Billion Years of Evolution from Our Microbial Ancestors (with Dorion Sagan), 1986

Origins of Sex: Three Billion Years of Genetic Recombination (with Dorion Sagan), 1986

Garden of Microbial Delights: A Practical Guide to the Subvisible World (with Dorion Sagan), 1988

Microcosmos Coloring Book (with Dorion Sagan), 1988

Mystery Dance: On the Evolution of Human Sexuality (with Dorion Sagan), 1991

HONORS AND AWARDS

Elected to the National Academy of Sciences: 1983

FURTHER READING

PERIODICALS

Current Biography Yearbook 1992
Los Angeles Times, July 23, 1991, p.E2
Montreal Gazette, Nov. 2, 1991, p.J11
New York Times Magazine, Jan. 14, 1996, p.21
Newsweek, Oct. 2, 1989, p.38
Science, Apr. 19, 1991, p.378
Scientific American, Jan. 1992, p.131; Aug. 1994, p.96
Sierra, May-June 1994, p.72
Smithsonian, Aug. 1989, p.72
Toronto Star, Nov. 2, 1991, p.D6
Whole Earth Review, Dec. 22, 1988, p.86

ADDRESS

Botany Department
University of Massachusetts at Amherst
Morrill Science Center
Amherst, MA 01003

OBITUARY

Iqbal Masih   1983?-1995
Pakistani Activist against Child Labor

EARLY YEARS

Iqbal Masih (ICK-bal mah-SEE) was born into an impoverished Christian family in the predominantly Muslim country of Pakistan. They lived in a two-room house in the village of Muridke, about 20 miles west of Lahore in northeastern Pakistan. His mother, Inayat Bibi, is a domestic worker. Her second husband reportedly abandoned the family, leaving her with the responsibility of supporting seven children. Many details about Iqbal's life remain sketchy, particularly about his father, his brothers and sisters, and his birth date.

When Iqbal was four years old his family sought a loan to pay for an older brother's wedding. (Traditionally, even poor people in Pakistan hold extravagant weddings.) They made arrangements with a local carpet factory owner to have Iqbal work there in order to pay off the loan for 600 rupees (about $12). He was paid one rupee a day (about 3¢), but his family's debt was extended to a much greater amount—13,000 rupees—because of the high interest rate attached to the loan and because the family allegedly continued to borrow money from the factory owner.

CHILD LABOR IN PAKISTAN

Iqbal is not the first child to be forced into slave labor. Children have been used—and exploited—as part of the labor force around the world for centuries. In the 20th century, the exploitation of child labor was acknowledged and curtailed in some countries. In the United States, laws limiting the work hours of children under 18 were enacted in 1938; by 1940 most European governments had taken similar action. In 1910 it became illegal to employ children under the age of nine in India. This same law also applied to what is now Pakistan, which seceded from India and became a separate nation in 1947. In 1933 the British government in India prohibited the use of children to make carpets. In 1991 the Pakistani government made it illegal for business owners to employ children younger than 13. Bonded labor of the sort that enslaved Iqbal was outlawed in 1992 under the Abolition of Bonded Labour Act.

Yet the practice continues. Even though it is illegal, children continue to be forced to work because the laws that would protect them are not enforced. Most reports agree that even today, from six to 10 million children work in Pakistani carpet factories, leather plants, farms, diamond-polishing shops, foundries, and kilns, and as construction workers and domestic servants. An estimated 30 percent of the children who work in the carpet industry are under the age of 10. The carpet industry prefers child workers because their small fingers can tie tighter knots, increasing the value of the carpet. Working children in Pakistan are often, like Iqbal, indentured servants—sold to work for a particular price and unable to leave their jobs until the price has been paid. Ultimately, it's a form of slavery. Poor families are often persuaded to sell their children into labor instead of sending them to school. According to Iqbal, "The factory owners tell the parents, 'If he goes to school, he will never get a job anyway. It's better for him to work now.'" And elementary school education is not required in Pakistan as it is in the United States.

IQBAL'S LIFE AS A CHILD SLAVE

For six years Iqbal went to work. Describing his working conditions, Iqbal said, "We had to get up at 4 and work 12 hours. There were 15 or 20 children where I was. We were chained to the looms, but after work, we were usually released and could go home to sleep." Injuries sustained on the job were met not with first aid but instead with a form of torture that was apparently designed to minimize a worker's off-time. Iqbal remembered, "if a child hurt his finger, they would dip it in hot oil." Iqbal's spine was curved from being forced to work in a hunched-over position, and he had a deep scar on his eyebrow from being beaten with a carpet tool by a supervisor.

Children are subjected to constant and harrowing pressure to maintain a steady level of production. "If the children fell asleep or were slow in their work, they would be punished by being beaten or starved," Iqbal said in an interview on American television, "If we were slow we often got lashed on our backs and heads." Many, like Iqbal, are afflicted with psycho-social dwarfism, a form of stunted physical growth caused by environ-mental and living conditions, rather than genetic problems. When he later came to the United States to accept a human rights award at the age of 12, he weighed 50 pounds and was the size of a six year old. Other children are crippled or suffer from tuberculosis and other diseases.

BECOMING AN ACTIVIST

When he was 10, Iqbal managed to slip away from the factory one day and attend a local rally held by the Bonded Labor Liberation Front (BLLF), a Pakistani organization committed to fighting against bonded labor and the illegal employment of children. There BLLF Chairman Ehsan Ullah Khan found Iqbal shying away in a corner, wheezing terribly. Khan told a reporter that "Iqbal was hiding himself. It was like he was trying to disappear, he was so frightened." Still, Iqbal gave a speech at that rally; it was printed in the local paper. Khan continued, "I felt there was something in this boy, that he had a strong will." He assured Iqbal that he didn't have to go to work because child labor was against the law. Iqbal replied that he had to go back to inform the other boys.

Iqbal was in effect rescued. Under the patronage of the BLLF he received medical assistance and went to school for the first time. He couldn't attend in his home village because the factory owner threatened the school if it admitted him. So Iqbal, his mother, and a younger sister moved to Lahore where he performed well in an accelerated program for two years.

Iqbal then became president of BLLF's children's wing. He grew into an ardent activist and one of the world's most outspoken voices against child labor. Iqbal would travel to factories employing children and talk to them about their rights and how to leave. According to BLLF Chairman Khan, he helped to free thousands of working children.

In November 1994 Iqbal went to Stockholm, Sweden, and spoke about Pakistani children's working conditions at an international labor conference organized by the Swedish Industrial Union and the BLLF. The following month, he traveled to Boston to accept the Youth-in-Action Award from Reebok. Iqbal planned to use the $15,000 prize money to go to school, become a lawyer, and work for the cause of freedom in his country. After the ceremonies, Brandeis University President Jehuda Reinharz offered Iqbal a full scholarship when he was ready to attend college. While in Boston, Reebok arranged for Iqbal to be examined at Children's Hospital—two years after he was freed from bonded labor, he still had pain in his fingers as well as breathing problems.

Iqbal also visited Boston-area schools where he spoke to children of his struggle, some of whom were moved to begin boycotting and letter-writing campaigns on behalf of his cause. At Broad Meadow Middle School in Quincy, Massachusetts, students remember that Iqbal held up a carpet-making tool and said to them, through an interpreter, "This should not be in the hands of a child." He then picked up a pen and said, "This should." They also remember the laughing child joining them for lunch in the school cafeteria. Many students lavished on him gifts of book bags, gum, baseball cards, and T-shirts. Later, back in Lahore, Iqbal would decorate his room with letters of support from American schoolchildren, a picture of Mickey Mouse drawn in crayon, and, hanging above the mat that served as his bed, a Teenage Mutant Ninja Turtle mask.

In an interview during his stay, Iqbal said of his former employer, "I'm not afraid of him any longer. Now he's afraid of me."

Iqbal was becoming an effective voice criticizing child labor practices and encouraging others to fight against child labor. He began to receive death threats from people in the carpet industry, according to the BLLF, because his efforts to publicize the industry's practices inspired people to quit buying Pakistani carpets. In 1993, the International Confederation of Free Trade Unions, based in Brussels, Belgium, organized a boycott of carpets from Pakistan, India, and Nepal because they knew that children were used to produce them. In early 1995, U.S. Senator Tom Harkin of Iowa introduced a bill that would make it illegal for the U.S. to import any product made by child or bonded labor. Many carpet stores throughout Europe and the United States decided to buy and sell only carpets that were not made by children. In Europe, the Rug Mark label attached to carpets was created to guarantee that child labor was not used in making the product, but some have questioned its reliability. Iqbal was publicly singled out by the Pakistan Carpet Manufacturers and Exporters Association (PCMEA) as the industry's most powerful and damaging critic. Its chairman, Imran Malik, has been quoted as saying, "Our position is that the government must avoid humanitarian measures that harm our competitive advantage." Iqbal received the most recent death threat two weeks before his murder, according to Khan.

IQBAL'S DEATH

During the evening of Easter Sunday, April 16, 1995, Iqbal and two relatives, Liaqat Masih and Faryab Masih, were traveling along a lonely road in Muridke. The three were taking dinner to another relative working in a nearby field. En route they had to pass a textile mill, a steel mill, some leather tanneries and a lead-recycling shed—all of which employ children. All three children were perched on one bike; Iqbal was riding on the handlebars, and his cousin Faryab was pedaling.

What actually happened next—and why—is unclear, buried in confusion and rumors of conspiracy and cover-up. According to the police report filed by Liaqat and Faryab, a man along their route lifted a shotgun, fired many rounds, and ran away. About the only undisputed facts seem to be that Faryab was wounded and that Iqbal took more than 100 shots to his back, buttocks, and legs, dying instantly. Two people were later arrested for the shooting, but both were released.

The validity of the police report was immediately questioned. According to the BLLF, local business leaders intimidated Iqbal's family into supporting the story in the police report. Iqbal's family appealed to the BLLF for protection, after which Faryab and Liaqat made a formal statement denying the story in the police report and asserting that they were coerced into going along with that account. To make matters more confusing, Iqbal's mother told Reuters news service, "I don't know who killed my son and why but I cannot blame carpet manufacturers." The fate of the $15,000 Reebok awarded Iqbal is unknown.

THE AFTERMATH

The murder of Iqbal has prompted international anger, and the official explanation has prompted widespread suspicion. Many believe he was killed by someone working for the carpet industry. A representative of the U.N. Working Group on Contemporary Forms of Slavery observed, "This courageous former child slave's tragic fate highlights the risks faced by those in many countries who reveal grave human-rights violations." From around the world came calls for a more thorough investigation. Within three weeks of Iqbal's death, carpet buyers throughout the world had canceled orders worth $10 million, according to the PCMEA.

By the end of May 1995, a Pakistani group, the Human Rights Commission, reported it found no evidence that carpet industry leaders were involved in Iqbal's murder. In June police arrested three BLLF workers, one on charges of allegedly aiding Indian intelligence in damaging Pakistan's carpet industry. Also detained were 13 members of Iqbal's family, though no reason for this was reported.

The seventh-grade class at Broad Meadows Middle School in Quincy, Massachusetts, which Iqbal visited while in the United States, was shocked and devastated at the news of his death. But the students soon transformed their anger into action and started a fund-raising campaign to build a school in Muridke. It is a difficult undertaking, but the students are determined to produce this memorial to Iqbal. So far, they've raised $27,000 of the $50,000 needed to complete the project. Amnesty International helped the students set up a page on the World Wide Web; it is currently listed as one of America Online's top ten Web sites. Their work has been praised by former President Jimmy Carter and the rock groups R.E.M. and Aerosmith. This year Reebok honored the students' efforts to continue Iqbal's work by giving them the Youth-in-Action award in December 1995. Two students, Amy Papile, 13, and Amanda Loos, 14, representing their class, spoke at the awards ceremony. Earlier, Amy told a reporter that the most important thing she's learned in the past year "is that you should open your eyes and care, whether it's across the street or across the world."

Iqbal's body rests in an unmarked grave in a Christian cemetery near his family's home. Whether his murder was related to his efforts to free other children may never be publicly resolved. What is certain is that in death, as in life, Iqbal not only helped to raise international awareness of child labor, but inspired others to crusade against it and the brutal conditions under which so many children work and live.

HONORS AND AWARDS
Reebok Youth-in-Action Award: 1994

FURTHER READING
PERIODICALS

Boston Globe, Apr. 18, 1995, p.A8; Apr. 19, 1995, p.A12; Apr. 20, 1995, METRO, p.29; Nov. 30, 1995, METRO, p.30
Buffalo News, Apr. 21, 1995, p.A13
Charlotte Observer, Apr. 19, 1995, p.1A
Chicago Tribune, Apr. 19, 1995, p.1; Apr. 20, 1995, p.1,19; May 3, 1995, p.2
Christian Century, May 24, 1995, p.557
Christian Science Monitor, June 22, 1995, p.15
Detroit Free Press, Apr. 20, 1995, p.1C; Apr. 26, 1995, p.2A
Independent (London), Apr. 19, 1995, p.10; Apr. 23, 1995, p.14; May 2, 1995, p.11
New York Times, Apr. 19, 1995, p.A16
Observer (London), Apr. 23, 1995, p.21
Philadelphia Inquirer, Dec. 9, 1994, p.H04
San Francisco Chronicle, Apr. 21, 1995, p.D5
Toronto Star, May 26, 1995, p.A18; June 23, 1995, p.B1
Vancouver Sun, Apr. 28, 1995, p.A21

OTHER

"Weekend Edition," Transcript from *National Public Radio,* December 2, 1995

[Donations to the "A School for Iqbal" fund can be sent to Hibernian Savings Bank, Quincy High School Branch, 731 Hancock Street, Quincy, MA 02170. The Broad Meadows Middle School students' Internet World Wide Web site is called "A Bullet Can't Kill a Dream." The address is: http/www.digitalrag.com/mirror/iqbal.html]

Mark Messier   1961-
Canadian Professional Hockey Player
with the New York Rangers
Winner of the 1990 and 1992 Hart Trophy
for Most Valuable Player in the National
Hockey League

BIRTH

Mark Douglas Messier, whose nickname is "Moose," was born January 18, 1961, in Edmonton, Alberta, Canada. He was the third of four children born to Doug and Mary Jean Messier. In 1966, the family moved to Portland, Oregon, where his father played minor league professional hockey in during Messier's childhood years. After his hockey career was over, Doug Messier earned his master's degree in special education from Portland University and returned with his family to Edmonton in the early 1970s, where he became a hockey coach.

YOUTH

Messier grew up in a very close-knit family that did nearly everything together. Each year his parents would take Mark and his three siblings—Paul, Jenny, and Mary Kay—on long vacations in the family station wagon. Destinations included Disney World, San Francisco, and the family cabin near Mount Hood in Oregon. When not traveling with his family, Messier could usually be found playing hockey with his brother or teaming up with his sisters in playground games of touch football. "Most brothers wouldn't choose their sisters for a team," says Mary Kay. "Not us. It was always family, together." In family "Olympics," it was always Mark and Mary Kay, the two youngest Messiers, against Paul and Jenny. "We won our share," recalls Mark.

Messier learned to appreciate the value of hard work on the family farm in Beaverton, Oregon, where he was responsible for cleaning the stalls of the Messiers' five horses. One of the horses—Billy—belonged to Mark, who was the only person who could ride him. Billy was an "ornery black Shetland pony," recalls Messier's mother. "The man next to us got rid of him because he used to bite everyone. He gave him to us. No one could ever do anything with that horse. Except Mark." Billy left a lasting impression on Messier. When he became a successful hockey player and bought his first sports car, he named it Billy.

Messier grew up in a hockey-loving household. In addition to his father's professional experience, Messier's maternal grandfather, Jack Dea, played goaltender for the Edmonton Eskimos, and his great-uncle Murray Murdoch once captained the New York Rangers in the National Hockey League (NHL). By the time he was six, Messier immersed himself in the game. Once, when he was eight, Messier stood behind his father's car and refused to move until his father relented and agreed to take him to practice with him.

Messier played Pee Wee hockey in Edmonton, and also served as stick boy for the Edmonton Monarchs, a senior league team that his father played for and coached. "I got a lot of hockey knowledge watching my dad play, and being around hockey all my life helped," says Messier.

At first, Mark was not even the best hockey player in his family—it seemed as if Paul would be the one to become a star. The brothers played street hockey constantly, and Paul always won, frustrating Mark to the point where he would lose his temper and take a swing at his brother, who would quickly fight back. "He used to cry so loud that when we first moved to Portland, the neighbors would come out of their houses to see what was wrong," says Paul. "Mark would be red as a tomato. After a while, they stopped coming outside. They knew it was that Messier kid."

A talented center with a nice scoring touch, Paul led his junior team, the Spruce Grove (Alberta) Mets, to the Canadian Tier II national championship in 1975. Mark was the stick boy on that team, and his experiences during this time helped him learn what it took to play team hockey and win a championship. "At a very young age, he got the opportunity to see a team that had a lot of togetherness," says his father, who coached the Spruce Grove championship team. "It was a good experience for all of us, Mark included. He saw firsthand that there are some things you have to do to win."

In 1976, at age 15, Messier made the jump to junior hockey, joining his father and brother on the St. Albert Saints Tier II team, a semi-pro group. "I still hadn't grown," recalls Messier. "I wasn't sure I could make the team, so I worked like crazy all summer." Initially afraid of being cut from the team, Messier instead became an excellent hockey player. In two years he bulked up from 155 pounds to 190, and while his brother remained a superior scorer, he earned a reputation as a physical player who would always back up his teammates and do whatever it took to win a hockey game.

After two seasons of Tier II hockey, Messier made the jump from amateur to professional hockey. Just two credits short of his high school diploma, Messier left school to join the Indianapolis Racers of the now-defunct World Hockey Association (WHA) for a five-game tryout. After the tryout, the Cincinnati Stingers obtained his rights, and Messier's professional career was underway.

CAREER HIGHLIGHTS

WORLD HOCKEY ASSOCIATION

Like many young hockey players in the 1970s, Messier found his first professional home in the World Hockey Association, a professional league that ran into financial difficulties and collapsed in 1978. As a member of the Cincinnati Stingers, Messier quickly enhanced his reputation as a physical player without much scoring touch. In 47 games with Cincinnati, Messier scored only one goal on a lucky shot from center ice that somehow went into the net. "Maybe I was in a little over my head, but I thought I could play well enough to get by," he admits.

Although he was not a scorer, Messier managed to attract a lot of attention on the ice. Edmonton Oilers head coach and general manager Glen Sather had tracked Messier's progress ever since he physically dominated one of the Oilers' key prospects in a junior game. When the WHA disbanded, he made Messier the Oilers' second draft choice in the 1979 National Hockey League draft. Sather recalls: "Coming off what he did in Cincinnati, he was no sure thing. But I had seen him play as a junior, and he had been a real leader. We were gambling on young players anyway, so we drafted him. When he made the team it was by design, not accident. We wanted players we could teach the game to."

Being drafted by Edmonton turned out to be the greatest thing that could have happened to Messier. Sather had a keen eye for talent, and the young players he gambled on in the draft turned out to be a dazzling collection of hockey talent that would go on to be one of the greatest teams of the era.

EDMONTON OILERS

At the start of the 1979-80 season, the 18-year-old Messier had a wild streak that quickly landed him in trouble with coach Sather. Bad attitude, tardiness at practices, and a missed team flight were just a few of the things that landed Messier in his coach's doghouse. In fact, Sather even sent Messier to the minor league Houston Apollos for four games, which turned out to be the only four games Messier ever played in the minor leagues. "He just wasn't dedicated to the game," says Sather. "He had a man's body but a kid's maturity." "I suppose I was pretty wild, " admits Messier. "I don't exactly go home after every game and bake cookies now, but I know there is a limit to how much you can do before it affects your hockey."

In Edmonton, Messier found himself in a situation that was very much like the one he had faced all his life. Used to playing in the shadow of his older brother Paul, Messier now found himself playing in the shadow of Wayne Gretzky, known as "The Great One." Many observers think Gretzky is the greatest hockey player to ever play the game. Already a teenage scoring machine by the time Messier arrived, Gretzky would prove to be a positive influence on Messier. "He saw the way Gretzky played and I think he was envious," says Doug Messier. "He always worked at his game, but that first season in Edmonton was as hard as I can ever remember Mark working. He'd work with Gretzky and he'd work on his own. He wanted that kind of game. He saw Gretzky's puck-handling and skating and he was determined to make it part of his game."

The extra work did not pay immediate dividends. His first season in Edmonton, Messier scored just 12 goals and 21 assists for 33 points in 75 games. By his second year, however, his scoring touch was beginning to develop. He nearly doubled his point output from his rookie season, totaling 63 points on 20 goals and 43 assists. Playing left wing on the line centered by Gretzky, Messier was quickly learning how to play the game at the highest level.

When the 1980-81 season ended, Sather decided it was time for Messier to expand the scope of his game. He asked the budding superstar to develop wrist and snap shots to complement his already booming slap-shot, and Messier did as he was asked. The result was a 1981-82 season that made Messier a household name in the NHL and marked him as one of the game's best young talents. He scored 50 goals for the first time and was named to the First-Team NHL All-Star team at left wing.

Messier continued to improve in 1982-83, when he notched his first 100-point season, scoring 48 goals and 58 assists for 106 points. Although he was surrounded by young teammates—Gretzky, Paul Coffey, Jari Kurri, Glenn Anderson, Kevin Lowe, and Grant Fuhr—who were maturing into one of the all-time great NHL teams, Messier began to emerge from Gretzky's shadow. "I don't think he ever played in anyone's shadow," insists Gretzky. "It's tough to hide a guy like that." Playing on a winning team for the first time in his career, Messier's rare combination of size, speed, skill, and determination helped the Oilers make it to the Stanley Cup championship finals for the first time, where they lost to the three-time defending champion New York Islanders. After the season, Messier was again named the First-Team NHL All-Star at left wing.

The following year proved to be a turning point in Messier's career. Moved from left wing to center during the season, Messier continued to produce offensively, totaling 101 points. Just as impressively, he continued to use his size to intimidate opposing players, and he led the Oilers in penalty minutes with 165. In the Stanley Cup finals, the Oilers met the Islanders once again, but this time the outcome was different. Messier scored 8 goals and 18 assists for 26 points and was named the Conn Smythe Trophy winner as the Most Valuable Player in the playoffs, leading the Oilers to their first-ever Stanley Cup.

Winning the Cup fulfilled a lifelong dream for Messier. "I've been rehearsing this moment for years," he said after the Oilers won. "Every night before I went to bed I went over what I'd do, how it would feel with the Cup in my hands. I've been dreaming about skating around with it since I was six years old."

After the 1984 season, Messier was a free agent. He could have left Edmonton for a bigger contract on another team. Instead, after a brief hold-out, he demonstrated how deeply he believed in the ideas of loyalty and leadership by signing a six-year contract extension with the Oilers. Messier sensed that the young Oilers team was about to become something special. "The guys we have together here, you have to think it's a miracle," he said at the time.

The "miracle" team just kept on winning. The 1984-85 season proved to be a tough one personally for Messier—he was injured for 15 games and suspended for 10 more for punching Jamie Macoun of the Calgary Flames—but the Oilers easily swept to their second straight Stanley Cup. Even though he played only 55 games, Messier still managed to contribute 54 points (23 goals, 31 assists), and he again was a dominant performer in the playoffs, scoring 25 points in 18 games.

With Messier and Gretzky leading the way, the Oilers were on the verge of a dynasty, but things came crashing down in the 1985-86 season. First, Messier was injured again, missing 17 games with a left foot injury. Then, the young Oilers fell apart in the playoffs, losing in seven games to the Flames in the divisional finals on a fluke goal—Oilers defenseman Steve Smith knocked the puck into his own net for the winning goal. Stunned by their failure to win the Stanley Cup, the team was also plagued by off-ice troubles. Messier was fined $250 for leaving the scene of an accident in which he hit three parked cars in his Porsche, and he was also sued by an automotive firm for failing to pay for services (the suit was later resolved). Rumors of drug use and other irresponsible behavior also dogged the team, and it seemed as if the dynasty in the making might be falling apart. "The club came too far, too young, too fast," says educational psychologist Maz Offenberger, who was hired by Glenn Sather to serve as a team consultant. "They had too much money and too much freedom. They did what they wanted to do. It was 'we want it and we want it now.'"

Messier responded to the team's troubles in the only way he knew how— he raised his game to an even higher level. In both the 1986-87 and 1987-88 seasons, Messier remained healthy for the entire year and scored more than 100 points, reaching 107 in 1987 and a then-career high 111 in 1988. Aided by Messier's strong performance, the Oilers recovered from the controversies that had swirled around the team and won the Stanley Cup championship both years, completing a streak of four Cups in five years.

The 1987 and 1988 seasons changed the way Messier was viewed by hockey experts. Gretzky was still considered the best skill player and scorer in the league, and he was unquestionably the NHL's top star attraction. But Messier was now considered by many observers to be the best overall player in the game, a ferocious competitor who combined offense and defense, size and skill, and power and finesse. As Calgary Flames coach Bob Johnson said at the time: "Messier is to hockey what Jim Brown once was to pro football. He's a bull—with finesse. What gives Messier an advantage is his ability to play any team, any style, over an 80-game schedule." Glenn Sather felt the same way about his star player. "You wouldn't notice Mark in the blowouts," he says, "but whenever we were in a battle, he'd be the guy to put the team ahead."

Just when it looked as if no one could beat Edmonton, team owner Peter Pocklington shocked the sports world after the 1987-88 season when he traded Wayne Gretzky to the Los Angeles Kings in a cost-saving move. Several other stars had already left Edmonton or been traded due to increasing player salaries that Pocklington could not afford. An angry Messier nearly called a team strike to protest the trade, but in the end he settled his differences with management and was named captain of the team, replacing Gretzky. The trade seemed to have a season-long effect on Messier and the Oilers, as the new captain scored only 94 points and the team was eliminated early in the Stanley Cup playoffs. It appeared the dynasty was over.

Messier, however, had other ideas. In 1989-90, he almost single-handedly rallied the Oilers and led them once more to the top of the National Hockey League. In his finest season, Messier scored 45 goals and 84 assists for a career-high 129 points. Leading a collection of young teammates through the playoffs, Messier tied for the lead in playoff scoring with 31 points in 22 games. In the division finals against the Chicago Blackhawks, Messier showed why he was considered the best overall player. Trailing the Blackhawks two games to one and playing in Chicago, Messier scored two goals and assisted on two others to lead Edmonton to a 4-2 win. The team went on to win the next two against the Blackhawks and then defeated the Boston Bruins in five games in the Cup finals. "Chicago was believing in themselves, and we had to win that game," Messier recalls. "It was a critical game. I thought the veterans had to step it up a notch and take control."

Teammate Craig MacTavish claims that Messier's grit was pivotal in that fourth game. "Mark took it upon himself to win that game," says MacTavish. "He was three hours early, quietly sitting in his stall, and he just had the Look. Of course I remember the game. He knocked out Denis Savard with an elbow and horrified [defenseman] Doug Wilson on two rushes and had two goals."

The Look, as MacTavish calls it, is probably Messier's best-known feature. Part glare, part scowl, Messier has been known to intimidate an opponent or teammate just by looking at them. It is probably the most famous stare in all of sports. "His game face is the most intimidating in hockey," says former teammate Craig Simpson. "Other guys are intense in the sense that they're absorbed in the game, but outwardly and physically, nobody is as intense as Mess." Hockey analyst Don Cherry goes a step further in describing the Look. "You look at his eyes, you think there's a screw loose."

As a reward for his great 1990 season, Messier swept almost every major postseason award, and secured his first Hart Trophy as the NHL's Most Valuable Player. He also won the Lester B. Pearson Award as Outstanding Player as voted on by the other NHL players, was a First Team NHL All-Star, and was named Player of the Year by both *The Sporting News* and the *Hockey News*.

The 1990 Stanley Cup proved to be the last hurrah for the Oilers, and for Messier as a member of the Oilers. In 1990-91, Messier was plagued by injuries and played in a career-low 53 games. The Oilers struggled all season, falling well short of the Stanley Cup. Seeing that the Oilers were committed to younger, cheaper players, Messier held out and asked to be traded. His request was granted on October 4, 1991, when he was traded to the New York Rangers.

NEW YORK RANGERS

The Rangers, one of the original six teams in the NHL, had failed to win the Stanley Cup since 1940, and general manager Neil Smith knew the team needed a strong leader who knew how to win. "This is the biggest day in the 66-year history of the New York Rangers," Smith said upon acquiring Messier. "I don't think the franchise has ever had a player like him." Two months after the trade, Smith was even more elated. "Seeing Mark Messier in a Rangers uniform seemed like a fantasy to me for a while after he got here. It took a lot of slaps in the face for me to realize it was true."

Messier was named captain of the Rangers, and he instantly accepted his new leadership role. He organized team functions, acted as spokesman, and continued his high level of play on the ice. The contract he signed with New York paid him approximately $2.5 million per year, and he knew that expectations were high. "When I first put on the Rangers' sweater, I knew I also took on that history, that tradition—and 1940," he recalls. "There were a lot of hurdles to overcome. In Edmonton we were kids. We didn't have history or anything to fall back on . . . . The toughest challenge in professional sports is to come here and try to win a championship."

In his first season in New York, Messier again won the Hart Trophy as the NHL's Most Valuable Player, scoring 107 points and leading the

Rangers to the division final. He also won the Pearson Award for the second time, was named a First Team All-Star, and was named Player of the Year by *The Sporting News* and *Hockey News*.

The 1992-93 season proved to be a disaster. Messier's point total slipped to 91, and the Rangers seemed to self-destruct. The team failed to qualify for the playoffs, finishing last in their division. Coach Roger Neilson preferred to play a defensive, tight-checking style that was the opposite of what Messier was used to in Edmonton, and the Rangers' captain became vocal in his criticism of Neilson's coaching. This led to dissension amongst the Rangers' players, and, for the first time in his career, Messier found his leadership being questioned.

Messier declared himself the "leader of the players" in dealings with Neilson, but this alienated some veteran players. "It was a declaration of war against Neilson," wrote *New York Times* columnist Robert Lipscomb, "and it tore the team apart. Older players, such as the gifted Mike Gartner, were less than charmed by Messier's Captain Dad approach." Neilson returned fire against Messier, even claiming that Messier was no longer leading by example on the ice. The crisis reached a conclusion when Neilson was fired midway through the season. Messier had won the power struggle.

For 1993-94, general manager Smith brought in an agressive coach to lead the Rangers. Mike Keenan had a reputation as a stern disciplinarian who could get results, and his arrival seemed to rejuvenate Messier and the Rangers. Messier scored 81 points during the season, despite playing with a severe wrist injury for much of the year, and he led the Rangers to the best overall record in the NHL during the regular season. When the playoffs started, Messier again took charge. In the Cup semifinals against the New Jersey Devils, the Rangers were trailing three games to two and were on the brink of elimination. Messier then took all the pressure off his teammates and put it on himself by boldly guaranteeing victory in the sixth game, a boast he backed up by scoring a hat trick (three goals) in the third period to lead the Rangers to a 4-2 victory. The Rangers went on to win game seven of the Devils' series and moved on to face the Vancouver Canucks in the Stanley Cup finals. Against the Canucks, Messier again came through when the pressure was greatest, scoring one goal and assisting on another in game seven of the finals to push the Rangers to a 3-2 victory. After a 54-year wait, the Rangers had finally won the Stanley Cup again, and Messier was hailed as a hero in New York.

Messier exercised a clause in his contract that allowed him to renegotiate if the Rangers won the Cup, and in January 1995, he became one of the highest paid players in the NHL when he signed a two-year extension worth an estimated $6 million per season. The contract took a long time to finalize, but Messier did not miss any playing time because the 1994-95 season was delayed for several months by a bitter lockout of the players by the owners over a new collective bargaining agreement. When the shortened season finally did begin, the Rangers had a new coach. During the lockout, coach Mike Keenan left the Rangers after a bitter dispute with the team's ownership. Under new coach Colin Campbell, the Rangers scrambled to make the playoffs, only to be eliminated by the Philadelphia Flyers. The following year, 1995-96, the Rangers rebounded from the previous season's playoff disappointment. They posted one of the league's best records, and Messier had his finest season in years, leading the Rangers in scoring. At press time, the Rangers were in first place in their division and looking forward to the playoffs.

FAMILY

Messier's family has always played an important role in his life. His father Doug is his agent, and his brother Paul and sister Mary Kay manage his business affairs through the company Messier Management International, Inc. Mary Kay also oversees Mark's involvement in the Tomorrow Children Fund, for which Messier has raised more than $400,000. Mark, Paul, and Mary Kay live on Manhattan's Upper West Side, while their parents live in the family's two-house complex in Hilton Head, South Carolina.

"The family has been my support system throughout my whole career," says Mark. "Because of it, your self-esteem becomes greater (as does) your confidence as a person. I don't think it's everything, but it gives you something to latch onto—your morals, your values, being compassionate toward other people."

Messier is unmarried himself, but he is considered to be one of New York City's most eligible bachelors. He has been romantically linked in the tabloids to singer Madonna and any number of supermodels. He does have one son, Lyon, from a previous relationship. Lyon, who was born in 1987, lives near Washington, D.C., with his mother.

HONORS AND AWARDS

First Team NHL All-Star: 1981-82, 1982-83, 1989-90, 1991-92
Conn Smythe Trophy: 1983-84
Hart Trophy (NHL Most Valuable Player): 1989-90, 1991-92
Lester B. Pearson Award: 1989-90, 1991-92
Player of the Year (*The Sporting News*): 1989-90, 1991-92
Player of the Year (*Hockey News*): 1989-90, 1991-92

FURTHER READING

PERIODICALS

Calgary Herald, Jan. 22, 1996, p.C2

Los Angeles Times, May 22, 1988, p.5
New York, May 4, 1992, p.47
The New York Times, Jan. 18, 1993, Section VIII, p.3
Newsday, Oct. 5, 1991, p.99; Oct. 13, 1991, p.28; Feb. 4, 1996, p.12
Ottawa Citizen, Oct. 5, 1991, p.C3
Philadelphia Inquirer, Dec. 18, 1991, p.D1
Sport, March, 1991, p.77
Sports Illustrated, May 12, 1986, p.32; May 9, 1988, p.53; Feb. 21, 1983, p.54; June 6, 1994, p.38; Feb. 12, 1996, p.66

ADDRESS

New York Rangers
4 Pennsylvania Plaza
New York, NY 10001

Larisa Oleynik 1981-
American Actress
Star of "The Secret World of Alex Mack"

BIRTH

Larisa Oleynik (pronounced oh-LAY-nick) was born in San Francisco, California, on June 7, 1981, to Lorraine and Roy Oleynik. Roy is a doctor and Lorraine is Larisa's manager. Larisa is an only child.

EARLY YEARS

EARLY ROLES

Larisa grew up in the suburb of Los Gatos, which is outside of San Francisco. She showed an early interest in performing and appeared in a production of "The Nutcracker" ballet when she was seven. At the age of eight, she went to an open audition for the touring company of "Les Miserables" and won a part. She appeared in the San Francisco production of the hit musical for one year. Larisa also took part in plays at her elementary school. She recently said that she thinks that kids who are interested in acting should give their school drama productions a try. "I really think school plays and after-school drama clubs are a good idea. Get an idea whether you really like it or if it's just a whim," she advises would-be actors.

When she was 10, Larisa found an agent, who got her auditions for commercials and bit parts in television. She appeared in an episode of "Dr. Quinn, Medicine Woman" and in an ad for Apple Jacks cereal. She also had a few lines in a voice part in the animated feature "The Swan Princess."

EDUCATION

Larisa attended Pinewood Elementary in Los Gatos and later a private academy in San Francisco. Her school schedule changed after she auditioned for and won the role for which she is famous, that of Alex Mack in the Nickelodeon hit, "The Secret World of Alex Mack."

CAREER HIGHLIGHTS

"THE SECRET WORLD OF ALEX MACK"

Larisa was only 12 when she auditioned for the role of Alex. The first time she read for the role, she was really nervous. The producer, Tommy Lynch, wanted to give her another chance. "We looked at 400 to 500 people. She came in and auditioned and was quite tentative with the material. But we liked her smile and asked her to read again. This time she relaxed and nailed it."

"The Secret World of Alex Mack" first appeared in the Fall of 1994 on Nick. Within a year, the show was one of the most popular on television with young viewers, and Oleynik was a star. In the show, Oleynik plays Alex, a middle school student who has developed special powers after being drenched with chemicals from a truck. With her super powers, Alex can "morph" into a puddle, send electric shocks through her fingers, and levitate people and things. Alex's best friend, Ray, and sister, Annie, are the only characters who know Alex's secret powers, and Alex uses her powers for good, not for evil. "This way it basically relates to more people," Oleynik says of her character's abilities. "I kind of like the way she uses them, because she's not really supposed to, but sometimes she sneaks them in basically just to annoy her sister."

Kids love to watch Alex use her powers, especially against snobby, nasty kids, but another appealing aspect of her character is that she is, in every other way, just a kid. "Alex is cool because a lot of people can relate to her," says Oleynik. "She's not the most popular girl in school, but she's also not a geek. I know what it's like to think you don't always fit in. I think kids can relate to Alex's feelings about being average."

Even with her magical powers, Alex can be hurt, like any other teenager. In one episode, she has a crush on a boy who already has a girlfriend, who is older and more sophisticated than Alex. At the school dance, the girlfriend confronts Alex: "Why don't you go home to your stuffed animals and stop embarrassing yourself? He's with me. Live with it." Alex responds by sending an electric charge toward the snobby girl, causing her dress to come apart and the heels on her shoes to break off.

Oleynik loves working with the special effects on the show. "Sometimes it's weird. The director will just yell, 'And lights go out, and now you're liquid.' The levitating thing is cool—everything is on fishing wire and it starts floating around me. Sometimes I forget it's on fishing wire because it looks so real."

After two years in the role, Oleynik still really likes the character she plays. "I liked her from the beginning when I read about her being embarrassed by her troll lunch box," claims the actress. "I think she's a lot like me in some ways—the way that we think and stuff." When the show's writers create situations and lines she thinks aren't accurate, Oleynik feels free to speak up. "Sometimes Alex would be scripted to say things that I didn't think she would say. There was one time she was supposed to say, "Get out." Alex isn't really a Valley Girl type or anything, and I thought that was a little un-Alexy." The line was changed.

"BABY-SITTERS CLUB" MOVIE

In the summer of 1995, Oleynik appeared in a movie featuring the characters from Ann Martin's popular "Baby-sitters Club" books. Oleynik played Dawn, who was always one of her favorite characters. She reread a lot of the BSC books so she could portray Dawn, described by one movie reviewer as the "all-natural granola girl" member of the club, as realistically as possible. Oleynik and the other actresses—Zelda Harris, Stacey Linn Ramsover, Tricia Joe, Rachael Leigh Cook, Bre Blair, and Schuyler Fisk—got along beautifully. "We got along really well—it was almost sickening! After the first couple of days, we just really hit it off." And they loved meeting author Ann Martin, who is something of a hero to all of them.

ON BEING A STAR

As a result of her popularity, Oleynik gets mobbed by adoring fans when she goes to the mall these days. Some people just can't separate the actress from the role she plays. "Some people actually believe I have super powers," she says. "They always come up to me, and they're like 'Hi, Alex, can you morph into a puddle for me?'"

FUTURE PLANS

As for future plans, Oleynik would love to appear in a movie with actress Claire Danes, who starred in the critically acclaimed but short-lived TV series "My So-Called Life," and in the movie version of *Little Women*. "Claire Danes is like the best actress in the world," she says. Oleynik would also like to appear in another movie: "I'd like to do some more serious work. A couple of scenes in BSC toward the end were serious. I'd really like people to see—I don't know—a different side of me."

HOME AND FAMILY

Oleynik and her mom live in the Los Angeles area in an apartment when she is filming episodes of "Alex Mack." When filming is over for the year, the family is reunited in San Francisco, as she and her mom move back to live with her dad. "I still have my friends at home. We have an apartment here in Los Angeles when I'm filming stuff. But I still have my other life at home with all my friends that I've known since I was 5. And so when I go home it's just totally different. It's like I'm nobody."

HOBBIES AND OTHER INTERESTS

Oleynik plays volleyball and soccer and likes a number of current music groups, especially nine inch nails. She also likes to play computer games, and to "watch TV, hang out with the kids, regular stuff like that." She stays in touch with her many fans through a column she writes for *Tiger Beat* magazine, and also takes part in chat groups on Nick's Web site. As one of the most popular stars on Nick, she has appeared on the Kids' Choice Awards and also on "The Big Help," a program that lets kids get involved with public service work in their communities.

CREDITS

TELEVISION

"The Secret World of Alex Mack," 1994—

FILMS

The Baby-sitters Club, 1995

FURTHER READING

PERIODICALS

Chicago Tribune, Aug. 1, 1995, Kidnews Section, p.1; Oct. 19, 1995, Tempo Section, p.12
Daily News of Los Angeles, Mar. 14, 1995, p.L1; Feb. 18, 1996, p.L16
Los Angeles Times, Oct. 2, 1994, TV Times Section, p.7; Aug. 18, 1995, p.F8
New York Times, June 2, 1996, Section 2, p.32
Newsday, Dec. 18, 1994, Section 2, p.2
TV Guide, Feb. 3, 1996, p.38
USA Today, Jan 12, 1996, p.D3

ADDRESS

"The Secret World of Alex
 Mack"
Nickelodeon Publicity Dept.
1515 Broadway
New York NY 10036

E-MAIL ADDRESS

NickMail02

Christopher Pike 1954-
American Writer of Thrillers for Young Adults
Author of *Slumber Party, Chain Letter,* and
the *Final Friends* Trilogy

BIRTH

Christopher Pike's real name is Kevin McFadden. He was born in Brooklyn, New York, in November 1954. He took his pen name from the character in the *Star Trek* television series who preceded James T. Kirk as captain of the Starship *Enterprise.*

YOUTH

Little is known about Pike's youth, aside from the fact that he grew up in Los Angeles. He is painfully publicity-shy and prefers not to give interviews or make public appearances.

FIRST JOBS

After dropping out of college, Pike worked for a while as a computer pro-
grammer. He spent several years writing science fiction that no one would
publish. Finally an editor at Avon Books who had seen some of his work
suggested that he try writing a teen thriller. In 1985 he published *Slumber
Party,* his book about a group of teenage girls who are stalked by a
murderer on a ski weekend. After that, he decided to abandon science
fiction and concentrate on horror stories.

CAREER HIGHLIGHTS

Slumber Party was quickly followed by two other successful novels: *Weekend*
and *Chain Letter,* both published in 1986. Pike's reputation spread rapidly
by word of mouth, and all three books became bestsellers for young adults,
or readers aged 12 to 16. Although his plots were occasionally far-fetched,
Pike was so good at building and maintaining suspense that his readers
didn't care. And unlike many other writers for young adults, Pike didn't
"talk down" to his teenage audience. His books presented well-defined
characters who, like teens everywhere, went to dances, threw parties, fell
in love, and had trouble communicating with their parents. But they often
chose extreme or unusual ways to deal with their problems. In *Gimme
a Kiss* (1988), for example, the main character tries to recover her stolen
diary by devising a complicated revenge strategy that ends up involving
her in a murder.

In his early books, Pike often relied on young female narrators whose
observations about people and events were essential to the novel's plot.
He was fascinated by females in general, because they seemed more complex, and it was easier for them to show their fear. But young adults of
both sexes started buying his books. Pike's thrillers eventually led to a boom
in the horror market for teenagers, replacing sports and adventure stories
for boys as well as the romances that had traditionally attracted young
female readers.

COMPLAINTS FROM PARENTS

In his novels, Pike speaks openly about teenage sex and drug use and
describes violent acts in graphic detail. This has led parents and educators
to question whether teenagers should be encouraged—or even allowed—to
read his novels. Several school libraries decided not to carry Pike's books
because parents found their content too disturbing for children in the
8- to 14-year-old age group. Such decisions, of course, have only added
to Pike's popularity. Because today's teenagers often have money of
their own to spend on books, there's nothing to prevent them from
buying what their friends recommend or what they know will offend
their parents.

Pike himself is the first to admit that his books are aimed at more mature teens. He seems to have an uncanny ability to zero in on topics that teenagers find fascinating, and he doesn't shy away from controversial subjects like suicide and life after death. In *Remember Me* (1989), for example, a teenage ghost who knows she didn't kill herself sets out to find her murderer. Pike claims to have received a number of letters from teenagers who said they had contemplated suicide before reading the book, and he believes that his novels have actually turned teens away from such desperate acts. His popularity, in fact, is largely due to his willingness to tackle issues that other young adult writers have considered taboo. While parents might not appreciate his treatment of sex and drug use, or the gruesome ways in which his characters often meet their deaths, Pike is more interested in appealing directly to his teenage readers. "My primary purpose is to tell a tale that will grip a reader until the last sentence is read," he says.

Librarians point out that Pike's thrillers often attract kids who might otherwise not read at all. Some teachers have even used Pike's books in the classroom. In his own defense, Pike claims that he never glorifies violence or suggests it as a way to solve problems, and that he tries to give his central characters a sense of right and wrong. But many of his books disregard morality and social values altogether, leading some critics to describe them as "novelizations of horror films that haven't been made yet."

WRITING FOR ADULTS

Now that Pike has conquered the young adult market, he's trying to do the same thing for adult fiction. His first novel for adults was *Sati*, published in 1990. *The Season of Passage* made an even bigger splash in 1992, with one reviewer saying that "it wriggles its way into the psyche like maggots in rotting flesh." In 1995 Pike published three adult horror thrillers: *The Cold One, The Listeners,* and *The Visitor.* But he is still known primarily as a master of suspense fiction for young adults.

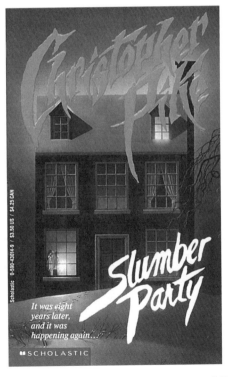

It was eight years later, and it was happening again...

269

MARRIAGE AND FAMILY

Pike is not married and has no children of his own. "I am prolonging my youth in books," he explains. "When I was at school, I never dated anyone, and I was really shy. I just used to read a lot."

One woman he dated recently left the relationship because he spent so much of his time writing. "I put her in *The Last Vampire*," Pike comments. "But then I killed her in the sequel."

MAJOR INFLUENCES

"Stephen King created my audience," Pike often says, referring to America's most successful horror writer. The *Wall Street Journal* has dubbed Pike "the Stephen King of young adult fiction." He also mentions the influence of novelist Anne Rice, the science fiction writer Arthur C. Clarke, and J. R. R. Tolkien, author of *The Hobbit* and *The Lord of the Rings*.

MEMORABLE EXPERIENCES

One day Pike saw a group of girls buying his book. He went up to them and told them that he was the author, but they thought he was trying to pick them up. They summoned a security guard, and their parents appeared soon afterward. Pike remembers this incident as particularly embarrassing because he normally goes out of his way to protect his anonymity.

HOBBIES AND OTHER INTERESTS

When he's not writing, Pike enjoys running, transcendental meditation, and studying astronomy. He also likes to read and surf.

SELECTED WRITINGS

FOR YOUNG ADULTS

Slumber Party, 1985
Chain Letter, 1986
Weekend, 1986
Last Act, 1988
Spellbound, 1988
Gimme a Kiss, 1988
Remember Me, 1989
Scavenger Hunt, 1989
Witch, 1990
Fall Into Darkness, 1990
See You Later, 1990
Bury Me Deep, 1991

Die Softly, 1991
The Last Vampire, 1994
Black Blood, 1994
The Cold People, 1996
The Dark Corner, 1996
Evil Thirst, 1996
The Starlight Crystal, 1996
The Witches' Revenge, 1996

"FINAL FRIENDS" TRILOGY

The Party, 1988
The Dance, 1989
The Graduation, 1989

FOR ADULTS

Sati, 1990
The Season of Passage, 1992
The Cold One, 1995
The Listeners, 1995
The Visitor, 1995

FURTHER READING

BOOKS

Children's Literature Review, Vol. 29
Contemporary Authors, Vol. 136
Something About the Author, Vol. 68

PERIODICALS

Daily News of Los Angeles, Oct. 14, 1991, Valley section, p.L4
Entertainment Weekly, Jan 31, 1992, p.68
Harper's Magazine, June 1991, p.55
The Times of London, Aug. 23, 1994

ADDRESS

Simon & Schuster, Inc.
1230 Avenue of the Americas
New York, NY 10020

David Robinson 1965-
American Professional Basketball Player
with the San Antonio Spurs
NBA Most Valuable Player in 1994-95
Member of the 1992 and 1996 Olympic
"Dream Teams"

BIRTH

David Maurice Robinson was born on August 6, 1965, in Key West, a resort beach community in the southernmost part of Florida. His mother, Freda, was a nurse. Ambrose, his father, was a career petty officer in the U.S. Navy.

Soon after David was born, the family—including David's brother Chuck and sister Kimberly—moved to Virginia Beach, Virginia,

272

another oceanside community. They lived there until David was 17, when the navy transferred Ambrose Robinson to Washington, D.C.

YOUTH

With their father often away on duty with the navy and their mother working, the Robinson children were called upon to take responsibility for their actions at an earlier age than many of their friends. David and his brother and sister were expected to help tackle household chores, and their parents insisted that they take their schoolwork seriously. Robinson once recalled that during junior high school he brought home a report card that included one A, two Bs, and one C. He was "grounded" for six weeks for getting the less-than-outstanding C grade.

Robinson's mother recalled that her youngest son was an intelligent and perceptive boy. Even as a small child, Robinson could total his mother's grocery bill before she got to the cashier, and he taught himself to play classical music by ear. He was also very curious about how machines and other things worked, and as he grew older he became known around the house for his knack for taking things apart and putting them back together again. On one occasion, his father bought a kit for a large-screen television. "It was state of the art, and I was looking forward to building it," Ambrose Robinson recalled. But when he returned home after spending three weeks at sea, he found the television up and running; David's curiosity had gotten the better of him, and he had put the television together himself. "Then he went down to the store," his father said, "and he helped them fix their display model."

EDUCATION

Growing up, Robinson attended public schools in Virginia Beach until his senior year, when his family moved to the Washington, D.C., area. Robinson was an excellent student, but he recalled that "I was lazy in high school; I don't know why. I knew I was smart, things like math came really easy to me. I took advanced placement courses all the way through school, but I somehow just didn't challenge myself." Instead, Robinson's interests in science fiction, tinkering with machines, and sports overshadowed his studies. Robinson played many sports as he grew up, but as a youngster basketball was no more important to him than tennis, golf, baseball, and other sports. In ninth grade he even quit his school's basketball team because he was not getting any playing time.

During high school, though, a tremendous growth spurt transformed Robinson into an imposing force on the basketball court. He grew nearly a foot between his freshman and senior years, when Art Payne, the basketball coach at Osbourn Park High School in Manassas, encouraged him to give basketball another try. "I didn't even notice how fast I was growing," Robinson said. "It just seemed that more and more people were looking at me and saying, 'Man, you must play basketball.'"

Robinson was named the starting center on the high school team during his senior season, and his height and coordination helped him overcome his unfamiliarity with the game. But his skills were limited, and only a few colleges extended scholarship offers to the slim center after he graduated in 1983.

The lack of attention from college scouts did not bother Robinson, though. His real ambition was to follow his father in the navy and become an engineer. His excellent scholastic record and his very high score of 1320 on the Scholastic Aptitude Test (SAT) secured his acceptance into the Naval Academy in Annapolis, Maryland. "I knew I liked the Academy and I could handle it [there]," Robinson later said. "It was a choice between the known and the unknown, and I just decided I was more comfortable with the known." Robinson also valued the discipline that the Naval Academy required, and he felt that the school's environment would make him a stronger person.

AT THE NAVAL ACADEMY

Robinson played basketball as a freshman at the Academy, but the game still was not a priority for him. "I didn't care if I played basketball at the Academy," he said. "I just wanted to get good grades and fit in." The Academy's basketball coach, Paul Evans, was anxious to get Robinson out on the court, but the tall center broke his hand in boxing class, an injury that caused him to miss the first four basketball games of the season. After his recovery, he saw only limited playing time. As the months passed, Coach Evans's frustration with Robinson's laid-back attitude toward basketball grew, for he believed that the player had a future in the NBA if he applied himself. "I felt I was coaching a freshman in high school, not college," Evans later said. "He'd do great things, then for five or six minutes he wasn't there. He was a terrific kid, but I had to be hard on him."

Robinson continued to grow during his years at the Academy. By his sophomore season he was a full seven feet tall. This size, coupled with his growing knowledge of basketball and his amazing coordination—he posted one of the Academy's highest scores in the obstacle course, and he occasionally dazzled onlookers with his ability to walk 100 yards on his hands—made him even more of a force on the basketball court. By the end of his sophomore year he had caught the attention of NBA scouts.

During Robinson's junior year, the towering center emerged as a dominant force. He scored nearly 23 points a game and led the nation in rebounding during the Midshipmen's 30-5 season, but after their last game Evans left the Naval Academy to become head coach at the University of

Pittsburgh. The new coach at the Academy was Pete Herrmann, who had a much more relaxed approach to coaching. Herrmann was the beneficiary of Robinson's continued growth as a basketball player. During his senior season Robinson smashed 33 school records as he led his team into the National College Athletic Association (NCAA) tournament for the third year in a row. He also set NCAA standards for the most blocked shots in a game (14), for a season (207), and for a career (516).

Opponents marveled at the quality of Robinson's all-around game as well as his attitude. He was a steady and accurate scorer, a relentless rebounder, and a talented defender, but people were equally impressed by the courtesy and manners he showed to the many people he encountered. He did not smoke, swear, or drink alcohol, and as *Washington Post* writer John Feinstein noted, Robinson's father "raised his son to respect discipline and not to be cocky. Because he was not a high school star, because he was not highly recruited and because he ended up at a military academy, Robinson never has been exposed to the kind of boot-licking that most high school stars come to expect by the time they are 16."

When Robinson graduated from the Naval Academy in 1987 with a bachelor's degree in mathematics, he had grown to a height of seven feet, one inch. As the owner of 12 NCAA player-of-the-year awards for his senior season, he was by far the number-one prospect in the 1987 National Basketball Association (NBA) college draft. His military obligations cast a cloud over his prospects for joining the NBA, however.

Students at the Naval Academy are required to serve active duty in the navy for five years after graduation. John F. Lehman, Jr., the secretary of the navy at the time, ruled that since Robinson was too tall for shipboard work, his obligation for active duty would be for only two years. Lehman also noted that Robinson had already generated great publicity for the Academy and helped its minority recruiting efforts. Some people complained that Robinson was getting special treatment, but the decision stood. Any team in the NBA could draft him in 1987, but the team would have to wait until 1989 for him to play. If it proved unable to sign him before the 1988 draft, the team would lose their rights to him.

Despite these uncertainties, the San Antonio Spurs used the first pick in the draft to select Robinson. The gamble paid off. They were able to reach agreement with Robinson and his agent on a contract, but the Spurs were forced to fork over a lot of money. Robinson got one of the biggest rookie contracts in all of sports history—$26 million to be paid over ten years, plus $1 million for each of the two years he was to spend in the navy fulfilling his military obligation. In addition, the contract was structured so that it guaranteed that Robinson would always be one of the highest-paid players in the league.

With his NBA future assured, Robinson began his two-year navy commitment. His situation was very unusual: he was a millionaire, but he found himself stationed at the King's Bay Naval Base in King's Island, Georgia, where he worked as a civil engineer and achieved the rank of lieutenant, junior grade. "I was living a normal life on a base," Robinson remembered. "It was strange. I would go to NBA things—go to the All-Star Game, for instance, where everyone was treated special—then come back to the base, where guys were going to the supermarket with their families, working jobs, doing all the normal things that people do. I had a foot in both worlds." Sometimes the contrast between the two worlds left Robinson nearly speechless. "People want to give me an incredible amount of money to play a game I enjoy. That boggles my mind. In the other world, I'm at the bottom of the totem pole. I might be asked to run out and get coffee for people. The whole situation is teaching me a lot. I'm learning about power and restraint."

While finishing out his tour of duty in the navy, Robinson continued to explore the world around him. He found time to study theology and Spanish, and he continued to indulge his interest in music. He was also able to play basketball competitively. In 1987, he was a member of the U.S. team in the Pan-American Games. It finished a disappointing second, and Robinson's performance was average. He was also a member of the 1988 U.S. Olympic team, which won a bronze medal for third place. Again, Robinson did not play up to expectations, and many observers wondered if his skills were getting rusty since he was not playing as many games as he had in previous years. Other critics complained that his heart was not in the game, or that he could not play well against really good players.

Robinson admitted that his performance in those two international competitions bothered him. "The Olympics were a tremendous experience up to the point that we lost," he said. "We never expected to. That was one of the biggest disappointments of my life. I haven't had a lot of big disappointments in life, but that was definitely one of the biggest, along with the Pan Am games. . . . For a while, I blamed myself. I was a big part of both of those teams, we were expected to win, and we didn't. I was the team leader. The responsibility, at least partially, was with me. I felt really bad. I got down on myself and felt like maybe I didn't have that special magic." As time passed and his NBA debut neared, however, Robinson gathered himself together, determined to prove that he belonged among basketball's elite.

CAREER HIGHLIGHTS

ROOKIE OF THE YEAR

Robinson delivered on his promise. Even after a few games of the 1989-90 season, it was clear that he had joined Hakeem Olajuwon and Patrick

Ewing as one of the NBA's top centers. "Some rookies are never really rookies, and he's one of them," said Lakers' star Magic Johnson. Other players and coaches agreed that the former Midshipman, who was nicknamed "The Admiral," was an unusual mixture of power and grace, and many observers commented on the poise that he maintained. During his rookie year, he averaged 24.3 points, 12.0 rebounds, and 3.9 blocked shots per game. He also made the All-Star team and finished fifth in the NBA's most-valuable-player balloting. Robinson was also a unanimous selection for the league's rookie of the year award.

In the year before Robinson's arrival, the Spurs had posted a miserable record of 21 wins against 61 losses; in the 1989-90 season, with Robinson's help, they went to 56 wins with 26 losses. That 35-game improvement was the best single-season turnaround in NBA history. Robinson's talents helped the San Antonio Spurs not only on the court but in the stands as well. During the 1989-90 season, the team drew 15,000 fans per game, up from 11,000 the previous year. Season ticket sales doubled, and B. J. (Red) McCombs, the owner of the team, estimated that the value of the Spurs had increased to $75 million in 1990 from the $47 million he had paid for the team in 1988.

RELIGIOUS FAITH DEVELOPS

In his second season (1990-91) Robinson improved in virtually all aspects of his game. He was one of the league leaders in nearly every statistical category, and he became known in other NBA locker rooms as one of the league's very best defensive players. Robinson led the Spurs to a division title, but they were upset in the first round of the playoffs by the Golden State Warriors, a heavy underdog. Robinson himself had a very strong series, averaging 25 points a game and shooting close to 70 percent from the floor. But even with Robinson's fine play, the outside shooting of Golden State's smaller players overwhelmed the Spurs.

Around this same time, Robinson felt that his personality was changing for the worse. "Money, time and youth can be a dangerous combination. It will all change you—for the worst, mostly—in incredible ways," he said. "What surprised me was that I wasn't happy. Here I had everything I ever wanted . . . and I wasn't happy at all. I looked at myself, and I didn't like the person I was becoming. I felt I was so important. I had a selfishness and arrogance. It was that thing: 'Oh, I'm 30 minutes late, but that doesn't matter, because they can't start without me. I'm the one who counts.' I found myself doing that more and more, and there were people encouraging me."

Unhappy with his sense that he was becoming more susceptible to the hard-partying lifestyle that some other NBA players fell into, Robinson finally agreed to talk with Greg Ball, an evangelist for a Christian group known as Champions for Christ. Their conversation stretched on for more than five hours, and Robinson subsequently began to read the Bible and think about his religious faith much more seriously than he ever had before. "His purpose, his life focus, wasn't established," Ball later said. "Here was this wonderful person, this superstar, but he was unhappy. He was a god of his own life. All these guys in the NBA are gods of their own lives. I told him it doesn't matter if you get all the Ferraris and Mercedes that are made—if you don't have a focus, you're still an empty Coke bottle rolling around the backseat of a '57 Chevy. It's like you're standing in front of a painted fire, trying to keep warm."

Robinson's new faith caused him to re-evaluate his life. He had recently broken up with a woman named Valerie Hoggatt, but he quickly realized that he had not fully appreciated her. He initiated a reconciliation and they were married three months later, in September 1991. "She was the same sweet, wonderful person she had been before and is now," Robinson said. "I just hadn't been paying attention."

Robinson continues to credit his religious faith with giving him the strength to cope with the pressures of living life so squarely in the public spotlight. "I'm not playing for the fans or the money, but to honor God," he said. "I know my motivation. I know where I'm headed. Every night I try to go out there to honor Him and play great."

DRIVE FOR THE PLAYOFFS

As the beginning of the 1991-92 season approached, Robinson became increasingly excited. He was finally content with his personal life, and he felt that the peace he had found would help him meet his basketball goals. As the season unfolded, Robinson posted another great year. But late in the season, on March 16, 1992, he tore a ligament in his left hand that required surgery. Forced to enter the playoffs without their most valuable player, San Antonio lost in the first round. The timing of the hand injury disappointed Robinson, but his performance prior to the mishap further solidified his place among the NBA's top players. He became only the third player in NBA history to finish in the top ten in five statistical categories for a season—first in blocks, fourth in rebounds, fifth in steals, sixth in field goal percentage, and eighth in scoring. He also was voted NBA defensive player of the year.

OLYMPIC GOLD

By August 1992, Robinson had recovered from his surgery well enough to play on the United States Olympic basketball team. In 1989, the international governing organization for Olympic basketball had ruled that professional athletes could compete in the Olympics. Olympic basketball had traditionally been dominated by the United States, even though the teams had always been composed of young college players rather than professionals. The American team's loss in the 1988 Olympics, though, spurred new calls for a team made up of the country's finest pro players. With the new mandate making professionals eligible to compete, the United States formed the so-called Dream Team. This Olympic team was made up of eleven NBA superstars, including Robinson, and one college player. As expected, the Dream Team trounced all their opponents and easily won the gold medal in Barcelona, Spain.

The 1992-93 season saw a number of changes on the Spurs team. The team struggled during the opening weeks under new coach Jerry Tarkanian, and injuries to key players further hampered the team. After 20 games the Spurs had a losing record, and Tarkanian resigned. He was replaced by John Lucas, a former NBA player with no head coaching experience. Under Lucas, though, San Antonio rediscovered its winning edge. Led by Robinson, the team ripped off a long winning streak and ended the regular season as one of the league's top teams. In the playoffs the Spurs defeated the Portland Trailblazers, who were the defending western conference champions, but eventually fell to the Phoenix Suns in six games in the conference finals. Once again, Robinson had been denied in his push to reach the NBA championship.

NBA'S LEADING SCORER

In the 1993-94 season Robinson posted his usual impressive rebounding and blocked-shots statistics. He averaged more than ten rebounds a game and was third in the league in blocked shots, with more than three a game. But he also led the entire NBA in scoring for the first time with a 29.8 points-per-game average. His total included a 71-point game on the final day of the regular season, which enabled him to edge out Shaquille O'Neal for league scoring honors. But Robinson's brilliant season and the Spurs' 55-27 regular season mark were quickly forgotten when they were dispatched from the playoffs by the Utah Jazz. John Lucas subsequently left the team, and he was replaced by Bob Hill.

As the 1994-95 season unfolded, the Spurs players worked hard to understand Hill's coaching strategy and philosophy, and to ignore the sometimes selfish and bizarre behavior of new forward Dennis Rodman. Robinson proved particularly adept at adjusting to the new atmosphere in the San Antonio locker room. Galvanized by Robinson's tough play at both ends of the court, the Spurs marched to a 62-20 regular season record, and their big center was named league Most Valuable Player. In the playoffs, though, the Spurs ran into the Houston Rockets. Houston had a star center of their own in Hakeem Olajuwon, who led them to victory over the Spurs with a tremendous performance. Losing to the Rockets "felt like falling off a cliff," said Robinson.

The 1995-96 season proved frustrating as well. After the Spurs traded Rodman to the Chicago Bulls, the atmosphere in the Spurs locker room became much calmer, and San Antonio once again enjoyed a successful regular season. Robinson led the team in scoring and rebounding, and on many nights he was as dominating as any other player in the league. But the season ended with another loss in the playoffs, this time to the Utah Jazz. The loss to the Jazz hurt Robinson, but he was happy to have the 1996 Summer Olympics to look forward to. The Dream Team of NBA stars

was formed once again. As expected, they easily rolled over their competition to win a gold medal in the basketball competition.

Despite past playoff disappointments, Robinson is determined to reach the league finals. He has noted that many famous NBA players have had to wait for years before reaching the championship, and he remains confident that his talent and desire will someday help push the Spurs to the top of the NBA.

THE NATURE OF FAME

Robinson recognizes that he has been a lucky man in many respects, and he often feels that other NBA players do not fully appreciate their good fortune. "I think I'm the luckiest guy in the world," he said. "I hear guys who sit at the end of the bench gripe about making $250,000. What are they talking about? . . . If I was making $250,000 to sit at the end of the bench and wave a towel, I'd be the best towel waver you ever saw."

The towering center also recognizes that fame can be a fleeting thing. "What good is putting my name in the record books when all I'm gonna be is a Trivial Pursuit answer 20 years from now?" Robinson once remarked. "So many guys have accomplished a lot, but, boy, where are they now? And who cares about them, to be honest with you. Who cares? A nasty guy, a guy who was mean to people and accomplished a whole lot? Big deal. How did your life really affect other people? The people's lives that I've been able to touch with God's help, that lasts forever."

MARRIAGE AND FAMILY

Robinson married Valerie Hoggatt in September 1991. They have two sons, David Maurice, Jr., and Corey. The Robinsons have homes in San Antonio and Aspen, Colorado, and Robinson loves to spend as much time with his family as he can. One time he remarked that while other men sometimes talk about finding ways to get out of the house, he is more interested in finding "ways to get back to the house."

HOBBIES AND OTHER INTERESTS

Robinson is well known for his active involvement in the San Antonio community. He supports many of the city's youth programs, and he has given his time to a number of national charities and foundations that are aimed at educating inner-city schoolchildren. He also established the David Robinson Foundation, which provides grants, game tickets, and other services to young people. During the first half of the 1990s the Foundation, which is operated by his parents, gave more than $1 million to various charitable organizations.

HONORS AND AWARDS

Adolph Rupp Award: 1987
College Player of the Year (*Sporting News*): 1987
John Wooden Award: 1987
Pan-American Games: 1987, silver medal
Olympic Basketball: 1988, bronze medal; 1992, gold medal; 1996, gold medal
NBA Rookie of the Year: 1990
NBA All-Rookie First Team: 1990
NBA All-Star: 1990-91, 1991-92, 1992-93, 1993-94, 1994-95, 1995-96
NBA Defensive Player of the Year: 1991-92
NBA Most Valuable Player: 1994-95

FURTHER READING

BOOKS

Aaseng, Nathan. *Sports Great David Robinson*, 1992 (juvenile)
Gutman, Bill. *David Robinson: NBA Super Center*, 1993 (juvenile)
Miller, Dawn M. *David Robinson: Backboard Admiral*, 1991 (juvenile)
Rothaus, James R. *David Robinson*, 1991 (juvenile)
Who's Who in America, 1996

PERIODICALS

Boys' Life, Feb. 1993, p.16
Current Biography Yearbook 1993
Gentleman's Quarterly (GQ), Feb. 1991, p.170
Jet, June 12, 1995, p.49
Los Angeles Times, Jan. 30, 1990, p.C2; Mar. 19, 1991, p.C1
New York Times, Dec. 7, 1986, p.10; May 18, 1988, p.A27; Oct. 16, 1989, p.C13; Jan. 12, 1990, p.A27
People, Feb. 23, 1987, p.85; Mar. 28, 1990, p.28
Sport Magazine, Nov. 1994, p.102; Jan. 1996, p.66
Sporting News, Nov. 8, 1993, p.12; Apr. 24, 1995, p.14
Sports Illustrated, Jan. 29, 1990, p.14; Feb. 17, 1992, p.77; Mar. 7, 1994, p.58; Apr. 29, 1996, p.90
Sports Illustrated for Kids, Mar. 1995, p.34

ADDRESS

San Antonio Spurs
600 E. Market St., Suite 102
San Antonio, TX 78205

WORLD WIDE WEB SITE

http://www.nba.com/spurs

Dennis Rodman 1961-
American Professional Basketball Player
with the Chicago Bulls
Winner of Four Consecutive Rebounding Titles

BIRTH

Dennis Keith Rodman was born May 13, 1961, in Trenton, New Jersey, to Shirley and Phil Rodman. Shirley was a homemaker at the time of Dennis's birth, and Phil was in the Air Force. The family soon moved to Dallas, Texas, where Dennis grew up. He has two younger sisters, Debra and Kim.

GROWING UP

When Dennis was three, his father left the family. Phil Rodman didn't make contact with any member of the family for almost 20 years. As a single mother, Shirley had to work two jobs to provide for her children. Dennis became a shy, sensitive kid, very withdrawn and longing to be close to his mother. "I felt shut out not having a father, always having to look out for myself," Rodman remembers. "And my mother just didn't have enough time to be with me. She was always more interested in my sisters."

EDUCATION

Rodman went to the public schools in Dallas and attended South Oak Cliff High School. Despite his current reputation as one of the great defenders in the NBA, Rodman didn't even play basketball seriously until he was 20 years old. He went out for football in high school, but was cut from the team. He also spent a half season warming the bench on the high school basketball team. "I couldn't even make a lay up right," Rodman says. At 5'11" and skinny, Rodman earned his nickname "Worm" around this time, for his wiggly contortions while playing pinball.

After graduating from high school in 1979, Rodman took a variety of odd jobs, busing tables, washing cars, and the like. Once, while working as a janitor at the Dallas-Fort Worth Airport, Rodman stole 15 watches from an airport store. He spent the night in jail, then returned the stolen goods.

Around this time, Rodman experienced an incredible growth spurt. In less than a year, he grew an astounding nine inches. He started to play basketball, and even as he was getting use to his new gangliness, his talent for the game emerged. Rodman's sisters, Debra and Kim, were both all-American basketball stars at their high school. They recognized their brother's gifts and arranged for him to try out for the Cooke County Junior College team.

But Rodman played only one semester at Cooke County, then dropped out. He moved back in with his family, but seemed to have no ambition to do anything. His mom got disgusted with him and threw him out of the house. Rodman moved from friend to friend. He spent a lot of time hanging out on the basketball courts of Dallas, and one day he was discovered by Jack Hedden, the coach of the Southeastern Oklahoma State basketball team. In 1983, Hedden offered Rodman a scholarship to play basketball. As a 22-year-old freshman, Rodman had a new start on a career, and he took advantage of it. "People said, 'You ain't gonna make it because you ain't got what it takes,'" says Rodman. "I said to myself, 'I'm never going to come back to Dallas until I make the NBA, prove all these people wrong.'"

COLLEGE

In his years at Southeastern Oklahoma State, Rodman was named a first-team NAIA (National Association of Intercollegiate Athletics) All-American for three straight seasons. He played in 96 games, making an average of 25.7 points in each game and showing his rebounding talent with an average of 15.7 rebounds per game. Rodman graduated from Southeastern Oklahoma State in 1986.

AN ALTERNATE FAMILY

During his years in Oklahoma, Rodman developed an unlikely friendship with the Rich family of rural Oklahoma. Pat and James Rich of Bokchito, Oklahoma, had sent their son Bryne to Southeastern Oklahoma State basketball camp, where he met Rodman. Bryne, 13 years old, was still in shock and grief over accidently killing his best friend in a hunting accident. His parents hoped that basketball camp would help the boy. Bryne was captivated by Rodman, and one day after camp asked his parents if Rodman could come to dinner. "By the way, he said, "Rodman is black."

"I almost swallered my tongue when I heard," says Pat Rich. But Rodman came to dinner and just about moved in. Over the next several years, he spent a lot of time on the family farm, even helping out with the harvesting. "Worm brought Bryne out of the depression he was in," says Pat Rich. "But at the same time, I think Bryne helped save Worm."

Much has been made in the media of Rodman and his "adoptive" family, some of it by the Rich family themselves. In the late 1980s, when Rodman had become an NBA star, Pat Rich tried to sell her story to magazines, television, and the movies. In 1994, Rodman, Pat Rich, and Alan Steinberg coauthored a book on the family's relationship with Rodman. Rodman's real mother, Shirley, resented the tone of the stories. "How dare people sit there and talk about Dennis's 'surrogate white family' or his second mother? He doesn't need another mother. He has one. I raised my son."

The Rich family lives in an area that is notoriously unfriendly to African-Americans. Rodman remembers driving to the Rich home on the weekends, with Pat Rich burying her head in a newspaper so that none of her neighbors could tell she was riding in the car with a black man. "I didn't want to be seen alone with Worm because I didn't want rumors to get started," said Pat Rich. Despite the evident contradictions in their backgrounds, Rodman and the Rich family continue to be close. In fact, he was with them when he received his first call from the NBA.

CAREER HIGHLIGHTS

DETROIT PISTONS

After graduating from college in 1986, Rodman was eligible for the NBA draft. He was picked in the second round by the Detroit Pistons, where he would play for seven years on the best team that franchise has yet put together. He spent most of the first year on the bench, averaging 4.3 points per game and 6.5 rebounds. The exuberant Rodman became an early favorite of the crowds.

Known as the "Worm," the nickname from his childhood days, Rodman was a player of tremendous energy and emotion. He would ride a stationary bicycle for hours before a game, go out and give his all, then go back to the bike for another hour after the game, just to burn off energy. Fans, sitting in a special section of the Pistons' arena called "Rodman's Roost," would delight in the emotional outbursts of their favorite player. He would punch his fists in the air after a key play, leap in the air to acknowledge the accomplishments of a teammate; he was an irrepressible spirit for the Pistons.

Former Pistons' coach and TV commentator Dick Versace remembers Rodman's early exuberance: "When he came into the league, he was this wide-eyed, frenetic, incredibly naive guy who just cherished it all. Dennis would get the ball two feet from the basket and give it up. He was so thrilled—it was like, 'Wow, I'm playing with Isiah Thomas'."

Rodman was making good money for the first time in his life, and felt he wanted to share his new-found wealth. He would sometimes drive through the streets of downtown Detroit and give whatever money he had—sometimes wads of bills amounting to hundreds of dollars—to the homeless.

But then Rodman made a comment that would dog him for years. Frustrated and angry over the Pistons' loss to the Boston Celtics in the NBA Eastern Conference finals in 1987, Rodman said: "Larry Bird is overrated in a lot of areas. I don't think he's the greatest player." When asked why Bird got so much publicity, Rodman responded, "Because he's white. You never hear about a black player being the greatest." The response to Rodman's outburst was immediate and negative. Pistons' Captain Isiah Thomas stepped in and took most of the flak, but Rodman was labeled a big mouth and a troublemaker.

The 1988-89 season saw Detroit emerging as a championship contender, with Rodman playing more games. His stats doubled, as he averaged 8.7 points per game and 11.6 rebounds. That season, he also led the league field goal percentage, with an average of 59.5 percent.

"BAD BOYS" AND TWO NBA CHAMPIONSHIPS

The Pistons of that era, coached by Chuck Daly, included Isiah Thomas, Joe Dumars, Bill Laimbeer, Adrain Dantley, Rick Mahorn, Vinnie Johnson, John Salley, and Rodman. The team developed a reputation as an aggressive, rough-and-tumble defensive team, tagged the "Bad Boys" by the media. Rodman and Laimbeer, especially, were fierce under the boards, using the force of their bodies to ground their opponents.

In the 1989-90 season, the Pistons began the first of five straight seasons in the conference finals. Rodman, now part of the starting line up, was also chosen for the NBA All-Star team and voted the league's best defensive player. As the Pistons roared to the NBA finals, their quest for the championship included a memorable series against the Chicago Bulls, during which Rodman successfully guarded superstars Michael Jordan and Scottie Pippen.

Coach Chuck Daly remembers the Worm: "There's never been an NBA player like him. I love him. I'll endorse him anywhere. As a coach you go to the wall for a guy like that. He'll win you six to 10 games a year without even scoring." Rodman explained his ability like this: "I have perfected the idea of following the flight of the ball. I know the arcs and can tell where it's going and most of the time how it will bounce."

The 1990-91 season brought another championship to the Pistons, and further evidence of their "Bad Boy" ways. In the playoff series against Chicago, Rodman shoved Scottie Pippen into the first two rows of the stands, causing a gash and scar that Pippen, now Rodman's teammate, still has today. Jordan was vocal in his disdain for the Detroit team, saying that the Pistons' style of play was "abhorrent" to him.

The 1991-92 season brought the emergence of the Chicago Bulls and the dominance of Michael Jordan to the NBA. The game was changing. John Salley, now a member of the Bulls, remembers it this way: "People wanted to see ballet in shorts. And Michael Jordan brought 'em ballet in shorts. Dennis brings you blue-collar; the Pistons brought you blue-collar. We did whatever was necessary to win without killing nobody." The Pistons lost to the New York Knicks in the playoffs at the end of the 1992 season.

In 1992, Vinnie Johnson, James Edwards, and John Salley left the Pistons. More importantly for Rodman, Chuck Daly was let go. Rodman, who considered Daly a close friend, was furious and hurt to see his team in disarray. "It's these kinds of things that I don't like and make me want to leave the game. It's like sometimes you don't have control of your own life, like you have to be a mechanical type of person because of your environment, and that's just not me." In the fall of 1992, Rodman skipped training camp entirely. He was suspended without pay. Rodman protested the suspension, claiming he was injured. He finally returned to the team in late November, playing great basketball. But by then some of his off-court activities were starting to attract attention, and were worrying those closest to him.

A CONTROVERSIAL CHARACTER

In early 1993 the police found Rodman in the parking lot of the Palace with a loaded shotgun under the seat. He hadn't broken any laws, but he had scared the Pistons players, coaches, and owners. Rodman remembers the incident. "Why was the rifle there? It's always there. I was depressed, but I wasn't going to kill myself. I was just hurting, ripped to shreds. You butt heads with reality and it's like having a stroke. I didn't lose touch with reality, but I put it on pause."

At the end of the 1992-93 season, the new Pistons coach, Ron Rothstein, was fired after the Pistons failed to make it to the playoffs. Rodman was ready to move. In the fall of 1993, he was traded to the San Antonio Spurs. By the time he left Detroit, Rodman was showing increasing signs of emotional strain. His marriage was falling apart, the team he had considered his family had disintegrated, and he felt abandoned.

SAN ANTONIO SPURS

In his two seasons with San Antonio, Rodman's ever more flamboyant personal life began to overshadow his professional career. He was becoming better known for his ever-changing hair color, his numerous tattoos, and the growing number of rings in his ears and nose than for his talent on the court. His much-publicized romance with Madonna made front page headlines as his arrogance and growing absences from practices made him more and more difficult to deal with. He would take car loads of sports writers to Las Vegas after games to gamble, reveling in a lifestyle purposely in contrast to that of a disciplined athlete.

By the 1994 season, Rodman seemed to be in a downward spiral emotionally, his behavior ever more manic both on and off the court. He missed planes, was chronically late for practice and games, and wound up getting suspended for the first 15 games in the fall of 1994. During that season, Rodman was called for 28 technical fouls and was ejected from five games. He had to meet with the commissioner of basketball and was reprimanded. But somehow his incredible defensive skills stayed intact. During the 1994-95 season, he won his fourth consecutive rebounding title. He was only the third person in history to do so, an honor he shares with basketball legends Wilt Chamberlain and Moses Malone.

Rodman was also angry over his salary. In a conference where many first-year players, without two championship rings, make $5 million a year, Rodman felt underpaid at $2.5 million a year. He claims he was promised that his salary would move upward if he played well, and he felt he did his best for the Spurs. "I want to be respected and rewarded for what I've done," he said. "All of a sudden you've got a guy like me who's controversial, and it's very interesting because they don't want to reward me for what I've achieved in basketball."

Rodman continued to flame the controversy, posing in women's clothing for a *Sports Illustrated* cover story in May 1995. Michael Silver, the author of the cover story, summed up the Rodman dilemma, writing that, depending on your point of view, he is "either a selfish problem child or an authentic genius who transcends the sport." Silver, like most players, commentators, and fans, is in awe of Rodman's prowess on the court. He describes Rodman's play like this: "He runs up and down the court like a gazelle, and his defense is a study in body control. Even the weakest part of Rodman's game, his offense, is deceptively potent." Rodman is able to alter the pace of the game, according to former teammate Doc Rivers. "He can control the tempo of a game without scoring, and that's amazing," says Rivers. "He's so smart, and he sees the floor like a guard. He'll set the key screen or make that great pass. His pass might not lead to the basket, but it's the pass that leads to the pass that leads to the basket."

The problem for the Spurs management became how to use Rodman and put up with the distractions. It just didn't work out.

CHICAGO BULLS

Then the Chicago Bulls came knocking on Rodman's door. After three spectacular NBA championships with Michael Jordan, the Bulls had languished while Jordan left basketball to pursue a career in pro baseball. When Jordan came back to the team in 1995, the Bulls seemed ready to dominate the league again. But they needed a power forward with strength under the boards. Despite his reputation, Rodman was their choice.

Rodman joined the Bulls in October 1995, and has performed brilliantly with the team. He was recently featured on another *Sports Illustrated* cover, this time as "The Greatest Rebounder of All Time." The Bulls are currently having the best season in the NBA, and it looks as if Rodman will be a key player in their next championship season.

How has Chicago taken to the former Piston they loved to hate? They have embraced him warmly. At Christmas time 1995, the hottest items for kids were Rodman jerseys and shoes. "It's just the way he plays," explains a 14-year-old Chicago fan. "He doesn't care about anything. He just does his job." The young fans like "the way he colors his hair, the tattoos. He's like no one else."

Rodman is also seeing dollars come his way through endorsements. In the eyes of companies like Nike and Pizza Hut, Rodman's in-your-face attitude plays well with teens and young adults, and he has signed lucrative contracts with both organizations. Tom Feuer, who manages public relations for Nike, says: "Dennis may be a little odd, but he's committed no crimes and he's very much a part of our future." The chairman of the ad agency that produces Rodman's Pizza Hut ads says that he thinks Rodman manipulates the media for his own ends. "Dennis has cultivated and created his bad-boy persona," says Philip B. Dusenberry. "He's decided to make himself marketable and not blend in with the NBA."

This may be an indication of Rodman's future. He claims he's "not an athlete, but an entertainer." He hopes to make films, and he's appeared on late-night TV, including "The Tonight Show with Jay Leno" and "The Late Show with David Letterman." "I could do something else, but show business is what I do on the court. So that'll be my next career," says Rodman. But most commentators agree that as long as he continues to play basketball, he will give it his all, racking up rebounds and titles for his teams. And as Phil Taylor of *Sports Illustrated* remarked recently, "It may be the knowledge that behaving himself for an entire year is the only way left for him to shock anyone."

MARRIAGE AND FAMILY

Rodman has been married once, to Annie Bakes, a former model and dancer. They have one daughter, Alexis. The marriage took place in 1993 and lasted less than a year. After Rodman and Bakes broke up, he had a tattoo of his daughter's face and name put on his forearm. Alexis lives with her mother in California, and Rodman visits often.

HOBBIES AND OTHER INTERESTS

Rodman owns a construction company in Dallas, Rodman Excavating, Inc. His flamboyant lifestyle includes an ever-growing number of tattoos, as well as a Harley Davidson motorcycle, a pickup truck, and a cigarette boat in his signature color—pink. "Pink shows power, bro'," says Rodman. He's also finishing an autobiography, tentatively titled *As Bad As I Want to Be*, scheduled for publication late in 1996.

WRITINGS

Rebound: The Enduring Friendship of Dennis Rodman and Bryne Rich, 1994 (with Pat Rich and Alan Steinberg)

HONORS AND AWARDS

NBA Defensive Player of the Year: 1990, 1991
NBA All-Star Team: 1990, 1992
NBA Rebounding Title: 1991-1995

FURTHER READING

BOOKS

Rodman, Dennis, with Pat Rich and Alan Steinberg. *Rebound: The Enduring Friendship of Dennis Rodman and Bryne Rich*, 1994
Thornley, Stew. *Sports Great Dennis Rodman*, 1996 (juvenile)
Who's Who in America 1996

PERIODICALS

Business Week, July 17, 1995, p.74
Chicago Tribune, May 27, 1990, p.D8; Apr. 19, 1992, p.D12; May 4, 1993, p.D5; Mar. 15, 1994, p.D7; Oct. 3, 1995, p.D1; Oct. 8, 1995, p.D1; Nov. 3, 1995, p.D1; Jan. 22, 1996, p.D10
Detroit Free Press, Dec. 13, 1988, p.D1; May 17, 1991, p.D1; Dec. 11, 1992, p.F1; May 5, 1993, p.C2; Jan. 19, 1996, p.F1
Interview, Nov. 1995, p.101
People, May 15, 1995, p.137
Reader's Digest, Jan. 1988, p.167
Sport, Mar. 1994, p.27; Nov. 1994, p.78
The Sporting News, Oct. 24, 1994, p.44
Sports Illustrated, May 2, 1988, p.58; Nov. 11, 1993, p.124; May 29, 1995, p.20; Mar. 4, 1996, p.21

ADDRESS

Chicago Bulls
1901 West Madison Street
Chicago, IL 60612-2459

OBITUARY

Selena   1971-1995
American Singer
The Queen of Tejano, or Tex-Mex Music

BIRTH

Selena Quintanilla Perez, the singing sensation known simply as
Selena who was tragically killed by one of her own fans, was born
on April 16, 1971, in Lake Jackson, Texas. Selena's entire family
was involved in her music. Her father, Abraham Quintanilla, Jr.,
a former musician, was the manager of her band, Selena y Los
Dinos; her mother, Marcela Quintanilla, provided guidance and
spiritual advice on the road; her brother, Abraham III, was the
bass player, songwriter, and later, producer; and her sister, Suzette,

was the band's drummer. For Selena, the youngest child of her family, music and family were so tied together that she eventually married her band's guitarist, Chris Perez.

Selena and her family were not recent immigrants to the United States. Selena's great-grandfather, Eulojio Quintanilla, came to the U.S. from Mexico soon after his birth; he eventually married a Mexican-American woman named Doloris who was born in this country. The Quintanilla family has continued to live and work in south Texas for over 100 years. Selena, along with the rest of her family, spoke English as her first language; she didn't learn to speak Spanish until years later.

YOUTH

Selena's father, Abraham Quintanilla, had been a musician in his youth. Beginning in high school, he sang and played bass guitar with a popular traditional Tex-Mex band called Los Dinos (slang for "the guys"). He stayed with the band from the late 1950s to the early 1970s, when he left the music business to take a comfortable job as a shipping clerk for Dow Chemical. Their facility was in Lake Jackson, where Selena was born, a blue-collar factory town south of Houston, near the Gulf of Mexico.

Selena's talent for music was obvious when she was still a little girl. One day when she was about five, her father was teaching her brother, Abraham III (known as A.B.), how to play bass guitar. Jealous of the attention her older brother was getting, Selena picked up a song book and started singing. Everyone in the family was amazed and impressed by "this huge voice coming out of this little bitty person," according to her sister Suzette. "Her timing, her pitch were perfect," her father adds. "I could see it from day one." Pretty soon, Selena was the one getting all the attention for her music.

She started out by singing country-western songs in English. Then her father began teaching her some traditional Mexican songs in Spanish. When she first started, he taught her the songs phonetically. She learned the individual sounds of the words without actually being able to speak or understand the language. Later, when she began touring in Mexico, Selena learned to speak Spanish.

By 1980, Abraham Quintanilla had saved up enough money to follow his dream: he quit his job at Dow Chemical and opened a Mexican restaurant, Papagallo's. The whole family helped out, doing chores around the restaurant. In addition, the family band, with A.B. on bass guitar, Suzette on drums, and Selena as the lead singer, often entertained customers at the restaurant and began playing at local weddings as well. But the following year, the economy throughout Texas underwent a recession, or economic downturn. Many Texans were employed by the oil industry, and when oil prices slumped, people lost their jobs. Many had to make serious changes in the way they spent money. In tough times, the luxury of dinner out in a restaurant is one of the first cutbacks people make. The Quintanilla family went bankrupt. They lost their restaurant and their home after only about one year.

By 1982, the family had packed up and moved to Corpus Christi, the hometown of the Quintanilla family. From there, the family began touring around Texas and eventually throughout the Southwest. Life on the road was really tough. They traveled in a broken-down bus with a foldout bed in the back. Their band, Selena y Los Dinos, played at weddings, bars, clubs, and anyplace else they could pick up a paycheck. "That's when we began our musical career," Selena once explained. "We had no alternative."

EDUCATION

Selena started school at Oran M. Roberts Elementary School in Lake Jackson. She was a good student: upbeat, easy to get along with, well-liked, and eager to learn. Even at a young age, she made an impression on those around her. Nina McGlashan, her first grade teacher, recalls: "What I remember is that big smile. Selena had a real perky personality. She was happy—she had a good attitude. Children who have a very cheerful 'up' personality frequently do go on to influence people, and that's the strength I saw in Selena."

After the family moved to Corpus Christi, Selena attended West Oso Junior High School. But by that time she was touring with the family band and was frequently pulled out of class to go on road trips. She dropped out of school in eighth grade and finished her education through a home-schooling program. She earned a high-school equivalency diploma through a correspondence course. Later, she became a strong advocate for education. She encouraged the Mexican-American children who looked up to her as a role model to stay in school.

CAREER HIGHLIGHTS

By her teen years Selena was already a professional musician, helping her family earn a living. Despite the hardships of those early years, she would say that she didn't mind. "I lost a lot of my teenage period," she once explained. "But I got a lot out of it too. I was more mature." Over time, Selena and the family band gradually became more successful and widely known. They started appearing in larger venues and drawing bigger crowds. They began releasing recordings as well, ultimately releasing almost a dozen albums for a small regional label. They also appeared on "The Johnny Canales Show," which showcases Latin music. Currently broadcast internationally, Johnny Canales was just getting started when

Selena first appeared on his show. In all these ways, Selena was bringing Tejano music to a larger and ever more appreciative audience.

TEJANO MUSIC

Tejano, which means "Texan" is Spanish, is a term used to describe a certain style of music that has been played in southern Texas and along the border of Mexico for almost 100 years. It is the music of Selena's childhood. Tejano music combines several different influences. The music is based on a traditional style called *conjunto,* or Tex-Mex music. (The term Tex-Mex is often used to describe the people, music, food, and other elements of life in the border region.) Conjunto relies on the drums, the *bajo sexto,* an acoustic bass guitar, and the accordian, which was brought to the area by the many German immigrants who settled in the region in the 19th century. Tejano music is a modernized form of conjunto that incorporates such diverse elements as polka (often using synthesizers to replace the accordion), country and western, rhythm and blues, and *cumbia* (red-hot Latin dance rhythms from Columbia). Above all, Tejano is dance music. As Selena herself once described it, "It's got polka in it, a little bit of country, a little bit of jazz. Fuse all those types of music together, I think that's where you get Tejano."

SUCCESS

When Selena first started touring with her band, Tejano music was a local phenomenon, popular only in the border region. Spanish-language music is very diverse, and people from different geographical areas and ethnic backgrounds tend to listen to very different types of music. In the late 1980s and early 1990s, though, interest in Tejano music gradually spread to Hispanic groups in other areas of the U.S., its popularity fueled in part by Selena. Her first big break came in 1986. She was only about 15 when she won the Tejano Music Awards for Female Vocalist of the Year and Performer of the Year, awards she

went on to win many more times. In 1989, she and Los Dinos signed a deal with the giant record company EMI, guaranteeing more aggressive promotion and widespread distribution of their records. Their career began to take off.

In 1992, the band had their first hit single. "Buenos Amigos," recorded with Alvaro Torres, reached # 1 on *Billboard* magazine's list of Hot Latin Tracks. After that hit, radio stations that played Tejano and other Spanish-language music began featuring Selena's records, and her music became much more widely known throughout the various Hispanic communities. Her songs began routinely hitting the top of the charts. Her 1993 album, *Selena Live!* earned her a Grammy Award for Best Mexican-American album. By the following year, her album *Amor Prohibido* (1994) was at the top of the *Billboard* Latin chart, and she was drawing 60,000 fans to her concerts in Texas.

SELENA'S IMAGE AND APPEAL TO HER FANS

Selena's live appearances contributed greatly to her image. A charismatic performer, Selena projected a certain image on stage. With her vivacious singing and dancing, suggestive smile, sizzling stage presence, and pro-vocative clothing, she was often compared to Madonna. Her flamboyant midriff-baring costumes became so popular, in fact, that she started a chain of boutiques to market her designs.

Despite Selena's sexy image, her fans saw another side of her. While enjoying her singing and stage shows, they also respected her strong emphasis on family, an important part of the Hispanic cultural tradition. Cheerful, sunny, friendly and approachable, down to earth and unpreten-tious, she still shopped at K Mart and ate rice and beans. At home in Corpus Christi, fans would see her in restaurants, shops, or at home washing her car, and she was always ready to stop and chat. Selena was proud of her heritage, and she shared that feeling of ethnic pride with her fans as well. Admired for her devotion to God and family as well as her vocal support for staying in school and staying off drugs, Selena was revered as a role model by Hispanics, and particularly by young women.

Selena was also broadening her appeal to the mainstream audience as well. In early 1995 she was working on a new album. For the first time, she would be singing in English. Selena had long dreamed of being a crossover success, an artist who could appeal equally to her long-standing Hispanic fans and to new mainstream English-language listeners as well. With her upcoming release, many believed that she was on the brink of achieving her dream. For her fans, that's what made the timing of her death so hard.

HER DEATH

On March 31, 1995, Selena was shot to death by Yolanda Saldivar. A long-time fan, Saldivar had been the founder of the singer's fan club and had, more recently, been employed by Selena in her clothing boutique. According to the family, they had recently come to suspect Saldivar of stealing money from the business, and they planned to fire her. On March 31, Selena went, alone, to the Days Inn motel in Corpus Christi to speak with her. Soon afterward, Saldivar shot Selena. Selena was rushed to the hospital, but she died shortly afterward. When the police arrived at the motel, they found Saldivar holed up in a car in the parking lot. She had a gun, and she was threatening to kill herself. The stand-off lasted almost 10 hours before she surrendered to police. When taken to police headquarters, she confessed to the crime.

The response to Selena's death was immediate. There was a huge outpouring of grief throughout Texas and elsewhere. Fans called in to radio stations, sobbing. They couldn't believe the devastating news. People created impromptu shrines to Selena—with flowers, signs, notes, and candles—at her home, her boutique, her recording studio, and at the Days Inn motel, the site of her death. Mourners held candlelight vigils and besieged her family with offers of condolence. Memorial services were held in many places, large and small, in Corpus Christi and elsewhere. At the Bayfront Plaza Auditorium in Corpus Christi, tens of thousands of mourners lined up to view Selena's casket, to pay their respects and to say goodbye.

Selena's fans paid close attention just a few months later, in October 1995, when Saldivar went on trial for murder. While the defense claimed that the shooting was accidental, the prosecution argued that Saldivar shot Selena because she was about to be fired for embezzling $30,000. The jury convicted Saldivar of murder and sentenced her to life in prison, the maximum punishment. Because of threats to her life, she will serve her time alone in her cell with no contact with the other inmates. Saldivar's lawyer has said that they will appeal the verdict.

Selena's final recordings were included in her posthumous release, *Dreaming of You* (1995). The album includes several cuts in English, two bilingual duets (one with David Bryne and one with the Barrio Boyzz), and six songs in Spanish, including several of her biggest hits: "Amor Prohibido," "Bidi Bidi Bom Bom," "Techno Cumbia," and "Como la Flor." Two of the Spanish songs are from her appearance in the 1995 film *Don Juan De Marco,* starring Marlon Brando and Johnny Depp. *Dreaming of You* became the second fastest-selling album by a female in pop history, selling 175,000 copies on its day of release. First-week sales of more than 331,000 copies put the album in the # 1 spot on the *Billboard* pop chart. Selena's first English-language release was a huge success. But it was bittersweet for her family, knowing that Selena had fulfilled her dream of crossover success only after her death.

SELENA'S LEGACY

In a moving tribute to the slain singer in *Hispanic* magazine, Catherine Vásquez-Revilla explained the phenomenal impact felt by so many when Selena died. "Selena was from a west side barrio in Corpus Christi, so for many of the children from lower-income families . . . Selena became a symbol of hope for their own success. Her devotion and obligation to her family and community were qualities that many Hispanics consider important in their own lives. . . .

"For Mexican Americans, Selena's success became their success. She inspired confidence and ethnic pride. The stage lights that shone on her also reached across to include Mexican Americans by highlighting their language, music, and culture. Her greatest gift was that her talent, beauty, and success empowered all Hispanics."

MARRIAGE AND FAMILY

Selena met her future husband, Chris Perez, when he joined the band as lead guitarist in the late 1980s. At first, they were just friends. Then Selena told her brother, A.B., that she was interested in Chris, and A.B. talked to him. Selena and Chris were going out together by 1991 and were married on April 2, 1992, in a simple private wedding. They lived next door to her parents in a small, two-bedroom house in Corpus Christi. When Selena died, they were planning to build a large home on 10 acres in a more secluded area outside of town. But Chris has abandoned those plans. "I gave up on that dream because that was a dream I had with Selena. I don't want it without her."

SELECTED RECORDINGS

Alpha, 1986

Dulce Amor, 1988
Preciosa, 1988
Selena y Los Dinos, 1990
16 Super Exitos Originales, 1990
Ven Conmigo, 1991
Entre A Mi Mundo, 1992
Selena Live! 1993
Mis Mejores Canciones—17 Super Exitos, 1993
Amor Prohibido, 1994
Dreaming of You, 1995

VIDEOS

"La Caracha"
"Amor Prohibido"
"No Me Queda Mas"
"La Llamada"
"Bidi Bidi Bom Bom"
"Dondequiera Que Estes" (with the Barrio Boyzz)
"Buenos Amigos" (with Alvaro Torres)

HONORS AND AWARDS

Tejano Music Awards: 1987, Female Vocalist of the Year; 1988, Female
Entertainer of the Year; 1989-95, Female Vocalist of the Year and Female
Entertainer of the Year (7 straight years); 1993-95, Album of the Year;
1995, also Song of the Year, Tejano Crossover, Record of the Year, and
Video of the Year
Premio Lo Nuestro a la Musica Latina: 1993, regional/Mexican category,
Female Artist of the Year and Album of the Year, for *Entre a Mi Mundo;*
Song of the Year, for "Como La Flor"; 1995, Female Artist of the Year
in Pop/Ballad and Regional Mexican Music, Best Song, Album of the Year
Grammy Award: 1994, for Best Mexican-American Album, for *Selena Live!*
Latin Music Hall of Fame (*Billboard* magazine): 1995

FURTHER READING

BOOKS

Novas, Himilce, and Rosemary Silva. *Remembering Selena: A Tribute in
Pictures and Words,* 1995 (a dual language edition; entitled in Spanish
Recordando Selena: Un Tributo en Palabras y Fotos)
Richmond, Clint. *Selena! The Phenomenal Life and Tragic Death of the
Tejano Music Queen,* 1995 (a dual language edition; entitled in Spanish
*Selena! La vida sensacional y la muerte tragica de la reina de la musica
tejana,* translated by Shawn Fields)

PERIODICALS

Entertainment Weekly, Apr. 14, 1995, p.20; Aug. 18, 1995, p.18
Good Housekeeping, Aug. 1995, p.26
Hispanic, May 1995, pp.12 and 96
New York Times, Apr. 1, 1995, p.A1; Apr. 2, 1995, p.A18; Apr. 3, 1995, p.A15; Apr. 4, 1995, p.C15
New Yorker, Oct. 30, 1995, p.35
People, Apr. 17, 1995, p.48; July 10, 1995, p.36
Texas Monthly, Sep. 1994, p.122; May 1995, p.110
Time, Apr. 10, 1995, p.91
USA Today, Apr. 6, 1995, p.D6
Washington Post, Apr. 1, 1995, p.A7; Apr. 2, 1995, p.A3; July 26, 1995, p.D1

Monica Seles 1973-
Yugoslav-Born American Professional
Tennis Player
Youngest Woman Ever to Achieve Top
Ranking in Pro Tennis

BIRTH

Monica Seles (SELL-es) was born December 2, 1973, at Novi Sad,
in the Vojvodina section of the former Yugoslavia, now part of
Serbia. She is, however, ethnic Hungarian. In Yugoslavia, her
father, Karolj Seles, was a political cartoonist and documentary
filmmaker, and her mother, Esther Seles, was a computer pro-
grammer. They left their jobs to move to the United States in 1986.
Monica's older brother, Zoltan, was once a Yugoslav junior tennis champion.

YOUTH

Seles was six years old when her father, who holds a degree in physical education, gave her a scaled-down tennis racquet. She practiced half-heartedly for a short time, but soon lost interest and returned to her dolls and toys. Then, when she saw her brother's winning trophy, she decided to give tennis another try. Karolj wisely geared the training this time to his daughter's extreme youth. He put his artistic skills to use by drawing "Tom and Jerry" cartoon characters on tennis balls, encouraging Monica to go after her opponent as a cat goes after a mouse. A second ploy was to place stuffed animals in strategic spots across the net in order to refine her accuracy. Still another of Karolj's maneuvers was the making of animated films to teach Monica the fundamentals of the game. Practice became sheer enjoyment as Karolj Seles cleverly guided his little left-handed daughter into the forceful two-handed swinging style that would define her future success.

The training was inspired enough to produce solid results. Monica won a junior tournament in Yugoslavia at the age of nine, competing against girls up to the age of 12. In 1984, months before her 11th birthday, she won the 12-and-under category at the European championships. After claiming the division victory again the next year, she then captured the European 14-and-under title. Yugoslavia honored 12-year-old Monica as Sportswoman of the Year in 1985; no one under the age of 18 had ever before been given this recognition.

There was time for more than tennis, though, in Seles's childhood. She loved to dance, to dress up in her mother's high heels, and to smear on lipstick, much as little girls everywhere do. Her enthusiasm for normal pursuits made her popular with playmates, some of whom she has kept in touch with all through her years in the limelight.

EARLY MEMORIES

The long scar that runs down Seles's forehead, reaching the bridge of her nose on the left side of her face, is not always apparent to the casual observer, but it triggers sharp memories for Seles. It is a permanent reminder of a childhood fall against the metal frame of a baby carriage at a moment that her grandmother was distracted from watching her. She still vividly recalls regaining consciousness in a hospital, and shrieking uncontrollably in fright. Seles plans no surgical removal of the scar, which she refers to now as "kind of neat."

EDUCATION

Seles started school in her native Yugoslavia. She continued her education in Bradenton, Florida, when she moved to the United States to begin training at the Bolletieri Tennis Academy in 1986. Later, she attended school in Sarasota, Florida. Her excellent record in the classroom—a straight-A average—matched her accomplishments on the court. Her dedication to academics as well as to tennis surprised many who initially regarded her as bubble-headed during her teens. Monica's fluency in languages and quick grasp of serious subject matter proved them wrong.

CHOOSING A CAREER

Seles had been playing on the junior circuit for three years when famed tennis coach Nick Bolletieri discovered her competing in Miami's 1985 Orange Bowl tennis tournament. He was so impressed by the 12-year-old's power and skill that he offered her a full scholarship to his high-profile tennis academy. She and her brother moved to Florida in 1986. Soon afterward they were followed by their parents, who left home and jobs in Yugoslavia to concentrate on preparing their gifted daughter for a tennis career.

"For two years, the Seles training tactics were shrouded in secrecy," reveals a *World Tennis* feature. "Monica played no junior tournaments, working instead to develop the power, finesse, and foot speed that would eventually carry her to the top of the women's game." No one was allowed to watch practice sessions as Karolj concentrated on drills, Bolletieri worked on strategy, and Seles's brother Zoltan, better known as "Z-Man," hit balls with his little sister. At about this time Monica developed the distracting grunt that remains her trademark, as she whacked the ball with all the force and intensity that her unorthodox two-handed approach could muster.

Finally, Seles's game was unveiled at the 1987 Virginia Slims of Florida tournament, where she competed as an amateur. She lost in the second round, but edged up in subsequent tournaments. Seles turned pro in early 1989, barely past her 15th birthday.

CAREER HIGHLIGHTS

A brash and flashy Seles won her first professional championship at Houston's Virginia Slims tournament in April 1989 with a show of animal instinct that stole the final match, 3-6, 6-1, 6-4, from top-seeded Chris Evert. She went on to the French Open, one of her sport's biggest annual events. In tennis, there are four tournaments, called the Grand Slam events, that are considered the major events of the year: the Australian Open in January, the French Open in May, Wimbledon (in England) in June, and the U.S. Open (in New York) in late August. "Seles's star potential and her flair for self-promotion was confirmed at the 1989 French Open, her first Grand Slam event," says *Current Biography Yearbook*. She was brought down in the third set of the finals by Steffi Graf, the top-ranked woman player of the time. In an earlier round, she had grandstanded shamelessly by flipping roses to the crowd and offering a bouquet to opponent Zina Garrison before their match, which Garrison lost. It was a poorly timed display of the type of the outrageous behavior that surrounded Seles as she ascended through the ranks.

A deflating loss to the experienced Graf that summer, this time a 6-0, 6-1 defeat in the fourth round at Wimbledon, saw Monica taking a two-month break to work on the weak spots in her game. She returned to play in time for the U.S. Open, but was roundly defeated by Evert in the fourth round. Nevertheless, in her first year as a professional, she reached the quarter-finals in all but two of the 10 tournaments she entered. By her 16th birthday, Seles had achieved the remarkable ranking of Number 6 in the world.

Seles began the 1990 season trying to adjust to her new height—she had stretched from 5'3" to over 5'9" in little more than a year. "The net seemed a different height," she explained when asked about her faltering game, "and the racket seemed lighter, like I was playing Ping-Pong." The rapid growth spurt was a problem that she was able to overcome, but tension was festering at the tennis academy. The Seles family began to resent the time and attention Nick Bolletieri was giving to another promising young player, Andre Agassi. Eventually, the relationship between the famous coach and the Seleses fell apart. Monica's offhand claims about her father being her only *real* coach prodded an offended Bolletieri to give a rundown of the hours and money he had spent in developing her skill and in providing expenses for her family. Monica countered that the publicity her success had generated for the academy was adequate compensation. It was a bitter parting as the Seles family moved to another tennis facility several miles away in Sarasota.

Despite the unpleasant dispute, Monica was on a roll by March 1990. She began collecting wins at the Lipton International Players Championships and quickly rose to third ranking. In May, she beat Martina Navratilova and took the Italian Open 6-1, 6-1. Steffi Graf was her next victim at the German Open in a straight-set victory that broke Graf's incredible 66-match winning streak. That summer, she again defeated Graf 7-6, 6-4 at the French Open, winning her first Grand Slam title and recognition as that event's youngest champion ever. Seles faltered in the quarterfinals at Wimbledon, then was ousted in the third round of the U.S. Open before fighting her way back to claim the Virginia Slims title later in the year.

REACHING THE PINNACLE

A string of successes followed, as the flamboyant teen sprinted her way to top ranking in women's tennis at the Australian Open in 1991. That year, Seles became the world's top-ranked female tennis player. At 17, she was the youngest player ever—male or female—to win the No. 1 spot, which she held for the next two years. She took the French Open again that year with a win in straight sets over the formidable Arantxa Sanchez Vicario. All the while, she was "taking a monstrous public bite of life," said Curry Kirkpatrick in *Sports Illustrated*, writing about her high-profile celebrity persona and burgeoning stardom. Seles was at the top of her game that summer when she mysteriously withdrew at the last minute from Wimbledon and went into seclusion. Ugly rumors, some fueled by disapproval and envy, surfaced about her departure. Her eventual statement about "shin splints and a slight stress fracture" failed to prevent the leveling of a hefty fine, mainly because of the delayed explanation and the ensuing secrecy. Monica returned to the circuit several months later, however, to capture her third Grand Slam title of the year, defeating Navratilova 7-6, 6-1 in the final of the U.S. Open.

The 1992 season brought Seles a second Australian championship, followed by a hard-fought victory over Graf to defend her title, 6-2, 3-6, 10-8, in the French Open. She was the first woman in 55 years to win three consecutive French titles. Seles was bested by Graf at Wimbledon that year and continued to have lackluster performances in other outings until the U.S. Open, which she won easily over Sanchez Vicario 6-3, 6-3. Her popularity began to fade, partly because of her puzzling behavior at Wimbledon the previous year but also, suggested *Vogue* in a 1992 feature story, because "most of her opponents are the underdogs. Grunting and grimacing, she attacks from the back of the court with murderous speed and accuracy, two-fisted, an assassin in her way." Envy played a part, too, as Seles accumulated lucrative endorsements, racked up millions in tournament wins, and made waves with her glamour poses in fashion magazines. "She is not your run-of-the-mill human being," Navratilova told *Vogue*. "She walks to a different drummer."

By 1993, Seles had won eight Grand Slam tournaments in just three years. A viral infection kept her off the tour for two months early that year. When she returned to tournament play, "her stranglehold on the women's game was loosened not by a racquet, but by a steel blade," wrote Peter Bodo in *Tennis* magazine.

A BIZARRE ATTACK

On April 30, 1993, in Hamburg, Germany, Seles was stabbed in the back by a delusional spectator during a changeover in a quarter final match against Magdalena Maleeva. Her attacker, an unemployed German lathe worker named Gunther Parche, was an obsessed Steffi Graf fan who later told authorities that he had stabbed Seles because he could not bear the fact that she held the No. 1 ranking. He said that he had no intention of killing her, and that he only wished to advance Graf's standing by hindering his victim's ability to compete. The harrowing incident was unprecedented in tennis, although other players, Graf among them, have had threatening and frightening experiences with fixated fans.

Unbelievably, Parche was given only a two-year suspended sentence for the assault; in an appeal last year, he was again set free. To the injustice of that verdict, complained sportswriters and Seles associates, was an added insult by the Women's Tennis Association (WTA). They refused to protect her top ranking during her convalescence.

Seles's physical recovery proved to be the easiest part of her rehabilitation; it was the psychological damage that held her prisoner for 28 months. She was so haunted by the memory of the attack that she had recurring nightmares. The nightmares were so bad that she couldn't sleep during the night at all; she could only sleep during the day. And she was forced to confront difficult and overwhelming issues.

"Why was it me?" she asked herself. "I didn't think at age 19 I would have to deal with this: I was playing, and suddenly I wasn't playing, and it changed my daily life. And all these emotions I didn't know I could feel. *How do I want to live my life?* You have to decide: If you live till 90 living this way, do you really want to live? Why do I have to face these questions? This is supposed to be fun, and here I am thinking about life-or-death issues. This guy stabbed me, he's out there, he can come to any tennis tournament, any place. And he's still obsessed. *What will it take for him not to do it again?''* With the help of a therapist, it took her over two years to rebuild her lost courage and confidence, and to find the fun in tennis again.

COMEBACK

Seles, who became an American citizen during her recovery, finally returned to tennis in a 1995 mid-summer exhibition match with Navratilova. She then made a dream comeback on the official tour that August at the Canadian Open, where she trounced South Africa's Amanda Coetzer in a 6-0, 6-1 final. She was also restored by the WTA to the special status of co-No. 1 ranking with Graf. Bolstered by her success in Canada, Seles blasted her way through the U.S. Open in September to meet Graf in the final, where she was beaten 7-6 (8-6), 0-6, 6-3 in a strenuous matchup.

More mature after her long absence, Seles is bouncy and confident again. She has grown still another inch to over 5'10", and claims she now has a "bigger and bolder game." The infectious giggle of her teens is intact, and the grunting is less noticeable. She is currently sidelined with a knee problem, but her return to top billing seems assured. "My life is not going to be the same as before," says Seles. "But everything is fine. Everything is going to be O.K."

MEMORABLE EXPERIENCES

Seles no longer looks only to her Grand Slam victories as memorable events. It is her triumphant comeback in capturing the Canadian Open in August 1995 that she counts as her moment of greatest fulfillment. "I can't believe this is real," she told center-court fans in an emotion-tinged voice after her win. "I just feel unbelievable, being back playing tennis again, being happy and doing something that I love so much."

MAJOR INFLUENCES

Nick Bolletieri was a defining influence in helping Seles mature into a complete tennis player, but it was Karolj Seles, Monica's father, who developed the champion within. He helped her create the unorthodox style that maximized her power and drilled her in timing and precision. Tennis parents exerting such influence on their children are normally looked upon as intrusive and overbearing, but Monica staunchly defends her father's training and nurturing as the key factors in her success.

FAMILY LIFE

Seles's home base is an estate in Sarasota, where she lives during the off-tour months with her parents and brother Zoltan, who handles her business interests. In the early months of her long hiatus from the tennis circuit, she spent much of her time in Colorado, working her way back to physical and emotional health. She says that living in hotels during this extended period made her all the more appreciative of the comforts and privacy of home.

Karolj and Esther Seles have been Monica's source of strength, even throughout their own debilitating health problems. Watching her parents' courage in rebounding from their recent illnesses—her mother from a complicated hysterectomy, and her father from stomach and prostate cancer—is said to have been the key to Monica's defeat of her own demons. The Seles family maintains a low-key existence in the face of wealth and publicity. Old friends visit the Florida house, and there is constant youthful activity in the pool, on the trampoline, and on the tennis and basketball courts. Brother, sister and a host of friends share the fun, and Astro (a Yorkshire terrier named for the dog in the old "Jetsons" TV cartoon) rounds out the family. Monica savors the joy and excitement and says, in a reflective moment, "I've got to the point where I live every day of my life like it's my last. Anything can happen. You never know."

HOBBIES AND OTHER INTERESTS

Leisure activities have changed considerably for Seles since the knife attack nearly three years ago in Hamburg. She has started to downplay her trendy clothing and hair fashions and free-spirited demeanor. Her once-prodigious magazine buying has given way to serious reading in the wake of her chilling experience.

Seles is known to enjoy other sports, including basketball and skiing, and friends say that she is fond of watching boxing matches. Movies interest her enough that she once hinted at someday doing some acting of her own. In fact, when she was a young girl in Yugoslavia, she tried out for every play her school produced, with the same unbridled enthusiasm she displayed on the tennis court.

HONORS AND AWARDS

Yugoslavia's Sportswoman of the Year: 1985
Italian Open: 1990
German Open: 1990
French Open: 1990, 1991, 1992
Virginia Slims: 1990, 1991, 1992
U.S. Open: 1991, 1992
Australian Open: 1991, 1992, 1993
Canadian Open: 1995

FURTHER READING

BOOKS

Great Athletes: The Twentieth Century, 1992 (juvenile)
Who's Who in America 1996

PERIODICALS

Current Biography Yearbook 1992
Forbes, Aug. 19, 1991, p.80
New York Times, May 2, 1993, Section VIII, p.1; Mar. 19, 1995, Section VIII, p.11

San Francisco Chronicle, Feb. 20, 1989, p.D4
Sports Illustrated, May 10, 1993, p.18; Apr. 10, 1995, p.44; July 17, 1995, p.22
Tennis, Mar. 1994, p.42; Mar. 1995, p.20; Aug. 1995, p.46
Vogue, May 1991, p.58; June 1992, p.164
Washington Post, July 30, 1995, p.D1
World Tennis, Aug. 1990, p.29

ADDRESS

International Management Group
1 Erieview Plaza
Cleveland, OH 44114-1715

Don Shula 1930-
American Professional Football Coach
Former Coach of the Miami Dolphins

BIRTH

Football coaching legend Don Shula was born on January 4, 1930, in Grand River, Ohio. He was the fourth of seven children born to Dan and Mary Shula, both of whom came from Hungarian Catholic families. Shula's father worked for a nursery and a fishing outfit while his mother looked after their children. Shula's siblings included twins Joseph and Josephine, sister Irene, and triplets Jane, Jim, and Jeannette.

YOUTH

Even as a youngster, Shula was drawn to sports. Nearly every day after school—and on most days during the summer—he could be found down at the local schoolyard, playing kickball, baseball, football, and other sports. It was on the dusty fields of Merrick Hutchinson School, which he came to regard as his home away from home, that his fierce competitive drive was first evident. "He wasn't the best athlete, but he was good and he hated to lose like nobody's business," said Roy Kropac, Shula's best friend during those childhood years.

Members of his family were familiar with young Shula's competitive hunger as well, and his grandmother recalled that she occasionally recruited her grandson to play cards when she and her friends needed a fourth player. If Shula found himself on the losing side, or if he even suspected that he was being teased, he would throw his cards across the table and stomp off angrily, tears in his eyes.

Shula himself recalls his childhood with fondness. He points to the lessons he learned during those early schoolyard games as important factors in his later coaching success, and he appreciates the sacrifices that his parents made for their children. "My father was one of those guys who just worked all his life," Shula said. "One of the things that makes me happiest now was that before he died I got to take them back over to the old country. We went to Budapest [Hungary], and then we drove about a hundred miles and found the little town he was from and looked up all the relatives. And then we went to Rome and while we were there the pope came out. That was everything he wanted."

EDUCATION

Shula attended Harvey High School in Painesville, Ohio. During his years at Harvey he established himself as a good student and a fine football player, although his high school football career was nearly derailed before it even started. When Shula was in ninth grade he came down with pneumonia shortly before football tryouts were to begin. Determined to make the team, Shula forged his mother's signature on a permission slip. Named a starter, Shula returned a punt for a touchdown in his first game and his parents promptly became football fans. "We never saw him much during those years," recalled one of Shula's sisters. "He was always gone, either at a practice or with his buddies."

After graduating, Shula was offered a scholarship to attend John Carroll University, a Catholic school outside Cleveland, Ohio, and he quickly made his mark on the gridiron there. A deeply religious person who continues to attend Mass every day, Shula considered to entering the priesthood, but he eventually decided that he loved sports too much. Shula went on to major in sociology and minor in math instead.

On the football field, Shula was a fierce player on both sides of the ball. He had many fine games at John Carroll, but it was during his senior season that he enjoyed his best game. Playing against powerhouse foe Syracuse, Shula led his school to a big upset victory. Paul Brown, the Cleveland Browns' head coach, was in the stands for the game. Aware that Shula was not the fastest player, Brown was nonetheless intrigued by his performance against Syracuse. Brown decided to take a chance and select him in the upcoming National Football League (NFL) draft.

CAREER HIGHLIGHTS

SHULA'S PLAYING DAYS

In 1951 the Cleveland Browns selected Shula in the ninth round of the draft. Brandishing his usual hard-nosed style of play, Shula managed to secure a spot on the team's roster as a defensive back. After two years with the Browns, though, he was traded to the Baltimore Colts as part of a whopping 15-player deal. Shula was stunned at the news, which he learned while reading the newspaper, for he had viewed playing for his home-state Browns as a dream come true.

Shula was determined to keep his career going in Baltimore, though, and he soon impressed his new coaches with his understanding of the game and his sound fundamental skills. One Baltimore reporter recalled that during the 1950s Shula "was one of the finest tacklers in the game. If you wanted to run a clinic on how to tackle, you'd get Don Shula." Shula called the plays for the Colts' defensive unit as well, and he enjoyed several productive seasons with Baltimore. Finally, though, NFL coaches came to see his slowness as a problem. He was cut by the Colts and, while he latched on to the Washington Redskins for the 1957 season, Shula knew that his playing days were coming to an end.

EARLY COACHING CAREER

In 1958 Shula was hired as an assistant coach by the University of Virginia, but the school's disorganized football program led him to look elsewhere. A year later University of Kentucky Head Coach Blanton Collier added Shula to his staff. Although Shula only worked with Collier for a year, he later called the cerebral Kentucky coach one of the two most influential people in his football career (the other was Paul Brown). "I don't want anyone to ever think I'm trying to act like somebody else," Shula later said, "but I'd be pretty stupid not to learn things from men I've played under or coached against."

In 1960 Shula moved into the NFL coaching ranks, securing a position as defensive backfield coach with the Detroit Lions. He quickly established himself as one of the bright young coaching talents of the NFL. Three years later, the Baltimore Colts raised eyebrows around the league when they decided to hire Shula as their head coach. Shula thus returned to Baltimore in 1963 at the age of 33 as the youngest head coach in pro football history.

Shula immediately put his own competitive imprint on the Colts. Even players who had been friends with Shula during his playing days with Baltimore found that their previous relationship with their new coach did not spare them if they failed to meet his exacting standards. "He was strong, demanding," remembered Baltimore halfback Tom Matte. "He didn't mince any words. You had to have thick skin to play for him."

Shula coached the Baltimore Colts for seven years, posting 71 wins in 98 games. He never had a losing season, but his tenure at Baltimore was marred by a painful loss in Super Bowl III to the AFL (American Football League) New York Jets. Many observers had previously dismissed the AFL as inferior to the established NFL, and the Colts 16-7 loss was a tremendous upset that gave the fledgling league instant legitimacy. The loss also embarrassed Colts owner Carroll Rosenbloom, and Shula's relationship with Rosenbloom quickly deteriorated.

SHULA JOINS THE DOLPHINS

In 1970 Shula left the Colts to become the head coach for the Miami Dolphins, a team that was struggling on the field and at the ticket office. He launched his trademark program of discipline and hard work with the Dolphins, and the results were immediately apparent. Miami had posted only three victories during the 1969 season, but in Shula's first season the team tallied ten wins. Observers pointed to Shula as the reason for the improvement. "I've never seen a guy with more energy," said Monte Clark, who was an assistant coach under Shula in Miami. "I think the church he goes to is called Our Lady of Perpetual Motion." Shula's intensity quickly assumed legendary status, and one Miami sports writer admitted that "everybody's afraid of Shula . . . . You've never seen him mad. His face changes. I mean, it doesn't look like the same person—it doesn't look like a person at all. It looks like a gargoyle, and when he gets like that he's merciless." Former Dolphin Dick Anderson, one of Shula's longtime friends, confirms that his old coach was a fiery sort. "He was completely consistent; he screamed at everybody."

Shula admits that he is an emotional coach, but he cites preparation and study as primary components of his success. "To me, coaching is finding out what makes an individual play to the best of his ability. I have to understand how best to motivate each and every one, and of the 45 players I'm going to be responsible for, . . . there are no two alike."

1972—MIAMI'S PERFECT SEASON

In 1971 Shula led the Dolphins to the Super Bowl, only to watch his team get squashed by the Dallas Cowboys. People began to whisper that the loss to the Cowboys, coupled with Shula's loss to the Jets several years before, might be an indication that the Miami coach was unable to win the really big games. Shula ignored the critics and went back to work, even more determined to win a Super Bowl.

Shula knew that he was bringing a talented football squad into the 1972 season, but the loss of starting quarterback Bob Griese to injury jeopardized the team's promising start. Shula's decision to add 38-year-old veteran Earl Morrall to the team earlier that year, however, proved to be an important one. Morrall stepped into the starting quarterback position and guided Miami to one victory after another. Shula's ball-control offense and stifling team defense combined to form a juggernaut that other NFL teams were unable to stop. The Dolphins finished the regular season with an unbeaten record and sliced through the playoffs, leaving battered teams in their wake. The team then beat the Washington Redskins in Super Bowl VII, topping off the only undefeated season in NFL history. More than 20 years later, that triumph has not been duplicated.

A year later, Miami again served notice that they were the class of the league. Stars Bob Griese, Larry Csonka, and Paul Warfield enjoyed banner years, and the Dolphins returned to the Super Bowl. In January 1974 Shula and the Dolphins won their second straight championship, ripping the Minnesota Vikings by a 24-7 score. Shula recognized that Miami's victory was a notable accomplishment. "Not only was it our second consecutive world championship, but it was the climax of what might have been the best two years that any team in the NFL ever put together," Shula said. "We won back-to-back Super Bowls and went 32-2, a two-year record that hasn't been broken yet."

HISTORIC CAREER UNFOLDS

Shula fielded tough and successful teams throughout the remainder of the 1970s and into the 1980s. Although they never won a Super Bowl, Miami tallied several divisional titles and became known as one of the most consistently winning organizations in the NFL. Players and assistant coaches came and went, but Shula maintained a standard of excellence that few other organizations could match. He proved adept at adjusting his strategy and playcalling in accordance with the talent he had, and Miami posted winning seasons with several dramatically different football philosophies.

Shula's approach to the game also contributed to his success. Never one to hold in his emotions, he even indicated that his emotional nature provided a much-needed outlet for the competitive pressures of professional football. "I've screamed so hard on the sideline, at players, coaches, and officials, that I don't even recognize myself when I see pictures of my face in that state," Shula admitted. "I've punched walls. I've stomped off from press conferences. My adrenaline flows, and everything just comes right out of me. I've always believed that you have to feel the disappointments, heartaches, and losses to be able to move on. You put so much time into it, you can't ever feel it too deeply. You've got to feel it down to your bones. You just can't allow yourself to get consumed."

As the 1980s gave way to the 1990s, players and coaches around the league marveled at Shula's longevity and success. Former football great Bubba Smith commented that "If a nuclear bomb is dropped, the only things I'm certain will survive are AstroTurf and Don Shula." In November 1993 Shula won his 325th NFL game as a head coach, surpassing legendary Chicago Bears head coach George Halas as the winningest coach in pro football history. "Honesty is at the heart of my success," Shula said. "I don't play games with players. Everything is based on years of solid facts. Sometimes it's not very flashy, and it's not exciting, but I look at the bottom line—winning—and that's all I'm interested in."

A LEGEND RETIRES

By the mid-1990s, however, growing numbers of Miami Dolphins fans began to grumble that Shula was not winning enough. They noted that while Shula had made more Super Bowl appearances than any other NFL coach, his last championship had been won back in the early 1970s. Critics contended that the legendary coach was having difficulty keeping up with the ever-changing nature of professional football, a charge that Shula's supporters felt was ridiculous. But after a rocky 1995 season during which the Dolphins lost in the first round of the playoffs, some Miami fans and media personalities grew increasingly vocal about their unhappiness with Shula.

In January 1996 Shula announced that he was stepping down as Miami's head football coach, taking a position in the organization's front office as Vice Chairman of the Board of the Miami Dolphins. He cited his desire to spend more time with his family as a primary reason for the decision, but many observers wondered if all the harsh public criticism finally got to him. After the retirement announcement, countless players and coaches rushed to praise Shula's professional accomplishments and to lament the shabby treatment he received at the end of his career. Carolina Panthers general manager Bill Polian said that "Don Shula represents everything good in our country. His integrity, character and competitiveness, and leadership are a positive example for all of us. The NFL is poorer for his leaving the sideline." Former Chicago Bears player and coach Mike Ditka agreed, stating that Shula's "contributions to the NFL are indescribable. I have so much respect for him as a man and a coach. He has dignity, class, and great character." Former Dolphins players chimed in as well, describing him as a father figure and a tremendously important influence on their lives. Former Miami linebacker Nick Buoniconti called him "probably the most highly principled, highly moraled individual the NFL has ever seen."

Shula left coaching with an overall record of 347-173-6. Under his leadership, the Dolphins compiled the best winning percentage in all of professional sports from 1970 to 1995, and observers point out that other NFL teams went through more than 200 head coaches combined during the time that Shula was at the helm in Miami.

FUTURE PLANS

In March 1996, Shula resigned from the NFL competition committee, which is the league's legislative body. He said "that without having a tie to a club, I felt I was just spinning my wheels." But it appears that his future will still be with the NFL. He may become a minority owner of the Cleveland Browns football team, which is moving to Baltimore and scheduled to begin playing in 1999. For now, Shula is considering the option. "I wouldn't close any door on the possibility," he said of the Browns deal.

MARRIAGE AND FAMILY

Shula has been married twice. He was first married on July 19, 1958, to Dorothy Bartish. They raised five children—David, Donna, Sharon, Annie, and Mike—who have given them six grandchildren. Both of the Shula boys grew up to follow their father into professional football careers. David became the head coach of the Cincinnati Bengals, while his younger brother Mike became an assistant coach in the NFL.

On February 25, 1991, after 40 years of marriage, Dorothy died after a long battle with cancer. The loss of his wife crushed Shula, who at one point prior to her death took Dorothy to a religious site halfway across the world to pray for her recovery. "I was always hoping for something positive to happen," he said. "I loved Dorothy. I wanted to do everything in my power to save her life. I would have gone anywhere for her."

Shula and his children became even closer after Dorothy's death, but it was still a difficult time for the family. As his daughter Donna admits, he was difficult to reach for a time. "It was terrible grief, beyond words. He was lost without my mother . . . . But these days he's very connected. He tells us he loves us a lot more."

In early 1992 Shula began dating Mary Anne Stephens, and they were married in October 1993. His marriage, says columnist Paul Attner, "transformed him off the field into sort of a teenage lovebird. They wink at each other and kiss in public. And he goes places and tries hobbies that he would never have even thought about 15 years ago." Shula and his wife continue to reside in Florida.

HOBBIES AND OTHER INTERESTS

Shula has long been known as a tireless worker on behalf of Florida charities, especially in the area of cancer research. He has received numerous awards from charity organizations in recognition of his efforts over the years.

WRITINGS

The Winning Edge, 1973
Everyone's a Coach: You Can Inspire Anyone to be a Winner, 1995

HONORS AND AWARDS

Coach of Year Award: 1964, 1966, 1970, 1971, 1972
Brotherhood Award (NCCJ, Florida region): 1977
Light of Flames Leadership Award: 1977
Coach of Decade (1970s), Pro Football Hall of Fame: 1980
Concern Award (Cedars Medical Center): 1992
Solheim Lifetime Achievement Award: 1992
Jim Thorpe Award: 1993
Sports Illustrated Sportsman of the Year: 1993
Horrigan Award (Pro Football Writers): 1994

FURTHER READING

BOOKS

Smith, Jay, *Don Shula,* 1974
Stein, R. Conrad, *Don Shula: Football's Winningest Coach,* 1994
Who s Who in America 1996

PERIODICALS

Esquire, Sep. 1983, p.80
Miami Herald, Sep. 11, 1988, p.8; Nov. 6, 1990, p.D1; Aug. 29, 1991, p.1D;
    Sep. 2, 1993, p.8
New York Times, Sep. 1, 1985; Jan. 6, 1996, p.27
Sport, Jan. 1983, p.48; Nov. 1984, p.17
Sporting News, Nov. 8, 1993, p.7; Oct. 3, 1994, p.12; Jan. 15, 1996, p.8
Sports Illustrated, July 26, 1993, p.60; Dec. 20, 1993, p.16; Oct. 10, 1994, p.44
Time, Jan. 15, 1996, p.62

ADDRESS

Miami Dolphins
7500 SW 30th St.
Davie, FL 33314

Kerri Strug 1977-
American Gymnast
Olympic Gold Medalist

BIRTH

Kerri Strug was born November 19, 1977, in Tucson, Arizona, to
Burt and Melanie Strug. Burt is a heart surgeon and Melanie is
a homemaker. Kerri has a brother, Kevin, and a sister, Lisa, who
are older.

GETTING STARTED IN GYMNASTICS

When Kerri was three, her parents started looking for an activity
for their busy little girl. At first they tried ballet, but, her mother
remembers, "Kerri didn't like it at all. So we put her in a gymnastics program. And that was it."

Kerri took part in a neighborhood meet and caught the eye of a family friend and gymnastic judge, Carol Jones. She told the Strugs that Kerri had a special gift that should be developed. So the Strugs enlisted the talents of Jim Gault, the women's gymnastic coach at the University of Arizona, in their home town of Tucson. "I could tell right away that Kerri was different than most," Gault remembers. "She's a very intense, intelligent young lady. Because of her intensity, mistakes are intolerable. She's a perfectionist."

Kerri trained alone in the afternoons, after Gault had finished working with the college gymnasts. She didn't get to meet any other young gymnasts her age. "It was the same way at meets," Strug recalled. "I didn't have any teammates when I went to competitions, so I didn't really make a lot of friends and I didn't have anybody else to push me. That was pretty hard."

TRAINING WITH BELA KAROLYI

Kerri is a fierce competitor. It was her idea, at the age of 13, to move to Houston, Texas, and begin training with Bela Karolyi, the controversial coach who had helped Nadia Comanici, Mary Lou Retton, and Kim Zmeskal develop into Olympic champions. In the world of gymnastics, it's common for the top young athletes to move away from home to train with a top coach. When Kerri moved to Houston, her mother visited her there once a month. "It wasn't easy," she says of her decision. "But I decided if I was going to move away, I was going to go to the best."

Karolyi, an emigre from Romania who became known to the world through his success with Comanici in the 1976 Olympics, was known for his tough methods and "winning is everything" approach to gymnastics. But Strug claimed that's what she wanted. "He is very disciplined and he does want you to be perfect all the time," she said after her move to Houston. "And sure, he gets upset with you when you do something wrong. He can get really upset. But it's always in the gymnast's best interest. . . . He wants us to be prepared so we can compete against the best."

The results were immediate. After six months with Karolyi, in July 1991, Strug placed in the top 10 at the U.S. Championships. In September 1991, Strug won a silver medal in the World Championships as part of the U.S. team. She had arrived at the top level of gymnastics.

EDUCATION

Kerri began her education in the public schools in Tucson, where she was always a straight-A student. As competitive in school as she was in gymnastics, Kerri couldn't stand not to get As, on a test or on her report card.

After she left home, her education continued wherever she was training. But unlike most gymnasts training away from home, Kerri did not receive her education through tutoring or by correspondence courses. Her parents insisted that she go to a regular school, and after six hours in the gym each day, Kerri took three hours to attend classes.

CAREER HIGHLIGHTS

By 1992, it was obvious that Kerri Strug was capable of competing with the best in the world. At the Olympic trials in June 1992, Strug placed third behind Kim Zmeskal and Shannon Miller, the two top U.S. gymnasts and Olympic favorites. From the beginning of her training, Kerri has excelled in each of the four individual areas of gymnastic competition: the balance beam, the uneven bars, the vault, and floor exercise. She is also outstanding in the all-around, an event that includes routines on all the apparatus as well as floor exercise. Her small, powerful body—she was 4'8" and 80 pounds in 1992—made her the preferred "munchkin" size favored in contemporary gymnastics.

1992 OLYMPICS

The 1992 Olympics took place in Barcelona, Spain. At 14, Strug was the youngest member of the entire 615-member American Olympic team.

Despite her youth, she performed brilliantly. After the first round of the all-around competition, Kerri was in third place. Kim Zmeskal, the gold medal favorite in several events, had fallen off the balance beam earlier and was in 32nd place. Only the top three athletes from each nation could compete in the all-around, and Strug wanted desperately to hold on to her third-place position. But in the finals to determine the team standing Zmeskal fought back to edge Strug out. Zmeskal went on to the finals in the all-around; Strug sat out after coming in fourth.

In the opinion of many, Zmeskal was able to beat Strug through the machinations of Karolyi, the head coach of the U.S. team. For the team finals, Karolyi placed Strug early in the competition. That placement, according to one reporter was a "disadvantage because judges tend to assign lower scores at the beginning of the order and higher ones at the end." So, by forcing Strug to compete before his favorite, he gave Zmeskal an unfair advantage.

The U.S. women went on to win a team bronze in the 1992 Olympics, but it was not enough to erase the sense of injustice Strug and her family felt. Kerri's mother Melanie wrote in a published diary that Karolyi had "sacrificed her daughter to ensure that Zmeskal would make the individual all-around."

The 1992 Olympics were a low point for U.S. gymnastics. Many journalists noted that all the U.S. gymnasts were under too much pressure, at too young an age. They claimed the girls had been robbed of their childhoods. Karolyi retired from the sport in disgrace, and many articles appeared featuring the U.S. gymnasts as manipulated, abused robots who were over-trained and bullied by their coaches, especially Karolyi. He was accused of forcing them to train while injured, and of emphasizing slimness until they developed eating disorders.

Strug returned to the U.S. and found another coach. She moved to Orlando, Florida, where she trained with Kevin Brown, who had coach-ed one of her Olympic teammates. In 1993 Strug moved again, this time to Oklahoma where she trained briefly with Steve Nunno, who has been Shannon Miller's coach throughout her career. Her parents, always sup-portive, said of their daughter, "Kerri is driven. It doesn't matter what it is. If she doesn't get As in class, she's unhappy. She gets lots of fan mail, but she's unhappy if she doesn't answer each one." After her move to Nunno's gym, Strug said, "My parents thought I needed to enjoy gym-nastics more, but I feel if I'm going to live away and sacrifice so much, I need to be where the best coaching is."

Under Nunno, Strug won a silver medal at the World Championships in 1994. But always in search of perfection, Strug made several more coaching changes. In 1995, Kerri's training found her home again in Tucson, where she finished up high school and graduated. She applied to and was accepted to the University of California at Los Angeles (UCLA), where she received a full scholarship to participate in gymnastics. Kerri deferred college for one year to devote herself to preparing for the 1996 Olympics.

RETURN TO KAROLYI

In January 1996, Strug shocked many in the gymnastic world when she returned to Karolyi to train. He had returned from retirement in 1994 to train elite gymnasts once again. His newest favorite and star was Dominique Moceneau, a 14-year-old emigre from Romania. Despite the competition for the spotlight, Strug considered training with Karolyi as her best chance for making the Olympic team and securing a medal. She made the Olympic team and was ready for the competition.

1996 OLYMPICS

Going into the 1996 Olympics, there were several clear favorites among the U.S. competitors. Shannon Miller, at 19 one of the oldest on the team and recovering from injuries, was still an experienced champion and veteran of the 1992 Olympics. At age 14, Dominique Moceneau was the youngest member of the team and the one who received some of the greatest pre-Olympic hype from the media.

But it was Kerri Strug's performance in the Olympics that was for many viewers the highlight of the games. In Olympic gymnastics, the team competition takes place before the individual events. In team competition, each of the seven women on the U.S. team competes in each of the four main events. The team members for 1996—Strug, Shannon Miller, Dominique Dawes, Dominique Moceneau, Emily Chow, J.C. Phelps, and Amanda Borden—each competed on each piece of apparatus. For each event, six of the seven scores were taken for the team totals and the seventh was thrown out. Midway through the team competition, the U.S. was in second place, behind the Russian team. Going into the vaults, the U.S. team looked as if it just might win the gold medal, for the first time in history. But then Dominique Moceneau fell on her landing for each of her two vaults. It was up to Strug.

A VAULT INTO THE HISTORY BOOKS

On her first vault, Strug fell on her landing. She had also landed on the side of her foot. Hobbling back to Karolyi, she told him. "I can't feel my leg." "Shake it out," he told her. "We need one more good vault." So with the eyes of the world on her, Strug made her final vault. She nailed it, soaring through the air and making a perfect landing, but only briefly. After she had secured her landing, she crumpled to the floor in pain. The score came up: a 9.712, good enough to put the U.S. in first place. For the first time in history, the U.S. women's gymnasts were gold medal winners. And Kerri Strug's gutsy move had won her the hearts and admiration of millions of people. After the vault, Strug was taken to the hospital, where her ankle was x-rayed, revealing a sprain. After her ankle was wrapped, she returned to the gymnastics venue to take part in the medal ceremonies. Karolyi carried Kerri to the podium for her gold medal, enjoying every minute of the acclaim.

Overnight, she became the star of the 1996 Olympics. While she was on the phone with CNN describing the event, Karolyi rushed into her room and interrupted her. "I'm on live TV," she told him. "Hang up!" Karolyi screamed. "The President is on the other line!" Strug's face appeared on newspaper and magazine front pages all over the world. The response was overwhelmingly positive, but there were some journalists who thought that Kerri's decision to compete when she was clearly injured was motivated by fear rather than the personal desire to win. Nonsense, said Strug. "I'm 18. I'm an adult and I make my own decisions," she claimed.

Later, it came to light that Kerri didn't have to make that final vault, that the total points accumulated up to that point were enough to assure a U.S. victory. But at the time she had to decide to make the vault, there was no way to know that the U.S. had all the points it needed. And it doesn't in any way detract from Strug's courage and spirit.

Because of her injury, Strug was unable to take part in any of the individual events. Instead, she sat and watched, cheering her teammates on. She was overwhelmed by the response to her final effort, but she still had some humor left. "It was a matter of pride," she said at one point. "I didn't want to be remembered for falling on my rear end."

After her amazing Olympic performance, Strug was surrounded by people who wanted to capitalize on her fame. She was told that she could earn as much as $3 million if she would turn pro. That would mean traveling with her Olympic teammates on a national tour and accepting lucrative endorsements for everything from cereal to makeup. It would also mean giving up her scholarship to UCLA and the chance to be a college gymnast. NCAA rules are firm on the matter: anyone receiving money through endorsements or paid as a professional is not allowed to receive scholarship funds or to compete in collegiate athletics. At first Kerri, who had never had an agent and had always refused all endorsements, gave a firm "no" to all offers. Then, on July 31, she announced that she would forego college at this time and take part in a professional gymnastics tour. She also signed with an agent. However, Kerri changed her mind about college in August and started classes at UCLA in September.

HOME AND FAMILY

Kerri's family lives in Tucson. Despite the time she has spent training away from home, Strug remains close to her family. Apparently, her quest for perfection extends to her closet. "You open Kerri's closet and all the short-sleeved shirts are with the short-sleeved shirts, and the long-sleeved shirts are with the long-sleeved shirts," says her mom. "Her room is always neat; the bed is always made." Kerri says she gets that streak of perfectionism from her dad. "We put everything into whatever we do," she claims. Strug may follow in her father's footsteps and study medicine.

HOBBIES AND OTHER INTERESTS

When she's not competing, Kerri likes to read, shop, and spend time with her family. She also likes to work with pottery.

HONORS AND AWARDS

World Gymnastics Championships: 1991, Silver Medal; 1992, Bronze Medal; 1995, Silver Medal (team); 1995, Bronze Medal

U.S. Gymnastics Championships: 1991, Gold Medal (vault), Bronze Medal (all-around and uneven bars); 1992, Gold Medal (vault and balance beam), Silver Medal (all-around an floor exercise)

U.S. Olympic Trials: 1992, Bronze Medal (all-around); 1996, Silver Medal (all-around)

Olympic Gymnastics: 1992, Bronze Medal (U.S. Team); 1996, Gold Medal (U.S. Team)

U.S. Olympic Festival: 1993, Gold Medal (uneven bars), Silver Medal (all-around, balance beam, and floor exercise); 1995, Gold Medal (all-around and uneven bars), Bronze Medal (balance beam)

FURTHER READING

PERIODICALS

Arizona Republic, Sep. 15, 1991, p.D10; July 29, 1992, p.D1; Nov. 2, 1992, p.D10; Apr. 17, 1993, p.E7; Dec. 16, 1994, p.F1; Oct. 2, 1995, p.D5; Jan. 14, 1996, p.C1; Mar. 3, 1996, p.C1
Atlanta Constitution, July 31, 1996, p.S4
Chicago Tribune, June 26, 1996, Sports, p.1
Daily Telegraph, July 27, 1996, p.25
Guardian, July 26, 1996, p.17
New York Times, July 25, 1996, p.B6
Newsweek, Aug. 5, 1996, p.42
People, Aug 5, 1996, p.118
Time, Aug. 28, 1995, p.73; Aug. 5, 1996, p.32
Times of London, July 27, 1996
USA Today, July 25, 1996, p.A2

ADDRESS

USA Gymnastics
201 S. Capitol Ave.
Indianapolis, IN 46225

WORLD WIDE WEB ADDRESS

http://www.usa-gymnastics.org/usag

Tiffani-Amber Thiessen   1974-
American Actress
Plays Valerie Malone on hit series
"Beverly Hills, 90210"

BIRTH

Tiffani-Amber Thiessen (THEE-son) was born on January 23, 1974, in Modesto, California. A fifth-generation Californian of Welsh, German, Greek, and Turkish descent, Tiffani-Amber was the second of three children born to Frank Thiessen, a landscape architect who designs parks, and his wife, Robyn, a homemaker. They gave their daughter a double name because they liked the name Tiffani and her grandparents liked the name Amber—and because, in her grandmother's words, "two names make a stronger person." Tiffani-Amber's older brother, Todd, is a professional cyclist. Schuyler, her younger brother, is a student at the University of California, Davis.

YOUTH

Thiessen grew up in Long Beach, just south of Los Angeles. Her mother enrolled her in dance classes at the age of five "for fun," and she stayed with it for ten years. If knee problems hadn't intervened, she might have grown up to be a professional dancer. Instead, she turned to modeling.

When she was still in grade school, Thiessen's uncle, a photographer, introduced her to a friend of his at a modeling agency. She started modeling at the age of eight, making Barbie doll commercials for Mattel, and landed her first acting job by the time she turned 11. Her parents entered her in a number of beauty pageants because they thought it would teach her poise. Thiessen won the title of Miss Junior America in 1987, when she was only 13 years old. That same year, she signed up for *Teen* magazine's Great Model Search—along with 27,000 other girls. Although she didn't win, Thiessen was one of the top 12 finalists. A year later, she entered the competition again and won. She became a *Teen* cover girl and quickly moved from modeling into television roles.

EDUCATION

Because she was involved in modeling and acting at such an early age, Thiessen never received a conventional high school education. Most of the time she had private tutors who worked with her on the set, but she also attended Valley Professional School when her schedule allowed. When she graduated in 1992, she was valedictorian of her class—she had earned the highest grade-point average in her graduating class. Although she does not regret her unusual upbringing, Tiffani-Amber admits that she "didn't get to go to the prom or be in the high school clubs and hang around with my friends a lot."

FIRST JOBS

Thiessen started out with guest appearances on the TV series "Step by Step," "Charles in Charge," "The Hogan Family," and "Married . . . With Children." In 1989, she landed the role of Kelly, the head cheerleader in the popular NBC Saturday morning teenage sitcom, "Saved by the Bell." She remained on the show for five years, during which it became one of the most popular young-teen programs in television history. Thiessen also played Kelly in "Saved By the Bell: The College Years," the show's prime-time spinoff, where the young cast from the original show turn up as students at the fictional California University. She also appeared in the 1994 TV movie, "Saved by the Bell: Wedding in Las Vegas."

Thiessen auditioned for the Fox network's nighttime soap, "Models, Inc." in 1993, but she didn't get the part. She did, however, make an impression on Aaron Spelling, the show's creator—a connection that would pay off later on.

CAREER HIGHLIGHTS

Thiessen's biggest break came in 1994, when she auditioned for the cast of "Beverly Hills, 90210," the Fox network hit about a group of upper-class white teenagers in southern California. Thiessen joined the show after Shannen Doherty was asked to leave the cast. Known for her on- and off-screen temper tantrums, her stormy personal relationships, and her chronic tardiness, Doherty had turned the set of "90210" into what one cast member described as "a war zone." It soon became clear to Aaron Spelling, the show's producer, that she would have to go. But who would replace Brenda Walsh, Doherty's character?

At the end of the 1993-94 season, when Doherty left the show, the writers sent Brenda off to acting school in London. They then introduced the character of Valerie Malone, a family friend of the Walshes who moves in with them after her father's suicide. Aaron Spelling, who remembered Thiessen from her audition for "Models, Inc.," invited her to read for the role. She was hired on the spot.

After playing a goody-two-shoes character on "Saved by the Bell," Thiessen was eager to tackle a more complex role. Although she moves into Brenda Walsh's old bedroom, Valerie is no mere replacement for Doherty's character. Thiessen describes Valerie as "a very troubled lady" with "a dark side." On the surface, she's a beautiful, smart, all-American girl; but she also lies, steals, drinks, smokes pot, steals other girls' boyfriends, and is sexually promiscuous.

Thiessen's convincing portrayal of Valerie Malone has helped boost the show's ratings to their highest level ever, but it has also made her a target for the tabloid press. Many persist in seeing her as a trouble-maker despite her sedate lifestyle and well-mannered behavior off-screen. Although she's only 21, Thiessen has learned to weather the media storms and the attention of her fans. She's had to deal with rumors about her alleged weight problem and her relationship with fellow "90210" castmember Brian Austin Green. But she's brought harmony and stability to the cast and crew. "Tiffani doesn't rock the boat," explains Aaron Spelling. "And frankly, after Shannen, it was important to have someone who would bring some quiet to the set."

Thiessen also hopes to branch out from her role as Valerie in "90210." Eager to prove that she's not just a teenage actress in a string bikini, Thiessen recently played sexual assault victims in two made-for-TV movies: ABC's "The Stranger Beside Me," and NBC's "Scared by Love." Although she's too busy with her career right now to continue her education, she's determined to graduate from college some day—"even if I have to wait until I'm 40!"

HOME AND FAMILY

Before Thiessen won the role of Valerie, she was already dating Brian Austin Green, who plays David Silver on "90210"; they had met in the late 1980s on the set of "Married . . . With Children." Eventually they moved in together, but their relationship ended recently after more than two years.

Right now, Thiessen is living in Los Angeles with her two golden retrievers, Bonnie and Clyde, and her cats, Sadie and Savannah. She claims that she stays "grounded" by maintaining close contact with her family in Long Beach.

MAJOR INFLUENCES

Her older brother Todd has been a major inspiration to Thiessen. "He's had a lot of problems," she explains, "and how he's come out of it is just amazing. Knowing someone who's been at the bottom and completely restructured himself . . . makes me think I could do anything. I have total respect for him."

HOBBIES AND OTHER INTERESTS

Thiessen stays in shape by taking kick-boxing lessons three times a week. She also enjoys rollerblading, running on the beach with her dogs, and dancing.

CREDITS

"Saved By the Bell," 1989-1993
"Saved By the Bell: The College Years," 1993-94
"Saved By the Bell: Wedding in Las Vegas," 1995
"Beverly Hills 90210," 1993-
"Stranger Beside Me," 1995
"Scared By Love," 1995

FURTHER READING

PERIODICALS

Daily News of Los Angeles, Sep. 12, 1995, "L.A. Life" Section, p.L8
Entertainment Weekly, July 28, 1995, p.22
New York Times, Aug. 7, 1994, Section II, p.33
People, Sep. 12, 1994, p.71
Teen, May 1993, p.92
TV Guide, Sep. 3, 1994, p.10; Aug. 26, 1995, p.12

ADDRESS

"Beverly Hills, 90210"
P.O. Box 900
Beverly Hills, CA 90213

Dave Thomas   1932-
American Businessman
Founder of Wendy's Restaurants

BIRTH

R. David Thomas was born July 2, 1932, in Atlantic City, New Jersey. He never knew his birth parents, who were unmarried. He was adopted when he was six weeks old by Rex and Auleva Thomas of Kalamazoo, Michigan. Auleva was a homemaker and Rex was a construction worker. They had no other children.

YOUTH

Auleva died of rheumatic fever when Dave was five. After her death, Dave and his dad lived in many different places, as Rex tried to find construction jobs. Dave remembers Rex as a man who didn't offer a lot of affection to his adopted son. "He was a hard worker and honest, but as far as being a father went, he didn't have the time or inclination," Thomas says. Their life was lonely. Dave didn't make many friends, because the family was always on the move. Rex remarried and divorced three times, adding to Dave's sense of rootlessness.

He and his dad ate in a lot of restaurants, and Dave began to notice what people liked and what they didn't. He paid attention to menus, decor, and the complaints of the customers. As one article stated recently, by the time he was nine, "he was already a restaurant critic." But Thomas says, "Most of all, I remember watching families sitting together, having a good time."

EARLY MEMORIES

Thomas spent many summers with his maternal grandmother, Minnie Sinclair, in Augusta, Michigan. Those are times he remembers with fondness. Minnie offered him his only sense of family warmth and formed his values. "She taught me early on about doing the right thing, working hard, doing a job well and having fun," Thomas remembers. She also offered him a glimpse of the life he would embrace as a career. His grandmother worked in a restaurant, and Thomas has vivid memories of the place, as he described in his autobiography *Dave's Way*: "The food was presented in big round and oblong bowls, pats of butter melting all over the mashed potatoes and green peas as they were carried out of the kitchen. They used to serve gallons and gallons of chicken and dumplings. And they served delicious pastries, which were always swimming in gooey icing."

FIRST JOBS

Dave knew he wanted to make money and to have a better life. "As early as the age of 8, I had a desire to live in better conditions than the way I was living," Thomas says. "Most everybody else had a family; I didn't. There were little things I wanted that I didn't have. I wanted money to go to the movies, to buy a hamburger when I was hungry. The right thing to do in my mind was to get a job."

Dave started to work when he was only 12 years old. He lied about his age, claiming he was 16, the legal age to begin working. When his first employer found out how young he was, he got fired. He found another job immediately, but when his new boss discovered his age, Dave lost his second job.

Dave's third job, which he also found at 12, was at a small restaurant in Knoxville, Tennessee. He again lied about his age. "They later told me they suspected the truth, but I worked so hard they decided not to make an issue of it," says Thomas.

EDUCATION

Dave attended the local public schools wherever he and his dad lived. When he was 15, they were living in Fort Wayne, Indiana, where Dave landed a job as a busboy at the Hobby House Restaurant. When his dad announced that they were moving again, Dave decided to stay put and live in the local YMCA. He was a sophomore in high school at the time. Working long shifts and attending school at the same time was exhausting him. So he decided to drop out of school and work full-time.

Later, he would complete his GED exam, but for now, Dave's formal schooling was over.

CAREER HIGHLIGHTS

Thomas worked at the Hobby House until he was 18, when he joined the army. Stationed in Germany, he put his restaurant talents to use working as a cook and baker. He was used to a heavy work load, so he volunteered to help out at the Enlisted Men's Club. Soon he was running the place. He revamped the menu, offering fried chicken and hamburgers to the men. And he began his remarkable string of successes in the restaurant world. "When I took over the club, we were doing $40 a day in business. When I left we were doing $1,000 a day," remembers Thomas. "And I was having fun. I learned a lot about getting ahead by giving the customer more of what he really wanted."

Returning to the U.S., Thomas went back to the Hobby House, where he worked as a short-order cook. Then, in 1956, Thomas and his boss, Phil Clauss, started a new restaurant, the Ranch House. Around this time he met Harland Sanders, the Colonel Sanders of Kentucky Fried Chicken fame. Sanders was traveling around the country selling franchises for his popular chicken restaurants. (A "franchise" is a store that is part of a larger chain of a business.) Phil Clauss bought a KFC franchise, and Thomas started in the chicken business. While he was with the KFC operation, he also helped to start the Arthur Treacher's Fish and Chips chain of restaurants.

In 1962, Thomas was given the opportunity to buy into the KFC franchise himself. Against the Colonel's advice, he took over four failing stores in Columbus, Ohio. It was a risk and a challenge, and Dave Thomas was ready for it. "The stores were practically bankrupt; I had four kids and a wife, and I was making $135 a week. But I made up my mind that I was going to be in business for myself."

It was incredibly hard work, and cash was sometimes a problem. But he had learned a little from the Colonel about unorthodox marketing. So when he didn't have the cash to buy radio advertising, he would swap a bucket of chicken for air time. It worked. Six years later, he sold the stores for $1.5 million. The former short-order cook was a millionaire at 35.

WENDY'S

In 1969, with the proceeds from the sale of his KFC stores, Thomas decided to start out on his own. And this time, he wanted to make burgers. "Even when I was in fried chicken, I wanted a hamburger restaurant," he says. "To tell the truth, I hated chicken and have since I was a kid. Give me a cooked-to-order hamburger, and I am happy."

That was the philosophy behind his new restaurant, Wendy's. Thomas named the restaurant for his then eight-year-old daughter, Melinda Lou, who was nicknamed Wendy. He wanted the store to have a cute, wholesome image, which he thought was represented by his daughter.

Wendy's had a niche: the restaurant offered a burger that was made with freshly ground meat, not frozen patties like the other fast-food chains. "I thought McDonald's was terrible," says Thomas. "The pickle was bigger than the meat." Under Thomas, Wendy's focused on high quality fast food, served in a clean atmosphere by a friendly staff. The burger was square, not round, so it stuck out of the bun. Thomas served baked potatoes and salads, which were unknown in fast food at the time. His restaurants were designed to look warm and inviting, with wooden tables and Tiffany-style lamps. And he refused to precook hamburgers and have them sit under a heat lamp. "People don't make sandwiches at home and put them under a heat lamp," says Thomas. "So we don't."

The restaurant took off. By 1982, Wendy's had 2,430 stores and revenues of $1.6 billion. The wealth that came with success was never a major concern to Thomas. "I liked to make money, but money wasn't the only thing. It was also the sense of accomplishment."

With the company going strong, Thomas decided to take some time off. The company was now a publicly held corporation, and the owners brought in a management team, while Thomas spent his time boating and dabbling in investments. At first, things seemed to go just fine. In 1984, the company ran a series of television ads that were wildly popular. Featuring an elderly actress, Clara Peller, the ads focused on the difference between a Wendy's hamburger and the regular skimpy burger found at most fast-food chains. These "Where's the Beef?" ads were a smash.

But the success of the ad made the Wendy's team complacent. The marketing and sales people had forgotten what had built the company: attention to product and service. "I thought we'd put in a smarter team to do a better job," said Thomas. "I was wrong."

In 1989, with sales floundering, Thomas asked James Near, a Wendy's franchise owner with a proven record in the business, to return to the company in a major role, as chief executive officer of the company. Near agreed, but he had one condition: Thomas had to return. So Thomas got back into burgers, this time as the star of the ad campaigns.

Thomas was immediately successful as the pitchman for his product. To date, he has appeared in more than 300 commercials for Wendy's. He presents a folksy, trustworthy image that people love. And Wendy's has never been more successful. As of 1995, there are more than 4,000 Wendy's restaurants in the U.S. and 33 countries, employing more than 130,000 people and generating more than $4.2 billion in revenues.

For Thomas, continued success means staying focused on a few simple truths: "There are a lot of guys in nice offices who get involved in complicated theories, but people want what they've always wanted. They want quality and their money's worth." And he believes that his years behind the grill have been crucial to his success. He is not above going into one of his restaurants, and if there's a long line, putting on an apron and getting behind the grill to serve his customers. "I'm not a celebrity," he claims, "I'm a hamburger cook."

BECOMING A SPOKESPERSON FOR ADOPTION

In 1990, Thomas was named national spokesperson for adoption by then-President George Bush. In the past several years he has devoted a great deal of his time to the cause of adoption, working "to raise awareness and to make adoption simpler and more affordable," he says. All the revenues from his two books, *Dave's Way* and *Well Done!*, go to support the Dave Thomas Foundation for Adoption. Thomas also donates all the money he receives from his speaking engagements to the cause of adoption. And he offers special incentives to his own employees to adopt, including paid time off and financial assistance. To Thomas, the bottom line on adoption is simple: "Every child deserves a home and love. Period."

His own story of being adopted took a painful personal twist a few years ago when he was finally able to locate the descendants of his birth family. By then, both his birth mother and father were dead, but his birth father had gone on to marry and have a family, including a son—Dave's half-brother—who was a very successful MIT-trained professor. But the professor wanted nothing to do with Dave Thomas. The rejection stung. "He might be very, very smart, but he doesn't have much common sense," Thomas says of the brother that rejected him.

MARRIAGE AND FAMILY

Thomas met his wife, Lorraine, while the two of them were working at the Hobby Horse restaurant in Fort Wayne. They got married in 1954 and are the parents of five children, Pam, Ken, Molly, Melinda (nicknamed Wendy), and Lori. The kids are all grown up now, and many of them are in the family business as owners of franchises. The Thomases have 14 grandchildren to date. Dave and Lorraine have four different homes, but their major base is Fort Lauderdale, Florida.

Despite his fervent belief in the importance of family, Thomas himself was not always around for his own kids. His job required him to travel constantly, and Lorraine took a up a lot of the slack. "He was always overtired," remembers daughter Pam. "He really didn't know how to go to a baseball game. My mom really held it together." In *Dave's Way*, Thomas says, "I have to confess that I cheated my kids by not being involved enough in raising them. I knew I had a responsibility to feed, clothe, and educate my children, and I did that 110 percent." But his kids harbor no bad feelings toward their dad. They know he is a man who loves to work and has a hard time sitting still. And, says Wendy, "he's a very giving guy. He's earned it, and he shares it."

HOBBIES AND OTHER INTERESTS

In addition to his work on adoption, Thomas is actively involved in other charities, including St. Jude Children's Research Hospital in Memphis, Tennessee, Children's Hospital in Columbus, Ohio, The Ohio State University Cancer Research Institute, and a new facility named for his wife, the I. Lorraine Thomas Emergency Children's Home and Family Support Center, in Ft. Lauderdale.

Thomas is also involved in national campaigns to encourage kids to stay in school and do well. While that may sound funny coming from a guy who dropped out of school, Thomas did finally finish his degree—in 1993. He completed the work for his GED—general equivalency diploma—through Coconut Creek High School in Fort Lauderdale, Florida. The graduating class held a special graduation for him, naming him "Most Likely to Succeed." And that spring, he escorted Lorraine to Coconut Creek's Senior Prom.

BUSINESS PHILOSOPHY

"I may not have a formal education, but I was lucky enough to find mentors who taught me about building a business and motivating people. You can't have a career until you get a job, and too many people want to start at the top. Just work hard and apply yourself. My recipe for success is hard work, patience, honesty, and total commitment."

WRITINGS

Dave's Way: A New Approach to Old-Fashioned Success, 1991
Well Done! Dave's Secret Recipe for Everyday Success, 1994

FURTHER READING

BOOKS

Thomas, Dave. *Dave's Way: A New Approach to Old-Fashioned Success,* 1991
Thomas, Dave. *Well Done! Dave's Secret Recipe for Everyday Success,* 1994

PERIODICALS

Barron's, Apr. 17, 1995, p.17
Cleveland Plain Dealer, Nov. 11, 1992, p.C1
Columbus Dispatch, Nov. 19, 1989, p.G1
Current Biography Yearbook 1995
Family Circle, Nov. 11, 1995, p.176
Ft. Lauderdale Sun Sentinel, Nov. 24, 1991, p.B6; May 28, 1995, p.C19
Forbes, Aug. 5, 1991, p.106; Jan. 3, 1994, p.149
Miami Herald, Feb. 8, 1995, p.E1
New York, Apr. 1, 1991, p.20
People, Aug. 2, 1993, p.86
USA Today, May 28, 1993, p,D2

ADDRESS

Wendy's International Inc.
P.O. Box 256
4288 West Dublin Granville Road
Dublin, OH 43017

Jaleel White   1977-
American Actor
Plays Steven Urkel in the TV Series,
"Family Matters"

BIRTH

Jaleel White was born in Los Angeles, California, on November 27, 1977. He is the only child of Michael White, a dentist, and Gail White, a homemaker. White's father claims he knew that Jaleel was special from the day he was born. "In the hospital," Michael White says, "all the babies were wrapped in their blankets, and Jaleel was the only one struggling to get his arms out. I watched him for about a half-hour, and even though his eyes were closed, he managed to wiggle his arms out of that blanket. . . . He was always extremely coordinated."

YOUTH AND EDUCATION

Growing up in Pasadena, California, neither White nor his parents expected him to go into show business. But his pre-school teacher recognized that he had talent and persuaded his parents to send him to a theatrical preschool in Hollywood, where he was spotted by an agent. The agent helped him get his first job in a commercial, when he was only three years old. From that time on, White combined his school work with various acting jobs.

White attended a private junior high school in southern California, where he was the only black student. He went on to become an honor student at a public high school, from which he graduated in 1995. Throughout his young years, the demands of his career necessitated hiring a private tutor, who worked with White while he was filming television shows. White is currently a business major at UCLA. His parents place a high priority on education and have steadfastly refused to let his work as an actor interfere with his studies.

White has always been self-motivated, according to his mother. "Once, when he was younger, I caught him one morning about 3 a.m. on the floor with a little light doing his homework," she recalls.

FIRST JOBS

Since appearing in his first commercial, for Goodyear Tires, at the age of three, White has made more than 30 commercials for television. He played his first role in a television movie when he was only in second grade, appearing in 1984 with Charlie Sheen in "Silence of the Heart." He went on to perform in a number of other TV movies, including "Kids Don't Tell," "Leftovers," and "Club Cucamonga." His first role in a series was playing Robert on "Charlie & Company" (1985-86), opposite Flip Wilson and Gladys Knight. He also guest-starred on "The Jeffersons," the pioneering television sitcom of the 1980s that portrayed the lives of a middle-class African-American family.

CAREER HIGHLIGHTS

"FAMILY MATTERS"

At the end of his eighth grade year, White promised his mother that he would get out of the business and concentrate on his studies. Then he auditioned for a guest appearance on "Family Matters," a series about a multi-generational black family living under the same roof in Chicago. Tom Miller and Bob Boyett, the producers, were worried about the show's cancellation at the end of its initial season (1989-90), and they knew they needed something to revive its sagging ratings. White wowed them with his spontaneous and unique portrayal of Steven Urkel, the nerd who lives next door to the Winslow family. Wearing his pants pulled up above his ankles by suspenders and oversized safety glasses that he'd borrowed from his dentist father, White invented the nasal voice, the snorting laugh, and the exaggerated walk that immediately defined his character. Looking back on the audition, White claims he was "temporarily possessed": "I went in, and this voice came out of me, and the stance just kind of flowed with it." He was hired on the spot.

What was supposed to be a one-shot appearance as Laura Winslow's five-foot-tall prom date in the spring of 1990 saved the show from extinction and changed its focus forever. People in the audience began chanting, "Urkel, Urkel, Urkel!" during the taping of the first episode featuring White, and the producers knew immediately that they would have to expand his role.

One of the show's writers recognized in Steven Urkel the potential for another "Fonzie"—the leather-jacketed character who started out in a supporting role and ended up stealing the show on "Happy Days," another hit series on which Miller and Boyett had collaborated. Since that time, Urkel has become a regular on "Family Matters," which airs on ABC during prime time Friday night.

With his bug collection, his passion for cheese and mice, his enduring crush on Laura Winslow (played by Kellie Williams), and his irritating voice and behavior, Steven Urkel is hardly the type of character one would expect to win a loyal following. On the show, he is the eager beaver who grates on everyone's nerves, barging in on the Winslows uninvited and showering Laura with pet names like "my little Jell-O mold." He has been described as the "nerd supreme" who spouts off irrelevant facts and uses a vocabulary that would challenge most adults. In one episode, for example, he tells Laura that he never expected her to ask him for a date "because that would be like asking (former Vice President) Dan Quayle to appear on 'Jeopardy.'" In another, he tries to win her affections by playing the sentimental pop song "Feelings" on his accordion outside her bedroom window. Despite his character's misguided attempts to win friends and romance, White receives so much fan mail that his family has had to hire someone to open it.

URKEL'S POPULARITY

White's rise to stardom as Steven Urkel has been followed by a string of commercial successes—including Urkel boxer shorts, sweatshirts, belts, suspenders, key rings, calendars, jigsaw puzzles, a board game, and a cereal called Urkel-Os. Most popular of all is the talking Urkel doll marketed by Hasbro. The doll comes dressed in a rugby shirt, beige-and-brown saddle shoes, pants pulled up by navy blue suspenders, and huge glasses. When you pull its voice cord, it says in a nasally whine, "Got any cheese?" There's even a dance named after Urkel, which begins with the instructions, "Hitch up your pants." Steven Urkel look-alike contests have been held throughout the United States.

WHAT LIES AHEAD

Although White is now 18 years old and 5 feet, 10 inches tall, ABC recently renewed "Family Matters" for its seventh season. He knows that his fame as Steven Urkel won't last forever. For the time being, however, White is enjoying his popularity on "Family Matters" and says he is particularly proud to play an African-American character known for his intelligence. In the future, he hopes to build on his television experience and combine it with his interest in writing. He calls the African-American movie maker Spike Lee his role model. White says that he would like to be "the next Spike Lee" because "he's an innovator and he's not afraid to come out and say what's on his and society's mind."

HOME AND FAMILY

On the set of "Family Matters," White's mother is always by his side. She is determined that her son not end up like other teenage actors who had trouble adjusting to adult life after their stardom faded. Michael and Gail White have gone out of their way to maintain a stable home environment for their son and to encourage his academic achievements. They have always limited how much time he spends on the phone or watching TV.

So far, his parents' strictness appears to be paying off. As a UCLA business student, White has been described as showing a maturity far beyond his years. He continues to earn top grades and credits his mother and father for instilling his work ethic early on. As for his transition to adulthood, White is matter-of-fact: "There are two different types of actors," he says, "one that looks at it like a business and enjoys what he does, and another who is concerned about the glamour end of it . . . . [I] don't get wrapped up in the perks. They're only there when you're a hit."

HOBBIES AND OTHER INTERESTS

Both as a fan and as a player, Jaleel White has always been passionate about basketball. When he's not working on the set of "Family Matters," he spends as much time as he can on the basketball or tennis court. His heroes include basketball greats Magic Johnson, Michael Jordan, and Charles Barkley, as well as tennis stars Andre Agassi and Michael Chang.

White is also an amateur cartoonist and writer. He loves making ice cream and hopes to market his own flavors some day.

CREDITS

"Silence of the Heart," 1984
"Charlie & Company," 1985-86
"Family Matters," 1990-

FURTHER READING

PERIODICALS

Chicago Tribune, Dec. 30, 1990, "TV Week" Section, p.3
Daily News of Los Angeles, July 24, 1991, "L.A. Life" Section, p. L19; Feb. 16, 1992, "TV/Book" Section, p.L5
Entertainment Weekly, June 30, 1995, p.42
Jet, June 3, 1991, p.58
Los Angeles Times, Jan. 4, 1991, "Calendar" Section, p.1
New Yorker, July 15, 1991, p.24
Time, Apr. 1, 1991, p.73
TV Guide, Jan. 19, 1991, p.28
USA Today, Feb. 20, 1992, "Life" Section, p.3D

ADDRESS

"Family Matters"
Warner Brothers Television
300 TV Plaza, Bldg. 137
Burbank, CA 91505

Photo and Illustration Credits

Aung San Suu Kyi/Photos: AP/Wide World Photos.

Ron Brown/Photo: AP/Wide World Photos.

Mariah Carey/Photos: Steven Meisel; Jo Ann Toy.

Jim Carrey/Photos: Marsha Blackburn; AP/Wide World Photos.

Larry Champagne/Photo: St. Louis Post-Dispatch.

Christo/Photos: John Chapman/*The Times*. Copyright © Times Newspapers Ltd.; RUETERS/Reinhard Krause/ARCHIVE PHOTOS; REUTERS/Kimimasa Mayama/ARCHIVE PHOTOS.

Chelsea Clinton/Photos: AP/Wide World Photos.

Coolio/Photos: Albert Watson; Byron J. Cohen.

David Duchovny/Photos: Michael Lavine/FOX; Michael Grecco/FOX.

Debbi Fields/Photo: Peter Garfield.

Chris Galeczka/Photo: Mark O. Thiessen.

Jerry Garcia/Photo: AP/Wide World Photos.

Jennie Garth/Photo: Timothy White/FOX.

Wendy Guey/Photos: Mark Bowen.

Tom Hanks/Cover: Copyright © 1994 Pocket Books. Photos: Ron Batzdorff; Copyright © The Walt Disney Company. All Rights Reserved.

Alison Hargreaves/Photos: Archive Photos/Express News.

Sir Edmund Hillary/Photos: AP/Wide World Photos.

Judith Jamison/Photos: Copyright © Michael Ahern; Copyright © Jack Mitchell.

Barbara Jordan/Photos: AP/Wide World Photos.

Annie Leibovitz/Photos: Robert Mapplethorpe; Annie Leibovitz.

Carl Lewis/Photos: AP/Wide World Photos.

Jim Lovell/Photo: NASA. Cover: Copyright © 1995 Pocket Books.

Mickey Mantle/Photos: AP/Wide World Photos; Archive Photos.

Lynn Margulis/Cover: Reprinted with permission of Simon & Schuster.

Iqbal Masih/Photo: AP/Wide World Photos.

Larisa Oleynik/Photos: NICKELODEON.

Christopher Pike/Photo: Martin Beddall/*The Times*. Copyright © Times
Newspapers Ltd. Cover: Scholastic Inc.

David Robinson/Photos: Nathaniel S. Butler/NBA Photos; R. Eckert/NBA
Photos.

Dennis Rodman/Photo: AP/Wide World Photos.

Selena/Photos: Maurice Rinaldi; AP/Wide World Photos; Kelly Jordan/
Sygma.

Monica Seles/Photo: AP/Wide World Photos.

Kerri Strug/Photos: AP/Wide World Photos.

Tiffini-Amber Thiessen/Photo: Timothy White/FOX.

Jaleel White/Photos: Bob D'Amico/ABC.

Appendix

This Appendix contains updates for individuals profiled in Volumes 1, 2, 3, and 4, and 5 of *Biography Today*.

* YASIR ARAFAT *

In 1996, Yasir Arafat continued to work for Palestinian autonomy, within the context of a very different political atmosphere in Israel. After the assassination of Yitzhak Rabin in November 1995, Israel elected a new prime minster, Benjamin Netanyahu. Netanyahu was elected in part for what his supporters believed was his tougher stance against the concept of Palestinians self- rule, which, under an accord signed when Rabin was in power, was to begin in the area of Israel known as the West Bank in 1996. There were a number of skirmishes between the Israelis and the Palestinians, culminating in the most deadly fighting to break out since 1967, in which 78 people were killed and over 1,500 were wounded. As the tensions between the two sides escalated, the two leaders met in Washington, DC, at the request of Bill Clinton to try to reach some kind of agreement on how the peace process would proceed. But no agreement was reached, and tensions between the two peoples continue.

* BENAZIR BHUTTO *

Benazir Bhutto's government was dismissed in early November 1996 by the President of Pakistan, Farooq Leghari. He charged that Bhutto's government was guilty of corruption, abuse of power, intimidation of the judiciary, and allowing a breakdown of law and order. Bhutto was placed under house arrest. Leghari also dismissed the ruling governmental body, the National Assembly, and called for new elections. This is the second time Bhutto has been removed from office. In 1990, she was also dismissed, also on charges of corruption.

* CONNIE CHUNG *

Connie Chung announced in June 1996 that she would return to broadcasting as a co-anchor with her husband, Maury Povich, on a news and information program slated to begin in 1998. The program will be produced by Dreamworks Television. In 1997, Chung will serve as a fellow at Harvard University's Joan Shorenstein Center on Press, Politics, and Public Policy.

* BILL CLINTON *

After being ahead in the polls throughout the campaign, Bill Clinton won reelection to the office of President with 49 percent of the vote. His opponent, Bob Dole, received 42 percent of the vote, and independent candidate Ross Perot received 9 percent. Clinton became the first Democrat since Franklin Delano Roosevelt to win reelection to the presidency. He says his priorities include focusing on campaign reform, education, crime, and the economy. There is also speculation that Clinton will make changes in his cabinet, in part to build a coalition with the Congress, which continues to be controlled by the Republicans. Clinton enters his second term with questions regarding his administration's involvement with Whitewater, possible illegal practices in fundraising, and other perceived ethical lapses.

* HILLARY CLINTON *

Hillary Clinton proved to be an able campaigner and fundraiser for her husband in the election campaign of 1996. Clinton won reelection with 49 percent of the vote to Dole's 42 percent and Perot's 9 percent. In the past year she has worked to improve children's television, to help children in foster care, and to anticipate the needs of children adversely affected by the changes in the welfare system. Also during 1996, Hillary Clinton continued to be part of the focus into the continuing investigation into the Whitewater affair.

* DIANA, PRINCESS OF WALES *

Princess Diana was divorced from Prince Charles in August 1996. She received a settlement of $23 million dollars and $600,000 a year in expenses, a nine-room apartment in Kensington Palace, a jewelry collection valued at $30 million, and the right to travel as a representative of the royal family. She lost the title Her Royal Highness and is now known simply as Diana, Princess of Wales. She resigned from many of the charities she used to head and will take a limited role in both charity work and as an official representative of the royal family.

* BOB DOLE *

After winning enough primary delegates to ensure his nomination as the Republican candidate for president, Bob Dole resigned his position as the U.S. Senator from Kansas in June 1996 and began his campaign. He formerly received the Republican Party's nomination at the convention in San Diego in July 1996. He named former HUD Secretary Jack Kemp as his running mate. Dole lost his bid for the presidency to Bill Clinton in November, receiving 42 percent of the vote to Clinton's 49 percent. Independent candidate Ross Perot received 9 percent. Dole is now a private citizen and will most likely return to Washington, where his wife, Elizabeth, will resume her job as head of the American Red Cross. At press time, Dole's future career plans were not certain.

* ELIZABETH DOLE *

Elizabeth Dole took a leave of absence from her job as president of the American Red Cross in 1996 to devote herself to her husband's campaign for the presidency. A popular and savvy politician in her own right, Dole gave a speech at the Republican convention in July 1996 that was considered a highlight of the convention and the Dole campaign. Dole lost the presidential race to Bill Clinton and is now retired from public office. Elizabeth Dole will now return to Washington and to her duties at the Red Cross.

* JANET EVANS *

Evans took part in the 1996 Olympics in Atlanta, her third Olympics. As a token of her contribution to American sports—she has four gold medals and one silver from past Olympics and three world records in swimming—she was chosen to hand the Olympic torch to former boxing champion Muhammad Ali during the opening ceremonies. At the age of 24, Evans was one of the oldest swimmers in the Olympics, and she placed sixth in her final bid for another medal in the 800-meter freestyle. Evans was happy to have competed: "I wouldn't give it up for the whole world," she said. "It's still been by favorite Olympics so far. It was fun to come to the Olympics and win gold medals, but this has been what the Olympics are all about, the highs and lows. It's been a heck of a ride, that's all I can say." Evans plans to go to law school next year, and she wants to try to run a marathon.

* MIKHAIL GORBACHEV *

Gorbachev ran unsuccessfully for the office of president of Russia in 1996, losing to Boris Yeltsin and receiving only a small percent of the vote. He is currently writing and lecturing, and is a frequent speaker in the United States.

* AL GORE *

As Bill Clinton's running mate, Gore was reelected to the office of the Vice President of the United States, with the ticket winning 49 percent of the vote. The Dole-Kemp ticket garnered 42 percent, and Ross Perot and running mate Pat Choate received 9 percent. Although he is not yet a declared candidate, Gore is expected to run for the presidency himself in 2000.

* SADDAM HUSSEIN *

Saddam Hussein was in the news in 1996 after President Clinton sent U.S. aircraft to bomb strategic targets in Iraq to defend Kurdish rebels in northern Iraq from attacks by Hussein's army. The U.S. move received little international support, and the bombings did little to curtail Hussein's aggression against the Kurds, which continues.

* JACKIE JOYNER-KERSEE *

Jackie Joyner-Kersee ended her Olympic career with a medal and a withdrawal. Much to the disappointment of her many fans, Joyner-Kersee was unable to compete in her third Olympic heptathlon because of an injured hamstring. After a painful run in the 100-meter hurdles, Joyner-Kersee and her husband and coach, Bob Kersee, decided that she could not continue in the grueling seven-event competition. She did, however, compete in the long jump, where she placed third and took home her sixth Olympic medal. In the fall of 1996, Joyner-Kersee began a new career as a professional basketball player with a newly formed women's team, the Richmond Rage. Her teammates include seven members of the U.S. Olympic team, which won a gold medal in Atlanta. Joyner-Kersee still plans to compete in track and field competitions in 1997.

* SHANNON MILLER *

In a superb ending to one of the greatest careers in gymnastics, Shannon Miller won two Olympic gold medals in Atlanta in 1996: one individual gold medal in the balance beam and one for the U.S. team's performance in the all-around competition. After the Olympics, Miller joined fellow U.S. team gymnasts in a nationwide tour, after which she plans to attend college at the University of Oklahoma. She retires as the most decorated gymnast in U.S. sports history.

* ROSS PEROT *

As he did in 1992, Ross Perot declared himself a candidate for president in 1996, with economist Pat Choate as his running mate. The two ran as the candidates of the Reform Party, which was formed by Perot in 1992. Unlike 1992, Perot was denied a place in the presidential debates. A committee formed to analyze the pre-election polls to assess Perot's chances of winning determined that he would receive less than 10% of the vote. They decided, therefore, that Perot should not receive the opportunity to debate with Clinton and Dole. The ruling made Perot furious and was widely criticized in the press and around the country. In October, Perot received an unexpected boost when Republican candidate Dole asked Perot to quit the race and give his support to the Dole/Kemp ticket. The move gave Perot more exposure than he had received, but it was not enough to help him in the election, where he received 9 percent of the vote. Clinton won the election, with 49 percent of the vote; Dole received 42 percent.

* BORIS YELTSIN *

In July 1996, Yeltsin won reelection as the president of Russia. He had appeared infrequently during the campaign, due to a dangerously weakened heart brought on by three heart attacks in the last year. By the fall of 1996, anxiety over Yeltsin's health and fitness to rule Russia was running high in Moscow and around the world. Planning to undergo multiple bypass surgery, Yeltsin had placed the country in the control of three men--Prime Minister Viktor Chernomyrdin, Chief of Staff Anatoly Chubias, and National Security Chief Alexsandr Lebed, his supposed political heir. But just weeks before his surgery, Yeltsin angrily dismissed Lebed, who had openly clashed with Chernomyrdin and Chubias. As Michael Specter of the *New York Times* stated, "With a sick President and no clear line of succession, it can only raise new questions about the future stability of the country."

Name Index

Listed below are the names of all individuals profiled in *Biography Today*, followed by the date of the issue in which they appear.

General Index

This index includes subjects, occupations, organizations, and ethnic and minority origins that pertain to individuals profiled in *Biography Today*.

Hill, Grant, 96/Sport
Johnson, Magic, 92/Apr
Jordan, Michael, 92/Jan;
 93/Update;94/Update
Olajuwon, Hakeem, 95/Sep
O'Neal, Shaquille, 93/Sep
Pippen, Scottie, 92/Oct
Robinson, David, 96/Sep
Rodman, Dennis, 96/Apr
Ward, Charlie, 94/Apr
"Beverly Hills, 90210"
Doherty, Shannen, 92/Apr;
 94/Update
Garth, Jennie, 96/Apr
Perry, Luke, 92/Jan
Priestley, Jason, 92/Apr
Thiessen, Tiffani-Amber, 96/Jan
biology
see also marine biology
          molecular biology
          neurobiology
          scientists
Margulis, Lynn, 96/Sep
McClintock, Barbara, 92/Oct
Ochoa, Severo, 94/Jan
Sabin, Albert, 96/Science
black
Aaron, Hank, 96/Sport
Abdul-Jabbar, Kareem, 96/Sport
Anderson, Marian, 94/Jan
Angelou, Maya, 93/Apr
Aristide, Jean-Bertrand, 95/Jan
Ashe, Arthur, 93/Sep
Baldwin, James, 96/Author
Battle, Kathleen, 93/Jan
Bearden, Romare, 96/Artist
Berry, Halle, 95/Jan
Boyz II Men, 96/Jan
Bradley, Ed, 94/Apr
Brandy, 96/Apr
Brown, Ron, 96/Sep
Champagne, Larry III, 96/Apr
Chavis, Benjamin, 94/Jan;
 94/Update
Childress, Alice, 95/Author

Coolio, 96/Sep
Cosby, Bill, 92/Jan
Dove, Rita, 94/Jan
Edelman, Marian Wright, 93/Apr
Ewing, Patrick, 95/Jan
Fielder, Cecil, 93/Sep
Gillespie, Dizzy, 93/Apr
Goldberg, Whoopi, 94/Apr
Griffey, Ken, Jr., 96/Sport
Guy, Jasmine, 93/Sep
Haley, Alex, 92/Apr
Hamilton, Virginia, 95/Author
Hammer, 92/Jan
Hill, Anita, 93/Jan
Hill, Grant, 96/Sport
Houston, Whitney, 94/Sep
Ice-T, 93/Apr
Jackson, Bo, 92/Jan;
 93/Update
Jackson, Jesse, 95/Sep
Jamison, Judith, 96/Jan
Jemison, Mae, 92/Oct
Johnson, Magic, 92/Apr
Jones, James Earl, 95/Jan
Jordan, Barbara, 96/Apr
Jordan, Michael, 92/Jan;
 93/Update;94/Update;
 95/Update
Joyner-Kersee, Jackie, 92/Oct;
 96/Update
Lawrence, Jacob, 96/Artist
Lee, Spike, 92/Apr
Lewis, Carl, 96/Sep
Mandela, Nelson, 92/Jan;
 94/Update
Marsalis, Wynton, 92/Apr
Marshall, Thurgood, 92/Jan;
 93/Update
Morrison, Toni, 94/Jan
Myers, Walter Dean, 93/Jan;
 94/Update
Ndeti, Cosmas, 95/Sep
Olajuwon, Hakeem, 95/Sep
O'Neal, Shaquille, 93/Sep
Parks, Gordon, 96/Artist

Carle, Eric, 95/Author
Handford, Martin, 92/Jan
Macaulay, David, 96/Author
McCully, Emily Arnold, 92/Apr;
   93/Update
Pinkney, Jerry, 96/Author
Ringgold, Faith, 96/Author
Scarry, Richard, 94/Sep
Sendak, Maurice, 96/Author
Seuss, Dr., 92/Jan
Van Allsburg, Chris, 92/Apr
Williams, Garth, 96/Author
"In Living Color"
Wayans, Keenen Ivory,
   93/Jan
inventors
Cousteau, Jacques, 93/Jan
Land, Edwin, 96/Science
Iraq, President of
Hussein, Saddam, 92/Jul;
   96/Update
Iraqi
Hussein, Saddam, 92/Jul;
   96/Update
Ireland, President of
Robinson, Mary, 93/Sep
Irish
Robinson, Mary, 93/Sep
Israel, Prime Minister of
Rabin, Yitzhak, 92/Oct;
   93/Update;94/Update
Israeli
Perlman, Itzhak, 95/Jan
Rabin, Yitzhak, 92/Oct;
   93/Update;94/Update;95/Update
Italian
Andretti, Mario, 94/Sep
Krim, Mathilde, 96/Science
Levi-Montalcini, Rita, 96/Science
Jamaican
Denton, Sandi
   see Salt 'N' Pepa, 95/Apr
Ewing, Patrick, 95/Jan
jockey
Krone, Julie, 95/Jan

Joint Chiefs of Staff, Chairman of
Powell, Colin, 92/Jan;93/Update
journalists
Anderson, Terry, 92/Apr
Bradley, Ed, 94/Apr
Chung, Connie, 94/Jan;
   95/Update;96/Update
Ellerbee, Linda, 94/Apr
Jennings, Peter, 92/Jul
Pauley, Jane, 92/Oct
Roberts, Cokie, 95/Apr
Walters, Barbara, 94/Sep
Jurassic Park
Spielberg, Steven, 94/Jan;
   94/Update
justices, United States
Supreme Court
Burger, Warren, 95/Sep
Ginsburg, Ruth Bader, 94/Jan
Marshall, Thurgood, 92/Jan;
   93/Update
O'Connor, Sandra Day, 92/Jul
Thomas, Clarence, 92/Jan
Kansas City Chiefs
Montana, Joe, 95/Jan
Kansas City Royals
Jackson, Bo, 92/Jan
Kenyan
Ndeti, Cosmas, 95/Sep
Ku Klux Klan
Duke, David, 92/Apr
Labor Party (Israel)
Rabin, Yitzhak, 92/Oct;
   93/Update;94/Update
Laker Girl
Abdul, Paula, 92/Jan
"Late Show with David Letterman"
Letterman, David, 95/Jan
lawyers
Babbitt, Bruce, 94/Jan
Boutros-Ghali, Boutros, 93/Apr
Clinton, Hillary Rodham, 93/Apr
Grisham, John, 95/Author
Reno, Janet, 93/Sep

Nirvana
Cobain, Kurt, 94/Sep
Nobel Prize
Aung San Suu Kyi, 96/Apr
Bardeen, John, 96/Science
de Klerk, F.W., 94/Apr
Gorbachev, Mikhail, 92/Jan
Levi-Montalcini, Rita, 96/Science
Mandela, Nelson, 94/Update
McClintock, Barbara, 92/Oct
Menchu, Rigoberta, 93/Jan
Morrison, Toni, 94/Jan
Ochoa, Severo, 94/Jan
Pauling, Linus, 95/Jan
Oakland Athletics, batboy
Hammer, 92/Jan
obituaries
Adams, Ansel, 96/Artist
Anderson, Marian, 94/Jan
Ashe, Arthur, 93/Sep
Asimov, Isaac, 92/Jul
Baldwin, James, 96/Author
Bardeen, John, 96/Science
Bearden, Romare, 96/Artist
Bourke-White, Margaret, 96/Artist
Brown, Ron, 96/Sep
Burger, Warren, 95/Sep
Calder, Alexander, 96/Artist
Candy, John, 94/Sep
Chagall, Marc, 96/Artist
Chavez, Cesar, 93/Sep
Childress, Alice, 95/Author
Cobain, Kurt, 94/Sep
Dahl, Roald, 95/Author
de Mille, Agnes, 95/Jan
Fossey, Dian, 96/Science
Garcia, Jerry, 96/Jan
Gillespie, Dizzy, 93/Apr
Haley, Alex, 92/Apr
Hargreaves, Alison, 96/Jan
Herriot, James, 95/Author
Jordan, Barbara, 96/Apr
Land, Edwin, 96/Science
Leakey, Louis, 96/Science
Mantle, Mickey, 96/Jan

Marshall, Thurgood, 93/Update
Masih, Iqbal, 96/Jan
McClintock, Barbara, 92/Oct
Moore, Henry, 96/Artist
Moses, Grandma, 96/Artist
Nevelson, Louise, 96/Artist
Nixon, Richard, 94/Sep
Nureyev, Rudolf, 93/Apr
Ochoa, Severo, 94/Jan
O'Dell, Scott, 96/Author
O'Keeffe, Georgia, 96/Artist
Oppenheimer, J. Robert,
  96/Science
Pauling, Linus, 95/Jan
Phoenix, River, 94/Apr
Rabin, Yitzhak, 95/Update
Rivera, Diego, 96/Artist
Rockwell, Norman, 96/Artist
Rudolph, Wilma, 95/Apr
Sabin, Albert, 96/Science
Salk, Jonas, 95/Update
Scarry, Richard, 94/Sep
Selena, 96/Jan
Seuss, Dr., 92/Jan
Speare, Elizabeth George, 95/Sep
Thomas, Lewis, 94/Apr
Travers, P.L., 96/Author
Warhol, Andy, 96/Artist
White, E.B., 95/Author
Williams, Garth, 96/Author
Wright, Frank Lloyd, 96/Artist
Zamora, Pedro, 95/Apr
oil executive
Bush, George, 92/Jan
Olympics
Baiul, Oksana, 95/Apr
Bird, Larry, 92/Jan
Blair, Bonnie, 94/Apr
Boulmerka, Hassiba, 96/Sport
Evans, Janet, 95/Jan;
  96/Update
Ewing, Patrick, 95/Jan
Griffith Joyner, Florence, 96/Sport
Harding, Tonya, 94/Sep
Hill, Grant, 96/Sport

Places of Birth Index

The following index lists the places of birth for the individuals profiled in *Biography Today*. Places of birth are entered under state, province, and/or country.

Birthday Index

January

1 Salinger, J.D. (1919)
2 Asimov, Isaac (1920)
4 Naylor, Phyllis Reynolds (1933)
  Shula, Don (1930)
8 Hawking, Stephen W. (1942)
9 Menchu, Rigoberta (1959)
  Nixon, Richard (1913)
12 Limbaugh, Rush (1951)
16 Fossey, Dian (1932)
17 Carrey, Jim (1962)
  Cormier, Robert (1925)
  Jones, James Earl (1931)
18 Messier, Mark (1961)
21 Domingo, Placido (1941)
  Olajuwon, Hakeem (1963)
22 Chavis, Benjamin (1948)
23 Thiessen, Tiffani-Amber (1974)
25 Alley, Kirstie (1955)
28 Gretzky, Wayne (1961)
29 Gilbert, Sara (1975)
  Winfrey, Oprah (1954)
31 Ryan, Nolan (1947)

February

1 Spinelli, Jerry (1941)
  Yeltsin, Boris (1931)
3 Nixon, Joan Lowery (1927)
  Rockwell, Norman (1894)
4 Parks, Rosa (1913)
5 Aaron, Hank (1934)
6 Leakey, Mary (1913)
  Zmeskal, Kim (1976)
7 Brooks, Garth (1962)
8 Grisham, John (1955)
10 Norman, Greg (1955)
11 Brandy (1979)
12 Blume, Judy (1938)
15 Groening, Matt (1954)
17 Anderson, Marian (1897)
  Hargreaves, Alison (1962)
17 Jordan, Michael (1963)
18 Morrison, Toni (1931)
20 Adams, Ansel (1902)
  Barkley, Charles (1963)
  Cobain, Kurt (1967)
  Crawford, Cindy (1966)
21 Carpenter, Mary Chapin (1958)
  Jordan, Barbara (1936)
24 Jobs, Steven (1955)
  Whitestone, Heather (1973)
25 Voigt, Cynthia (1942)
27 Clinton, Chelsea (1980)
28 Andretti, Mario (1940)
  Pauling, Linus (1901)

March

1 Rabin, Yitzhak (1922)
  Zamora, Pedro (1972)
2 Gorbachev, Mikhail (1931)
  Seuss, Dr. (1904)
3 Hooper, Geoff (1979)
  Joyner-Kersee, Jackie (1962)
  MacLachlan, Patricia (1938)
5 Margulis, Lynn (1938)
10 Guy, Jasmine (1964)
  Miller, Shannon (1977)
12 Hamilton, Virginia (1936)
13 Van Meter, Vicki (1982)
15 Ginsburg, Ruth Bader (1933)
16 O'Neal, Shaquille (1972)
17 Nureyev, Rudolf (1938)
18 Blair, Bonnie (1964)
  de Klerk, F.W. (1936)
  Queen Latifah (1970)
20 Lee, Spike (1957)
22 Shatner, William (1931)
25 Lovell, Jim (1928)
  Steinem, Gloria (1934)
26 O'Connor, Sandra Day (1930)
27 Carey, Mariah (1970)
28 James, Cheryl

March, continued

28 McEntire, Reba (1955)
30 Hammer (1933)
31 Chavez, Cesar (1927)
   Gore, Al (1948)

April

2 Carvey, Dana (1955)
3 Garth, Jennie (1972)
   Goodall, Jane (1934)
4 Angelou, Maya (1928)
5 Powell, Colin (1937)
6 Watson, James D. (1928)
12 Cleary, Beverly (1916)
   Doherty, Shannen (1971)
   Letterman, David (1947)
13 Brandis, Jonathan (1976)
14 Rose, Pete (1941)
16 Abdul-Jabbar, Kareem (1947)
   Selena (1971)
   Williams, Garth (1912)
17 Champagne, Larry III (1985)
18 Hart, Melissa Joan (1976)
22 Levi-Montalcini, Rita (1909)
   Oppenheimer, J. Robert
   (1904)
26 Pei, I.M. (1917)
28 Baker, James (1930)
   Duncan, Lois (1934)
   Hussein, Saddam (1937)
   Leno, Jay (1950)
29 Agassi, Andre (1970)
   Seinfeld, Jerry (1954)

May

2 Spock, Benjamin (1903)
7 Land, Edwin (1909)
9 Bergen, Candice (1946)
10 Jamison, Judith (1944)
13 Rodman, Dennis (1961)
14 Smith, Emmitt (1969)
15 Johns, Jasper (1930)
   Zindel, Paul (1936)
17 Paulsen, Gary (1939)

18 John Paul II (1920)
21 Robinson, Mary (1944)
23 Bardeen, John (1908)
   O'Dell, Scott (1898)
26 Ride, Sally (1951)
27 Kerr, M.E. (1927)

June

1 Lalas, Alexi (1970)
4 Kistler, Darci (1964)
5 Scarry, Richard (1919)
6 Rylant, Cynthia (1954)
7 Oleynik, Larisa (1981)
8 Bush, Barbara (1925)
   Edelman, Marian Wright
   (1939)
   Wayans, Keenen Ivory (1958)
   Wright, Frank Lloyd (1869)
10 Sendak, Maurice (1928)
11 Cousteau, Jacques (1910)
   Montana, Joe (1956)
12 Bush, George (1924)
13 Allen, Tim (1953)
   Christo (1935)
14 Bourke-White, Margaret
   (1904)
   Graf, Steffi (1969)
15 Horner, Jack (1946)
16 McClintock, Barbara (1902)
17 Gingrich, Newt (1943)
   Jansen, Dan (1965)
18 Morris, Nathan (1971)
   Van Allsburg, Chris (1949)
19 Abdul, Paula (1962)
   Aung San Suu Kyi (1945)
20 Goodman, John (1952)
21 Bhutto, Benazir (1953)
   Breathed, Berke (1957)
22 Bradley, Ed (1941)
23 Rudolph, Wilma (1940)
   Thomas, Clarence (1948)
25 Carle, Eric (1929)
26 LeMond, Greg (1961)
27 Babbitt, Bruce (1938)

September, continued

2 Galeczka, Chris (1981)
5 Guisewite, Cathy (1950)
7 Lawrence, Jacob (1917)
  Moses, Grandma (1860)
  Pippig, Uta (1965)
8 Prelutsky, Jack (1940)
  Thomas, Jonathan Taylor (1982)
13 Taylor, Mildred D. (1943)
15 Marino, Dan (1961)
16 Dahl, Roald (1916)
17 Burger, Warren (1907)
18 de Mille, Agnes (1905)
  Fields, Debbi (1956)
21 Fielder, Cecil (1963)
  King, Stephen (1947)
23 Nevelson, Louise (1899)
24 Ochoa, Severo (1905)
25 Locklear, Heather (1961)
  Lopez, Charlotte (1976)
  Pippen, Scottie (1965)
  Smith, Will (1968)
  Walters, Barbara (1931)
26 Stockman, Shawn (1972)
27 Handford, Martin (1956)
29 Berenstain, Stan (1923)
  Guey, Wendy (1983)

October

1 Carter, Jimmy (1924)
2 Leibovitz, Annie (1949)
3 Herriot, James (1916)
  Winfield, Dave (1951)
5 Hill, Grant (1972)
  Lemieux, Mario (1965)
7 Ma, Yo-Yo (1955)
8 Jackson, Jesse (1941)
  Ringgold, Faith (1930)
  Stine, R.L. (1943)
11 Perry, Luke (1964?)
  Young, Steve (1961)
12 Childress, Alice (1920?)
  Ward, Charlie (1970)

13 Kerrigan, Nancy (1969)
  Rice, Jerry (1962)
14 Daniel, Beth (1956)
15 Iacocca, Lee A. (1924)
17 Jemison, Mae (1956)
18 Marsalis, Wynton (1961)
  Navratilova, Martina (1956)
20 Mantle, Mickey (1931)
21 Gillespie, Dizzy (1956)
23 Pele (1940)
26 Clinton, Hillary Rodham (1947)
27 Anderson, Terry (1947)
28 Gates, Bill (1955)
  Salk, Jonas (1914)
29 Ryder, Winona (1971)
31 Candy, John (1950)
  Pauley, Jane (1950)

November

2 lang, k.d. (1961)
3 Arnold, Roseanne (1952)
9 Denton, Sandi
  Sagan, Carl (1934)
11 Vonnegut, Kurt (1922)
12 Andrews, Ned (1980)
  Harding, Tonya (1970)
13 Goldberg, Whoopi (1949)
14 Boutros-Ghali, Boutros (1922)
15 O'Keeffe, Georgia (1887)
16 Baiul, Oksana (1977)
17 Fuentes, Daisy (1966)
18 Mankiller, Wilma (1945)
19 Strug, Kerri (1977)
21 Aikman, Troy (1966)
  Griffey, Ken, Jr. (1969)
  Speare, Elizabeth George (1908)
24 Ndeti, Cosmas (1971)
25 Grant, Amy (1960)
  Thomas, Lewis (1913)
26 Pine, Elizabeth Michele (1975)
  Schulz, Charles (1922)

November, continued

27 White, Jaleel (1977)
29 L'Engle, Madeleine (1918)
30 Jackson, Bo (1962)
   Parks, Gordon (1912)
 ? Pike, Christopher (1954)

December

 2 Macaulay, David (1946)
   Seles, Monica (1973)
 3 Filipovic, Zlata (1980)
 7 Bird, Larry (1956)
 8 Rivera, Diego (1886)
12 Bialik, Mayim (1975)
   Frankenthaler, Helen (1928)
13 Fedorov, Sergei (1969)

16 McCary, Michael (1971)
18 Sanchez Vicario, Arantxa (1971)
   Spielberg, Steven (1947)
21 Evert, Chris (1954)
   Griffith Joyner, Florence (1959)
22 Pinkney, Jerry (1939)
23 Avi (1937)
26 Butcher, Susan (1954)
27 Roberts, Cokie (1943)
28 Washington, Denzel (1954)
30 Woods, Tiger (1975)

People to Appear in Future Issues

Actors
Trini Alvarado
Gillian Anderson
Richard Dean
  Anderson
Dan Aykroyd
Tyra Banks
Drew Barrymore
Zachary Ty Bryan
Levar Burton
Cher
Kevin Costner
Courtney Cox
Tom Cruise
Jamie Lee Curtis
Brittany Daniel
Cynthia Daniel
Patti D'Arbanville-
  Quinn
Geena Davis
Ozzie Davis
Ruby Dee
Michael De
  Lorenzo
Matt Dillon
Michael Douglas
Larry Fishburne
Harrison Ford
Jody Foster
Morgan Freeman
Richard Gere
Tracey Gold
Graham Greene
Mark Harmon
Michael Keaton
Val Kilmer
Angela Lansbury
Joey Lawrence
Martin Lawrence
Christopher Lloyd
Heather Locklear
Kellie Martin
Steve Martin
Marlee Matlin
Bette Midler
Alyssa Milano
Demi Moore
Rick Moranis
Tamera Mowry
Tia Mowry
Kate Mulgrew
Eddie Murphy
Liam Neeson
Leslie Nielsen
Leonard Nimoy

Rosie O'Donnell
Sean Penn
Phylicia Rashad
Keanu Reeves
Jason James Richter
Julia Roberts
Bob Saget
Arnold
  Schwarzenegger
Alicia Silverstone
Christian Slater
Taran Noah Smith
Jimmy Smits
Wesley Snipes
Sylvester Stallone
John Travolta
Mario Van Peebles
Damon Wayans
Bruce Willis
B.D. Wong
Malik Yoba

Artists
Mitsumasa Anno
Graeme Base
Maya Ying Lin
Yoko Ono

Astronauts
Neil Armstrong

Authors
Jean M. Auel
Ray Bradbury
Gwendolyn
  Brooks
John Christopher
Arthur C. Clarke
John Colville
Paula Danziger
Paula Fox
Patricia Reilly
  Gibb
Jamie Gilson
Rosa Guy
Nat Hentoff
Norma Klein
E.L. Konigsburg
Lois Lowry
Stephen Manes
Norma Fox Mazer
Anne McCaffrey
Gloria D. Miklowitz
Marsha Norman
Robert O'Brien

Francine Pascal
Daniel Pinkwater
Ann Rice
Louis Sachar
John Saul
Shel Silverstein
Amy Tan
Alice Walker
Jane Yolen
Roger Zelazny

Business
Minoru Arakawa
Michael Eisner
David Geffen
Wayne Huizenga
Robert Johnson
Donna Karan
Phil Knight
Estee Lauder
Sheri Poe
Anita Roddick
Donald Trump
Ted Turner
Lillian Vernon

Cartoonists
Lynda Barry
Roz Chast
Greg Evans
Nicole Hollander
Art Spiegelman
Garry Trudeau

Comedians
Billy Crystal
Eddie Murphy
Bill Murray
Richard Pryor

Dancers
Debbie Allen
Mikhail
  Baryshnikov
Gregory Hines
Twyla Tharp
Tommy Tune

**Directors/
Producers**
Woody Allen
Steven Bocho
Tim Burton
Francis Ford
  Coppola

Jody Foster
Ron Howard
John Hughes
George Lucas
Penny Marshall
Leonard Nimoy
Sean Penn
Rob Reiner
John Singleton
Quentin Tarantino

**Environmentalists/
Animal Rights**
Marjory Stoneman
  Douglas
Kathryn Fuller
Lois Gibbs
Wangari Maathai
Linda Maraniss
Ingrid Newkirk
Pat Potter

Journalists
Christiane
  Annenpour
Tom Brokaw
Ed Gordon
John Hockenberry
Ted Koppel
Jim Lehrer
Dan Rather
Nina Totenberg
Mike Wallace
Bob Woodward

Musicians
Ace of Base
Babyface
George Benson
Bjork
Clint Black
Ruben Blades
Bono
Edie Brickell
Toni Braxton
James Brown
Ray Charles
Natalie Cole
Cowboy Junkies
Sheryl Crow
Billy Ray
  Cyrus
Melissa Etheridge
Aretha Franklin
Evelyn Glennie

Green Day
Guns N' Roses
P.J. Harvey
Hootie & the
 Blowfish
India
Janet Jackson
Michael Jackson
Winona Judd
R. Kelly
Anthony Kiedis
Lenny Kravitz
James Levine
LL Cool J
Andrew Lloyd
 Webber
Courtney Love
Lyle Lovett
Madonna
Barbara Mandrell
Branford Marsalis
Paul McCartney
Midori
Alanis Morissette
Morrissey
Jesseye Norman
Sinead O'Connor
Joan Osborne
Luciano Pavoratti
Pearl Jam
Teddy Pendergrass
David Pirner
Prince
Public Enemy
Raffi
Bonnie Raitt
Red Hot Chili
 Peppers
Lou Reed
L.A. Reid
R.E.M.
Trent Reznor
Kenny Rogers
Axl Rose
Paul Simon
Smashing
 Pumpkins
Sting
Michael Stipe
Pam Tillis
TLC
Randy Travis
Terence Trent
 d'Arby
Travis Tritt
U2
Eddie Vedder
Stevie Wonder
Trisha Yearwood

Dwight Yoakum
Neil Young

**Politics/World
Leaders**
Madeleine Albright
Harry A. Blackmun
Jesse Brown
Pat Buchanan
Mangosuthu
 Buthelezi
Violeta Barrios
 de Chamorro
Shirley Chisolm
Jean Chretien
Warren Christopher
Edith Cresson
Mario Cuomo
Dalai Lama
Mike Espy
Tipper Gore
Alan Greenspan
Vaclav Havel
Nancy Kassebaum
Jack Kemp
Bob Kerrey
Kim Il-Sung
Coretta Scott King
John Major
Imelda Marcos
Kweisi Mfume
Slobodan Milosevic
Mother Theresa
Ralph Nader
Benjamin
 Netanyahu
Manuel Noriega
Hazel O'Leary
Leon Panetta
Federico Pena
Simon Peres
Ralph Reed
Robert Reich
Ann Richards
Richard Riley
Phyllis Schlafly
Pat Schroeder
Donna Shalala
Desmond Tutu
Lech Walesa
Eli Weisel
Vladimir
 Zhirinovsky

Royalty
Charles, Prince
 of Wales
Duchess of York
 (Sarah Ferguson)

Queen Noor
William, Prince

Scientists
Sallie Baliunas
Avis Cohen
Donna Cox
Stephen Jay
 Gould
Mimi Koehl
Deborah
 Letourneau
Philippa Marrack
Helen Quinn
Barbara Smuts
Flossie Wong-
 Staal
Aslihan Yener
Adrienne Zihlman

Sports
Jim Abbott
Muhammad Ali
Michael Andretti
Boris Becker
Barry Bonds
Bobby Bonilla
Jose Canseco
Jennifer Capriati
Michael Chang
Roger Clemens
Randall
 Cunningham
Eric Davis
Clyde Drexler
John Elway
Chris Evert
George Foreman
Zina Garrison
Anfernee Hardaway
Rickey Henderson
Evander Holyfield
Brett Hull
Raghib Ismail
Jim Kelly
Petr Klima
Willy Mays
Paul Molitor
Jack Nicklaus
Joe Paterno
Kirby Puckett
Pat Riley
Mark Rippien
Daryl Strawberry
Danny Sullivan
Vinnie Testaverde
Isiah Thomas
Mike Tyson
Steve Yzerman

**Television
Personalities**
Andre Brown
 (Dr. Dre)
Katie Couric
Phil Donahue
Kathie Lee Gifford
Ed Gordon
Bryant Gumbel
Arsenio Hall
Ricki Lake
Joan Lunden
Bill Maher
Dennis Miller
Diane Sawyer
Alison Stewart
Jon Stewart
Vanna White
Montel Williams
Paul Zaloom

Other
James Brady
Johnnetta Cole
David Copperfield
Jaimie Escalante
Temple Grandin
Jack Kevorkian
Wendy Kopp
Sister Irene Kraus
Jeanne White